Political Liberalization and Democratization in the Arab World

Volume 1

Political Liberalization and Democratization in the Arab World

Volume 1
Theoretical Perspectives

edited by

Rex Brynen,
Bahgat Korany, Paul Noble

Consortium interuniversitaire pour les études arabes
Inter-University Consortium for Arab Studies
إتحاد جامعات مونتريال للدراسات العربية

(Montréal)

LYNNE
RIENNER
PUBLISHERS

BOULDER
LONDON

To
Chloe, David, Vanessa, Leyla,
Mark Ramzi, Michael, Patrick, Peter, and Paul

Published in the United States of America in 1995 by
Lynne Rienner Publishers, Inc.
1800 30th Street, Boulder, Colorado 80301

and in the United Kingdom by
Lynne Rienner Publishers, Inc.
3 Henrietta Street, Covent Garden, London WC2E 8LU

Library of Congress Cataloging-in-Publication Data
Political liberalization and democratization in the Arab world /
    edited by Rex Brynen, Bahgat Korany, Paul Noble.
        p.   cm.
    Includes bibliographical references and index.
    Contents: v. 1. Theoretical perspectives
    ISBN 1-55587-559-9 (hc : alk. paper)
    ISBN 1-55587-579-3 (pb : alk. paper)
        1. Arab countries—Politics and government—1945–   2. Civil
society—Arab countries. 3. Democracy—Arab countries.
4. Political culture—Arab countries. I. Brynen, Rex. II. Korany,
Bahgat. III. Noble, Paul.
JQ1850.A91P65   1995
306.2'0917'4927—dc20   95-17941
                                                           CIP

British Cataloguing in Publication Data
A Cataloguing in Publication record for this book
is available from the British Library.

Printed and bound in the United States of America

⊗ The paper used in this publication meets the requirements
of the American National Standard for Permanence of
Paper for Printed Library Materials Z39.48-1984.

5 4 3 2 1

Contents

Tables and Figures

Tables

Figure

Preface

Long dominated by authoritarian regimes,the Arab world faces the challenge of change posed by a variety of internal and external factors. In recent years, significant degrees of political liberalization have already been evident in a number of Arab states—although the extent to which this presages an eventual democratization of their political systems is far from evident. Elsewhere, regimes have made more modest (perhaps only cosmetic) reforms or resisted demands for expanded public freedoms and participation. In still otherArab states, experiments in liberalization and even democratization have been slowed, suspended, or aborted.

This book is the first of a two-volume work addressing these important issues. In this volume (*Theoretical Perspectives*), contributors from the Middle East, North America, and Europe focus on the major factors shaping liberalization and democratization in the Arab context, focusing on questions of culture, civil society, political economy, and international relations, and highlighting key analytical debates within each of these areas. Drawing on these theoretical insights, a forthcoming volume (*Arab Experiences*) will examine the processes and prospects for political reform in key Arab states, selected to demonstrate a broad range of contexts, trajectories, and political potentialities.

This research project has been conducted under the auspices of the Inter-University Consortium for Arab Studies (ICAS), established jointly by scholars at McGill University, the Université de Montréal, and other Canadian institutions. Many of the chapters published herein were presented in draft form to a conference organized by ICAS in Montreal in May 1993. We wish to thank all the participants who enriched that conference, as well as contributors who joined the project at a later stage. We would also like to thank the Université de Montréal, McGill University, the Social Sciences and Humanities Research Council of Canada, the Fonds FCAR (Québec), the International Centre for Human Rights and

Democratic Development, and the Cooperative Security Competition Program for financial support. Gratitude is also due to students of the Programme d'études arabes (Université de Montréal) and the Middle East Studies Program (McGill University) who assisted with the original conference; to a bevy of helpful ICAS Research Fellows, including Pete Moore, Bassel Salloukh, Keith Martin, James Devine, Tamer Anis, and Anik Finkel; to Susan Bartlett and Eric Laferrière; to Alex Brynen (for the index); to Adam Jones (itinerant speed-typist); and to Joëlle Zahar (efficient ICAS administrative assistant) for efforts above and beyond the call of duty.

—*R.B.*
—*B.K.*
—*P.N.*

Introduction

1

Introduction:
Theoretical Perspectives on Arab
Liberalization and Democratization

Rex Brynen, Bahgat Korany, and Paul Noble

Analysts of liberalization and democratization must steer between two dangerous shoals. On the one hand, there is much to be gained from engaging in comparative study aimed at highlighting and explaining the similarities and differences evident across different political systems. On the other hand, scholars must avoid the ethnocentric dangers of reading processes deriving from one specific set of historical and political circumstances into other, very different, contexts. Yet democracy is presumably not entirely in the eye of the beholder, and some conceptual rigor is necessary if the notion of democracy is not to be debased to mean all things to all people.

This chapter is intended to provide an introductory exploration of the key theoretical issues involved in the analysis of political liberalization and democratization in the Arab world. Particular effort is made to identify the key areas of agreement and disagreement among scholars, and to set such debates (and the chapters within this volume) within the broader context of comparative politics. Given the warnings above, however, it is important to first make clear some of the essential terminology and assumptions of this project—starting with the terms "liberalization" and "democratization" themselves.

Although commonly intermixed in both popular and academic discussions, this project is rooted in the view that these two processes are not synonymous. *Political liberalization* involves the expansion of public space through the recognition and protection of civil and political liberties, particularly those bearing upon the ability of citizens to engage in free political discourse and to freely organize in pursuit of common interests. *Political democratization* entails an expansion of political participation in such a way as to provide citizens with a degree of real and meaningful collective control over public policy.

3

The distinction is an important one, since it is possible to have elements of one without the other. Political repression can be relaxed without expanding political participation. Indeed, far from automatically preceding or accompanying democratization, such partial liberalization can be intended to stave off democratic pressures. Conversely, some political systems may claim widespread popular participation (for example, revolutionary regimes that empower previously marginalized groups) while restricting political freedoms (for example, repressing those deemed counterrevolutionary).

Around the world, *elections* have been the most common way of expanding political participation in government decisionmaking. It is important not to confuse the appearance of elections with the substance of democratic politics, however. Elections conducted under a limited franchise, under highly distortional systems of electoral representation, or amidst widespread electoral fraud may not in fact provide citizens with any effective say in political decisionmaking. Similarly, elections held amidst repression may be meaningless as an indicator of public preferences. Here, the important linkage between liberty and democracy (and between liberalization and democratization) becomes clear: Without a context of political freedom, citizens are unable to effectively participate, organize, or freely choose among political alternatives.

This connection is at the heart of democratic theory, and in our view it is likely to be an incontestable characteristic of any meaningful democratic system. This having been said, it is important not to presume that all democracy must necessarily follow a Western *liberal democratic* model. Whenever and wherever it operates, democracy is fundamentally shaped by the historical and cultural context out of which it emerges. Moreover, many elements of liberal democracy are open for serious debate and alternative interpretations. Is liberal democracy solely based on individual rights, or can it recognize group rights too? If so, what relative weightings are to be given to these? From which sources do rights derive, and by what processes are they defined? Should the legislative powers of liberal democratic institutions be constrained by constitutional protections of rights, and if so, when and how? What of the dangers of majoritarianism in liberal democratic systems? Is there a necessary connection between political democracy and a market economy? Is economic equality a requirement for political equality? In short, a variety of shades and variants of democratic politics are possible.

The Study of Liberalization and Democratization in the Arab World

Since the early 1980s there has been an upsurge in academic interest in the processes and potentialities of democratic transition. This attention was spurred in large part by democratization of the remaining authoritarian regimes in southern Europe as well as ongoing processes in Latin America. Combined with regime openings in East and Southeast Asia, to a lesser extent in Africa, and then most dramatically the transformation of former communist regimes in Eastern and Central Europe, this sustained an explosion of new scholarship on the so-called third wave of global democratization.[1]

Initially scholars of comparative politics devoted relatively little attention to, or hope for, processes of democratization in the Arab world. This was evident in the two most important and influential research projects on the subject published in the 1980s. The first—O'Donnell, Schmitter, and Whitehead's influential comparative study of transitions from authoritarian rule—does not mention a single Arab country anywhere in its 710 pages.[2] Similarly, Diamond, Linz, and Lipset's massive four-volume study of democratic politics in the developing world explicitly excluded consideration of most of the Middle East, noting that "the Islamic countries of the Middle East and North Africa generally lack much previous democratic experience, and most appear to have little prospect of transition to even semi-democracy."[3] Another influential scholar, Samuel Huntington, agreed, arguing that "among Islamic countries, particularly those in the Middle East, the prospects for democratic development seem low."[4]

Western specialists on the Middle East were equally likely to overlook the subject, due in part to the lack of sustained democratic practice in the Arab world, in part to the presence of other political preoccupations (notably the Arab-Israeli conflict), and in part due to the general analytical weaknesses of Middle East studies. When Michael Hudson decided to deliver his 1987 presidential address to the Middle East Studies Association on the subject of "democratization and the problem of legitimacy in Middle East politics," he reported that most of his colleagues were "incredulous" at the prospect.[5] A 1990 survey of the field barely mentioned political liberalization—let alone democracy—as an area of research.[6] Similarly, a 1990 study of the content of contemporary Middle East studies courses in the United States revealed comparatively little attention to the subject in the classroom.[7] Finally, within the region itself scholarly attention to democracy and human rights was distracted by other preoccupations or discouraged by government repression.[8] Indeed, when Arab intellectuals undertook to organize a seminar on "The Crisis of Democracy and Human Rights in the Arab World" in 1983, the meeting had to be held in Limassol, Cyprus, since no Arab government would agree to host it.[9]

With time, however, this situation has begun to change. Part of this change was undoubtedly motivated by academic fad, as the general concern with democratization within contemporary social science percolated into Middle East studies. For many scholars, the shift was also fed by the normative preference—implicit or explicit—for democratic government. Increased attention to the subject was also spurred by greater attention to

democracy by Arab intellectuals and nongovernmental organizations (the
Arab Organization for Human Rights, the Centre for Arab Unity Studies,
the Arab Thought Forum, among others) starting in the mid-1980s, and by
the consolidation or initiation of political openings in Egypt, Sudan, Algeria, Tunisia, Jordan, Yemen, and elsewhere.

By the early 1990s, interest in the processes of, and prospects for, political liberalization and democratization had become widespread among
social scientists studying the Middle East. This has been manifest in a
sharp increase in the number of papers, articles, and conferences on the
subject. Most of this attention remains ad hoc, however.

While partial case studies abound, there have been relatively few attempts to identify the key theoretical issues arising from the study of political change in the Arab world, to systematically explore those debates,
and to engage in comparative examination across Arab political systems.
This project is an attempt to address this deficiency. In this volume, contributors concentrate their attentions on four key "clusters" of conceptual
and analytical issues: the role of religion and culture; the nature, development, and role of Arab civil society; the political economy of Arab authoritarianism and reform; and the interaction of domestic change with
forces within the broader regional and international system. Throughout,
particular attention is paid to identifying the impact of liberalization not
only on dominant elites, but also on subaltern and marginalized groups. In
a companion volume, these theoretical explorations inform a series of
comparative case studies of the prospects and processes (current or potential) of political change in different Arab countries.[10]

Democracy and Political Culture

Among the many sets of issues addressed by contemporary scholarship on
Arab democracy—and perhaps the most intensely debated of all of them—
is that of the role played by Arab and Islamic culture. This debate raises
critical questions not only about how we should approach (methodologically and theoretically) the study of Arab politics, but also regarding the
preconceptions and prejudices that are sometimes brought to scholarship.
Within the debate, three essential positions can be discerned.

The first position suggests that important aspects of Arab and/or Islamic political values are incompatible with, or at least in tension with, the
fundamental principles of democratic practice. It has been suggested, for
example, that Islam's emphasis on divine rather than popular sovereignty—with the former being expressed in an established body of Islamic
law resistant to change, and generally interpreted by an elite of religious
scholars—puts many of the most important issues of public policy outside

the realm of public, participatory decisionmaking. Scholars often point to a long tradition in Islamic (especially) Sunni political thought upholding the importance of maintaining order in the potential face of anarchy. A lack of fundamental equality within Islam for various groups, notably women and religious minorities, is also emphasized.[11]

At times the problem is located within Middle Eastern or specifically Arab, rather than Islamic, political culture. This, it is suggested, is characterized by primordialism (strong clan, tribal, and sectarian loyalties), which inhibits a sense of common citizenship, by the lack of a tradition of liberal tolerance of pluralism and dissent, by a conspiratorial mentality, and by patterns of authoritarianism and submissiveness.[12]

Other analysts provide a rather different view of the impact of culture on political liberalization and democratization in the Arab world. Here it is argued that political culture has considerable utility as an explanatory variable, but only if it is dealt with in a nuanced way, sensitive to effects of history, social structure, and context. It is suggested, for example, that both authoritarian *and* participatory strands exist within the political culture of the region, with the latter expressed in Islamic principles of *shura*, the bond of obligation between ruler and ruled (represented by the *bay'a*), and in traditions of accountability and (limited) participation in tribal decisionmaking.[13] Moreover, such scholars see political culture as far from fixed. Rather, it is subject to constant change, whether due to "modernization" and its associated processes (economic changes, urbanization, education, the freer flow of people and ideas) or because of the "diffusion" of democratic ideas into the Middle East from the West. It is suggested that Islam in particular is in practice a far more varied, changing, and flexible religion than a narrow, doctrinal reading of it would suggest—thus leaving room for a liberal interpretation.[14] Hence, notions of democracy—whatever their origins, ancient and modern—have become firmly established in Islamic political discourse.[15]

Still another position in this debate responds to charges of an antidemocratic bias in Arab or Islamic political culture not by focusing on the truth or untruth of such a claim, but rather by asserting that political culture itself should not be seen as the prime or overriding variable in any process of regional democratization. Cultural attitudes, it is suggested, not only influence political realities but are also themselves influenced by political context. Hence, Arabs may be deferential to authoritarian rule not because of some ingrained cultural disposition, but as a consequence of a quite rational response to authoritarian repression. Were a more democratic system of governance instituted, it would facilitate the emergence of a more democratic political culture.

Another variant on this position is to suggest the important degree of flexibility between the doctrinal foundations of movements and their actual political behavior.[16] This view would suggest that whatever their authoritarian bent, electoral competition and the expectations of electorates would force most political actors to behave in a democratic way once a system was fully democratized. Hence the danger is not that Islamic fundamentalists or others will use the electoral process to subvert democracy, but rather that the absence of democracy creates the conditions under which antidemocratic political forces thrive.[17] Finally, several critics of a political culture approach point as well to what they see as its methodological failings. Specifically, they suggest that attitudinal variations (across countries, classes, and communal groups), the absence of sound survey data for most populations, and the tendency to use "culture" as an explanatory catchall for political behavior all restrict the value of such analyses. Consequently, they point to what they see as more useful areas of investigation, such as historical processes of state formation and the contemporary impact of political economy.[18]

Despite the intensity of the debate over these issues, none of them is simply resolved. They are further complicated by the political and intellectual consequences of Western colonialism and an often conflictual relationship between the Western world and Islam. This leads to the accusation that Western concern with the supposed authoritarian characteristics of Arab-Islamic political culture simply reflects a contemporary Orientalism, with all of its attendant emphasis on the cultural "alienness" of the region and a narrow ahistorical reading of Islam. Or, even more simply, perhaps it reflects Western ethnocentrism (and an assumption that democracy is inevitably tied to Western cultural values) or racism (and a denigration of things Arab and Muslim).[19]

Such accusations are not without foundation. Yet although some of the scholarly literature may be ethnocentric, much or most of it is probably not. Indeed, it must be recognized that attention to these sorts of issues is not confined to scholarship by Western scholars on the Arab world. It is common to find Arab intellectuals and activists, in discussion with their non-Arab counterparts, attributing the crisis of human rights and democracy in the region to cultural obstacles.[20] It is also evident that many of those scholars in the West who either emphasize Arab/Western cultural differences or who find evidence of authoritarian components of Arab or Islamic political culture are themselves of Arab origin.[21] Within the Arab world itself, one hardly needs to look very far to find debates over, for example, secularism, Islam and democracy, the status of women, or the values sustaining (or inhibiting) democratic politics. Such themes represent central preoccupations in virtually every Arab conference on democracy and human rights. Indeed, the assassination of Farag Fawdah in Egypt and terrorism against both secular intellectuals and Islamists in Algeria suggest the tragic intensity that these debates have sometimes attained.[22]

It might also be added that much of the debate in the West over Arab political culture echoes similar debates with regard to other regions, including the West itself. There is, for example, a lengthy literature associating Christianity (especially Catholicism) with the maintenance of authoritarian rule in Europe and Latin America, or suggesting contradictions between it and important aspects of social equality (particularly regarding the status of women).[23] There is also an emerging literature, spurred in recent years by both ethnic separatisms and the reemergence of European fascist movements, on the tensions between individual and collective rights or the connections between nationalism and intolerance.

Most importantly, accusations of bias do not really solve the puzzle. Does culture matter? If so, how and when does it matter—and how do we assess its impact? Are we ethnocentric or reductionist if we emphasize the importance of an Arab political culture? Or are we being ethnocentric if we do not emphasize cultural differences? If it does not matter (or does not matter all that much) what else should we be looking at?

Such questions are addressed directly by the contributors to Part 1 of this volume. For Michael Hudson, political culture is an important and necessary part of any effort to understand politics, whether in the Arab world or elsewhere. Cultural value shapes the valuations placed on desired goals, notions of political community, and criteria of legitimacy. They cannot, moreover, be reduced to epiphenomenal expressions of some other underlying social, structural, economic, or other set of variables. Thus, while recognizing the shortcomings of previous analyses, Hudson asserts that it is important that scholars not "throw out the political culture baby with the Orientalist bathwater." In order to do this, he argues that analysts should avoid reductionist conceptualizations; disaggregate subcultures; distinguish between deeply rooted value orientations and more transitory ideologies and opinions; focus on certain key elements of political culture, notably "group identities, orientations toward authority, and principles of equity and justice"; and adopt multiple complementary methodological techniques. By contrast, Lisa Anderson is much more doubtful of the advantages of focusing attention on political culture, suggesting that although it "can be very seductive, particularly to policymakers looking for short, neat explanations of the complexities they face," it is, in its most common forms, "unusually susceptible to distortion and bias." She does not assert that culture does not have some role to play in shaping political realities. For Anderson, however, there are much more important variables—notably structural aspects of the economy and political system— that need to be addressed first.

The notion of "democracy" in contemporary Arab discourse is explored in Part 1 by Salwa Ismail. It is clear from her survey that although the term *dimuqratiyya* has come to occupy a central place in contemporary

Arab political and intellectual debates, there is by no means a consensus on how democracy should be understood or implemented. In particular, differences arise over how to reconcile the protection of individual rights within the framework of a broader project of Arab societal renovation. The tensions that this generates are particularly evident in the different societal views on secularism, pluralism, and the role of the state. In terms of the sorts of analytical issues raised above, Ismail's discussion is salutary in two key respects. First, it underscores the dangers of analytically imposing outside definitions of democracy on actors and social groups that may in fact use the term in very different ways. Second, it highlights the intellectual concern, energy, and tumult generated by questions of political reform in the contemporary Arab world—a picture very different from portrayals of the region as somehow intrinsically disinterested in political liberalization and democratization.

The specific question of Islam and political pluralism is taken up in greater detail by Gudrun Krämer. She notes that it is possible to identify both antipluralist and pluralist tendencies within Islamic political theory, the former emphasizing the unity of the Islamic community and the dangers of internal division, and the latter rejecting any human claim to monopoly of truth. This second position, she suggests, is a minority view. It is also qualified by its acceptance of the unassailable character of certain foundations of Islamic faith, as well as its attitude to those (non-Muslims or atheists) outside the Islamic framework. This having been said, however, she also suggests that it would be a mistake to attempt to discern the compatibility of Islamic movements (or Islam in general) and pluralist politics solely from a narrow and abstract reading of doctrine. In practice—as her case studies of Egypt and Tunisia suggest—the role and attitude of Islamist groups is shaped by regime policies, by the movement's own internal dynamics and debates, by the members' actual experiences, and by the balance of other political forces. This theme is one that is returned to later in the volume, as other contributors—notably al-Sayyid, Clark, Brumberg, and Ben-Dor—return to offer varying perspectives on Islamic movements and democratic politics.

Civil Society

Another common preoccupation of the recent literature on democracy and democratization has been the concept of "civil society." This is as true of scholarship on the Middle East as with any other region of the world, as evidenced by the existence of a number of major projects devoted to the question.[24]

The notion of civil society usually revolves around three different dimensions. The first is an organizational one, with civil society being defined as "how society organizes itself at the level between the family and the state"[25] or the "mélange of groups, associations, guilds, syndicates, federations, unions, parties, and groups that come together to provide a buffer between state and citizen."[26] A second, more abstract dimension emphasizes the "civility" of civil society—that is to say, a social milieu characterized by pluralistic discourse, tolerance, and moderation. A third dimension emphasizes a certain quality of state-society relations.

Different scholars emphasize these elements to different degrees. For some, what is particularly important about civil society is its organized existence. Social organization outside the auspices of the state is important because it counterweighs the power of the state, dilutes its control over society, and articulates and advances various societal interests vis-à-vis the dominant political elites. At times of political crisis, the organized manifestations of civil society pressure authoritarian elites to open up the regime through strikes, demonstrations, petitions, and propaganda. Once an opening has been initiated, a resurgent civil society emerges into newly liberalized public spaces, creating both momentum toward a further expansion of the opening and a "ratchet" effect that, by increasing the costs of repression, makes it more difficult for political authoritarian elites to reverse course.[27]

Other scholars emphasize the "civility" of civil society, tracing the emergence and consolidation of ideas of pluralism and tolerance within society and emphasizing the role that these ideas play in sustaining democratic interaction.[28] Historically, scholars associated the emergence of this form of civil society in Europe with the rise of modern bourgeois society. Modernity and modernization bring with them economic development, urbanization, and an expansion of education, communication, and transportation. This sustains a complex societal division of labor, generating a variety of cross-cutting economic and other interests and undercutting the ascriptive, primordial identifications of religion, ethnicity, tribe, or clan. These changes—and more particularly, the growth of capitalism—also sustained new patterns of state-society relations, characterized by concepts of individualism, citizenship, and legal personhood, and by a complex web of rights protecting political association and economic activity.[29]

To a large extent, these three dimensions of civil society—as a pattern of social organization, a set of attitudes and ideas, and a qualitative relationship between society and the state—are mutually reinforcing. The civil organizations of democratic society thus act both to promote societal interests vis-à-vis the state and to inculcate democratic values among their members; the state protects, by upholding established rights, the public space within which such activities occur.

But these different components of the concept also reveal a degree of ambiguity and even contradiction. An "organizational" definition tends to exclude informal politics.[30] It also suggests that even groups characterized by authoritarian or primordially based organization might have an important role to play in opening authoritarian regimes, provided they can mobilize the appropriate pressures. Indeed, centralized authoritarian groups might have a greater effect than more decentralized and democratic ones, since they may be able to more effectively escalate or de-escalate pressures as the situation warrants, as well as being more able to negotiate and implement the political pacts (with both the regime and other political actors) that have proven important in many transitions from authoritarian rule.[31] Primordial, authoritarian, or extremist groups might also prove more cohesive and durable under regime repression.

Should, therefore, tribes, clans, and religiously based groups be considered part of civil society? While those who emphasize the importance of civility would not see such groups as the building blocks of a new democratic political system, those who stress the contingent nature of the democracy—the extent to which, particularly in its early years, it is likely to be a compromise among warring parties, based on a series of agreements, tacit red-lines, and a complicated political balance of power—may not be so concerned. This in turn raises the question of where an appropriate balance between state and society is to be found. A vibrant civil society—understood in organizational terms—may so constrain state power as to render effective governance impossible. Indeed, the vibrancy of civil society may well be a symptom of the collapse, rather than success, of the political order: It may indicate weak national integration and a proliferation of ideological or communal organizations committed to protecting the interests of their members amidst a collapse in the constitutional order, or even civil war. Those who emphasize the importance of civility (rather than social organization) might see this as confirmation of the view that moderation is sustained by political culture rather than the political balance of power. But this only raises the question of where "moderate" or "democratic" social attitudes come from: whether they foster democratic governance, are fostered by it, or—least analytically elegant, but most probably the case—a bit of both.

Such issues and ambiguities within the study of civil society and democratic politics all have relevance to the study of democracy in the Arab context. In particular, much attention has been given to the implications of Islam for the development of Arab civil society. One leading Western scholar of civil society, for example, argues that Muslim societies "manifest at most a feeble yearning for civil society," due largely to the transcendent demands of Islam.[32] Another argues that "tribalism combined with a powerful and virtually unchangeable doctrine to make political rule alien, transitory and predatory," thereby inhibiting the development of autonomous capitalism and the social relations it sustained in the West.[33]

Still another points to the historical absence in Islamic societies of "any legal recognition of corporate persons," which served as an obstacle to the emergence of "the innumerable parliaments, councils, synods, diets, chambers and assemblies of every kind" that existed in the West since classical antiquity.[34] Others scholars dispute these accounts of civil society in the Middle East on both historical[35] and theoretical[36] grounds.

As is readily apparent, these issues are intimately intertwined with many of the debates over political culture discussed earlier. Are Islamist groups inherently antiliberal by virtue of their religious foundations and their commitment to an absolute truth resistant to political and social compromise? Or can elements of a tolerant Islamic liberalism be detected? Does Islam justify political authoritarianism, or does it subvert political legitimacy? Is Arab civil society too weak, as powerful states and repressive limitations on social organization would suggest, or are Arab societies too strong and unruly, resulting in governments that must depend on force to maintain their control? At another level, does the doctrinal content of Islam matter—as those emphasizing "civility" would suggest—or is the fact of opposition to existing authoritarian rule more important? Indeed, what is the connection between doctrine and political activities, especially those activities at the level of civil society?

Other questions are raised about the extent of family-, tribal-, or other primordially based organizations within Arab societies, and the impact that these might have on any possible process of liberalization and democratization.[37] Is democratization possible in communally divided societies? Again, the question partly depends on how one conceives of civil society. If democracy requires a civil society which itself sustains moderate interaction, divisions and intolerances within Arab societies can be seen as problematic. Yet if democracy is the product of a particular balance between the state and various competing social groups, communal divisions may in fact be particularly suited to democratic solutions based on accommodation and compromise between the contenders. Actual Arab experiences in Lebanon, Sudan, and now Yemen—which have sustained wild swings between parliamentary politics and civil war—seem to confirm both contentions.

These issues are explored at length in Part 2 of this volume. Mustapha Kamel al-Sayyid explores the dilemma of using the concept of civil society in the Arab context. He argues against any formulation of a specifically "Arab" notion of civil society on the grounds that this would dilute the comparative analytical value of the concept. Adopting a definition that emphasizes organization, civility, and a certain quality of state-society relations, he finds at most a nascent civil society in the region. The future of Arab civil society, moreover, is uncertain, given pressures from authoritarian states and a doubtful commitment to pluralism on the part of some emergent political forces.

The subsequent chapters in this section all explore key sectors of civil society. Lise Garon assesses the role of the press in supporting political openings, arguing that in cases where liberalization opens spaces for a long-suppressed civil society, the press too will move into those spaces—but more reactively than proactively. In turn, Janine Clark addresses the question of the connection between doctrine and political activities, raised earlier in this introduction and also addressed in Part 1. Her fieldwork among Islamic clinics in Cairo finds that despite emphasis on the principle of *shura*, there was little conscious effort to create new models of group decisionmaking or societal empowerment. Moreover—and contrary to the presumptions of much of the literature—she found little signs of Islamic political mobilization or of a grassroots political battle against the state. Finally, Mervat Hatem explores the impact of political liberalization on women's organizations in Tunisia, Egypt, and Sudan. She suggests that, despite the assumptions usually made about democratization and empowerment, the practical effect has often been quite different. True, there may be greater tolerance of pluralism and autonomy. Yet in many regimes (such as Egypt), governments have retreated from their former commitment to gender issues. For their part, Islamist movements have sought to "socialize" gender issues, redefining women's place out of the political arena and back in the family.

Political Economy

There is a long-established intellectual tradition, dating as far back as Aristotle, linking wealth and democracy.[38] More recently, a major contemporary research project on democracy asserts that "over the past three decades, a large number of quantitative analyses have supported the thesis of a positive relationship between socioeconomic development and democracy."[39] Attempts to explain this have pointed to a number of factors, including the disruptive impact of modernization (which breaks down old authority structures and introduces the possibility of political change), higher degrees of education, greater satisfaction of social demands (and hence a less conflictual political environment), a more equal distribution of wealth, the development of a more complex society, and the growth of a bourgeoisie.[40]

According to recent statistics, the Arab world has an average gross national product (GNP) per capita of $1,730, a figure approaching that of the (generally democratic) states of Latin America and well ahead of the average of $810 for the developing world as a whole.[41] These aggregate figures, however, mask the unique economic characteristics of the Arab region, characteristics largely associated with subregional petroleum wealth.

Thus, while most Arab countries are classified as "middle" or "lower-middle" income countries by the World Bank, the major Arab oil producers are unique among developing countries in the high levels of economic resources available to them. Indeed, the disparities between Arab "haves" and "have-nots" represent the greatest regional disparities in the world.

Since the early 1980s a number of scholars have posited a connection between Arab oil wealth and the lack of democracy in the Arab oil-producing countries.[42] It is argued that these countries constitute "rentier" states in which access to large amounts of externally generated economic resources serves to strengthen state autonomy. Because state revenues are not dependent on domestic production, but rather on the international market, state decisionmakers are much less constrained by the interests of domestic actors. The availability of financial resources not only supports the coercive apparatus of the state but also sustains massive social welfare programs and fuels powerful neopatrimonial networks based on family, tribe, and proximity to the ruling elite. Indeed, coercion becomes less important as political legitimacy is, in a very real sense, "purchased" through economic rewards.

All of this has important implications for the development of civil society. The narrow base of the economy (centered on the petroleum and public sectors) deprives most societal actors of any degree of economic leverage vis-à-vis the state. Society is atomized into individual rent- and reward-seekers, and the development of the autonomous institutions of civil society is severely stunted. Finally, the absence of domestic appropriation by the rentier state may alter the very nature of collective political demands made upon it. In most developing countries, state appropriation of societal resources ("taxation") typically spurs the population to seek a greater voice in the allocation of state expenditures ("representation"). Indeed, in the Western political experience at least, the proto-institutions of liberal democracy (parliamentary bodies and legal-constitutional limits on executive power) were frequently won in struggles of citizens and social classes against the extractive power of the state.[43] Such pressures, however, are much less likely in rentier states. The social contract here is of a very different sort: The state is expected to provide a certain level of economic security, in exchange for which society grants state leaders considerable political autonomy. Indeed, if anything, the slogan of the American Revolution—"no taxation without representation"—is reversed: In a rentier state, state-society relations seem predicated on the principle of "no taxation, no representation."[44]

The concept of "rentier politics" represents a powerful analytical tool to explain the absence of democratic politics in the major oil-producing countries. Indeed, given the existence of a broader Arab oil economy in the 1970s and 1980s that linked rich and poor states in the region through a web of migrant labor and petrodollar foreign aid, it can even be argued that poorer "semi-renters" like Jordan were able to blunt demands for increased representation during this period through a combination of economic buoyancy and enhanced state financial resources. Similarly, the onset of political liberalization in countries like Jordan and Algeria can be explained by reference to mounting economic crises that rendered the old style of rentier politics increasingly untenable.[45]

There are, however, a number of difficulties inherent in the rentier model. It can be seen as overdeterministic in linking oil wealth with authoritarian rule, while failing to adequately value the importance of historical and cultural context.[46] The model holds out few possibilities for change (other than economic crisis) and might have difficulty explaining Kuwait's return to limited parliamentarianism, the modest openings in Oman and (more questionably) in Saudi Arabia, the trajectory of crisis in Algeria, or the ups and downs of the liberalization process in semi-renters like Egypt and Jordan. Finally, rentierism—however well it might fit in the Arab context—does not seem to travel well to other oil-producing states. In Iran, oil wealth is often credited with causing, rather than blunting, revolutionary pressures from below.[47] In Venezuela, by contrast, oil wealth is often credited with having cemented the transition to democracy.[48] In Nigeria, oil income seems to sustain neither stability nor democracy.

Nonetheless, the concept continues to have validity, especially in light of the mounting pressures on many Arab governments to curtail expenditures, institute structural adjustment programs, and generally accommodate themselves to the forces of a global market. Some critical scholars studying processes of market reform and globalization suggest that these have "dramatically increased poverty and skewed income distribution," resulting in a rapid erosion of political legitimacy, the growth of antiregime "movements of rage," and a "profound redrawing of political boundaries along definitely illiberal lines."[49] Still others suggest a mixed and even contradictory relationship between economic and political liberalization, while highlighting the limited and manipulative nature of both in the Middle East.[50]

Most of the orthodox literature, however, suggests that the dominant role of the government in many Arab economies has had antidemocratic effects, bolstering the power of state over society. In this view, the prospects for a political opening are closely linked to a shift to a market economy. As the latest edition of the most widely used American textbook on Middle East politics asserts:

> Political systems will be more profoundly affected by the course of economic liberalizations. Authoritarian government in the Middle East, as elsewhere, must have control over the bulk of economic resources to

sustain itself. Otherwise, it will be challenged by those who do. If economic growth is rapid and private sectors of national economies prosper, resources beyond the control of the state will be available to reinforce political liberalization. The state's retreat from the economy would be paralleled by the expansion of civil society.[51]

Such a perspective looks to the long-term growth of the middle class and of a new Arab bourgeoisie, which serves to weaken the autonomy of state elites and stimulate the organization of new, pluralist associations and interest groups within civil society.[52]

Another, shorter-term perspective focuses on the immediate politics of structural adjustment measures. It suggests that Arab governments have been forced by economic circumstances to offer "a new ruling bargain by which popular acquiescence to difficult economic reform is obtained through the creation of a new democratic bargain."[53] This is particularly likely when economic reform involves a shift away from an earlier pattern of rentierism, statist development, and the provision of social welfare services. In addition, it is often argued that political reform facilitates, rather than hinders, economic reform. Political liberalization improves information flows, and hence the efficiency of both economic and political decisionmaking. Expanded political participation serves to distribute more widely the responsibility for painful economic measures, facilitates revenue-generation through taxation, and increases the credibility of the shift away from old economic policies.[54] Indeed, despite the frequent assumption that democracies find it difficult to adopt and implement hard economic choices, some comparative evidence suggests that they are as successful—or more successful—than authoritarian regimes in this regard.[55] At the same time, however, it is clear that there is no automatic connection between economic performance and regime type,[56] nor is political reform a prerequisite for economic liberalization.[57]

In Part 3 of this volume, all of these issues are further explored. Giacomo Luciani, accepting the view that rentierism has helped to support Arab authoritarianism, explores what may follow from it. He suggests that, in principle, economic structural adjustment can be undertaken without endangering political stability. In the Arab world, however, reform has been very late, making economic change more difficult. The persistence of established authoritarian regimes (associated with old economic policies), moreover, undermines the credibility of economic reform. Democratization, by replacing old elites, might enhance the credibility of economic reform—although there is certainly no automatic connection between political and economic reform. The question of these reforms is also taken up by Daniel Brumberg. He suggests that the initial response of regimes to economic failure has not been far-reaching economic and political reform, but rather, more cautious economic and political "survival strategies." These, he suggests, are rooted in the legacies of populist authoritarianism, which render it difficult for elites to move away from old statist policies or strike dramatically new democratic bargains. However, such survival strategies have failed to address the underlying roots of economic malaise and, unless supported by external financial resources, only temporarily postpone economic structural adjustment. This, in turn, requires deeper political changes, either exclusionary or inclusionary in nature. Interestingly, Brumberg suggests that Arab monarchies, because they are not bound by the legacies of populist authoritarianism, may find these economic adjustments easier to make.

Samih Farsoun and Christina Zacharia have greater doubts than either Luciani or Brumberg about the benefits of structural economic adjustment, emphasizing the extent to which it benefits the rich and foreign capital, while its burden falls disproportionately on subordinate socioeconomic classes. The political effects of this, in turn, imperil—rather than advance—the prospects for building a societal consensus. Farsoun and Zacharia also have doubts about contemporary political reforms, critically suggesting that "political neoliberalism—whether in Latin America, the Arab world, or the rest of the Third World—is only for those indigenous elites, classes, or groups (and political parties) who are willing and able to support economic liberalism." At this point, however, their analysis begins to converge with that of Brumberg, suggesting that coalition building under political liberalization is intimately tied to maintaining a constituency for economic policy reforms—and, furthermore, that even cautious and controlled openings may ultimately begin to acquire, unforeseen by elites, a political momentum all their own.

Regional and International Context

In emphasizing the impact of globalization and international financial pressures, many of the contributors to Part 3 point to a fourth area of analytical concern: the impact of forces at the regional and global levels on the prospects for liberalization and democratization.

This area is one that is comparatively understudied within the general literature on democratization. To the extent that a literature exists, much of it focuses on global "diffusion" (that is to say, the spread of democratic values) or on democratic "demonstration effects" (transitions in one country hastening transitions elsewhere in its region).[58] Economic globalization and technological change (including, variously, such things as fax machines, television satellite dishes, and the global computer Internet) are generally held to have accelerated this process by breaking down international barriers, loosening the authoritarian grips of governments over the free flow of information, and empowering grassroots democratic activists. At the same time, however, it is important to note that these same sorts of pressures may reinforce the tendency toward authoritarian retrenchment by beleaguered regimes (as in China since Tiananmen Square). Insofar as they are seen as spearheads of a Western cultural invasion, they may also provoke a defensive reaction within the affected societies themselves—possibly delegitimizing whatever liberal democratic messages they may carry at the same time.[59] Others have focused on the general role of the United States and other actors in shaping democratic change. Strong differences exist between those who see Western countries playing a genuinely supportive role and critics who see Western policies on democracy as ultimately driven by the desire to secure economic or strategic advantage.[60]

The impact of regional and international forces on democratization in the Arab world is also understudied. There does exist some literature linking the persistence of authoritarianism in the Arab world to regional conflict, which is said to have spurred the militarization of the *mukhabarat* state, diverted resources away from social priorities, and justified domestic repression in the name of national unity against an external enemy.[61] There is also significant attention—much of it more rhetorical than analytical—on the impact of extraregional support for authoritarian regimes and contemporary Western (especially U.S.) attitudes toward Arab democratization. On this issue, most scholarly opinion is critical, albeit spanning a range from "it is unfair to say that American policy has been consistently hostile to democratic movements *per se* in the Middle East,"[62] through "foreign governmental policies, principally US, toward reform have not played significant positive roles in the past,"[63] to "in its 20th century engagement with the Middle East, Washington has consistently opposed and subverted those forces pursuing any measure of a democratic program."[64] Most Arab opinion clearly concurs with the latter view.

There has been little attention, however, to the role that regional forces and foreign policies may play in facilitating or inhibiting political openings in neighboring states. That question is taken up in this volume by Gregory Gause, who suggests that high degrees of international conflict in the Middle East, the power of transnational ideology, and the economic importance of exogenous rents all serve as obstacles to liberalization. At the same time, however, increased attention to issues of repression, human rights, and effective governance among Arab intellectuals may come to represent a significant transnational regional force in support of future political liberalization.

There has also been little attention—other than to note its importance—directed to the salience of democratic diffusion and the complex interaction of external and internal variables in shaping the prospects for democracy. Herein, Gabriel Ben-Dor addresses those very issues, suggesting that the post–Cold War international environment has created improved conditions for democratic experiments in the Arab world. He is less confident, however, that domestic conditions are equally ripe—although a reduction of Arab-Israeli tensions may have an important moderating effect on domestic political processes. Indeed, both Gause and Ben-Dor ultimately underline the primacy of internal conditions in shaping political openings.

By Way of Conclusion

This introduction has suggested that four themes—political culture and discourse, civil society, political economy, and the regional and international context—lie at the core of any theoretically informed study of political liberalization and democratization in the Arab world. It is for that reason that this book has been organized around them. Before moving on to the insights offered by contributors, however, two other observations should be made.

The first of these observations concerns the differential impact of liberalization and democratization, and the importance of focusing particular attention on the impact of political reform on subaltern groups within society. To what extent do the middle and upper classes reap disproportionate benefit from political reform by virtue of their superior access to such critical resources as money, connections, education, organizational skills, and spare time? Herein, Farsoun and Zacharia suggest important class dimensions to current programs of economic and political liberalization. What are the differential implications of political liberalization and democratization for men and women in the Middle East? Comparative scholarship on democratic transitions suggests important gendered dimensions of this process.[65] Herein, Hatem suggests that the decline of authoritarian developmental regimes may hurt the interests of many women, insofar as such regimes—whatever their limited participatory character—were at least formally committed to gender equality and social welfare. Finally, how might religious or ethnic minorities be affected by democratization? How can their interests best be protected? The issue is a highly sensitive one.[66] Liberal democracies tend to presume that the salience of communal identities will be removed by a system that emphasizes primacy of individualism and individual rights. Yet, as is amply evident in contemporary politics around the world, this prescription fails to work in cases where groups wish to preserve a distinctive cultural identity or achieve a greater degree of communal self-determination. This being so, democratic polities are forced to adopt one or more of several possible strategies for "managing difference": Communal groups (whether majorities or minorities) can act outside a liberal framework to repress other groups; communal majorities can use their majoritarianism within the democratic process to exert control over minorities through legislative means; democratic authority can be decentralized (through some form of federalism or cantonization) and efforts made to match local authority to the geographic distribution of communal groups; some form of consociationalism and institutionalized power sharing can be adopted among communal groups; and/or external parties may be called upon to arbitrate communal differences, or may intervene to assume the task.[67] Because of its importance, this issue—among others—will be explored in detail in the second volume of this project, in the context of case studies of Lebanon (characterized by external intervention and uncertain stability of its consociational political structures), Sudan (where such issues are manifest in both civil war and debates over federalism), Yemen (with its regional tensions and endemically weak national integration), and other Arab countries where minorities may fear majoritarian politics.

The second observation to be made concerns the need to integrate both theoretical and substantive insights in our work. Just as ad hoc treatments of Arab politics have tended to inhibit the generation of appropriate theoretical tools, so too theorizing in abstraction from the historical setting and real experience of politics is a sterile exercise. It is for this reason that the second volume of this project devotes itself to a range of country case studies, of rich and poor economies, of more and less homogeneous societies, of republics and monarchies, and of liberalizing and nonliberalizing regimes. It is for that reason too that we begin our exploration in this first volume with Saad Eddin Ibrahim's overview of the contemporary status of liberalization and democratization in the Arab world.

Notes

1. Samuel Huntington, *The Third Wave: Democratization in the Late Twentieth Century* (Norman: University of Oklahoma Press, 1991).
2. Guillermo O'Donnell, Philippe C. Schmitter, and Laurence Whitehead, eds., *Transitions from Authoritarian Rule: Prospects for Democracy* (Baltimore: Johns Hopkins University Press, 1986).
3. Larry Diamond, Juan J. Linz, and Seymour Martin Lipset, eds., *Democracy in Developing Countries, Volume Two: Africa* (Boulder: Lynne Rienner Publishers, 1988), p. xix.
4. Samuel Huntington, "Will More Countries Become Democratic?" *Political Science Quarterly* 99, 2 (Summer 1984), p. 216.
5. Michael Hudson, "Democratization and the Problem of Legitimacy in Middle East Politics," *MESA Bulletin* 22, 2 (December 1988), p. 157.

6. Anderson, "Policy-Making and Theory Building: American Political Science and the Islamic Middle East," in Hisham Sharabi, ed., *Theory, Politics and the Arab World: Critical Responses* (New York: Routledge, 1990).

7. The issue of "experiments in democracy and the birth of political parties" received a "high" degree of attention in 16 percent of the courses surveyed, and "little" or "no" attention in 29 percent; the issue of "political dissidents and social protest" received a "high" degree of attention in 16 percent of the courses surveyed, and "little" or "no" attention in 43 percent. Instead, the most studied political issues were "nationalism," "religious and ethnic factionalism," "revolutions," "ideologies," and the "fundamentalist resurgence." Lori Anne Salem, "The DANTES Survey of Courses in Contemporary Middle East Studies," *MESA Bulletin* 26, 2 (December 1992), pp. 174–175.

8. Joe Stork and Steve Nida, "Academic Freedom in the Middle East," MERIP Special Publication (December 1989).

9. For the impact of government controls on academic enquiry, see Joe Stork and Steve Nida, *Academic Freedom in the Middle East* (Washington, DC: Middle East Research and Information Project, 1989).

10. Bahgat Korany, Rex Brynen, and Paul Noble, eds., *Political Liberalization and Democratization in The Arab World: Experiences* (Boulder: Lynne Rienner Publishers, forthcoming).

11. See, for example, Daniel Pipes, *In the Path of God: Islam and Political Power* (New York: Basic Books, 1983), pp. 144–147; Amos Perlmutter, "Islam and Democracy Simply Aren't Compatible," *International Herald Tribune*, 21 January 1992; Elie Keddourie, *Democracy and Arab Political Culture* (Washington, DC: Washington Institute for Near East Policy, 1992), pp. 5–8.

12. David Pryce–Jones, *The Closed Circle: An Interpretation of the Arabs* (New York: Harper & Row, 1989); Daniel Pipes, "Dealing with Middle Eastern Conspiracy Theories," *Orbis* 36, 1 (1992).

13. Michael Hudson, *Arab Politics: The Search for Legitimacy* (New Haven: Yale University Press, 1977).

14. John Esposito, *The Islamic Threat: Myth or Reality?* (Oxford: Oxford University Press, 1992), pp. 184–189; Leonard Binder, *Islamic Liberalism: A Critique of Development Ideologies* (Chicago: University of Chicago Press, 1988). Ann Elizabeth Mayer (*Islam and Human Rights: Tradition and Politics* [Boulder: Westview Press, 1993]) finds that, although rights have been narrowed rather than expanded in most Muslim countries, this is due largely to political manipulation rather than the intrinsic content of Islam. She does, however, express concern over the status of women and minorities. Bernard Lewis also explicitly notes the actual and potential variation within Islam. However, his analysis generally seems to suggest that the emergence of a successful Islamic democratic liberalism is very unlikely. See, for example, Bernard Lewis, "Islam and Liberal Democracy," *Atlantic Monthly* (February 1993). Similarly, see John Waterbury, "Democracy without Democrats? The Potential for Political Liberalization in the Arab World," in Ghassan Salamé, ed., *Democracy without Democrats: The Renewal of Politics in the Muslim World* (London: I. B. Tauris, 1994), pp. 30–32, 39–44.

15. John Esposito and James Piscatori, "Democratization and Islam," *Middle East Journal* 45, 3 (Summer 1991); Gudrun Krämer, "Islamist Notions of Democracy," *Middle East Report* 183 (July–August 1993).

16. Michael Collins Dunn, "Islamist Parties in Democratizing States: A Look at Jordan and Yemen," *Middle East Policy* 2, 2 (1993).

17. Augustus Richard Norton, "Inclusion Can Deflate Islamic Populism?" *New Perspectives Quarterly* 10, 3 (Summer 1993); John L. Esposito, "Islamic Movements, Democratization, and US Foreign Policy," in Phebe Marr and William Lewis, eds., *Riding the Tiger: The Middle East Challenge after the Cold War* (Boulder: Westview Press, 1993), p. 207.

18. Lisa Anderson, "Absolutism and the Resilience of Monarchy in the Middle East," *Political Science Quarterly* 106, 1 (1991).

19. Edward Said, *Covering Islam* (New York: Pantheon, 1981); Said, *Orientalism* (New York: Pantheon, 1978).

20. See, for example, Kevin Dwyer, *Arab Voices: The Human Rights Debate in the Middle East* (Berkeley: University of California Press, 1991), pp. 87–98; Peter Ford, "The Dilemma for Arab Democrats," *Christian Science Monitor*, 7–13 May 1993.

21. One obvious example is Fouad Ajami; see Ajami, *The Arab Predicament: Arab Political Thought and Practice since 1967,* 1st ed. (New York: Cambridge University Press, 1981), p. 182, and his comments to the Jerusalem Foundation, 3 June 1992 (transcript). Although Ajami's work has been criticized—often on ideological grounds—there is no shortage of other scholars (of differing political persuasions) who could be pointed to. Hisham Sharabi, in his *Neopatriarchy: A Theory of Distorted Change in Arab Society* (New York: Oxford University Press, 1988), places great emphasis on what might be termed political culture, although he does not assign it prior or overwhelming weight. As'ad AbuKhalil finds Islam—and indeed all three monotheistic religions—as antithetical to gender equality and democracy, but only insofar as they are fully applied in pure doctrinal form. As'ad AbuKhalil, "A Viable Partnership: Islam, Democracy and the Arab World," *Harvard International Review* 15, 2 (Winter 1992/93), and "Toward the Study of Women and Politics in the Arab World: The Debate and the Reality," *Feminist Issues* 13, 1 (Spring 1993). Fatima Mernissi is more ambiguous as to whether it is the text, context, or interpretation of Islam that accounts for authoritarianism and gender subordination, but clearly frames much of her analysis in terms of Arab-Islamic political culture. See Mernissi, *Islam and Democracy: Fear of the Modern World* (Reading, MA: Addison-Wesley, 1992). Hilal Khashan, "The Quagmire of Arab Democracy," *Arab Studies Quarterly* (1993), argues that lack of national integration and democratic political culture are among the major obstacles to successful democratization in the region.

22. Indeed, the contemporary Arabic literature on the question of Islam, pluralism, liberty, and democracy is voluminous, as suggested by both Salwa Ismail and Gudrun Krämer in their respective contributions to this volume. For recent representative examples, see Fahmi Huwaydi, *al-Islam wa al-dimuqratiyya* [Islam and Democracy] (Cairo: al-Ahram, 1993); Rashid al-Ghannushi, *al-Hurriyyat al-'amma fi al-islam* [Public Liberties in Islam] (Beirut: Center for Arab Unity Studies, 1993).

23. Of even more direct relevance is the debate within Israel over the tensions between that country's aspirations to be both "Jewish" and "democratic." In fact, given some of the doctrinal parallels between Islamic and Jewish concepts of religious jurisprudence, this debate could be useful if studied by those interested in the question of religion and democratic development in the Arab world. Israel has not been the object of comparative study in this way, of course, because of the tensions and taboos generated by the Arab-Israeli conflict.

24. These include, for example, the collaborative research project on "Civil Society in the Middle East," directed by Augustus Richard Norton (Boston University);

the newsletter *Civil Society and Democratic Transition in the Arab World* and other activities of the Ibn Khaldoun Center for Development Studies in Cairo, directed by Saad Eddin Ibrahim; and the "Civil Society Working Group" of the Initiative for Peace and Cooperation in the Middle East/Search for Common Ground.

25. Dwyer, *Arab Voices*, p. 146.

26. Augustus Richard Norton, "The Future of Civil Society in the Middle East," *Middle East Journal* 47, 2 (Spring 1993), p. 211.

27. Guillermo O'Donnell and Philippe Schmitter, *Transitions from Authoritarian Rule: Tentative Conclusions about Uncertain Democracies* (Baltimore: Johns Hopkins University Press, 1986), pp. 48–56.

28. Ernest Gellner, "Civil Society in Historical Context," *International Social Science Journal* 129 (August 1991).

29. See, for example, John Hall, *Powers and Liberties: The Causes and Consequences of the Rise of the West* (London: Penguin, 1985); David Blarney and Mustapha Kamal Pasha, "Civil Society and Democracy in the Third World: Ambiguities and Historical Possibilities," *Studies in Comparative International Development* 28, 1 (Spring 1993).

30. Feminist scholars have complained that this notion of civil society privileges male-dominated formal organizations and hence understates the political role of women. "Organizational" notions of civil society also tend to exclude patron-client networks or diffuse kinship-based groups, although both of these could conceivably blunt the power of an authoritarian state.

31. See, for example, Samuel Valenzuela, "Labor Movements in Transitions to Democracy: A Framework for Analysis," *Comparative Politics* 21, 4 (July 1989). The danger of "democratic" civil society is that its resurgence, propelled forward by the anger and aspirations of its mass membership, will so alarm already skittish authoritarian elites that they will halt or reverse the liberalization/democratization process. Guillermo O'Donnell and Philippe Schmitter, *Transitions from Authoritarian Rule: Tentative Conclusions*, pp. 26–27, 70–71.

32. Ernest Gellner, "Civil Society in Historical Context," p. 506. In particular, Gellner suggests that toleration emerges from a clash and stalemate between an established clerical class and religious enthusiasts, a "Reformation" that he finds absent in the Middle East.

33. Hall, *Powers and Liberties*, pp. 84–110.

34. Lewis, "Islam and Liberal Democracy," pp. 93–94.

35. Ellis Goldberg, "Private Goods, Public Wrongs, and Civil Society in Some Medieval Arab Theory and Practice," in Ellis Goldberg, Resat Kasaba, and Joel Migdal, eds., *Rules and Rights in the Middle East: Democracy, Law and Society* (Seattle: University of Washington Press, 1993). Goldberg argues that individuals in medieval Islam were able to use various instruments, legal and otherwise, to protect their economic resources from the power of monarchs.

36. For an examination of these issues within recent writings on civil society in the Middle East, see Yahya Sadowski, "The New Orientalism and the Democracy Debate," *Middle East Report* 183 (July–August 1993).

37. Or, for that matter, the impact that electoral politics might have on primordial groups. See Linda Layne, *Home and Homeland: The Dialogics of Tribal and National Identities in Jordan* (Princeton: Princeton University Press, 1994), pp. 108–127.

38. Aristotle, *The Politics*, Book 6, Chapter 5.

39. Larry Diamond, Juan Linz, and Seymour Martin Lipset, eds., *Politics in Developing Countries: Comparing Experiences with Democracy* (Boulder: Lynne Rienner Publishers, 1990), pp. 18–19.

40. For a discussion see Huntington, "Will More Countries Become Democratic?" Zehra Arat, *Democracy and Human Rights in Developing Countries* (Boulder: Lynne Rienner Publishers, 1991), pp. 33–43.

41. United Nations Development Program, *Human Development Report 1993* (Oxford: Oxford University Press, 1993), p. 213. Data are for 1990.

42. Giacomo Luciani, "Allocation vs. Production States: A Theoretical Framework," and Hazem Beblawi, "The Rentier State in the Arab World," in Luciani and Beblawi, eds., *The Rentier State* (London, New York: Croom Helm, 1987). See also the discussion in Rex Brynen, "Economic Crisis and Post-Rentier Democratization in the Arab World: The Case of Jordan," *Canadian Journal of Political Science* 25, 1 (March 1992), from which much of this section is drawn.

43. Charles Tilly, "War Making and State Making as Organized Crime," in Peter B. Evans, Dietrich Rueschemeyer, and Theda Skocpol, eds., *Bringing the State Back In* (Cambridge, UK: Cambridge University Press, 1985), p. 183.

44. Giacomo Luciani, "Economic Foundations of Democracy and Authoritarianism: The Arab World in Comparative Perspective," *Arab Studies Quarterly* 10 (1988). A parallel argument has also been made by scholars who suggest that the development of representative institutions enhances the efficiency of revenue collection by revenue-maximizing states. See Robert Bates and Da-Hsiang Donald Lien, "A Note on Taxation, Development, and Representative Government," *Politics and Society* 14 (1985); Margaret Levi, *Of Rule and Revenue* (Berkeley: University of California Press, 1988).

45. Brynen, "Economic Crisis and Post-Rentier Democratization in the Arab World;" Laurie Brand, "Economic and Political Liberalization in a Rentier Economy: The Case of the Hashemite Kingdom of Jordan," in Iliya Harik and Denis Sullivan, eds., *Privatization and Liberalization in the Middle East* (Bloomington: Indiana University Press, 1992).

46. Eric Davis, "Theorizing Statecraft and Social Change in Arab Oil-Producing Countries," in Eric Davis and Nicolas Gavrielides, eds., *Statecraft in the Middle East: Oil, Historical Memory and Popular Culture* (Miami: Florida International University Press, 1991).

47. Theda Skocpol, "Rentier State and Shi'a Islam in the Iranian Revolution," *Theory and Society* 11 (1982); Afsaneh Najmabadi, "Iran's Turn to Islam: From Modernism to Moral Order," *Middle East Journal* 41, 2 (Spring 1987). In the Iranian case, oil wealth aggravated the tensions of rapid social change, while the autonomy of the petroleum-financed state generated societal alienation from the Shah's regime.

48. Terry Lynn Karl, "Petroleum and Political Pacts: The Transition to Democracy in Venezuela," *Latin American Research Review* 22, 1 (1987).

49. Kiren Aziz Chaudhry, "The Myths of the Market and the Common History of Late Developers," *Politics and Society* 21, 3 (September 1993), p. 263.

50. David Pool, "Observations on the Connections between Economic and Political Liberalization," xerox; Nazih Ayubi, "Political Correlates of Privatization Programs in the Middle East," *Arab Studies Quarterly* 14, 2–3 (Spring–Summer 1992), pp. 47–54.

51. James Bill and Robert Springborg, *Politics in the Middle East,* 4th ed. (New York: HarperCollins College Publishers, 1994), p. 450. Although rejecting a "direct causal link," Iliya Harik also finds that "economic and political liberalization reinforce one another," in Harik and Sullivan, eds., *Privatization and Liberalization in the Middle East,* p. 21.

52. Robert Springborg, "The Arab Bourgeoisie: A Revisionist Interpretation," *Arab Studies Quarterly* 15, 1 (Winter 1993), pp. 31–33. See also Alan Richards and

John Waterbury, *A Political Economy of the Middle East: State, Class and Economic Development* (Boulder: Westview Press, 1990), pp. 436–437.

53. Daniel Brumberg, "Democratic Bargains and the Politics of Economic Stabilization: The Case of Egypt in Comparative Perspective," paper presented to the 1989 MESA annual conference, pp. 1–2.

54. See Giacomo Luciani's chapter in this volume.

55. Karen Remmer, "The Politics of Economic Stabilization: IMF Standby Programs in Latin America, 1954–1984," *Comparative Politics* 19, 1 (October 1986); Marc Lindenberg and Shantayanan Devarajan, "Prescribing Strong Economic Medicine: Revising the Myths about Structural Adjustment, Democracy, and Economic Performance in Developing Countries," *Comparative Politics* 25, 2 (January 1993).

56. Larry Sirowy and Alex Inkeles, "The Effects of Democracy on Economic Growth and Inequality: A Review," in Alex Inkeles, ed., *On Measuring Democracy: Its Consequences and Concomitants* (New Brunswick, NJ: Transaction Publishers, 1993).

57. Steven Heydemann, "Taxation without Representation: Authoritarianism and Economic Liberalization in Syria," in Goldberg, Kasaba, and Migdal, eds., *Rules and Rights in the Middle East.*

58. For a discussion of the potential role of "democratic diffusion"—albeit one that ignores the Middle East entirely—see Giuseppe DiPalma, *To Craft Democracy: An Essay on Democratic Transitions* (Berkeley: University of California Press, 1990), pp. 14–26, 183–199. See also Harvey Starr, "Democratic Dominoes: Diffusion Approaches to the Spread of Democracy in the International System," *Journal of Conflict Resolution* 35, 2 (June 1991); Larry Diamond, "The Globalization of Democracy," in Robert Slater, Barry Schutz, and Steven Dorr, *Global Transformation and the Third World* (Boulder: Lynne Rienner Publishers, 1993), pp. 49–61.

59. For an insightful discussion of the complex effects of new information technologies on democratization, see Adam Jones, "Wired World: Communications Technology, Governance, and the Democratic Uprising," in Edward Cornor, ed., *The Global Political Economy of Communication* (London: Macmillan, 1994).

60. See, for example, the contrasting assessments offered by Larry Diamond, "Promoting Democracy," *Foreign Policy* 87 (Summer 1992), and William Robinson, *A Faustian Bargain: US Intervention in the Nicaraguan Elections and American Foreign Policy in the Post–Cold War Era* (Boulder: Westview Press, 1992).

61. Rex Brynen, "Palestine and the Arab State System: Permeability, State Consolidation and the Intifada," *Canadian Journal of Political Science* 24, 3 (September 1991), pp. 607–610; Bahgat Korany, Paul Noble, and Rex Brynen, eds., *The Many Faces of National Security in the Arab World* (London: Macmillan, 1993), pp. 206–213.

62. William Quandt, "American Policy toward Democratic Political Movements in the Middle East," in Goldberg, Kasaba, and Migdal, eds., *Rules and Rights in the Middle East*, p. 164.

63. Pete Moore, "The International Context of Liberalization and Democratization in the Arab World," *Arab Studies Quarterly* (forthcoming), p. 28 (ms). This article is noteworthy for its attempt to address a range of international factors, including diffusion, foreign policies, and the activities of human rights organizations.

64. The editors, "The Democracy Agenda in the Arab World," *Middle East Report* 174 (January–February 1992), p. 47.

65. Georgina Waylen, "Women and Democratization: Conceptualizing Gender Relations in Transition Politics," *World Politics* 46, 3 (April 1994).

66. Such sensitivity extends to the whole question of minorities in the Arab world. Evidence of this was provided by a conference on that subject organized in Cairo by the Ibn Khaldoun Center for Development Studies in May 1994. A number of influential commentators in Egypt attacked the focus on minority rights, fearing that it served to divide the Arab-Islamic world. Subsequently, the venue of the conference was moved to Cyprus. For details, see *Civil Society* 3, 30 (June 1994).

67. This schema derives largely from John McGarry, presentation to the conference "From Transition to Consolidation: Contexts of Democracy in the Late 20th Century," McGill University, October 1994.

2

Liberalization and Democratization in the Arab World: An Overview

Saad Eddin Ibrahim

Much of the literature circulating in recent years on the prerequisites, requisites, and modalities of transition from nondemocratic to democratic rule[1] finds a fertile ground for testing in the Arab world. While belonging to one general political-cultural area, the 21 Arab countries represent a wide variety of cases in terms of the variables often associated with such transition—for example, the nature and evolution of the state,[2] political regimes, class structure, political culture, levels of socioeconomic development, and civil society.[3]

A Theoretical Overture

The concept of civil society has emerged in the last decade as an overarching category linking democracy, development, and peaceful management of domestic and regional conflict. While there are a variety of ways of defining the concept, they all revolve around *maximizing volitional, organized, collective participation in the public space between individuals and the state.* In its institutional form, "civil society" is composed of nonstate actors or nongovernmental organizations (NGOs), including political parties, trade unions, professional associations, community development associations, and other interest groups.[4] Normatively, "civil society" implies values and behavioral codes of tolerating—if not accepting—others and a tacit or explicit commitment to the peaceful management of differences among individuals and collectivities sharing the same "public space" —that is, the polity.[5]

Civil society, as so defined, emerged organically out of modern socioeconomic formations such as classes, occupational categories, and other interest groups. In the West, this process unfolded simultaneously with the processes of capitalization, industrialization, urbanization, citizenship, and the nation-state. While the ultimate loyalty of citizens was supposedly to the nation-state as the natural sovereign embodiment of all society, subloyalties were to follow interests focused in class, occupation, and residential community. Volitional associations emerged and expanded around the many interests of citizens—political parties, trade unions, professional associations, clubs, community organizations, and so on. While loyalty to the sovereign state was emotive, abstract, and only occasionally invoked, solidarities of volitional associations were interest-based, concrete, and more frequently invoked. While loyalty to the state was supposedly universal and consensual among all citizens, solidarity with a volitional association was particularistic and variable in intensity and duration. That is to say, while citizens rarely change their ties to a nation-state, they frequently alter the structure of their volitional associations: Class, occupation, status, and residence change due to vertical and horizontal mobility. With competing, or even conflicting, interests of various socioeconomic formations in the same nation-state, governance ideally evolves gradually along participatory lines—toward democracy. Some socioeconomic formations are more conscious of their interest and quicker than others in organizing their ranks to retain, seize, or share political power within the state. The less conscious and less organized formations learn over time, by emulation, the art of associational life. Thus, the organs of civil society in the West have multiplied in numbers and organizational sophistication.

The state apparatus is supposedly a neutral arena for all units of civil society. The competition among the latter is often over "government"— that is, the decisionmaking nerve center of the state. The neutrality of the state may be debatable and the boundaries between state, government, and regime are often blurred in theory and practice, as well as in the minds of ordinary citizens. But because civil society has evolved simultaneously with the nation-state, both have been more concordant than discordant. Neither has been completely autonomous from the other—only relatively so. Hence, the positing of the relationship between state and society in "zero-sum" terms may be a misleading dichotomy. A strong state does not necessarily imply a weak civil society or vice versa. In fact, most stable Western democracies represent cases of strong civil society and strong state. Similarly, as we will observe in the Arab world, a more common situation is that of weak civil societies and weak states.

The link between civil society and democratization should be obvious. Democracy, after all, is a set of rules and institutions designed to enable governance through the peaceful management of competing groups and/or conflicting interests. Thus the normative component of "civil society" is essentially the same as that of "democracy." Aside from the Athenian or "town-hall" model of direct democracy, organs of civil society are believed to be the optimum channels of popular participation in governance. Couched in different terminology, this is the essence of how the concept of civil society has been used by theoreticians of the "Social Contract," down through Hegel, Marx, Tocqueville, and Gramsci.[6] The modern-day users of the concept have merely refined or elaborated its manifestation in contemporary complex societies.

Some area observers contend that the lagging democratization of the Arab world is due to the absence or stunting of its "civil society" and its corresponding "political culture." Some Orientalists and ethnocentric analysts go so far as to totally dismiss even the potential for the evolution of an Arab civil society, and hence any prospect of genuine democratization. These assertions will be examined in the context of both premodern and contemporary Arab realities to argue a counterproposition—that despite noted distortion and time lags, the Arab world is currently going through civil society building and democratization. The relationship between the two processes is essentially symbiotic: As modern socioeconomic formations sprout and take shape, they create their civil society organizations, which in turn strive for participatory governance.

Traditional Arab Civil Formations

Premodern society in what is now called the Arab world was fairly closely ordered around a political authority[7] whose legitimacy was derived from a combination of conquest and religious sources. But the public space was immediately shared by *ulama*, merchants, guilds, sufi orders, and sects (*millat*).[8] Outside this first concentric zone, the public space was populated by peasants and tribes, where political authority asserted itself most clearly. Outside the first zone, its assertion varied markedly—in most cases it was hardly felt. Other collectivities, especially the tribes, were quite autonomous from, if not outright defiant of, the central authority.[9] Even in the first concentric zone, often within city walls, various groups coexisted and interacted with a great deal of autonomy. Guilds, religious sects, and ethnic groups ran most of their own internal affairs through elected or appointed leaders. The latter were accountable to both the political authority and their own communities. Tension, no doubt, existed within each category but was of low intensity. Equally, tension may have existed between or among two or more of these communities, but was often resolved intercommunally. Only occasionally did it warrant the direct intervention of the political authority.[10]

This traditional equilibrium of governance was maintained by a multitude of mechanisms; for example, clear hierarchies, occupational and residential segregation, and autonomous resources (mostly from *awkaf* or *hubus* religious endowments). Social solidarities existed along occupational, religious, and ethnic lines. Central authority collected taxes, administered justice through the *shariʿa*, maintained public order and defense, and occasionally patronized the arts and sciences. Social services and direct economic functions were not expected obligations of the "state," but were mostly left to local communities. In this sense, traditional Arab society not only knew the equivalent of civil formations but also depended on them for survival. Individuals relied on these formations for their identity and most of their basic needs. In this manner they were insulated from direct dealing with political authority.[11] In the traditional equilibrium, the public space in which civil formations interacted coincided with the physical space in which they lived and worked.

This traditional equilibrium of governance was occasionally disrupted by seditions (*fitan*, singular *fitna*) or calamities (*nakabat*, singular *nakba*). The Arabic political vocabulary referred to *fitna* as sharp internal strife, usually accompanied by armed conflict. A *nakba*, meanwhile, referred to an invasion by an alien (non-Muslim) power, often accompanied by mass looting, destruction, and dislocation.[12] Both *fitan* and *nakabat* would lead to a disintegration of this traditional equilibrium for a shorter or longer time. Often, however, the equilibrium would be pieced together and would reassert itself. At least this seemed to be the case for much of the first 12 centuries of Arab-Islamic history.

The last two centuries have witnessed what seems to be an irreversible disintegration of the traditional equilibrium of governance and its accompanying socioeconomic symbiosis, a direct function of Western penetration of Arab-Muslim societies and those societies' coercive integration into the budding world system. Most of the traditional civil formations were to wither away: New ones were born through the hardest of labor. Among the latter was the new Arab "state."

The New Arab State: Expansion and Retreat

In the birth of the new Arab states the Western colonial powers acted as midwife.[13] The states bore numerous deformities—ranging from artificial borders to the internal weaknesses of their institutions. From the start, they have faced severe problems and challenges from within and without. The new states neither tapped the reservoir of traditional wisdom of premodern civil formations nor adequately allowed sufficient public space for new ones to sprout and flourish. As a result, the new Arab state found itself embattled on many internal and external fronts.

The Arab world shared some, but not all, of the processes that had accompanied the emergence of the modern state and civil society in the West

—such as the withering away of traditional equilibria, rapid population growth, and urbanization. But the processes of capitalization and industrialization lagged far behind. Hence the new socioeconomic formations, which are the backbone of the modern state and civil society, have not grown progressively or evenly.

Erratic State Building and Development

The Arab world witnessed phenomenal socioeconomic growth in the three decades following World War II, the birth period of most independent Arab states. But the growth was erratic or sluggish—resulting, among other things, in a distorted stratification. The bearing of this distortion on the development of Arab civil society will be obvious from the account sketched below.

In the 1950s and 1960s, many of the newly independent Arab states embarked on ambitious educational and industrial expansions. As a result, two sprouting classes grew steadily: the new middle class and the modern working class. Central planning and command socioeconomic policies were the order of the day in most Arab countries. But the two subsequent decades witnessed a mix of inconsistent or outright confused socioeconomic policies. The initial oil boom of the 1970s tempted many of the poorer and larger countries to introduce what came to be known as liberal "open-door" policies, without successfully phasing out the command socioeconomic policies of the previous decades. Since that time, three formal sectors—public, private, and mixed—have been operating—or rather failing to operate—simultaneously. In addition, a growing informal or "underground" sector has appeared. Multiple and extremely varied levels of efficiency, skill appropriation, and salary scales prevailed in the same national economy, polity, and society. Distortions were inevitable. Inflationary pressures, worsening equity, and mounting external debt became rampant in most Arab countries.[14]

From a stratification point of view, two social formations grew rapidly in the 1970s and 1980s—a nouveau riche class and a lumpenproletariat. The first appropriated an increasing share of the national GNP without adding much to national wealth. It also engaged in conspicuous consumption and capital flight. The second, the lumpenproletariat, has grown tremendously in size, adding to unemployment and spawning deep feelings of relative deprivation. The poverty belts around major cities represent an ominous time bomb. Meanwhile, the new middle class and the modern working class, on fixed salaries and wages, have been hard pressed by rampant inflation. These two classes would steadily be alienated from the ruling regimes in their respective countries. The urban lumpenproletariat, on the other hand, would be easily manipulated by masters of street politics.[15]

The State and Conflict Management

The predicaments of the state in the Arab world are further compounded by old unresolved regional and internal conflicts, as well as by new ones. Relevant to our main concern—civil society and democratization—is the dismal failure of postindependence ruling elites in managing conflicts.

Among the old persistent problems are protracted conflicts—such as the Arab-Israeli, the Iraqi-Iranian, the Libyan-Chadian, the Lebanese, the Sudanese, the Somali, and the Saharan conflicts. Some of these (like the Arab-Israeli) are over 40 years old, and the relatively more recent ones are already several years old (the Iraqi-Iranian). Some have flared up into armed conflicts on and off for four decades (including the Arab-Israeli and the Sudanese). All of them are nevertheless costly in material and human terms. The Middle East region is the principal buyer and consumer of lethal arms in the Third World, spending an average of *$100 billion annually* over the last two decades. Overall spending on defense is twice as high. Some $4 trillion has been spent, or rather wasted, on defense purposes without settling most of the above-mentioned conflicts (including the $2.3 trillion spent in intrastate conflicts, as shown in Table 2.1). The number of those killed, wounded, disabled, and displaced is estimated at 13 million during the same period (see Table 2.1). With the rapid introduction and spread of arms of mass destruction (e.g., nuclear and chemical), the human and material costs of these protracted conflicts, if unsettled, is bound to be astronomical in the 1990s.[16]

Equally relevant is the fact that intrastate armed conflicts outweigh interstate ones in terms of human losses and population uprooting. Entire local communities have been partially or completely destroyed. Many of these were ethnic and minority group–based. The heavy losses, measured in economic terms alone as "opportunity cost," indicate what could have been achieved with these squandered resources. Development has clearly been a major victim of such protracted conflicts. But more detrimental to the development of civil society have been the deep psycho-sociopolitical cleavages created by protracted intrastate armed conflicts. They have forced individuals and groups to reentrench themselves behind primordial walls of solidarity. Traditional loyalties to ethnic, religious, sectarian, and tribal groups would take primacy over loyalty to modern formations of civil society or to the state itself.[17]

The dismal failure of the new Arab states in managing internal and external conflict was a cause and an effect of the dubious legitimacy accorded many of them by substantial sectors of their own citizenry (as in Lebanon, Iraq, Jordan, and South Yemen).[18] More often, however, the failure was due to the questionable legitimacy of the authoritarian ruling regimes in the new Arab states. While the legitimacy question of the state

Table 2.1   Cost of Armed Conflicts in the Middle East, 1948–1992

Type of Conflict	Period	No. of Casualties	Estimated Cost in Billions of U.S. $ (1990 Value)	Estimated Population Displacement
Interstate Conflicts				
Arab-Israeli	1948–1990	160,000	300.0	3,000,000
Iraq-Iran	1980–1988	300,000	300.0	1,000,000
Gulf War	1990–1992	120,000	650.0	1,000,000
Other	1945–1991	20,000	50.0	1,000,000
Subtotal		**600,000**	**1,300.0**	**6,000,000**
Intrastate Conflicts				
Sudan	1956–1991	500,000	20.0	4,000,000
Iraq	1960–1991	300,000	20.0	1,000,000
Lebanon	1958–1990	150,000	50.0	1,000,000
N. Yemen	1962–1972	100,000	5.0	500,000
Syria	1975–1985	30,000	0.5	150,000
Morocco (Sahara)	1976–1991	20,000	3.0	100,000
S.Yemen	1986–1987	10,000	0.2	50,000
Somalia	1989–1992	110,000	0.3	500,000
Other	1945–1991	30,000	1.0	300,000
Subtotal		**1,250,000**	**1,000.0**	**7,600,000**
Grand Total (All Armed Conflicts)		**1,850,000**	**2,300.0**	**13,600,000**

Source: Files of the Arab Data Unit, Ibn Khaldoun Center for Developmental Studies.

seemed amenable to resolution over time, regime legitimacy steadily deteriorated; hence the mounting pressure for more participatory politics, especially over the last decade. Much of the latter would either take the form of random outbursts by the lumpenproletariat through street politics or of less sensational but more sustained pressures from civil society.[19]

New Civil Society: The Difficult Birth

Despite the authoritarian nature of governance in many Arab states for much of their postindependence history, the seeds of modern civil society have sprouted in nearly all of them. Some of these new civil organizations, especially in the northern tier of the Arab world, date back to the second half of the nineteenth century; but they increased in number and thrived in the interwar period (1918–1939). The embryonic new middle class was the backbone of these civil organizations. Under colonial rule, many of them took on the explicitly political role of liberating their respective countries. From the ranks of these organizations emerged the leaders of independence.

Stunting of an Embryonic Civil Society (1950s–1960s)

A few years after independence, several Arab states witnessed a wave of radical politics, mostly through populist military coups d'état (Syria, Egypt, Iraq, Sudan, Yemen, Algeria, Libya, Mauritania, and Somalia). These "radical" regimes ended the liberal experiments that some of their societies had engaged in briefly before and immediately after independence. One-party rule, or rule by a junta, became the dominant pattern of governance. The new populist regimes gave the state an expansionist socioeconomic role. An explicit or implicit "social contract" was forged under the terms of which the state was to effect development, ensure social justice, satisfy the basic needs of its citizens, consolidate political independence, and achieve other national aspirations (e.g., Arab unity, the liberation of Palestine). In return, citizens were to forgo, at least for a while, the quest for liberal participatory politics. Pan-Arab nationalist and socialist ideologies were used to popularize this social contract and to generate political mobilization in support of ruling regimes. The majority of citizens accepted or acquiesced. So attractive did this populist trade-off social contract seem at the beginning that even traditional Arab monarchies, including Jordan, Saudi Arabia, the Gulf States, and Morocco,[20] adopted it in part since the 1960s.

The populist social contract had, among other things, a detrimental impact, not only on existing political parties, but also on other organizations of civil society. The latter were either prohibited or severely restricted by an arsenal of laws and decrees or were annexed outright to the single party in power.[21] In other words, under populist rule organizations of civil society lost all or much of their autonomy. As a result, many of these organizations withered away due to aging membership and the disinterest of younger generations. Some became merely paper organizations, and only a very few adapted to the new populist formula and managed to remain active within the existing political constraints.

The defeat of populist regimes at the hands of Israel in 1967 and successive reversals, culminating in the 1990–1991 Persian Gulf crisis, led to the discrediting of the populist social contract and the steady erosion of the legitimacy of most Arab regimes. Clinging to power, many populist regimes escalated their oppression; others engaged in external adventures, while some did both. Some, as will be elaborated upon later, engaged in the token or substantial revision of their systems of governance.

Mismanagement and Retreat of the State

The expansionist role of the Arab state seems to have reached its zenith in the 1970s, in rich and poor countries alike. Since then, the course of socio-political events internally, regionally, and internationally has forced the state to retreat from several socioeconomic functions. In most cases that retreat has been disorderly, leaving in its aftermath structural and situational misery that could have been avoided or reduced, had civil society been in better shape. Instead, some of the public space vacated by the state has been filled either by extremist Islamic tendencies (as in Egypt and Algeria), or by separatist primordial tendencies (as in Sudan, Somalia, and Iraq).

Using a typology that pairs and crosses the variables bearing on the strength of state and civil society, as indicated in Table 2.2, most Arab countries have oscillated among cells B, C, and D. None has ever been firmly established in cell A—both a strong state and a strong civil society. Countries like Somalia, Sudan, and Iraq are currently located firmly in cell D—the worst possible combination of a weak state and a weak civil society.

Table 2.2 State and Society in the Arab World

		The State	
		Strong (+)	Weak (−)
Civil Society	Strong (+)	A Conflict management through accepted participatory politics and democratic consensus	B Governance imposed through interest groups manipulating the state at the expense of other groups (early years of independence)
	Weak (−)	C Governance imposed by an autonomous state and an autocratic elite (height of populism in the 1950s–1960s)	D Disintegration or governance imposed by regional and international events or dictate (the 1970s, 1980s, and early 1990s)

Revitalization of Arab Civil Society

In the years of the Arab state's retreat (in the 1970s and 1980s), some of the prepopulist civil formations revitalized themselves, while new ones were created. A case in point is human rights organizations. In the aftermath of the 1982 Israeli invasion of Lebanon, one of the most severe reversals since the 1967 defeat, such organizations sprang up on a Pan-Arab or national scale.[22] Equally, hundreds of private voluntary organizations (PVOs) and community development associations (CDAs) have mushroomed in the last two decades. The number of Arab NGOs is estimated to have grown from less than 20,000 in the mid-1960s to about 70,000 in the late 1980s.[23]

Enhancing this phenomenal quantitative growth of Arab civil organizations in the last two decades are several factors, among them:

• *Growing unmet needs of individuals and local communities.* For the lower and lower middle classes these needs were mainly socioeconomic services the state was no longer able or willing to provide, such as housing, health, more income generation, better quality education, and food supplies. For the middle and upper classes, needs were of the expressive, cultural, professional and political variety.

• *Expansion of the educated Arab population.* Whatever the faults of populist regimes, one of their undeniable achievements was free mass education. Though lacking in quality, this expansion of education has nevertheless created higher levels of consciousness, expectations, and rudimentary organizational skills. Such attributes have been instrumental in building formal associations.

• *Growing individual financial resources.* The 1970s and early 1980s were years of financial boom for many Arab individuals due to skyrocketing oil revenues and the unprecedented interstate movement of labor that accompanied them, as well as the introduction of economic liberalization policies in formerly command economies. Thus, while governments mismanaged or wasted financial resources, many individuals earmarked some of their new fortunes to newly created associations. The Arab world witnessed for the first time the creation of American-style foundations, such as the Sabbagh, Shuman, and al-Hariri foundations.

• *Growing margins of freedom.* Either de facto or by default, margins of freedom expanded gradually in many Arab countries. This was due partly to state fatigue or incompetence in controlling society. But it was also due to citizens' growing repertoire of strategies to circumvent the state. International travel, Arab media abroad, and Arabs' individual bank accounts in foreign countries were expressions of such expanded boundaries. In fact, many civil Arab organizations were conceived or established abroad before transferring activities to their home countries.

Some Specificities of Arab Civil Society

Political parties in civil society. Political parties have been part of the rapid multiplication of Arab civil organizations in the last two decades.

While some old parties—those predating independence—have endured under autocratic governance (e.g., Istiqlal in Morocco, Umma and Ittihadi in Sudan), most other parties did not survive the populist phase of Arab politics. But with increasing freedom some old political parties resurfaced from the late 1970s onwards (e.g., the Wafd and Young Egypt Socialists in Egypt). More important, however, was the mushrooming of new parties, once it became legal to establish them—46 in Algeria, 43 in Yemen, 23 in Jordan, 19 in Morocco, 13 in Egypt, 11 in Tunisia, and 6 in Mauritania.[24]

The quantum leap in Arab civil organization, however, should not imply that all such organization is equally effective. In fact, the majority of civil organizations, including many of the new political parties, are too small to be significant in the public life of their respective countries. Egypt is a case in point: Claiming about one third of the estimated 70,000 Arab civil associations, most of Egypt's 20,000 NGOs are inactive or only moderately active.[25] The same applies to Arab political parties. Parliamentary elections in Yemen (April 1993) and Morocco (June 1993) revealed the political insignificance of most parties in building or attracting constituencies of any size. Only 7 of Yemen's 43 political parties won seats, and 3 captured more than 80 percent of those seats. In Morocco, of 19 parties, only 9 appeared on the electoral scoreboard, with 4 capturing 75 percent of the contested seats.[26]

Professional syndicates. Professional associations are probably the most active civil organizations in the Arab world at present. Partly because they provide unionlike benefits to their membership, partly because of their constituents' higher level of education and political consciousness, and partly because of their relatively independent financial resources, Arab professional associations or syndicates (*niqabat* in Arabic) have spearheaded the resurgence of civil society in their respective countries. In Sudan, they managed twice (in 1964 and 1985) to oust from power a ruling military regime. In Egypt, Morocco, and Tunisia they proved to be potent pressure groups during the 1970s and 1980s.

Enhancing the social and moral power of professional syndicates are two additional factors. First, the syndicates are organized on the Pan-Arab level as federations, and linkages to their international counterparts are strong. This has given them not only broader fora but also added moral support and protection. Second, Arab professional syndicates are organically and strategically located at the heart of production and service institutions, including those administered by the state. They cannot be easily dissolved or dismissed by ruling elites. Hence, when they all decide to go on strike, for example (as actually happened in the Sudan in 1985), the entire society and state can be paralyzed. Among the most influential syndicates are those of doctors, engineers, and teachers. More recently, business associations have joined these ranks.[27]

Politics by proxy. In Arab countries where political parties are still prohibited or severely restricted, some civil associations have served many
of their functions by proxy—for example, by articulation and debating
of public issues, formulation of public policy alternatives, and exertion of
pressure on decisionmakers. Kuwait's University Graduates Society, Qatar's
Jassrah Cultural Club, and the UAE's Association of Social Professions
have been performing such functions.

Possibly for these reasons, some Arab civil associations (other than
political parties per se) have recently become arenas of intensive political
activity. Their elections, generally fair and honest, are very competitive,
and are widely followed by the public at large. This phenomenon was evident in Egypt, Jordan, Kuwait, Tunisia, and Morocco during the 1980s
and early 1990s. More recently in Egypt, the Muslim Brothers, denied a
political party of their own, have systematically taken over, by electoral
means, the boards of the most important professional syndicates—doctors,
engineers, and lawyers.[28]

Traditional formations in modern garb. A sizable number of Arab civil organizations are still tainted by remnants of their society's traditional formations. The typical case would be the establishment of an apparently
modern civil association in an urban center, whose membership belongs
for the most part to the same tribe, village, or religious sect. The trappings
of modernity may all be there—formal registration, licensing, lofty by-
laws, elections, boards, committees, and so on—but in effect, the association is headed and run in the same traditional manner sketched earlier.

This observation should not detract from the importance of this type
of civil association. The fact that its initiators have founded it along modern lines to enhance "traditional" loyalties and/or serve traditional functions attests to the need to reconcile tradition and modernity during a period of societal transition. When established in big urban centers, this
associational type not only enhances traditional leaders but equally helps
their kin and followers to land on their feet in an otherwise alien or im-
personal environment. This associational type also has a latent protective
function in both modern civil society and the state. Without it, newcomers
to Arab cities from hinterland areas are bound to be consigned to the amor-
phous urban lumpenproletariat, the fastest-growing socioeconomic formation in the Arab world in the last two decades. It represents the most
volatile form of demagogic street politics. Urban riots spawned by this formation were vividly displayed in Egypt (1977, 1986, 1992), Tunisia (1976,
1987), Morocco (1974, 1981, 1987), Jordan (1988), and Algeria (1988).

Civil society and crisis situations. Like many other dimensions of development in the Arab world, the advance of civil society has not been uniform. But to the extent that civil formations existed and were relatively

solid, rumblings for democratization were felt or heard, as we will explore further later. More important is the fact that in Arab countries recently subjected to severe crises, the presence or absence of civil formations has made a tremendous difference in how the country withstands a crisis.

Lebanon, Kuwait, and Somalia are cases in point. In all three, the "state" nearly vanished under catastrophic or overpowering circumstances—Lebanon and Somalia because of protracted internal strife compounded by regional and international factors, Kuwait because of a lightning Iraqi invasion. Different as they were in many ways, Lebanon and Kuwait had in common the presence of fairly well-developed civil formations—some 600 and 200 of them, respectively. While many of these organizations were reduced to total impotence, scores remained active during the crises. These active civil associations provided material and moral support to many Lebanese and Kuwaiti citizens at home and abroad. Even sectarian-based Lebanese NGOs extended help across sectarian lines on many occasions. Also, many new neighborhood-based associations emerged at the height of the 16-year civil strife.

In Kuwait it was, of all things, the consumers' cooperatives that came to perform many of the functions previously provided by the state—such as food rationing, health, social welfare, education, mail, and an informal communication network. Other civil organizations that could not operate openly for fear of the occupation authorities used the less suspect food cooperatives and mosques as covers for their activities.

In contrast, Somalia had very few civil organizations. For many years of populist military rule, many Somalis who lived away from their villages or tribes relied almost exclusively on the state for work and services. When the state machinery collapsed totally in 1991, they found themselves without a base or cover. As the ensuing internal conflict expanded, the very fabric of even primordial formations was severely ruptured and quickly disintegrated. The massive famine that struck Somalia in 1992 occurred not just because of the fighting, or even a lack of food supplies (much was sent by foreign donors), but mainly because of difficulties in distribution. Had there existed civil organizations similar to those of Lebanon and Kuwait, much of the starvation, disease, and death would have been avoided or markedly ameliorated. Somalia represents a tragic and extreme case—not only of disorderly retreat, but of a total disintegration of the state without a civil society to provide a "safety net" or pick up the pieces.

Regimes, Civil Society, and Democratization

No longer able to honor the terms of the old social contract, assuage new socioeconomic formations with the tired language of political discourse, or forge a new participatory social contract (for fear of being toppled from power), Arab ruling elites resorted either to coercive repression at home or to risky adventures abroad. Since 1980, Saddam Hussein's regime in Iraq has followed both these tacks, which reached their peak on 2 August 1990 with the invasion of Kuwait, triggering what came to be known as the "Gulf crisis." During the crisis it was predicted that more participatory governance in the Arab world would be among the outcomes. This prediction was based on the proposition that the crisis was as much an internal Arab political crisis as it was a regional international crisis. In fact, elements of participatory governance did materialize in a number of Arab countries, but the trend was already underway before the crisis. What the crisis has done is to expedite it. That some countries are proceeding faster than others can be ascribed to numerous domestic and external factors. Among the former is the relative size and degree of maturation of civil society in each country. It was among civil society organizations that rumblings were first heard, and these were followed by advances in democratization. In some countries, the march toward democracy was set back; in others it proved stillborn. What follows is a sketch of these three modal conditions of current Arab politics.[29]

Democratization: The Rumblings

In the years immediately preceding the Gulf crisis, several Arab regimes were already sensing their deepening loss of internal legitimacy. This was expressed in increasingly frequent violent confrontations between regimes and one or more of the major socioeconomic formations. The upper rungs of the new middle class engaged regimes in nonviolent battles over basic freedoms, human rights, and democracy. On the Pan-Arab level, and within several Arab countries, the quest for democracy took the form of establishing human rights organizations and more autonomous professional associations, thus revitalizing stunted civil societies. There were varying levels of popular demands vis-à-vis Arab regimes. On one level, the demands were for greater "liberalization," such as freedom of the press and association, as well as the right to travel abroad. Nearly all regimes made some concessions in response to these demands. On a more elevated level, the demand was for serious and explicit democratization, such as legalized political parties, equal access to the mass media, and free and honest elections. None of the regimes fully responded to these demands in the 1980s.

The lower rungs of the new middle class adopted Islamic political activism to challenge ruling elites. The modern working class opted more often for strikes or other forms of work slowdown and industrial sabotage. The urban lumpenproletariat resorted to "street politics" such as demonstrations, rioting, and looting. Whichever formation started a confrontation, and however its discontent was expressed, other equally alienated socio-economic formations joined in to advance their own demands. During the 1980s and into the 1990s, this phenomenon occurred across the region: in Algeria in 1988; Egypt in 1981 and 1986; Jordan in 1989; Kuwait in 1989 and 1990; Mauritania in 1986 and 1988; Morocco in 1984, 1988, and 1990; South Yemen between 1986 and 1990; Sudan in 1985; and Tunisia in 1984 and 1988. The ruling elites in these countries all responded to mounting discontent with promises of economic and political reform. In fact, some began to honor such promises before the outbreak of the Gulf crisis. Others took advantage of the crisis to renege on or delay honoring them.

Algeria, Jordan, and Yemen had embarked on serious democratization processes before the Gulf crisis. All three held national or municipal elections between 1987 and 1990, with few or no complaints regarding their integrity. The fact that antiregime Islamist candidates performed well and captured more seats than expected added to the credibility of the process. That democratically elected representatives in all three countries vocally supported Saddam Hussein during the Gulf crisis perplexed Western observers espousing democratization in the Third World.

The support for Hussein is an irony to be pondered on its own. These newly elected members in the opposition were expressing discontent not only with regard to their own rulers, but also with regard to the overall Arab order and, for that matter, the much-talked-about "new world order." Although no less despotic than some other Arab rulers on both sides of the crisis, Saddam Hussein tapped into and manipulated that discontent outside Iraq. He was able to do this in part because Iraqi citizens had not flaunted the country's oil wealth in other Arab lands as had their counterparts in the Gulf states. The emphasis of the United States and other Western countries on the issue of international legitimacy seemed insincere to many Arabs; in view of the Palestinian question, it smacked of a double standard.

In 1987, a few years before the Gulf crisis, the Tunisian leadership changed peacefully—although via something of a constitutional coup—from Habib Bourguiba to Zein al-'Abidin Bin 'Ali. The new leader promised political reforms to secular opposition parties, but continued to deny legitimacy to the Islamist al-Nahda Party. A series of bloody confrontations took place between the regime and followers of al-Nahda in late 1989 and early 1990. The Gulf crisis, on which all Tunisian parties saw eye to eye, froze these confrontations for nearly a year, but they subsequently resumed. Other secular opposition parties remain disdainful of the ruling Rassemblement Constitutionnel Démocratique, but their fear of the Islamist trend makes them view the status quo as the lesser of two evils.

Limited democratization in Egypt and Morocco several years prior to the Gulf crisis did not progress further in 1990–1991. Although the Moroccan government sided with Kuwait and the U.S.-led coalition during the crisis, the opposition condemned foreign intervention and mobilized Moroccan public opinion. Indeed, the biggest demonstration in support of Iraq was staged in Morocco. The crisis gave the opposition a chance to show its ability to mobilize—a fact that did not go unnoticed by the regime, whose immediate response was to scale back Moroccan military involvement. A year after the crisis, King Hassan announced political reforms, which he would honor, as discussed below.

In Egypt, there was less discordance between the ruling elite and the public over the crisis. In fact, the regime issued a call for a parliamentary election in October 1990, as if to show that life in Egypt was orderly despite the crisis. While two major opposition parties, the Wafd and the Labor-Islamic Alliance, boycotted the elections, this was for reasons unrelated to the crisis—namely, the government's refusal to guarantee fairness in the political competition. The Egyptian regime's self-assuredness was, however, shaken by two events: the October 1990 assassination of former parliamentary speaker Rif'at al-Mahgub, supposedly by Islamic militants, and the protests of thousands of Egyptian university students against what seemed to be the systematic destruction of Iraq.

In the countries directly involved in, or close to the heart of, the crisis—Iraq, Syria, and the six states bordering the Persian Gulf and the Gulf of Oman—ruling elites claimed a "legitimate" excuse to delay moves toward democratization, and one must wonder if any such moves were ever seriously intended. It was a full year after the crisis before Arab elites showed a serious inclination toward genuine participatory politics, although promises had been extracted from them in some instances, such as in Kuwait and Saudi Arabia. During 1991, it became obvious that something had to be done.

One positive development among the many negative aspects of the Gulf crisis has been the unprecedented political mobilization of the Arab masses. Popular expressions of support for one Arab side or the other in the crisis were not always in accord with the official positions of regimes. This had the effect of breaking the wall of fear between many Arabs and their ruling elites. Iraq is a dramatic example of this trend. The Shi'a in the south and the Kurds in the north rose up against the regime of Saddam Hussein—emboldened, it could be argued, by Iraq's crushing defeat and the prospect of aid from the victorious allies. Even the Gulf elites on the winning side faced mounting demands from their intelligentsia for more political participation.

Political Liberalization: The Advances

Since the Gulf War, political liberalization has unfolded in a number of Arab countries only slowly and reluctantly. In others, it has been set back.

In Jordan, King Hussein resumed his country's political reforms shortly after the Gulf War. In March 1992, the Hashemite monarch scrapped the emergency legislation that had been in effect since the 1967 war. This was followed in July by the reinstating of a multiparty system after a 35-year suspension. In September 1992 the Jordanian parliament passed a new printing and publication law that lifted restrictions on the press. Parliamentary elections for the 80-seat Lower House took place in November 1993, and by all standards were fairly democratic. Although a number of blocs emerged in the new parliament, only the Islamic Action Front (IAF) can be said to be cohesive.[30] With parties themselves having been formally legalized only in 1992, it remains to be seen whether larger, more organized, and more effective political groups might eventually form out of these nascent blocs. Taken together, these developments indicate that Jordan's democratization continues on the trajectory begun in November 1989 with the election of a new parliament. King Hussein has launched an experiment that may prove to be a bellwether for the Arab world. He also seems to have calculated that the long-term survival of his regime must be based on broad support. If so, the steps he has permitted to date are vital. At the same time, there were also developments in Jordan that gave rise to concern about the pace of any future reform. Prior to the 1993 election the electoral law was amended—to the obvious disadvantage of the IAF—by executive fiat rather than parliamentary procedure. Legal measures were taken against two Jordanian newspapers for reporting accusations of torture against the security services. Finally, many parliamentarians voiced complaints that their role was marginalized in domestic and especially foreign policymaking. With the acceleration and successful conclusion of Jordanian-Israeli peace negotiations these concerns were further reinforced. In the event of significant domestic dissent on this issue, the regime is likely to be more cautious about further political opening.

Lebanon and Kuwait are two countries with longer parliamentary traditions. Beset by internal strife and external threats, Lebanon had not been able to conduct parliamentary elections since 1972. Thanks to the 1989 Ta'if agreement, regional and international efforts, and a modicum of stability, the Lebanese held their first parliamentary elections in 20 years in August–September 1992. The elections were based on the Ta'if formula of Muslim-Christian parity, with the 128 parliamentary seats distributed among Lebanon's various confessional groups. Most Maronite Christians boycotted the elections because of Syria's failure to redeploy its forces in September 1992 as required by the Ta'if agreement. Nevertheless, the government, under Syrian tutelage, disregarded Maronite objections and proceeded on schedule with three rounds of elections. The showing of Islamist forces, Shi'i and Sunni alike, was striking, and reflected an impressive campaign to build political support at the grassroots. Among the Shi'a, several of the long-reigning *zu'ama* (political bosses) went down to stunning defeats. A new government headed by a newcomer to Lebanese political life, billionaire businessman Rafiq al-Hariri, was named by President Ilyas al-Harawi in October 1992. With these steps, Lebanon appeared to be on the road to the restoration of its pre-1975 consociational-style democratic system. However, the Maronite-led boycott has undermined the mandate of the new parliament. The renewed Lebanese democratic experiment thus remains a qualified one, subject to significant internal and external constraints and pressures.

In Kuwait, parliamentary life was resumed with a heated and spirited campaign during the summer and fall of 1992. In October, elections were held with few or no complaints about irregularities. Several new faces won seats in the National Assembly, where the opposition forces won a clear majority and Sunni and Shi'i Islamist forces won at least one third of the 50 seats.[31] The significance of the Kuwaiti elections is that they were the first to be held after the experience of the Iraqi invasion and occupation, and the first since the 1986 suspension of parliament. The new parliament represented a victory for democratic forces that had never accepted the 1986 suspension or the regime's tampering with the constitution and signaled significant dissatisfaction with the performance of the regime during the Gulf crisis.

The most recent success story of Arab political liberalization is Morocco. Though the fifth since independence, the June 1993 Moroccan parliamentary elections attracted disproportionate attention. They were held, under judicial supervision, after more than one year of intensive open debate among major political forces, and subsequent constitutional and administration reform. More than 11 political parties participated in the race to elect 212 parliamentary deputies, along with about 200 independent candidates. No major complaints were registered, nor did international observers note serious irregularities. No single party obtained an absolute majority of the contested seats. But the fact that two opposition parties, the Socialist Union of Popular Forces (SUPF) and Istiqlal (Independence), took first and second place (with 48 and 43 seats respectively) added to the credibility of the elections.[32]

But there was more to this Moroccan exercise in liberalization. First, it came nearly one and a half years after the abortion of the democratization experiment in neighboring Algeria. These two countries, similar in population size and importance in the Arab-African world, have competed for regional leadership in the Grand Maghreb. The successful reform exercise in Morocco will, no doubt, tilt the race in its favor for years to come. Second, the Moroccan elections and the national debate preceding it are a model of the disposition toward "power-sharing" in the transition from autocratic to democratic rule with a minimum of sociopolitical instability. Third, the Moroccan elections were more than an expression of political pluralism. They were also an embodiment of the country's sociocultural diversity. The Berber-based parties obtained a reasonable number of seats (45 out of 212). Thirty-three Moroccan women ran for seats and two of them won, for the first time in the country's parliamentary history. Also for the first time, the percentage of women voters nearly equaled that of men (about 60 percent). Young people showed a similar inclination—voting among 22- to 24-year-olds exceeded 60 percent.[33]

In Mauritania in 1991 a multiparty system was reinstated. In the January 1992 presidential elections, incumbent Mu'awiya Wild Tayi' was re-elected. In parliamentary elections in March 1992, his party won a comfortable majority. Several major opposition parties boycotted the elections amid charges of vote-rigging, but more serious was the pattern of voting in both sets of elections. Tayi' and his ruling party mobilized and obtained the support of Arab and Arabized Mauritanians in the rural and northern areas of the country, while his opponents mobilized black Mauritanians in the capital and southern areas of the country. This quite obvious and disturbing ethnic cleavage, if not contained, could threaten not only Mauritania's political opening but also the country as a whole.[34]

In Saudi Arabia, in the midst of the Gulf crisis, leaflets and cassette tapes circulated underground criticizing the royal family for its ineptitude in defending the country and its reliance on non-Muslims for the task despite massive military spending over the two previous decades. More accountability was demanded, and the long-awaited political reforms were finally announced by King Fahd in March 1992—one year after the war. While modest by Western or even some Third World standards, these reforms represent a notable step in the political evolution of the kingdom. The reforms are akin to a constitution, providing a formalization of the basic system of rule in the country, a system of local governance in the provinces, and a national consultative council. This last item is by far the most important measure.[35]

Comprising 60 members chosen by the king, the council is to carry out all the activities usually performed by parliaments elsewhere except the enactment of laws. The council may initiate debates, discussions, and deliberations on public matters; it may question members of the executive and may recommend new laws and policies to the cabinet, which, in turn, would forward the recommendations to the king (who is invested with the powers of lawmaking within the bounds of *shari'a*). In September 1992, Fahd decreed the naming of the president and members of the council. Many among the Saudi intelligentsia thought these measures too little, too late. In response, they circulated petitions during the summer of 1992 calling for further, deeper reforms. The petitions were leaked and published in the Arab press outside the kingdom. Proregime elements then countered with a campaign of their own through paid advertisements in the same newspapers, reprimanding the petitioners and commending the king for his wise gradualist approach to political reform. Even this practice, "politics by petition," was new to the Saudis.[36]

The establishment of the Committee for the Defense of Legitimate Rights (CDLR) in April 1993 was another new development in the kingdom. However, once the committee was announced, the founders, mostly university professors and intellectuals, were put in jail and expelled from their jobs. Some of the founders were later released in October 1993 as a result of the kingdom's desire to ease growing internal tensions and to improve its conservative image internationally.[37] Nevertheless, the measures, taken together with the heavily qualified moves toward greater political accountability and participation, suggest that the extent of the political opening has been limited.

Democratization: Retreats and Blockages

Despite advances in Arab political liberalization after the Gulf crisis, there were also important reversals. The most dramatic among these occurred in Algeria and Yemen. Tunisia and Egypt also have had some difficult moments in their democratization processes.

In 1988, Algeria seemed to be a promising contender for the transition from autocratic to democratic rule. After nearly 30 years of one-party rule by the National Liberation Front (FLN), and in the aftermath of widespread rioting in the fall of 1988, the regime of President Chadli Bin Jadid embarked on a series of political reforms. A multiparty system was introduced in 1989, under which municipal elections were held in the spring of 1990, shortly before the August eruption of the Gulf crisis. Of the many parties competing in those elections, the Islamic Salvation Front (FIS) emerged as the most threatening to the FLN, scoring victories in about 50 percent of the country's municipalities. National parliamentary elections were scheduled for the summer of 1991.

Internal division within the FLN, however, and FIS's insistence on modifications of electoral rules and its resort to militant confrontations with the government, led to the arrest of FIS leaders and the postponement of elections for several months. When elections finally were held in December 1991, FIS emerged with a landslide first-round victory. Out of 599 contested seats, FIS won more than 300, compared to only 25 seats for the secular, Berber-based opposition Front of Socialist Forces and 16 seats for the FLN. A round of run-off elections for some 250 undecided seats was scheduled for mid-January 1992.[38] With its decisive victory in the first round, FIS would have had a sufficiently large majority to form the government without winning more seats in the second round. Many forces in the country—in particular the army, the FLN, the Berbers, and organized women's groups—found this prospect ominous. Their apprehensions were reinforced by FIS's ambitions to restructure Algerian sociocultural life. A few days before the second round of elections, President Bin Jadid resigned, the army took over, and a provisional presidential council was established that appointed an interim head of state, Muhammad Boudiaf. This was clearly a coup d'état. With the democratic experiment aborted, Algeria witnessed the widespread arrest of FIS leaders and violent confrontations between FIS followers and the government. At the end of June 1992, Boudiaf, an elderly statesman and former freedom fighter, paid with his life. At present, with the country beset by increasingly bloody civil war, the future of Algerian democracy looks dim.[39]

In Yemen, shortly after the unification of the north and south in March 1990, the regime—made up of an alliance of the two parties that had ruled in the two Yemens—announced its intention to introduce a multiparty system in a fully fledged democracy. An interim period not exceeding 30 months was to culminate in parliamentary elections in the united, politically pluralistic Republic of Yemen. By the spring of 1992 a democratic environment was flourishing. Forty-six political parties and organizations were operating in the political arena, and the number of daily and weekly newspapers and magazines had multiplied severalfold. Observers visiting Yemen in 1992 were impressed by the open atmosphere in which opinions and criticism were expressed without fear of retribution.[40]

Still, there were justifiable apprehensions about the situation. Mounting incidents of violence, especially against leading figures of the Yemeni Socialist Party (one of the partners in the ruling alliance), threatened the entire experiment, since none of the offenders in these incidents were arrested by the authorities. The precariousness of the situation apparently explains the regime's decision to postpone elections, originally scheduled for November 1992, until the spring of 1993. The regime did, however, honor its promises. The first multiparty parliamentary election was held in April 1993. It was a marked success. No party won a majority of seats, but all major parties were reasonably represented. Some 50 women ran, and two of them won. The overall results reflected the sociocultural pluralism of Yemen.[41] Despite the important achievements, the situation soon began to unravel. The leaders of the YSP, worried about possible marginalization in the new coalition, refused to participate actively in the government and retreated to their southern base. In this climate of political tension, periodic clashes erupted between North and South Yemeni military units. Ultimately civil war broke out in May 1994 and culminated in the victory of the northern forces of President 'Ali 'Abdullah Salih. This, for the time being at least, put a hold on Yemen's brief experiment with political liberalization and democratization.

In Tunisia, a multiparty system has been in effect since the coming to power of President Bin 'Ali in 1988. The ruling party, however, continues to monopolize power, although it engages in democratic rhetoric and dialogue with secular opposition parties. Meanwhile, the regime has been forceful in isolating and oppressing the followers of al-Nahda and other Islamists. Gross human rights violations have been recorded by Amnesty International and Middle East Watch. The regime has not only ignored such criticism but has endeavored to curb the activities of the Tunisian League for Human Rights by making it illegal to hold simultaneous memberships in that organization and a political party. By July 1992, the League found it impossible to operate, and dissolved itself. Its dissolution was a serious setback not only for the democratization process, but for the evolution of civil society in Tunisia.[42]

In Egypt, the Mubarak government has continued to muddle through with little, if any, marked change in its attitude toward further democratization of the system. The press continues to enjoy a reasonable degree of freedom, and three new parties have been established by court order since the Gulf crisis; of these, the most important is the Arab Democratic Nasserite Party, established in April 1992.[43] Not much else has happened to make the system more participatory. Meanwhile, new bouts of violent confrontations with Islamist groups broke out. The assassination of Farag Fawdah, a notable secular thinker, along with sectarian strife in Asyut and assaults on foreign tourists, were among the more ominous developments.[44] The regime's reactions to the violence and strife have been more of the same: tighter security measures and additional antiterrorism laws. At present, the situation remains a low-level war of attrition between the regime and Islamists. With the greater freedom in Egypt, however, other, more moderate Muslim Brothers continued their peaceful attempts to secure greater influence in the major organizations of civil society, such as professional unions. Through democratic elections, they gained control of the boards of doctors, engineers, and lawyers' associations. The last eventuality was particularly stunning, given that the lawyers' association has been called Egypt's "fortress of liberalism."[45]

In Iraq, Syria, Libya, and the Sudan, regimes have shown no discernible change in their autocratic methods. Iraq, a three-decade-long authoritarian state, emerged from the Gulf crisis as a tragic mixed case. Having been the immediate cause of the crisis, and having suffered a serious defeat at the hands of the U.S.-led multinational coalition, the regime of Saddam Hussein was substantially weakened. It was challenged internally by the Kurds in the north, the Shi'a in the south, and by reported coup d'état attempts at the center. Nevertheless, the regime has clung doggedly to power in Baghdad and the center of the country by maintaining its traditional authoritarian-repressive methods of governance. Thanks however to the Western-protected zone in the north, Kurdish opposition parties were able to set up democratically elected bodies in May 1992 to run their "liberated areas" and to negotiate with Baghdad over a possible final settlement regarding self-rule. The reluctance of Saddam Hussein to meet some of the basic demands of the Kurds induced Kurdish leaders to rally other Iraqi opposition groups in the summer and fall of 1992, in a quest to form a national united front to oust the Saddam regime. This effort is backed by the United States and other Western powers, who in the summer of 1992 declared a "no-fly" zone in the south to reduce military pressure on Shi'i rebels. The rebels, however, are unable to emulate their Kurdish counterparts in the north by setting up some kind of interim home rule.[46]

Syria, for its part, conducted another presidential plebiscite early in 1992 with the usual "four nines"—99.99 percent of voters approving Hafiz al-Asad for six more years in office. Having mended his fences with Egypt, the West, and the oil-rich Arab states during the Gulf crisis, Assad has been under no significant regional or international pressure to change his ways. With his Ba'thist rival in Iraq much weakened and isolated, his participation in the Middle East peace talks endearing him to Washington for the time being, assistance from Gulf states, and Syria's new oil discoveries filling his coffers, the Assad regime has been able to present to Syrians as strong a front as ever. It is rumored that Assad may initiate some democratic measures in preparation for signing a peace agreement with Israel, but there is little evidence to support this contention. It is based on an analogy with Egypt's late president Anwar Sadat, who accompanied his opening to the West and the launching of negotiations with Israel with a policy of economic liberalization, *infitah*, and a modicum of new political freedoms.

In Libya since the fall of 1991, Muammar Qaddafi's regime has been embroiled in a dispute with the West over the 1988 Pan Am bombing over Lockerbie, Scotland. UN sanctions and confrontations with the United States and Britain have allowed the regime to mobilize Libyan public opinion. Several anti-West mass rallies, marches, and demonstrations have drummed up support. Qaddafi has portrayed Libya as just one more Arab country (after Iraq) targeted for destruction by the West in its ongoing campaign of "vengeance" against the Arab nation, for which the Pan Am episode merely serves as a pretext. The opposition, which is fragmented, has opted for silence both at home and abroad.

In Sudan—where the 1989 overthrow of a democratically elected government set back democratization—'Umar Hasan al-Bashir's military regime has been able to break out of its internal, regional, and international isolation since the Gulf crisis. Feelers were extended hurriedly to Libya and Iran, which for reasons of their own have responded with financial and military aid. The Sudanese regime, which is backed by the National Islamic Front, has been using this aid to pressure rebels in the south. Losing their sanctuary in Ethiopia after the collapse of the Mengistu government in

1991 and suffering serious internal divisions, the southern Sudanese rebels were dealt several military blows at the hands of government forces. Bolstered by these victories, the regime has tightened its grip on the home front. Much of the vocal northern Sudanese opposition is now operating from Cairo and London with little prospect of overthrowing the military-Islamic dictatorship in the foreseeable future. It is possible, however, that with neighboring Ethiopia and Eritrea on fast tracks to democratization Sudan may be affected.[47]

Conclusion

Organizations of civil society are playing growing roles in the political arenas of a score of Arab countries. Professional associations and organized interest groups, nominally nonpartisan, are becoming increasingly politicized. The elections of Kuwait's Chamber of Commerce in the spring of 1992—dubbed a dress rehearsal for parliamentary elections to take place later that fall—attracted much public attention. As stated earlier, Egypt's medical, engineering, and legal associations have been equally politicized, with Muslim Brothers dominating their respective elections in 1992. The same thing has been occurring in Jordan, where Islamists have used civil society organizations as proxy arenas for political discourse and schooling in the arts of articulation and mobilization. They also have learned the imperative of appealing to circles wider than their own if they are to win elections, perform well in office, and be reelected. Egypt's Muslim Brothers learned this lesson when they lost a reelection contest in the pharmacists' association in 1992, gracefully conceding their first defeat in 10 years. The case of the pharmacists has shown that the march of Islamists is reversible, not only in professional associations but also in political contests at large. There is some evidence of this from Jordan in both municipal politics and the 1993 parliamentary election. Even the dazzling victory of Algeria's Islamic Salvation Front concealed the fact that the FIS lost one million votes between the municipal elections of 1990 and the parliamentary elections of December 1991.

The global wave of democratization is helping the process of opening up Arab polities, as is the prominent role being played by international and Arab human rights advocates such as Amnesty International, Middle East Watch, and the Arab Organization for Human Rights. These organizations are making it more and more difficult for Arab elites to draw upon their traditional coercive impulse and apparatus. Thus, while the Gulf crisis may not have led to a "democratic revolution" in the Arab world, it has definitely contributed to an erosion of Arab authoritarianism.

During recent years, there have been two indigenous processes unfolding in the Arab world: democratization and an escalating Islamic activism. Discordant as they may appear at first glance, the two processes intersect at their edges through the moderate variety of Islamic groups that are opting to engage in "politics as usual." Incorporation of these moderate Islamists into the mainstream of Arab politics would be much enhanced if civil society were permitted to develop naturally; but this process still is highly restricted in several Arab countries, as is democratization itself. In extreme cases, such as Iraq, forming an association inside the country or joining one outside the country without written governmental approval can expose a citizen to nothing less than the death penalty. Even in countries with a longer history of civic organization, such as Egypt and Tunisia, not only is governmental approval required, the authorities reserve the right to monitor and dissolve such organizations almost at will.

Needless to say, in the Arab world as elsewhere, there are other requisites for sound and smooth democratization that have not been discussed in this chapter. Among them are steady, even if modest, economic development, and a greater measure of social equity. Without these, the road to democracy will be quite rocky and reversals likely. Unemployment, especially among youth, and income disparities tend to breed fanaticism and violence. This encourages demagoguery and entices an authoritarian military to step in and derail the democratization process. Thus civil society, economic development, and social equity must proceed hand in hand. They are mutually reinforcing and bolster, as well, the prospects for democratization in the Arab world.

Equally important to reinforcing democratization would be positive regional developments, especially regarding the Arab-Israeli conflict. The signing of the historic peace accord between Israel and the Palestinian Liberation Organization is potentially of great importance, not only in bringing peace and stability to the region, but also in promoting the process of democratization and the development of civil society in the Arab world. The agreement stipulates that any Palestinian authority must be freely elected. If this plan bears fruit, Palestine would be the first Arab state to be born democratically. Beyond the agreement itself, a close look at Palestinian society reveals that in the previous absence of a ruling state as such, the institutions of civil society have attained considerable prominence. The PLO itself has been a federation of nonstate actors. The Fatah group with its subsidiaries, the Islamic Hamas movement and its subdivisions, and numerous voluntary organizations are examples of active instruments of civil society.

On a broader scale, the Gaza-Jericho accord could bring the Arab-Israeli armed struggle to a final phase. This would deliver a logical rebuff to the claims of most Arab regimes, which have suspended democracy until a solution for the Palestinian question is reached—"No voice can be louder than that of the struggle." Substantial Arab resources and capacities were directed toward the liberation of occupied Arab lands. Syria is one such example of the suspension of democracy and basic human rights. The end of the Arab-Israeli conflict would mark the end of all pretexts to delay the onset of democracy.

Yet the importance of an end to the Arab-Israeli conflict extends beyond the discourse and rhetoric of Arab regimes. A large proportion of Arab budgets was indeed funnelled into strengthening military capabilities to confront a massively armed enemy. This has diverted funds away from essential needs such as development and the building of a primary infrastructure. Many Arab regimes have also taken the Palestinian case as a source of their legitimacy and a scapegoat for economic and social failures. As the conflict subsides and development priorities shift to meeting basic needs, other, more articulated demands—such as democracy and respect for human rights—are likely to be advanced more vociferously by the Arab people. Thus Arab priorities will move from basic needs such as food, shelter, clothes, and security to calls for political participation and other basic freedoms.

If the Palestinian-Israeli agreement is fully implemented, Palestine will join the ranks of those Arab countries that have already begun to explore greater political pluralism. The experiences of Jordan, Morocco, and Kuwait may be fortified by the Palestinian experience, and this may act in turn as a catalyst for greater democratization in other Arab countries. This domino effect is exemplified in Algeria, where, in the wake of the Moroccan experience, calls for reinstitution of the drive toward democracy are being aired more volubly. The Kuwaiti example also echoes that of Saudi Arabia and other Gulf countries. But more prominent is the status of Lebanon, where an enduring democracy is bound to generate pressure for democratization in Syria. Still-obstinate Syria might need the example of Palestine to push it toward further pluralism.

The Gaza-Jericho accord, in its sum and substance, has sparked a debate in Palestinian society and throughout the Arab world. The Islamist forces, represented in Palestine by Hamas, argue that the treaty with Israel is "treason" and a capitulation to the Israeli aggressor. Yet to date, most Palestinians, along with the majority of Arab regimes, accept the agreement as a landmark step toward peace. Even Syria, which might not agree with the accord ideologically, has vowed not to stand in its way. Debate and pluralistic opinion thus have created an environment akin to that of democracy.

The Israeli-Palestinian agreement has broken down long-entrenched psychological barriers, entailing as it does the acceptance of past enemies and an embrace of alternative programs and ideas. If successful, it may serve as a stimulus to other Arab states to implement the broad themes of the peace accord in their own societies. Conversely, delay or reversal in settling the conflict will only play into the hands of extremists disinterested in reconciliation.

Notes

A similar version of this chapter has been published in *Civil Society in the Middle East*, Volume 1, edited by Augustus Richard Norton (Leiden: E.J. Brill, 1995). We are extremely grateful to Professor Norton and E. J. Brill for their kind permission to include the chapter here.

1. See, for example, Larry Diamond and Marc Plattner, eds., *The Global Resurgence of Democracy* (Baltimore: The Johns Hopkins University Press, 1993); Samuel Huntington, *The Third Wave: Democratization in the Late Twentieth Century* (Norman: Oklahoma University Press, 1991); Gerald Schmitz and David Gillies, *The Challenge of Democratic Development: Sustaining Democratization in Developing Countries* (Ottawa: The North-South Institute, 1992).

2. See Saad Eddin Ibrahim et al., *al-Mujtama' wa al-dawla fi al-watan al-'arabi* [Society and State in the Arab World] (Amman: The Arab Thought Forum, 1988); and Giacomo Luciani, ed., *The Arab State* (Berkeley and Los Angeles: University of California Press, 1990).

3. Huntington, *The Third Wave*.

4. Saad Eddin Ibrahim, ed., *al-Mujtama' al-madani wa al-tahawwul al-dimuqrati fi al-watan al-'arabi* [Civil Society and Democratic Transformation in the Arab World] (Cairo: Ibn Khaldoun Center, 1992), pp. 12–13.

5. Richard Norton, guest editor's introduction to a special issue on civil society in the Middle East, *Middle East Journal* 47, 2 (Spring 1993).

6. See a review of how the concept of "civil society" was used in Anthony Orum, *Introduction to Political Sociology* (Englewood Cliffs, NJ: Prentice-Hall, 1978), pp. 24–26; Brian Redhead, ed., *Plato to Nato: Studies in Political Thought* (London: BBC Books, 1984).

7. See Younan Labib Rizk, *Misr al-madaniyya* [Civil Egypt] (Cairo: Tiba, 1993); Manfred Halpern, *The Politics of Social Change in the Middle East and the Arab World* (Princeton, NJ: Princeton University Press, 1962).

8. See Ilya Harik, "The Origins of the Arab System," in Luciani, *The Arab State*, pp. 1–28; Patricia Crone and Martin Hinds, *God's Caliph: Religious Authority in the First Century of Islam* (Cambridge: Cambridge University Press, 1980).

9. For an elaboration on this traditional mode of governance, see the classic of A. Ibn Khaldoun, *Al-Muqaddima* [The Introduction] (Baghdad: Al-Muthanna, 1980); Elbaki Hermassi, *al-Mujtama' wa al-dawla fi al-maghrib al-'arabi* [Society and State in the Arab Maghreb] (Beirut: Center for Arab Unity Studies, 1987).

10. Rizk, *Misr al-madaniyya*, pp. 40–48, 90–91.

11. Rizk, *Misr al-madaniyya*, pp. 141–142.

12. On the Arab political usage of the two terms (*fitna, nakba*) see Saad Eddin Ibrahim, *al-Khuruj min zuqaq al-tarikh: durus al-fitna al-kubra fi al-khalij* [Exiting the Blind Alley of History: The Arabs and the Current Sedition in the Gulf] (Cairo: Ibn Khaldoun—S. Al Sabah, 1992), p. 12.

13. Ibrahim et al., *al-Mujtama' wa al-dawla*, pp. 45–78; Harik, "The Origins of the Arab System," pp. 19–24.

14. See Hazem Beblawi, "The Rentier State in the Arab World"; Jean Leca, "Social Structure and Political Stability: Comparative Evidence from Algeria, Syria, and Iraq," in Luciani, *The Arab State*, pp. 85–98 and 150–188.

15. Ibrahim et al., *al-Mujtama' wa al-dawla*, pp. 342–369.

16. See Saad Eddin Ibrahim, *Ta'amulat fi mas'alat al-aqalliyyat fi al-watan al-'arabi* [Reflections on the Question of Minorities in the Arab World] (Cairo: Ibn Khaldoun—Al Sabah, 1992), pp. 17–18; and, by the same author, "Minorities and State-Building in the Arab World," a paper presented to the Annual Meeting of the American Sociological Association, Pittsburgh, August 1992.

17. Ibrahim, *Ta'amulat fi mas'alat al-aqalliyyat*, pp. 243–244.

18. Ibrahim et al., *al-Mujtama' wa al-dawla*, p. 334.

19. Ibrahim et al., *al-Mujtama' wa al-dawla*, pp. 347–375.

20. See the account of how Arab monarchies responded to radical ideologies in Michael Hudson, *Arab Politics: The Search for Legitimacy* (New Haven: Yale University Press, 1977).

21. For an elaborate account, see the proceedings of the Conference on Arab Civil Organizations (in Arabic), Cairo, 31 October–3 November 1989; the papers of a seminar on *al-Mujtama' al-madani al-'arabi* [Arab Civil Society], Beirut, 21–24 January 1993, and later published under the same title (Beirut: Center for Arab Unity Studies, 1993).

22. On the birth of the Arab Human Rights Organization and similar civil formations in the 1980s, see Ibrahim, ed., *al-Mujtama' al-madani*, pp. 9–12.

23. This estimate was aggregated from the country papers of the Conference on Arab Civil Organizations.

24. For a detailed account, see Ibrahim, *al-Mujtama' al-madani*.

25. According to a recent field study, only about 40 percent of Egypt's NGOs were judged active and effective. See *Grass-roots Participation and Development in Egypt*, a study by the Ibn Khaldoun Center, commissioned by UNICEF, UNDP, and UNFPA (Cairo, 1993).

26. See the *Civil Society and Democratic Transformation in the Arab World Newsletter* (hereafter, *CSDT Newsletter*), an Ibn Khaldoun Center monthly publication (in English and Arabic), May, June, July 1993.

27. Ibrahim, ed., *al-Mujtama' al-madani*.

28. For facts, figures, and analysis, see *CSDT Newsletter*, May, October 1992.

29. Much of what follows is adapted from an earlier paper by the author, "Crises, Elites, and Democratization in the Arab World," *Middle East Journal* 47, 2 (Spring 1993), pp. 292–305.

30. Ibrahim, ed., *al-Mujtama' al-madani*, pp. 318–335; *CSDT Newsletter*, May, June 1992.

31. *CSDT Newsletter*, November 1992 and January 1993.

32. *CSDT Newsletter*, May, November 1993.

33. *CSDT Newsletter*, July 1993.

34. For facts, figures, and analysis, see *CSDT Newsletter*, February, April 1992.

35. For details, see *CSDT Newsletter*, March 1992.

36. The latest such episode is the defiant establishment of a Saudi Human Rights Organization in April 1993. Unhappy, but unable to punish the founders for fear of public opinion abroad and at home, the Saudi government mobilized its

own media and religious establishment (led by the famous Shaikh Ben-Baz) to counterattack the new organization. See *CSDT Newsletter*, May 1993.

37. See *CSDT Newsletter*, May, November 1993.

38. For the background since 1988 and events into January 1992, see *CSDT Newsletter*, January, February 1992.

39. *CSDT Newsletter*, July, August 1992; and *al-Musawar*, 1 July 1993, in which the Algerian president, Ali Kafi, was quoted as declaring to a group of Egyptian intellectuals that "the future of Algeria is far more important than democracy."

40. *CSDT Newsletter*, February, April 1992.

41. See the detailed results and analysis in *CSDT Newsletter*, May, June 1993.

42. *CSDT Newsletter*, September 1992.

43. *CSDT Newsletter*, May 1992.

44. *CSDT Newsletter* has kept a monthly scoreboard and detailed accounts of these confrontations since the June 1992 issue.

45. *CSDT Newsletter*, October 1992.

46. *CSDT Newsletter*, April, October 1992, January 1993.

47. *CSDT Newsletter*, "Special Report on Eritrea," June 1993, p. 3.

1

The Domestic Setting: Culture, Discourse, and Politics

The Political Culture Approach to Arab Democratization: The Case for Bringing It Back In, Carefully

Michael C. Hudson

The abuse and misuse of the political culture concept to "explain" Arab politics has been so egregious that it is hard to resist the temptation to consign it without further ado to the dustbin of political science. So many sins have been committed: gross overgeneralization (Patai), crude Orientalism (Pryce-Jones), Eurocentric chauvinism (Kedourie), anthropologic reductionism (Gellner), not to mention media sound-bites ("Shi'is are suicidal but Sunnis are homicidal"). In academic political science the "political culture approach," much admired as part of the dominant modernization–political development paradigm in the 1960s, retreated with the decline of that paradigm under the onslaught of political economy, "statism" and corporatism, rational choice, and the new institutionalism. In Middle East political science, even though there is a certain time-lag in intellectual fashions, one can observe a similar shift in attention: Today, socioeconomic rather than sociocultural approaches seem to be enjoying the greatest favor, while institutional approaches have yet to receive the attention they perhaps deserve.

Until fairly recently the main dependent variable for students of Middle East and Arab politics was authoritarianism. Each explanatory approach to this condition had its own conventional wisdom. There were easy political culture explanations: fatalism, individualism, primordial chauvinism, a herd instinct, and more. Political economy explanations focused on the dependency of the "peripheral" societies on the developed "center," the historic hegemony of wealthy elites, and the peculiar properties of oil-driven economies. Those who advocated "bringing the state back in" had no problem ascribing the authoritarian condition to the overdeveloped *mukhabarat* [national security] state. Economistic and institutional approaches were even combined with the application of the model of the "bureaucratic-authoritarian state," drawn from Latin America. Culture in general, and political culture in particular, seemed superfluous.

The crisis of authoritarianism sweeping across the Middle East since the 1970s, however, has forced political scientists to rethink their enterprise. The situation to be explained is now more complex than the seemingly permanent authoritarianism of the past. Experiments in liberalization, even democratization, are occurring in several countries. The conventional wisdom, in its several variations, did not predict these experiments; instead, it showed us why liberalization would be highly unlikely. Indeed, if we continue to adhere to such conventional wisdom, we would have to conclude that these liberalization cases are "exceptional" and likely to fail. It is, of course, quite possible that the liberalizing trends we have observed in countries such as Jordan, Yemen, Kuwait, Lebanon, and Morocco are only ephemeral; our conventional wisdom that explains the permanence and ubiquity of authoritarianism may be correct. But suppose, for the sake of argument, that liberalization is a more durable phenomenon. How, then, are we to explain it?

It is not my purpose to propose a general theory of liberalism for the Arab world. My more modest task is to ask whether the new liberalism can be adequately explained *without* invoking political culture. My answer is a somewhat reluctant "no": Despite its conceptual untidiness and empirical difficulties, political culture is an important variable; it cannot be reduced to other factors such as economics, institutions, or externalities; it is necessary for helping explain how authoritarianism is losing its legitimacy. The political culture concept, then, must be "brought back in"—but carefully. Obviously, the egregious abuses of the term must be avoided. Recently among political scientists there has been a "return" to the approach in general and an effort to address earlier weaknesses. Among Middle East political scientists too there are new efforts to rethink political culture in terms of an emerging "civil society." The attack on "Orientalism" led by Edward Said was unquestionably salutary, but a side effect was the discrediting of political culture analysis in general. Notwithstanding all the problems it poses for empirical analysis, it seems too important to be ignored. Without factoring in the complexities of culture, values, beliefs, ideology, and legitimacy, we risk being left with arid economistic reductionism. This is not a claim for the uniqueness or exceptionality of Arab politics, nor is it a denial of the significance of other factors. I would merely suggest that we need—and can develop—more sophisticated, less biased formulations of political culture(s) in Arab politics that will help us understand the possibilities and limits of alternatives to authoritarianism.

Political Culture Revisited

Almond and Verba's *The Civic Culture* (1963) was a major step forward in American political science, as Inglehart and others have noted, notwithstanding its flaws.[1] It marked an obvious advance over the old impressionistic "national character" analyses. Philosophically, in a tradition going back to Plato and Tocqueville, it sought to provide empirical grounding for the idea of "community" as a determinant of political performance. Their study offered new support for the proposition that a constellation of habits and attitudes marked by mutual trust was an essential condition for the development of associational life, political participation, and a loyal opposition. A torrent of debate and criticism raised serious methodological questions about *The Civic Culture*. The use of individual survey data to depict a society's political culture was faulted. The study was heavily criticized for proposing a direct causal linkage between political culture and democratic stability. Critics also raised the problem of ahistoricity inherent in a "snapshot" of attitudes at a single point in time. The authors themselves later accepted the validity of some of these criticisms.

Partly as a result of these criticisms the "political culture approach" faded during the 1970s and 1980s. Its retreat was also due to the decline of the larger political development and modernization paradigm in which it had been embedded. Ambiguities in the political culture concept were exposed. On the one hand, if political culture constellations were essentially permanent, how could they account for change in the dependent variables of stability and democratization? On the other hand, some political culturalists assumed or implied that attitudes and habits would in fact be easily modified by the forces of modernization; and yet empirical observation failed to show that more participant, inclusive political cultures were actually emerging. In the ensuing paradigmatic struggles, political economy, dependency, and the state pushed aside political culture approaches.

But the basic proposition of *The Civic Culture* is, if anything, even more central in comparative politics today—as we witness a certain "wave" of democratization around the world—than it was three decades ago. And, as we shall see, it rests at the heart of the contemporary debate about civil society and political liberalization in the Arab world. Some of the newly ascendant approaches do not seem to account satisfactorily for these outbreaks of liberalism. Dependency and statism, for example, would appear to predict the opposite. Rational choice and political economy approaches do better, but rational choice can offer only arbitrary utilitarian explanations for the values to be maximized, and economistic independent variables don't appear to discriminate between contradictory political outcomes: Economic crises can give rise to democratic experiments and also

kill them. And the causal connection between economic and political liberalization is hardly less problematic than that between the "civic" culture
and democratic stability.

Perhaps these conundrums help account for what Inglehart calls "the
renaissance of political culture" in mainstream comparative politics. "Renaissance" may be too expansive a term, but there does appear to have been
a modest movement toward rehabilitating the political culture approach.
Elkins and Simeon conceive of political culture as common assumptions
(about order, causality, goals, communal identity, the political sphere, and
the trustworthiness of others) pertaining to collectivities, not individuals,
and they distinguish between the term as a descriptive category and as explanation.[2] Used in conjunction with structural factors, political culture
has a residual explanatory function. Political culture—especially as a single factor—is not likely to "explain" dependent variables as general as stability, democracy, or authoritarianism. But it may help explain why certain
institutions (such as legislatures) function as they do. Noting the distinction made by Brian Barry between sociological (or cultural) and economic
approaches, they suggest that economistic categories like self-interest and
utility are shaped by cultural configurations.

The same point is developed by Wildavsky, who argues that the political preference configurations essential for rational-choice analysis are
rooted in political culture and not simply exogenous "givens."[3] Conflict
may arise as different subcultures in a given political system clash over issues. In the same vein, Berntzen and Selle argue that "qualitative knowledge of the content of politics," by which they mean the historical cultural
or ethnographic context, along with external structural factors, are essential to knowing "what is really going on."[4] Similarly, Lane stresses the importance of disaggregating "culture" into subcultures and locating them
precisely in the social structure.[5] For students of Middle East politics, concerned as we must be with multiple cultures within or across state boundaries, and within or between elites (as well as masses), the point would
seem to be obvious. The problem, rather, is to avoid the excessive generalizations that marked political culture studies in their heyday: artificial di-
chotomization between "traditional" and "modern," the oversimplification
of "subject-parochial-participant" classifications, and the application of a
single "culture" to a whole nation. Laitin's rejoinder to Wildavsky, while
stressing the complexity of culture(s), notes that people with strongly opposed views can share a culture, while people from different cultures can
have similar views. Taking the view (held by Geertz and Gramsci, among
others) of political culture as a control mechanism, Laitin urges that we
see it as a set of symbols that "constitute a political resource that can be
effectively exploited by political entrepreneurs."[6]

Notwithstanding the weaknesses of the political culture approach in its
heyday a generation ago, many political scientists today feel that the concept

cannot be abandoned altogether. They also have made some specific proposals for remedying these earlier deficiencies. It is possible, therefore, that political culture may also deserve to be brought back in to the analysis of Arab politics. But before we jump to that particular conclusion let us look briefly at the uses and misuses of political culture in the literature on Arab politics. Then let us examine the current interest in "civil society" and "democratization" in the Arab world from an enlightened political culture perspective.

Applications to Arab Politics

In the problematic epistemological relationship between political science and "area studies" one would have thought that "political culture" would be the indispensable linking concept. The gap between global generalizations and regional particularities would be bridged through careful empirical analyses of the given regional context in such a way as to enhance the explanatory power of general propositions while avoiding the blind alley of regional "exceptionalism." It is unfortunate, therefore, that the treatment of political culture in the Arab world has lagged behind general work on this subject as well as applications to other regions, notably Europe. While we shall mention below a number of notable exceptions, we have not moved as far as we should have beyond the level of long-discredited "national character" approaches. Political science on the Arab world has yet to produce a watershed study equivalent in theoretical importance to what Almond and Verba's *The Civic Culture* did to advance the study of political culture in general. A new generation of Arab-world political scientists is indeed rightly guided in its rejection of reductionist biased and ethnocentric readings of what Said called Orientalist political culture, but we should be careful not to throw out the political culture baby with the Orientalist bathwater.

Writers on political culture in the Arab world fall, it seems to me, into two categories: the reductionists and the empiricists. The reductionist "school," of which "Orientalism" is a big part, is the oldest and—notwithstanding the attack of Said and a new generation of scholars—the most influential, having seeped into the popular, and policy, discourse. The empiricists, to my mind a more interesting and diverse group, represent a salutary advance over the reductionists, but their work still suffers to some extent from the weaknesses of the 1960s.

"Reductionist" Approaches

The reductionist approach, whose practitioners have mainly been philologists, historians, anthropologists, and essayists, is given to grand generalizations.

It begins but does not end with Islam. The Islam presented by major scholars like von Grunebaum, Lewis, and Gellner is a disembodied essence, oddly disconnected from history, seemingly unadaptable to changing circumstances. To be sure, their Islam is (unto itself) complex, but its political implications are fairly simple: Both textually and historically it supports authoritarianism by rulers and submission by followers. Islamic political culture (in the reductionist presentation) permits no autonomous public sphere, no separation of the spiritual and temporal.

Then there are the Arabs. Jacques Berque is one of the few non-Arab scholars with the erudition and immersion to produce a profound presentation of Arab culture: He reveals the complexities of "the unitary and the plural."[7] Eschewing the too-broad generalization, the historian Albert Hourani describes multiple and changing Arab cultures over time.[8] Hourani is remembered as well for an oft-quoted characterization of "Levantine" culture: "To be a Levantine is to live in two worlds or more at once without belonging to either. . . . "[9] The implied political consequence is instability.

Lesser analysts, however, have slipped into reductionist stereotyping, sometimes unwittingly. In his well-known book, *The Arab Mind*, Patai evokes Ibn Khaldun: "The Arabs are least willing of nations to subordinate themselves to each other, as they are rude, proud, ambitious, and eager to be the leader."[10] From there he examines (among other things) child-rearing practices, "the spell" of the Arabic language, "the Bedouin substructure of the Arab personality," shame, honor, the "fahlawi" personality, the "Islamic component of the Arab personality," "extremes and emotions, fantasy and reality," "conflict proneness," and hatred of the West. If national character approaches have long since been discredited in political science they linger on in some of the other disciplines. Fouad Ajami, starting from Orientalist assumptions, goes beyond simply elaborating the image of a closed Arab-Islamic culture immune to Westernization and asserts that Arab culture has become hopelessly pulverized by the West. The result? A collective desire "to escape from politics, to entrust it all to grand schemes."[11] Communalism and sectarianism, he declares, prevail over integration and progress; Arab Muslims are yearning for a Mahdi rather than democracy (but Islamism probably won't bring cultural coherence); the Arab citizenry lacks the institutions and "habits of mind" to become more than "sheer spectators" in the political drama.[12]

Such notions are then vulgarized for general consumption, often for political purposes. Elie Kedourie, in a book written for a pro-Israel think tank, asserts that " . . . there is nothing in the political traditions of the Arab world—which are the political traditions of Islam—which might make familiar, or indeed intelligible, the organizing ideas of constitutional and representative government."[13] David Pryce-Jones caricatures the received wisdom in a 400-page "interpretation" of the Arabs that blames

Islam, tribalism, a shame-and-honor culture, and a total inability to be Western for the lamentable condition of Arab politics: "At present, an Arab democrat is not even an idealization, but a contradiction in terms."[14] One could cite other examples but to no useful purpose.

"Empirical" Approaches

The "reductionist" treatment of Arab political culture offers some wheat and a great deal of chaff. The insights of a Berque or Hourani resonate with independent empirical observation and other informed analysis, and the sense of contemporary *political* culture incoherence that most of these writers depict is hard to gainsay. Valid conclusions, however, can sometimes be reached for the wrong reasons. Two factors stimulated the attempts by social scientists to specify the contours of Arab political culture more precisely and empirically. One was a healthy skepticism about traditional epistemological premises and methods. The other was the pathbreaking work on political culture in comparative politics, discussed above. But how successful these attempts have been is another matter.

Reviewing political culture approaches to Middle East politics, Ben-Dor is somewhat dissatisfied with the state of affairs, but perhaps not dissatisfied enough.[15] He rightly observes that the political culture "movement" in comparative politics was unfocused: Themes exposed in *The Civic Culture* were not consistently developed in subsequent work, notably Almond and Verba's collection, *Political Culture and Political Development* (1965). Not surprisingly, therefore, the scope of Middle East political culture scholarship (as Ben-Dor sees it) is capacious, including textual studies of Islam; anthropological "findings" about personality traits, socialization, and language; and structural studies focusing on families and elites. The generalizations on Islam and politics he finds (correctly) to be somewhat impressionistic.[16] He notes (without comment on their validity) Morroe Berger's (1964) generalizations about the primacy of family and other primordial units, the hostility, lack of trust, formality, and political quietism of the Arabs. Waterbury's study of Morocco[17] is cited as a contribution to our knowledge about factionalism and clientelism. But there are more questions than answers: How do alleged negative attitudes toward government vary from place to place, class to class, and sect to sect? What precisely are the bases of solidarity groupings? What exactly are the political implications (if any) of the so-called honor and shame culture? In what way does culture affect political participation? And in what way does it support (or retard) democratic legitimacy? In the Arab world we are a very long way indeed from being able to specify and empirically test a formal model, with correlation coefficients, as Inglehart does for the European and Anglo-Saxon countries.[18]

Far away as they may be from quantifying the impact of Arab political culture(s) on a range of political outcomes (such as legitimacy, stability, or democratization), the empirical social scientists have improved upon the more reductionist and Orientalist formulations (even if they are better at questions than answers) in several ways. One is their consideration of social and cultural change. Leonard Binder, for example, in one of his earlier essays (during his "political development" period) looks beyond the texts to ask (following Karl Deutsch) whether social mobilization will increase the pressures for traditionalism or radicalism. What will be its effects upon minorities, irredentism, and "sleeping nationalities"?[19] Dankwart Rustow, more historically knowledgeable than many Middle East political scientists, was able to portray the cultural milieus of specialized elites in Turkey, thus moving the analysis beyond global country-level generalizations.[20] He also made a conceptual contribution by proposing that the investigation of political culture be focused on issues of identity, authority, and equality. Clement Henry Moore's old but still valuable study of North Africa, while not quantitatively rigorous, offers insightful contrasts between the "rationality" of the Tunisian "political formula" compared with the emerging institutionalized tradition of Morocco and the artificial "order" of Algeria disconnected from an incoherent political culture.[21]

The latest edition of Bill and Springborg's textbook on Middle East politics for the most part eschews sweeping cultural generalizations and wisely focuses on structures.[22] Despite certain misleading phrases (such as "the genes of politics") and some tenuous historical propositions (such as the Prophet Muhammad as the model for today's "patrimonial" leaders), political culture is not explicitly advanced as an explanatory factor for contemporary tensions—indeed, the term does not even appear in the index or chapter headings. Social structure and political economy receive greater attention. Cultural *content* is less important than the *configuration* of social units like family, clan, sect, and client grouping. The balancing behavior and competition for "collective goods" among such groupings is what politics is all about, and the overarching, multifaceted dynamics of economic change ("modernization") intensify the uncertainty and the competition. In a loose sense, of course, this book—emblematic of the "political development" school of the 1960s—is "cultural" in its basic proposition: "the dialectical clash between the challenging forces of modernity and the persistent strength of tradition."[23] While the singular noun "tradition" might appear as the ultimate cultural reductionism, a closer reading of these "neomodernization" authors—who are not oblivious to two decades of often-valid criticisms of that paradigm—reveals a more discriminating and sophisticated depiction of enduring Middle Eastern political "realities." Certainly their work represents a significant advance over the Islamic essentialism and national character stereotyping that unfortunately still dominate the public discourse.

In any inventory of political culture work by social scientists mention should be made of attitude surveys and micro-level, often anthropological case studies of ethnic, tribal, and sectarian communities. Both in their different ways aspire to a degree of specificity and empiricism absent in the nation-level studies. Attitudes and opinions, as measured by questionnaires and systematic interview data, may not be the best way of tapping into deep collective value orientations, but they are not perhaps inherently less valid than textual extrapolations or armchair speculation. Compared to other regions, empirical survey work on the Arab world is meager, but there is some and it is increasing.[24] Validity and reliability, not to mention interpretation, are often problematic, however; particularly when polling designs are polluted by "the authorities" or when the survey methods and even the identities of the poll-takers cannot be specified.[25] Lerner's groundbreaking work in the 1950s used attitude surveys to support an imaginative if flawed proposition about modernization and cultural transformation in which the mediating variable was the psychological property of empathy.[26] Marvin Zonis discovered on the basis of systematic interviews with a sample from the Iranian political elite a culture of cynicism that (rightly) suggested a certain hollowness in the legitimacy of the Shah's regime.[27] Farah brought together a number of studies from social psychology and survey research that empirically demonstrated an authoritarian socialization process and challenged conventional views about hierarchies of group identification in several Arab countries.[28] Saad Eddin Ibrahim directed a large-scale, cross-national survey of Arab public opinion that confirmed that Arabs remained deeply concerned about "all-Arab" national problems, but also discovered significant subregional variations.[29]

Among more recent work is Suleiman's survey of young Tunisians' political attitudes. He finds not one but three distinct subcultures: Arab-Islamic, secular (French), and a "mixed" stratum that is (in Hourani's term) acutely "Levantinized."[30] A U.S. government information specialist, writing under the auspices of a pro-Israel think tank, takes to task both scholars who "underrate" and those who "exaggerate" the power or consistency of Arab popular opinion, and expresses moderate optimism (based on a private Jordanian poll) that there is an attitudinal change in Arab opinion toward acceptance of a compromise with Israel.[31] In contrast, on the basis of a survey of professionals and academics in the Gulf during and after the Iraq-Kuwait crisis, Ismael and Ismael discern an antagonism between (regime) politics and popular political culture and conclude that the Arab state system "cannot be sustained any longer."[32]

The "ethnographic" approach to political culture typically involves the application of anthropological or historical methods to particular social groupings. A fruitful recent example is the collection edited by Khoury and Kostiner, in which scholars examine the complex relationship between tribes and the development of the modern state in the Middle East.[33] An underlying concern of these writers is compatibility of identification between these deeply rooted structures and the newer, overarching state, with all of its demands. The legitimacy of the political order depends to an important degree on this congruence—or, in the Middle East, the lack of it. "Because the nominal nation-state has not met the challenge [of development]," writes one of the contributors, "society has resorted to its prenational ties as a solution. . . . The 'ethnicization of conflict' suggests that tribalism has been revived under a new cover and that it obstructs the process of state formation."[34] In the same vein but more categorically, the editors of a volume on ethnicity in the Middle East make the following cultural assertion: "The Middle East is a congeries of ethnic communities, most of which are fated to coexist with others under the same political authority within the boundaries of the same territorial state."[35] One of the editors states that the Middle East is generally similar to other Third World regions, except that "the salience of the religious definition of communal solidarity" is more acute. He concludes that modernization has exacerbated ethnic solidarities and conflict rather than erasing them, and that consequently ethnic solidarities are too strong to permit the management of conflict by assimilation, that is, developing allegiance to nonethnic symbols.[36] Coercive domination by the strongest ethnic group tends to be the prevalent pattern. Such observations rest on a certain image of Arab or Middle Eastern political culture, which in turn rests on an interpretation of a certain historical "reality."

To try and derive such images and interpretations from empirical observation is an improvement over *ex cathedra* Orientalism or armchair psychology; yet there is still room for disagreement. Subjectivity, unwitting bias, conceptual reification, factual selectivity, and even hidden agendas may also play their part. Serious scholars can and do have honest disagreements. For example, contrast Barakat's interpretation of roughly the same empirical materials with some of the writers discussed above. Arguing from what the dust jacket explains is "an Arab perspective," he skillfully dispatches the national character reductionists.[37] Like several of the "ethnographers" just mentioned, he is sensitive to the pull of parochial subcultures and "primordial" loyalties; but he sees much more development in the "secular" sector than they do, and he ascribes much of the stagnation not to cultural factors but to structural political conditions—authoritarian regimes and their powerful external supporters. Reversing the explanation of the cultural reductionists who ascribe the lack of democracy to cultural factors, Barakat and many other Arab intellectuals blame the current sociocultural malaise—including stifled creativity, a "traditional mentality," the absence of "scientific and future-oriented rationalism," the "subjugation of women," and what Sharabi calls "neopatriarchy" (a deformed, authoritarian, dependent, imitative condition neither truly traditional nor modern)[38]—on "a devastating condition of alienation" engendered by the Arab citizen's exclusion from the political process.[39] Which comes first: the democratic chicken or the cultural egg?

Civil Society and Democratization

With the collapse of the Soviet system and the end of the Cold War came a wave of experiments in democratization around the world.[40] There has been as well a renewed interest on the part of comparative politics theorists in democracy.[41] Although the Arab-Islamic world seems to some to be the major exception to this trend, even here there has been some cautious movement toward liberalization, if not democratization.[42] In the search for explanations, some political scientists have returned to old concepts, among them political culture. A recent volume on political culture and democracy in developing countries celebrates "the return of political culture" after two decades of banishment at the hands of neo-Marxism and dependency theory.[43] Indeed, the larger paradigm of liberal political development and modernization may also be making a return, although with slightly different labeling. The concept of "civil society" has emerged as a key condition for democratization, and now a number of the most able political scientists of the Middle East are investigating whether the reality is emerging as well, and why.[44]

Most of these analysts would agree that civil society is an autonomous space between the domain of the state and society at large and that it has links with both. It is a structural concept whose hallmark is a plethora of voluntary associations. But it is a cultural concept too: As al-Sayyid puts it, there must be an "ethic of tolerance."[45] When Norton speaks of "the vibrancy of civil society" in some Middle East countries, he is not just saying that they have many voluntary associations, but also that there are habits of cooperation and an acceptance of pluralism. Economic explanations alone will not do the trick; nor will reliance on exogenous political factors. From this Tocquevillian perspective the appropriate habits of the mind are deeply rooted—cultural—and they take time to grow. They do not vary with short-term changes in per capita income. In their empirical study of civic traditions in Italy, Putnam and his collaborators trace the origin of civic traditions (and democratic behavior) in northern Italy to the twelfth century and chart the growth of civic involvement from the mid-nineteenth century.[46]

If one is interested in understanding conditions such as legitimacy, liberalism, or democracy it is hard to ignore culture (and Tocqueville) even if it is a residual variable after structural, economic, and exogenous factors. But if we decide to exhume the political culture concept in application to the Arab world (some would prefer to leave it buried), we must confront again old arguments. Some Orientalists would claim that the requisite "civic" associational structures and habits of mind certainly have not existed over time, nor do they now; on the contrary, there is an unbroken and unchanging cultural predisposition toward authoritarianism, submission, and fatalism.

But a respectable number of social scientists read "reality" very differently. Hermassi, for example, rejects the prerequisite of unbroken historical continuity, observing that the colonial experience created a kind of cultural *tabula rasa* in which civic culture can indeed take quick root.[47] He criticizes what he calls the Orientalist depiction of Arab-Islamic political culture as basically responsible for the lack of liberalism and democracy in the Arab world. Objecting to the "cultural essentialism" of Lewis, he observes that equally reputable scholars "have shown that in the Arab and Islamic world, the historic experience of freedom is much larger than a textual analysis would lead one to believe." He also challenges the Orientalist assumption of historical and cultural continuity in the Middle East state: What they miss, he contends, "is the obvious and profound discontinuity in the social formation of the Middle Eastern state introduced by colonialism."[48] He goes on to argue that neither Islam nor Arab cultural patterns are inherently hostile to liberalism and democracy and, indeed, that democratic norms may be gaining importance as a source of political legitimacy. Similarly, Saad Eddin Ibrahim, on the basis of empirical investigations, is convinced that associational life is growing significantly throughout the Arab world and that a new civic space is emerging to curb the authoritarian *mukhabarat* (national security) state. Barakat (unlike some of the ethnographers) argues that a "progressive secular" future is possible, despite formidable obstacles. He cites Gramsci's observation on the double-edged character of civil society: " . . . at once the political terrain on which the dominant class organizes its hegemony and the terrain on which opposition parties and movements organize, win allies and build their social power."[49]

The key question (except perhaps for radical and postmodern analysts) is how to deal empirically with civil society and political culture in general. Our survey of past and present applications suggests that there are no simple answers. Definitions are imprecise and elastic. Methods and evidence include everything from cerebral intuition and texts to historical narratives and quantitative survey data. It may be, as Diamond argues, that "the return of political culture" is welcome, and that it cannot be ignored in any attempt to explain the enlargement of democracy.[50] But in a book designed to fill part of the void on applications to the developing world there are only three Middle Eastern studies—Turkey, Egypt, and Israel—

of which only two are thoroughly indigenous political cultures and only one is Arab. The analysis of Egypt proposes that Egypt's current malaise is rooted in a deep antagonism between "modern instrumental rationality and indigenous value rationality,"[51] the latter represented by the Islamist movement. While political Islam challenges the authoritarian modalities of "modern instrumental rationality," it refuses to accept the ethic of tolerance required for civil society, leaving Egypt with both an opening for and an obstacle to democracy. If the conclusion sounds familiar, so is the methodology: a qualitative interpretation of historical events and Islamist texts, with some emphasis on "Islamic praxis in the field of political economy."[52] But the effects of Islamism on democratization or liberalization in Egypt or elsewhere need more careful examination than they receive here, and one wonders whether we have advanced much beyond the kind of work that was being done 30 years ago.[53]

The uneven evolution of political culture studies provides us with a few epistemological lessons: (1) Avoid reductionist concepts and essentialist assumptions. (2) Disaggregate political culture: Look at subcultures (vertical and horizontal); look at elite cultures and mass cultures. (3) Political culture is a multilayered phenomenon, amenable therefore to "geological" study: Look at formal ideologies (on the "surface"), then at opinions (easily changeable), then at attitudes (less so), and finally try to plumb the deep structure of enduring collective values and orientations. (4) Focus on group identities, orientations toward authority, and principles of equity and justice. (5) Be methodologically multifaceted: Texts (from scripture and philosophy to newspapers, cassettes, and graffiti), despite their occasional misuse in our field, remain a fundamental (and fundamentalist) primary source; traditional historical narratives are indispensable, as are comparative case studies; interview and survey data should be more widely utilized.

The return of political culture to the study of Arab politics is, as W. S. Gilbert might have put it, a cause for "modified rapture." No Middle East area specialist (if only out of professional self-interest) would quarrel with the notion that culture is a good thing to know about: On a purely descriptive level, cultural knowledge no doubt improves political analysis in some intangible way. It is on the explanatory level that the concept seems at once indispensable yet problematic. It is important to specify what political condition or behavior one wants to explain. If asked to explain the decline of the U.S. automobile industry, economists might invoke models of supply and demand, factor costs, comparative advantage, and aggregate growth. If asked to explain General Motors' loss of market share, however, they might hire an anthropologist to analyze the "culture" of General Motors' management. Austere rational-choice models or macro-level economic variables may be sufficient to explain certain kinds of domestic and even foreign policy decisionmaking. Structures and institutions (formal and informal) will help explain the powers of and constraints on politicians. But can economics or structures alone carry us far enough toward understanding those enduringly interesting dependent variables: legitimacy and stability, trust and effectiveness, authoritarianism and despotism, liberalism and democracy? Dogan remarks that "[p]ower, legitimacy, trust and effectiveness do not have identical meanings in London and Jakarta, or in Washington and Cairo."[54] Some comparative understanding of political culture surely is necessary to save us from egregious ethnocentrism. The discourse of Arab politics is, if anything, increasingly moral in tone and value-laden: There has been no "end of ideology." Today's debate over political Islam conceivably is no more than coded language for "pure" economic and political behavior. Is it old-fashioned to sometimes take things at face value—or is it prudent?

Notes

For research assistance, I would like to thank Stephen Day, a Ph.D. candidate in the Department of Government at Georgetown University.

1. Ronald Inglehart, "The Renaissance of Political Culture," *American Political Science Review* 82, 4 (December 1988), p. 1204.

2. David J. Elkins and Richard Simeon, "A Cause in Search of Its Effect, or, What Does Political Culture Explain?" *Comparative Politics* 11, 2 (January 1979), pp. 127–145.

3. Aaron Wildavsky, "Choosing Preferences by Constructing Institutions: A Cultural Theory of Preference Formation," *American Political Science Review* 81, 1 (March 1987), pp. 3–21.

4. Einar Berntzen and Per Selle, "Plaidoyer for the Restoration of the Concept of Political Culture, or Bringing Political Culture Back In," *International Journal of Comparative Sociology* 31 (January–April 1990), p. 47.

5. Ruth Lane, "Political Culture: Residual Category or General Theory?" *Comparative Political Studies* 25 (October 1992), pp. 362–387.

6. David Laitin, "Political Culture and Political Preferences," *American Political Science Review* 82, 2 (June 1988), p. 591.

7. Jacques Berque, *Cultural Expression in Arab Society Today* (Austin: University of Texas Press, 1978), Ch. 3.

8. Albert Hourani, *A History of the Arab Peoples* (Cambridge, MA: Harvard/Belknap, 1991).

9. Albert Hourani, *Syria and Lebanon Under French Mandate* (London: Oxford University Press, 1946), pp. 70–71.

10. Raphael Patai, *The Arab Mind* (New York: Scribners, 1973), p. 20.

11. Fouad Ajami, *The Arab Predicament* (Cambridge: Cambridge University Press, 1981), p. 20.

12. Ajami, *The Arab Predicament*, p. 182.

13. Elie Kedourie, *Democracy and Political Culture* (Washington, DC: Washington Institute for Near East Policy, 1992), p. 15.

14. David Pryce-Jones, *The Closed Circle: An Interpretation of the Arabs* (New York: Harper and Row, 1989), p. 406.

15. Gabriel Ben-Dor, "Political Culture Approach to Middle East Politics," *International Journal of Middle East Studies* 8, 1 (January 1977), pp. 43–63.

16. Ben-Dor, "Political Culture Approach to Middle East Politics," p. 51.

17. John Waterbury, *The Commander of the Faithful: The Moroccan Political Elite* (New York: Columbia University Press, 1970).

18. Inglehart, "The Renaissance of Political Culture," p. 1216.

19. Leonard Binder, "Islam, Arabism, and the Political Community in the Middle East," Ch. 5 in Binder, *The Ideological Revolution in the Middle East* (Chicago: University of Chicago Press, 1964), p. 150.

20. Dankwart A. Rustow, "Turkey: The Modernity of Tradition," in Lucian W. Pye and Sidney Verba, eds., *Political Culture and Political Development* (Princeton: Princeton University Press, 1965), pp. 171–198.

21. Clement Henry Moore, *Politics in North Africa* (Boston: Little, Brown, 1970), Ch. 3.

22. James A. Bill and Robert Springborg, *Middle East Politics*, 4th ed. (New York: HarperCollins, 1994), esp. Chs. 2–4.

23. Bill and Springborg, *Middle East Politics*, p. 1.

24. Monte Palmer, Mima S. Nedelcovych, Hilal Khashan, and Debra L. Monro, *Survey Research in the Arab World: An Analytical Index* (Boulder: Westview Press, and MENAS Press, Ltd., 1982); Mark Tessler et al., *The Evolution and Application of Survey Research in the Arab World* (Boulder: Westview Press, 1987).

25. David Pollock, "'The Arab Street'? Public Opinion in the Arab World," *The Washington Institute Policy Papers* No. 32 (Washington, DC: The Washington Institute for Near East Policy, 1992), pp. 21–27 and appendices.

26. Daniel Lerner, *The Passing of Traditional Society* (Glencoe, IL: Free Press, 1958).

27. Marvin Zonis, *The Political Elite of Iran* (Princeton: Princeton University Press, 1971).

28. Tawfic E. Farah, ed., *Political Behavior in the Arab States* (Boulder, CO: Westview Press, 1983); Tawfic E. Farah and Vasumasa Kuroda, eds., *Political Socialization in the Arab States* (Boulder, CO: Lynne Rienner, 1987).

29. Saad Eddin Ibrahim, *Ittijahat al-ra'iyy al'am al-'arabi nahwa mas'alat al-wahda* [Trends in Arab Public Opinion Toward the Problem of Unity] (Beirut: Center for Arab Unity Studies, 1980).

30. Michael W. Suleiman, "Political Orientations of Young Tunisians: The Impact of Gender," *Arab Studies Quarterly* 15, 1 (Winter 1993), pp. 61–80.

31. Pollock, "'The Arab Street'?" pp. 57–65.

32. Tareq Y. Ismael and Jacqueline S. Ismael, "Arab Politics and the Gulf War: Political Opinion and Political Culture," *Arab Studies Quarterly* 15, 1 (Winter 1993), p. 10.

33. Philip Khoury and Joseph Kostiner, eds., *Tribes and State Formation in the Middle East* (Berkeley: University of California Press, 1990).

34. Bassam Tibi, "The Simultaneity of the Unsimultaneous: Old Tribes and Imposed Nation-States in the Modern Middle East," in Khoury and Kostiner, *Tribes and State Formation in the Middle East*, p. 149.

35. Milton Esman and Itamar Rabinovich, eds., *Ethnicity, Pluralism, and the State in the Middle East* (Ithaca: Cornell University Press, 1988), p. 23.

36. Milton Esman, "Ethnic Politics: How Unique Is the Middle East," in Esman and Rabinovich, eds., *Ethnicity, Pluralism, and the State in the Middle East*, p. 272.

37. Halim Barakat, *The Arab World: Society, Culture, and State* (Berkeley: University of California Press, 1993), Ch. 9.

38. Hisham Sharabi, *Neopatriarchy: A Theory of Distorted Change in Arab Society* (New York: Oxford University Press, 1988).

39. Barakat, *The Arab World*, pp. 270–271.

40. Samuel P. Huntington, *The Third Wave: Democratization in the Late Twentieth Century* (Norman: University of Oklahoma Press, 1991).

41. Guillermo O'Donnell and Philippe C. Schmitter, *Transitions from Authoritarian Rule: Tentative Conclusions About Uncertain Democracies* (Baltimore: Johns Hopkins, 1986).

42. Michael C. Hudson, "Democratization and the Problem of Legitimacy in Middle East Politics," *Middle East Studies Association Bulletin* 22, 2 (December 1988), pp. 157–172.

43. Gabriel A. Almond, "Foreword: The Return to Political Culture," in Larry Diamond, ed., *Political Culture and Democracy in Developing Countries* (Boulder, CO: Lynne Rienner, 1993), p. x.

44. See Augustus Richard Norton, "The Future of Civil Society in the Middle East," *The Middle East Journal* 47, 2 (Spring 1993), pp. 205–216; and Saad Eddin Ibrahim, in this volume.

45. Mustafa K. al-Sayyid, "A Civil Society in Egypt?" *The Middle East Journal*, 42, 2 (Spring 1993), pp. 228–242.

46. Robert D. Putnam, with Robert Leonardi and Raffaella Y. Nanetti, *Making Democracy Work: Civic Traditions in Modern Italy* (Princeton: Princeton University Press, 1993), Ch. 5.

47. Elbaki Hermassi, "Political Culture and Democratization in the Middle East," paper presented at the Conference on Democratization in the Middle East, Antalya, Turkey, 14–16 November 1991.

48. Hermassi, "Political Culture and Democratization in the Middle East," pp. 3–4, 8.

49. Barakat, *The Arab World*, Ch. 12, p. 274.

50. Larry Diamond, "Introduction: Political Culture and Democracy," in Diamond, ed., *Political Culture and Democracy in Developing Countries*.

51. Gehad Auda, "The Islamic Movement and Resource Mobilization in Egypt: A Political Culture Perspective," in Diamond, *Political Culture and Democracy in Developing Countries*.

52. Auda, "The Islamic Movement and Resource Mobilization in Egypt," pp. 403–404.

53. See, e.g., Leonard Binder, "Egypt: The Integrative Revolution," in Pye and Verba, eds., *Political Culture and Political Development*, pp. 396–449.

54. Mattei Dogan, "Conceptions of Legitimacy," in Mary Hawkesworth and Maurice Kogan, eds., *Encyclopedia of Government and Politics*, Vol. 1 (London: Routledge, 1992), p. 125.

4

Democracy in the Arab World: A Critique of the Political Culture Approach

Lisa Anderson

In the aftermath of the Cold War and the apparent worldwide embrace of the values and institutions of the victors, the virtually complete absence of liberal democracy in the Arab world seems quite remarkable. Political scientists do not ordinarily concern themselves with accounting for negatives—that is, with explaining what did not happen or is not there—for it is difficult enough to interpret what did happen without also trying to explain what might have been. Democracy is an exception to this general rule, however, because it is what might be called a "sentimental favorite" of Western social scientists. Most European and North American students of social and political life (almost all of whom, it should be noted, live and work in democracies) more or less secretly believe that the democratic states were victorious because they deserved to be. In other words, they believe that what was always self-evident to its beneficiaries—that democracy is the most desirable form of government—has now become apparent to the rest of the world as well.

Social theorists have failed to distinguish their normative biases from their analytical frameworks since social theory began; indeed, ethical values animate much truly important social science. Unfortunately, however, many of today's partisans of democracy have assumed not only that the superiority of democracy is self-evident, but that the converse is also true: A country's failure to embrace it is evidence of political perversity or moral obtuseness on the part of its citizenry. From this perspective, the inability or unwillingness of people elsewhere in the world to install and maintain democratic governments is to be explained by assigning some kind of handicap or immaturity to the people themselves.

In fairness, much of the literature examining the prospects for democracy in various parts of the world often does address what might be called "objective conditions": the economic organizations and levels of development that seem to be most propitious for development of democratic government, for example, or the importance of international support of various kinds to the installation of democratic institutions.[1] Nonetheless, and particularly in examinations of the Middle East, resort is frequently had to psychosocial or cultural explanations to account for the ease or difficulty with which countries adopt and sustain democratic political procedures.

As a result, a sort of stylized literature on politics and political change in the Middle East has developed over the last several decades. It has two notable aspects. First, violating the ordinary conventions of social science methodology, it often addresses the absence of a phenomenon in a particular place—20 years ago it was "the search for legitimacy"[2] in the Arab world, while more recently it has been the failure of democracy there. Thus are journals devoted to political science and, particularly, to Middle East studies replete with discussions of the possible precursors to and prospects for political democratization and the impetus and impediments to liberalization in the Arab world.[3] Second, much of this social science literature treats the Arab world as congenitally defective, "democratically challenged" as it were, and seeks to find biological, cultural, and/or religious causes for this disability.

I do not subscribe to this view. In my estimation, the nature of the political regimes in the Arab world, like those elsewhere in the world, can best be understood as reflections of the political economy of the countries in question, particularly the character of their integration into the world economy. Because it is my purpose here to examine critically the assumptions and conclusions of political culture theorists, however, I do not now offer alternatives, which are provided elsewhere in this volume by others.

Before proceeding to examine some of this literature, it is necessary to clarify the terms of the title of this chapter. There is inevitably debate about the universal applicability of any definition of so normatively laden a notion as democracy but, following the conventional definitions of empirical democratic theory, I understand the term to mean a system in which the "most powerful collective decisionmakers are selected through periodic elections in which candidates freely compete for votes and in which virtually all the adult population is eligible to vote."[4] I have chosen a definition based on the Western liberal institutional tradition (thereby excluding "people's democracies" in which electoral competition is circumscribed, for example) because that is what most students of democracy and democratization mean by the term today. The definition is intentionally minimalist and leaves open for analysis possible correlates and conditions, including whether particular values or orientations are necessary to the proper working of these kinds of institutions.

By "political culture," I (and most of the authors who employ the term) mean precisely those values that might support or undermine a particular set of political institutions: "the particular distribution of patterns of political orientations—attitudes toward the political system and its various parts, and attitudes toward the role of the self in the system"[5]—within the population in question. As originally conceived by the authors of the term, a particular people's political culture is ascertainable through survey research. Relatively little such research has been conducted in the Arab world, however, and, as we will see, most analysts who have recourse to political culture analysis either draw their data from general (and usually unsystematic) observations of political behavior or extrapolate from other realms of belief and behavior—notably religion—to ascertain values and habits that might bear on politics.[6] Obviously, this quite relaxed approach to the standards of social science methodology raises important questions of testing and verification, but these concerns do not deter proponents of cultural analyses of Middle Eastern politics.

Finally, it is worth noting that even the term "Arab world" is contestable. In privileging "Arab" as the criterion by which we select our universe of cases, we are highlighting linguistic and ethnic identities at the expense of, say, a role in the world economy or a geostrategic position on the globe as crucial elements of politics and political action. Whether this is appropriate to the endeavor of understanding the conditions in which democracy takes root and flourishes is obviously debatable. Nonetheless, despite these qualms, because they are the terms of reference for so much of the discussion of politics in this region today, "democracy," "political culture," and "Arab world" will be used in this essay without further apology.

Linguistic and Biological Theories: Arabs as Aliens

Although it is no longer acceptable in most scholarly company to treat Easterners with the overt racism that passed for scholarship during the heyday of imperialism, there are still audible echoes of that posture in works published today. The notion that Arabs are qualitatively different from Westerners (and almost always worse) is still fairly widespread in policy and journalistic circles.

In an essay published in 1992, for example, by a professor of philosophy and religious studies at a respectable American university who is described as "lecturing extensively for the U.S. Navy," and who describes his work as based on documents produced for the naval chaplaincy, Arabs are portrayed as fundamentally unlike Westerners:

> Over a period of many years, some of the tribes of Arabia developed a certain social philosophy, partly in reaction to their desert way of life. This social philosophy is still a very powerful force in Arab civilization, and attempts to understand it in Western terms have led to confusion and misunderstanding.[7]

To illustrate his point, he spells out a comparison:

> To this day, the noble bedouin raider is an heroic prototype within Arab
> culture, and the "manly" talents of riding, shooting, fighting and raiding,
> as well as writing poetry and being cleverer and trickier than the enemy,
> are highly admired. To the Western mind, this is an odd combination.
> Riding, shooting, and fighting fit well with the knightly tradition; they
> are an extension of chivalry and manliness. Writing poetry is marginal.
> Seducing, marauding, tricking and lying to gain advantage are not part of
> that chivalric tradition. The two traditions are, in fact, altogether differ-
> ent, and it is an error to see one as a mere version of the other. They must
> each one be approached with a sense of its own integrity.[8]

The "integrity" of seducing, marauding, tricking, and lying is difficult to
fathom. More importantly perhaps, it is not apparent that such traits are
completely foreign to the Crusaders of the age of chivalry or even, in light
of the recent revelations about the Tailhook Association Convention of
1991, the American naval officers in this consultant's audience.

Should it be assumed that this kind of assessment is limited to aca-
demically marginal government consultants, John Entelis, whose works on
Lebanon and North Africa have appeared on many a North American university reading list over the last several decades, examines the literature on
the "Arab personality" and reports that

> researchers have assembled a compendium of essentially negative and
> deficient characteristics: suspiciousness, excessive hostility alternating
> with excessive politeness, negative individualism, a large reservoir of
> free-floating hostility, efforts to keep conflicts suppressed or at least
> manageable, a high degree of mistrust and hostility toward others, secre-
> tiveness about the self and curiosity toward others, and, as a result of the
> unpredictable and arbitrary patterns of parental relations with children, a
> resulting wish to ingratiate oneself with those in authority.

Although he is aware of the "essentially negative and deficient" characterization he describes, Entelis goes on to accept it in its broad outlines:

> Without getting bogged down in the many theoretical and normative as-
> sumptions associated with such controversial studies, one can agree that
> some of the traits described above do apply to large categories of Arab,
> as well as non-Arab people.[9]

Entelis makes a gesture toward questioning the utility of this kind of characterization in his reference to "non-Arab people" as well as to Arabs. Yet,
in adopting this perspective in its broad outlines he suggests that it provides a useful and appropriate analytical approach.

Indeed, the conviction that Arabs and Westerners are fundamentally
unalike seems to be a difficult one to shake, in part perhaps because it is a

belief shared by policymakers and analysts in the Arab world as well. The argument that a fundamental dissimilarity between Arabs and Westerners should inhibit comparison is put forward by Arabs quite often, usually to account for the failure of some feature of Arab politics to meet a Western standard. Thus is the Jordanian representative at the United Nations quoted as observing that "in the Arab world, it's wrong to judge democracy by western criteria. Comparing western democracy with Islamic democracy is like comparing silver with gold."[10]

Most writers go beyond merely asserting an unfathomable divide between East and West, however, and explore the content of Arab culture as it influences politics. Two features of Arab political tradition and history caught their attention: the egalitarian, informal, and personal character of tribal organization, and the patriarchal authoritarian nature of the imperial governments of the region, from the Byzantines to the Ottomans. Neither of these legacies of custom and history is thought to be conducive to democracy.

Families and Tribes: Too Democratic to Be Democratic?

In part because they have been professionally preoccupied with tribes, anthropologists have devoted special attention to the influence of kinship, family, and tribal relations on other realms of social life, including politics. Western journalists and policymakers have been quick to adopt this perspective as well, perhaps because it offers fairly simple propositions. Indeed, in many versions, the characterization of tribal politics is entirely too simple.

Although Arab tribes are sometimes thought to embody many democratic principles, notably a predisposition toward equality and consultation, tribal social structures are usually thought to inhibit the development of democratic values, habits, and institutions. Indeed, in an intriguing but somewhat puzzling finding, Ahmad Dhaher posits a correlation between tribal identity and leisure activities that might have some bearing on politics:

> Gulf Arab culture has been determined by two closely related factors: tribal tradition and Islam. Tribal tradition enshrined certain virtues—generosity, loyalty, honor—which were of paramount importance for survival in the harsh desert environment. Not that foresight or persistence, for example, are not considered virtues in Arab tradition; but necessity dictated which considerations were to be stressed. This code of ethics still has a strong influence on the Arab mind and in many ways complicates efforts to introduce innovations into Arab countries. For example, the response given by Gulf states students to questions about their leisure activities showed reading to be one of their last choices. There is no strong tradition

of reading per se and the students have not developed an appreciation for it on their own.[11]

While high levels of literacy do correlate closely with democratic values and attitudes, the causal relationship between tribal traditions and the devaluation of reading can be said to be undeveloped in the general literature.

In an effort to find more direct political implications of tribalism, David Pryce-Jones recently argued in a heavily promoted book on the Arab world that "the tribal legacy . . . has everywhere perpetuated absolute and despotic rule, preventing the evolution of those pluralist institutions that alone allow people to participate in the processes of the state and so to identify with it."[12] He gives several reasons: Tribalism makes members of tribes incapable of impartiality, resistant to authority, and prone to resort to violence to resolve conflicts. Indeed, on the last point, he argues, "tribalism is completely at the mercy of its lack of organizing principle other than custom."[13] That custom itself always embodies organizing principles escapes Pryce-Jones; what he means to say is that in the absence of clear criteria for establishing leadership and ensuring regular succession, violence may become a mechanism for asserting claims to power and resolving conflicts: "violence is an essential ingredient in the process of decisionmaking, it is proof of serious intention, of the will to proceed in the group interest, no matter what the right or wrong."[14]

Pryce-Jones gives only anecdotal evidence to support this contention but it is worth noting that there is a fairly widespread conviction among those who employ political culture to explain politics in the Middle East that violence is endemic to the region and that there is a proclivity toward violence that needs to be explained, most likely by cultural predispositions. These propositions are contestable, of course; for better or worse, the Arab world has seen less violence over the course of the last century than have most of Europe and Asia, and much of what violence has occurred there has been with the active connivance of foreign arms suppliers.[15] Interestingly, however, the debates about the sources of violence in the Middle East usually exclude assessment of outside comparisons or influences and concern themselves with the relative importance of tribal traditions, Ottoman legacies, or Islamic dictates, all of which have been credited with encouraging violent conflict resolution.

In addition to its putative role in promoting violence, reliance on kinship ties has also been assigned responsibility for the absence or weakness of the associational life of civil society, long considered the bedrock of democratic politics. In their very influential textbook, for example, James Bill and Robert Springborg argue that "Middle Eastern societies and political systems grew out of tribal constellations, and the personalism that prevailed in the family and the clan has had a pervasive and protracted influence."[16] This influence has meant that

> associational and institutional groups that have played a critical role in Western political systems have been considerably less significant in the Middle Eastern context. The dominant group structure in the Islamic world has been the informal group. Group organization hardens around particular individuals and kinship structures. Small shifting clusters of individuals form cliques that resemble one another only in their personalistic, informal, fragmented mode of organization. . . . Formal groups exist either as extraneous facades or as general structures within which small, informal groups carry out their important activities. . . . Decisions attributable to the formal organization may in fact be the product of a parasitical informal group within it.[17]

As is apparent from their choice of words—shifting clusters, cliques, fragmented modes of organization, facades, parasitical informal groups—the authors do not view these organizational patterns with favor.

Not only do such proclivities appear morally questionable to Bill and Springborg but also politically suspect, for they inhibit the kind of political participation required by democratic politics. As they continue:

> The formation of a viable formal group structure requires a certain level of organizational skill, a minimal degree of trust and cooperation, a reservoir of funds for equipment and staffing, and a willingness on the part of political elites to tolerate the existence of such groups. In Middle Eastern societies, these conditions of organization are seldom all present at once.[18]

Ordinarily maintaining a cohesive family unit, not to say the complex collection of families that constitute a tribe, should probably be thought to entail considerable organizational skill (ask any "homemaker"!), fairly high levels of trust and cooperation, and adequate funds. It is thus only the fourth condition—political tolerance—that has been wanting in the Arab world. This suggests both that political democracy and the flourishing associational life of civil society interact and reinforce each other, but also that it is not lack of sufficient skill, trust, and cooperation among Arabs so much as deliberate government policy that accounts for the weakness of formal group organization. Certainly it seems implausible to maintain that in the Middle East, which is home to at least as much ideological politics as anywhere else on the face of the earth, "commitments are more often to individuals and family units than to ideas."[19]

From this vantage point, perhaps Albert Hourani's more generous interpretation is salutary. He argues that Ibn Khaldun's emphasis five centuries ago on *'asabiyya*, or the "group feeling" born of shared kinship and religious conviction, continues to be appropriate. Political (or any other) success is not guaranteed by "group feeling," but its likelihood is certainly enhanced:

> Ties of interest were reinforced by those of neighborliness, kinship or intermarriage; the tradition of Middle Eastern and Maghribi society was that other kinds of relationship were stronger if expressed in terms of kinship.[20]

Patriarchy and Patrimonialism:
Sultanism as an Ideal-Type

Although the apparently informal, ad hoc nature of political affiliation and decisionmaking in extended kin networks is often called to account for the character of Arab politics, in fact the problem is equally often characterized not as too little authority, but too much. Indeed, so closely associated in Western political theory are the Middle East and arbitrary and capricious rule that Max Weber dubbed his ideal-type of personalistic and unconstrained rule "sultanism."[21] Traditions of domination are seen as permeating social and political life in the Arab world. According to Hisham Sharabi, a major proponent of this approach, contemporary "neopatriarchy" in the Arab world reflects the interaction of what he calls "Arab patriarchy" and modernity.

> A central psychosocial feature of this type of society, whether it is conservative or progressive, is the dominance of the Father (patriarch), the center around which the national as well as the natural family are organized. Thus between ruler and ruled, between father and child, there exist only vertical relations: in both settings the paternal will is the absolute will, mediated in both the society and the family by a forced consensus based on ritual and coercion. . . . Thus in social practice, ordinary citizens not only are arbitrarily deprived of some of their basic rights but are virtual prisoners of the state, the objects of its capricious and ever-present violence, much as citizens once were under the classical or Ottoman sultanate.[22]

Bill and Springborg—who, as we have seen, also place great store in the influence of tribalism—agree with Sharabi's characterization, saying that "patrimonialism has been the dominant pattern of leadership in Middle Eastern politics for centuries." The leader is the source of authority and his advisors, ministers, and confidants are all beholden to him. They in turn have their own circles of clients and a system of personal dependence extends downward throughout society. In part to maintain such a system, the powerholders encourage rivalry among their dependents, say Bill and

Springborg, who attribute much of what Pryce-Jones sees in tribalism to patrimonialism: "the personal rivalry that has always been central to patrimonial society has led to numerous schisms and divisions within the Islamic community."[23]

In an interesting (and one has to assume inadvertent) admission that political analysis in the Middle East (as, presumably, elsewhere) can be frustrating and confusing, Bill and Springborg attribute to patrimonial patterns of politics a high level of "informality." The patrimonial leader's need to keep his followers dependent leads him to discourage creation of formal organizations in which they might gather to oppose him; the inclinations previously attributed to tribalism are reinforced.

> Informal patterns of control and authority have been responsible for a great deal of uncertainty in the decisionmaking environment. Middle Eastern political processes reflect a high level of intrigue and counter-intrigue as leaders at various levels maneuver in secret and semi-secret settings. . . . In Middle Eastern politics, an informal personal organization has tended to rest behind the formal institutional organization. Oftentimes, observers are confused because of the presence of the identifiable leader at the center of both organizations.[24]

It is equally plausible that both the informality and confusion these analysts see in Middle Eastern politics are a reflection of the enormity of the changes wrought in the region in recent decades and the consequent absence of stable institutions, political or otherwise. To take but one simple example: For the proponents of "patriarchy" as an explanatory device, the enormous population shifts occasioned by urban migration within countries and labor migration within the region and to Europe should be very troubling. More and more children are being raised in households in which the father is absent 11 months a year and in villages or neighborhoods in which the only men are aged or infirm. When combined with the marked decline in the average age of the Arab population (thanks to the rising birth rates in the region), this has meant that adult men—not to say "patriarchs"—are an increasingly small proportion of the general population in many parts of the Arab world. That this will unleash changes in family structures is virtually certain; will it change political attitudes as well?

Among the very few full-scale efforts to assess the impact of instability and change on attitudes in the Arab world and of the impact, in turn, of those attitudes on politics, was Michael Hudson's examination of the causes and consequences of the absence of legitimacy. He observed that

> if one were called upon to describe the contemporary style of politics in the Arab world . . . the adjectives that immediately spring to mind include mercurial, hyperbolic, irrational, mysterious, uncertain, even dangerous.

Arab politics are not just unstable, although instability remains a prominent feature, they are also unpredictable to participants and observers
alike.

Leaders are playing by rules that are constantly changing, and they are
frustrated by recalcitrant bureaucracies and insatiable popular aspirations.
The people themselves are cynical and fearful. As Hudson acutely observes, however, certainly at the popular level, "such attitudes cannot be
satisfactorily explained simply by the superstitions of 'traditional' people
but rather appear to be rationally derived from unhappy prior experience
with 'the authorities.'"[25] Hudson's point—that most people "reality test,"
to use the jargon of the psychologists, and adjust their beliefs, perceptions,
and attitudes on the basis of experience—is a very simple and profoundly
important one. Attitudes are not "uncaused" or unchanging. In fact, change
itself may engender particular values and attitudes, perhaps fostering con-
servatism, cynicism, anxiety, or skepticism. That it is infinitely more difficult to govern in the face of a hostile, recalcitrant, skeptical populace is
half of Hudson's insight; that, given their recent experience, most of the
people of the Arab world are quite right to be angry, reluctant, and suspicious participants in politics is the other half. To examine the causes and
consequences of political change through the lens of political culture
rather than structure may not be the most parsimonious vehicle, nor the
easiest to test and verify, but certainly if it is to be done, it should be done
this way, in all its complexity.

Despite the intelligence of Hudson's interpretation of the nature of political culture's relationship with political institutions and incumbents,
however, many observers prefer to ascribe the absence of stable, transpar-
ent institutions to essentially permanent cultural inclinations. In fact, Bill
and Springborg argue that patterns of patrimonialism "have existed
throughout Islamic history and can be traced to the days of the Prophet
Muhammad, himself the model par excellence of political leadership."[26]

"Islam Is the Solution": Religion as Impediment

Authoritarian politics in the Arab world is very often attributed to Islam.
Despite the fact that many politically active Islamists, not to say many politically inactive Muslims, pay lip service to democracy, skepticism
abounds. As *New York Times* correspondent Judith Miller recently put it
in *Foreign Affairs*, a journal widely cited in policy circles, "Why should
one suspect the sincerity of the Islamists' commitment to truth, justice, and
the democratic way? In short, because of Arab and Islamic history and the
nature and evolution of these groups."[27]

Miller cites for support works by Martin Kramer and Bernard Lewis, both noted historians of the Muslim world and advocates of the position that Islam is ill-suited to democracy. Islam's failure to distinguish the realms of Caesar and God, its insistence that sovereignty rests with God and that the essence of the law is divinely revealed and therefore beyond human emendation, its discriminatory treatment of women and non-Muslim minorities all appear quite inconsistent with democratic politics. As Elie Kedourie put it, "the idea of democracy is quite alien to the mind-set of Islam" because "there is nothing in the political traditions of the Arab world—which are the political traditions of Islam—which might make familiar, or indeed intelligible, the organizing ideas of constitutional and representative government."[28]

The political significance of Islamic dictates is not clear, however, even for those analysts who advocate cultural analysis. Far from being unable to distinguish between the worldly and otherworldly realms, as is so often assumed to be the case among Muslims (believers and nonbelievers alike), some authors find that Muslims compartmentalize their lives all too easily. In a widely used textbook, for example, David E. Long and Bernard Reich argue that

> the fixation on the omnipresence of divine will has enabled Middle Easterners to view events as separate exercises of God's will or fate, having little or no association with related events. This view has made it relatively easy for them to hold more than one position on the same issue that Westerners might find too contradictory. It has also tended to keep problems over conflicting loyalties or interest to a minimum. For example, hostile political relations in the Middle East need not rule out good commercial relations, for the two are viewed quite separately.[29]

Interestingly, the conflicting interpretations of the "experts" about the role of Islam have led political scientists like Samuel P. Huntington, a leading American student of comparative politics, to be somewhat skeptical of this kind of argumentation. In an early examination of the relationship between culture and the prospects for democracy, Huntington was fully in agreement with the notion that Islamic precepts are important impediments to the development of democracy. Having examined statistical correlations between various religious traditions and democracy, he observed that "significant differences in their receptivity to democracy appear to exist among societies with different cultural traditions," and his conclusion about the influence of Islam was categorical: "Islam . . . has not been hospitable to democracy." Huntington then speculated that this could be explained because, "in Islam, no distinction exists between religion and politics or between the spiritual and the secular, and political participation was historically an alien concept."[30]

Several years later, Huntington revisited this question. This time he concluded that "Islamic doctrine . . . contains elements that may be both congenial and uncongenial to democracy." Moreover, and perhaps more importantly, he was less sure that culture is so powerful an influence in democratization. As he explains it,

> great cultural traditions like Islam . . . are highly complex bodies of ideas, beliefs, doctrines, assumptions, and behavior patterns. Any major culture . . . has some elements that are compatible with democracy, just as both Protestantism and Catholicism have elements that are clearly undemocratic. . . . The real question is which elements in Islam . . . are favorable to democracy, and how and under what circumstances these can supersede the undemocratic aspects.[31]

Survey research in Egypt confirms Huntington's later position that Islam is not a strong influence on political attitudes: As the investigator put it, "religiosity, as the practical understanding of Islam, is a neutral factor in its relationship with development: it neither hinders it nor furthers it."[32]

Assessing Political Culture Approaches to Democracy in the Arab World

The works selected for discussion in this chapter reflect the variety of literature that regularly cross the desk of anyone in the United States interested in Middle East politics; it includes work by journalists, policy analysts, and academic historians, political scientists principally concerned with the Middle East, as well as general comparativists. While hardly exhaustive, these citations are fairly representative of the various positions about what "Arab political culture" encompasses and what influence it may have on the prospects for democracy in the region.

Probably the characteristic of this literature most likely to strike an uninitiated observer is the negative tone of most of the assessments. Not only are Arabs thought to be dismal prospects for democratic politics, but they appear to be fairly dismal people all around: illogical, untrustworthy, passive before domineering rulers while given to intrigue and violence —all in all, an unsavory lot. It is possible to find other stereotypical characterizations of Arab culture—the generous, loyal, honorable traits mentioned by Ahmad Dhaher, one of the researchers cited earlier, for example—but the preponderance of contemporary Western writing appears to be negative.

That so many people with such an apparent aversion to their subject study the Arab world professionally is puzzling, but it is clear that the professional Arabists are doing little to dissuade the general Western public from their negative stereotypes about Arabs. Almost equally disturbing is the remarkably cavalier attitude exhibited by these professionals to the norms and standards of "scientific discourse." There is very little concern with testing and verification in this literature and a marked willingness to make categorical statements without regard to evidence.

Finally there are logical and epistemological flaws in most of the cultural analyses. As we have seen, rather than simply survey the attitudes and behavior of the population in question, most analysts begin with an effort to explain the absence of something desirable—democracy—by the presence of something undesirable—in this instance, "bad attitudes." Perhaps, however, this lacuna is more appropriately attributable to the absence of other desirable traits—full national sovereignty, for example, or greater economic prosperity—rather than the presence of some kind of congenital defect. There are two mistakes here and together they compound the problems they separately create. First, as we have seen, accounting for what is absent, while not impossible, is extremely difficult and requires very rigorous specification of the feature whose absence is to be explained. Second, when that feature is something so simultaneously intricate and value-laden as democracy, that requirement for rigor is almost guaranteed to be relaxed in the face of the complexity and desirability of the phenomenon itself.

We therefore find ourselves faced with a body of literature composed, not of closely reasoned or carefully researched arguments, but of self-fulfilling prophecies. There is virtually no effort to examine the actual causal connections between apparently correlated phenomena, such as attitudes, behavior, and institutions, nor is there any capacity for dynamic analysis in which change in one realm of human life could be predicted to precipitate change in another. Indeed, the implicit (and sometimes explicit) assumption that attitudes and beliefs born in the desert in the era of the Prophet are timeless, unchanging, and overwhelmingly powerful—in contrast to, say, the ideas and values of contemporaneous seventh-century Europe—is a reflection of an inability to think critically about change. We happily hypothesize that cultural attitudes play a causal role in fostering or inhibiting installation and maintenance of democratic institutions, when in fact the attitudes correlated with democracy might be a *result* of habituation to these kinds of institutions. Similarly, we know that transformations in one part of social life—the economy, technology, education are often cited—will alter other aspects of social life, but we content ourselves with resorting to "timeless beliefs" to account for popular reactions to the quite profound changes in politics in the Arab world in the last half century and the now quite varied political regimes and political oppositions that operate there.

This is not to say that values and attitudes do not play a role in politics. Obviously they do, but we must consider far more carefully how best to assess when and where they have their impact. Just as no economists would deny the importance of consumer "confidence" in influencing market fluctuations, neither would they begin an analysis of how an economy works with an inventory of attitudes. Understanding the role played by psychological factors in economics must be preceded by analysis of the proportion of production devoted to subsistence as opposed to trade, how much money has replaced barter, the relationship between agriculture and industry, the nature of property relations, and so forth. So too, in studying politics, we need to know about institutional structures, sources of government revenue, population growth rates, class relations, regime constituencies, government policy biases, and a host of other things before we can assess the appropriate context and real significance of political attitudes.

Political culture analysis can be very seductive, particularly to policymakers looking for short, neat explanations of the complexities they face but, at least as it is currently done, it is unusually susceptible to distortion and bias. If we are not careful to specify its context and limits, we not only risk analytical confusion, we set the stage for sloppy, self-indulgent, or even damaging prescription. Given the widespread consensus today that democracy is indeed desirable, we should be far better at exploring and promoting its prospects in the Arab world.

Notes

1. Among the recent classics, see Robert Dahl, *Polyarchy* (New Haven: Yale University Press, 1971); Dankwart Rustow, "Transitions to Democracy," *Comparative Politics* 2, 3 (1970); Guillermo O'Donnell et al., eds., *Transitions from Authoritarian Rule* (Baltimore: Johns Hopkins University Press, 1986); Samuel P. Huntington, "Will More Countries Become Democratic?" *Political Science Quarterly* 99, 2 (Summer 1984); Samuel P. Huntington, "Democracy's Third Wave," *Journal of Democracy* 2, 2 (Spring 1991).

2. The phrase is the subtitle of Michael Hudson's *Arab Politics* (New Haven: Yale University Press, 1977), probably the single most widely read book on the Arab world of its time.

3. Among the more sophisticated treatments is that of Ghassan Salamé, who recognizes the methodological problem, in "Sur la causalité d'un manque: pourquoi le monde arabe n'est-il donc pas démocratique?" in *Revue Française de Science Politique* 61, 3 (June 1991). Also see Muhammad Muslih and Augustus Richard Norton, "The Need for Arab Democracy," *Foreign Policy* 83 (Summer 1991); Michael Hudson, "After the Gulf War: Prospects for Democratization in the Arab World," *Middle East Journal* 45, 3 (Summer 1991).

4. This particular wording is from Huntington, "Will More Countries Become Democratic?" p. 195.

5. This is the definition provided by Gabriel Almond and Sidney Verba of the term they themselves coined in *The Civic Culture* (Boston: Little, Brown, 1963), pp. 12–13.

6. Among the exceptions to the general neglect of survey research are the studies collected in Mark A. Tessler et al., *The Evaluation and Application of Survey Research in the Arab World* (Boulder: Westview Press, 1987); and Tawfic Farah and Yasumasa Kuroda, *Political Socialization in the Arab States* (Boulder: Lynne Rienner Publishers, 1987). Several of these studies are discussed later in this essay but it is worth noting that, in an interesting variation on this theme, at least one author treats the "cultural" considerations that may inhibit survey research in the Arab world. See Iliya Harik, "Some Political and Cultural Considerations Bearing on Survey Research in the Arab World," in Tessler et al., *The Evaluation and Application of Survey Research in the Arab World*.

7. Allen Howard Podet, "The Gulf War: Religious and Cultural Considerations," in Carole Rae Hansen, ed., *The New World Order: Rethinking America's Global Role* (Flagstaff: The Arizona Honors Academy Press, 1992), p. 216.

8. Podet, "The Gulf War: Religious and Cultural Considerations," p. 217.

9. John Entelis, *Culture and Counterculture in Morocco* (Boulder: Westview Press, 1989), pp. 27–28.

10. Adnan Abu Odeh, quoted in Timothy D. Sisk, *Islam and Democracy: Religion, Politics, and Power in the Middle East* (Washington, DC: United States Institute of Peace, 1992), p. 47. This volume is a report of a symposium that brought together policymakers and academics to discuss the topic described in the book's title in May 1992.

11. Ahmad J. Dhaher, "Culture and Politics in Arab Gulf States," in Farah and Kuroda, *Political Socialization in the Arab States*, p. 65.

12. David Pryce-Jones, *The Closed Circle: An Interpretation of the Arabs* (New York: Harper & Row, 1989), p. 26.

13. Pryce-Jones, *The Closed Circle*, p. 26.

14. Pryce-Jones, *The Closed Circle*, p. 22.

15. See Yahya Sadowski, *Scuds or Butter: The Political Economy of Arms Control in the Middle East* (Washington, DC: Brookings Institution, 1993).

16. James A. Bill and Robert Springborg, *Politics in the Middle East*, 3rd ed. (Glenview, IL: Scott, Foresman/Little, Brown, 1990), p. 161.

17. Bill and Springborg, *Politics in the Middle East*, p. 88.

18. Bill and Springborg, *Politics in the Middle East*, p. 89.

19. Bill and Springborg, *Politics in the Middle East*, p. 97.

20. Albert Hourani, *A History of the Arab Peoples* (New York: Warner Books, 1991), p. 449.

21. See Bryan S. Turner, *Weber and Islam* (London: Routledge and Kegan Paul, 1974).

22. Hisham Sharabi, *Neopatriarchy: A Theory of Distorted Change in Arab Society* (New York: Oxford University Press, 1988), p. 7.

23. Bill and Springborg, *Politics in the Middle East*, pp. 157, 161.

24. Bill and Springborg, *Politics in the Middle East*, pp. 166–167.

25. Hudson, *Arab Politics*, pp. 2–3.

26. Bill and Springborg, *Politics in the Middle East*, p. 138.

27. Judith Miller, "The Challenge of Radical Islam," *Foreign Affairs* 72, 2 (Spring 1993), p. 47.

28. Elie Kedourie, *Democracy and Arab Political Culture* (Washington, DC: Institute for Near East Policy, 1992), pp. 1, 5.

29. David E. Long and Bernard Reich, *The Government and Politics of the Middle East and North Africa* (Boulder: Westview Press, 1986), p. 19.

30. Huntington, "Will More Countries Become Democratic?" p. 208. He cites Daniel Pipes, *In the Path of God: Islam and Political Power* (New York: Basic Books, 1983) as his sole source on Islam.

31. Huntington, "Democracy's Third Wave," pp. 28–30.

32. Kamal El-Manoufi, "Islam and Development: A Field Study," in Farah and Kuroda, *Political Socialization in the Arab States*, p. 153.

5

Democracy in Contemporary
Arab Intellectual Discourse

Salwa Ismail

The purpose of this chapter is to examine how the concept of democracy is formulated in the discourse of contemporary Arab intellectuals. Specifically, it seeks to investigate the primary issues and concerns, both theoretical and practical, that underlie the articulation of democracy. In this regard, it deals with how the discourse addresses the fundamental questions of democratization in the Arab world, such as the definition of the principles of the political community, the role of the state in a democratic society, and the relation between secularism and democracy.

Integral to our discussion of the various dimensions of the discourse is the proposition that the concept of democracy is developed within the problematic of a new Arab *nahda* (renaissance). In this sense, the elaboration of the concept is governed by the mechanisms operative in the problematic of *nahda*. In the overriding objective to transform the Arab reality, the general interest that guides the problematic (that is, the search for a new project of civilization) connects with the particular interest behind the discussion of democracy (defining the principles that are to regulate the mode of relations in the political community).

The writings that form the core of this discussion span the last two decades—a period marked by junctural events that, to some extent, shaped intellectuals' concern with democracy. Many of these writings have come out of conferences and seminars dedicated to the examination of democracy in the Arab World. The analysis presented in this chapter also draws on a number of works dealing with themes closely related to democracy. Several of these themes have come to occupy an important place in the ongoing debates on democracy as a result of sociopolitical changes taking place in many Arab countries. The emergent configurations of Islamist politics have posed a challenge to secular ideologies and regimes. Thus the question of the relation of secularism to democracy has moved to the fore of the discussion. Given the dialogic nature of the intellectual discourse— that is, its development in relation to a discourse that articulates notions of the polity and society in Islamist terms—attention is given to the formulation of democracy within Islamist discourse. The chapter's examination of the Islamist articulations is thus limited to the elements that bear directly on the Arab intellectuals' discussion of democracy.

The chapter is structured into two sections. The first part discusses the context for the rise of the discourse on democracy, its articulation within the problematic of *nahda,* and its broader relationship to Arab-Islamic and Western thought. The second part outlines the specific issues that arise in discussion of the principles of the democratic community, namely the role of the state, state-society relations, secularism, and intellectual freedom.

Conceptualizing and Defining Democracy

Democracy and the Problematic of Nahda: *The Early Context*

The construction of the problematic of *nahda* is conventionally situated at the time of the encounter between the West and the countries where Islam constituted an intellectual force.[1] The problematic is grounded in the search for the elements behind the progress of the West ("Other") and the retardation of the Arab world ("Self"), and how to create the conditions for a new Arab civilization. The problematic was thus constructed on the basis of a reading of the encounter as taking place between unequal forces. In this context, the lesser side attempted to remove the charge of inferiority. Thus, the onus on a thinker like Muhammad 'Abduh was to prove that Islam was compatible with progress, a state of being identified with the West.

The opposing side was conceived of as a form of government, among other things, and democracy was one of its defining features. Hence Islam, as a religion and "state," had to be proven compatible with that form of government—that is, it had to be shown to have the necessary qualifications for progress. The negation in 'Abduh's statement that "Islam will never stand as an obstacle on the road to civilization"[2] indicates the presence of a counterdiscourse affirming the contrary. Proof of the compatibility between Islam and democracy (understood as an element of civilization) was sought through the establishment of equivalences in conceptual terms. The field of meaning that defined democracy was found to have its counterpart in Islamic terminology. The constellation of equivalent terms included *shura* (consultation), *ijma'* (consensus), and *bay'a* (oath of allegiance). The concern with the form of government constituted an aspect of the discourse devoted to discovering the means for achieving progress and, more precisely, of creating the conditions required for the Arab and Islamic *nahda*.

The Crisis of Democracy: The Contemporary Context

As noted by Muhammad 'Abid al-Jabiri, in the 1950's the problematic of *nahda* gave way to the discourse of revolution.[3] The 1967 defeat and the subsequent assessment of the revolution as a failure set the stage for the rise of the new *nahda* discourse. The need for a new Arab project was propelled by the sense of crisis encompassing all aspects of the Arab condition. Against this background, the discussion of democracy in contemporary Arab intellectual discourse develops within the problematic of a general crisis. This crisis is defined as a civilizational one, encompassing economic, political, and social difficulties. In addressing the general crisis democracy, or its absence, is put forward as a partial explanatory factor. The analysis begins with a diagnosis: Democracy is in crisis, or there is a crisis of democracy in the Arab world. The notion of crisis (*azma*) denotes a threat to something that is already there but, as used in this context, it evokes another meaning, that of shortage, lack, or absence. One point on which Arab intellectuals agree is the diagnosis; namely, that there is a shortage of democracy in the Arab world.

The immediate context for the rise of the discourse of *azmat al-dimuqratiyya* (the crisis of democracy) is woven by critical events: the 1967 defeat, the 1982 Israeli invasion of Lebanon, and the Gulf War of 1991—the same events that unleashed a flood of self-criticism, debates, and conferences devoted to the study of the general crisis.[4] What does democracy have to do with these junctures? In diagnosing the disease as *azmat al-dimuqratiyya*, some symptoms exhibited by the Arab masses are explained, mainly apathy and a refusal to get involved. These symptoms were noted in the aftermath of the Israeli invasion and again during the Gulf War. From the diagnosis, an analysis of the features and causes of the *azma* unfolds. A multitude of causes including dependency, unequal social relations, social and cultural retardation, illiteracy, and the relation between contemporaneity and authenticity constitute the background of the *azma*, whose main features are limited participation and repressive practices by the state.[5]

Thinking Democracy

The question of democracy thus far appears to emerge out of the real conditions of Arab society. It has posed itself as an element of the general crisis and in this respect must be dealt with. However, as an absence or a lack, it remains in search of a presence; hence the call for a model. Thus, while the debates on democracy in Arab societies focus on present empirical

conditions, their analytical framework is developed with reference to experience somewhere else or at some other time. One model emerges out
of the Western experience, another is grounded in the Arab-Islamic past.

In the first instance, the problematic of democracy is constructed and
thought of within a reading of the history of democracy in the West. Most
of the studies concerned with democracy in the Arab world begin with an
outline of the story of Western democracy, commencing with the Renaissance and extending through the Enlightenment to the present period. Here
a familiar narrative unfolds: the narrative of church absolutism during the
European Middle Ages and the opposition it engendered, the rise of social
forces struggling for political rights, and the revolutionary events that
brought about the institutions enshrining these rights. Once this is put forward, a comparative analytic framework is set up for the purpose of determining the possibility of democracy in the Arab world. A taxonomy of
similarities and differences between the Western model and the Arab reality is the result of this comparative effort. Differences are constituted as
absence and lack; thus the existence of a different configuration of social
forces in Arab countries is expressed in terms of the absence of a developed bourgeois class capable of pressing for political rights. In the trajectory of Western development, the colonies play the role of helper; the
resources of the colonies allowed for economic prosperity and better distribution of wealth in the colonizing countries and, in turn, it was possible
to expand the arena of political participation. Given the lack of these conditions (namely, the impossibility and undesirability of having colonies),
the question is: How does the West serve as a model? As will be shown
below, what is retained from the image of Western democracy is its definitional content as a system of government and as a set of values.

In sum, the problematic of democracy is thought of in terms of the experiences of the "Other." This is true of the intellectuals who use the West
as a model to emulate as well as those who reject that model. While rejection is articulated in terms of difference and specificity, emulation is
posited as an obligatory step for joining in the march of humanity, catch-
ing up, and staying in history. Democracy in this sense becomes a historical imperative dictated by the necessity/desire to remain in history and to
be historical agents. This formulation is embedded in the problematic of
the Renaissance and the civilizational project for the future.

Another model for democracy is constructed out of Arab-Islamic history, particularly the early period of the Prophet and the four Rightly
Guided Caliphs, and is supported by a reading of Islamic tradition. For instance, in his analysis of that period of Islamic history Muhammad 'Imara
attempts to show the importance of various Islamic institutions. In particular, *shura* is understood as participation in the management of the affairs
of state and society, and is underlined in quranic verses.[6]

Similarly, Khalid Muhammad Khalid has found democracy to be synonymous with *shura*. Khalid's reading of Islamic history advances the claim that the political liberties associated with democracy had their antecedents in the Islamic society from the time of its foundation. The right of the *umma* (Islamic community) to choose its leader is evidenced in the event of Saqifa and the *bay'a* given to 'Umar, 'Uthman, and 'Ali.[7] As proof that just rule is a principle governing the polity in Islam, Khalid invokes certain quranic verses and the example of the Rightly Guided Caliphs. In his account of that period, 'Umar, the third caliph, emerges as the symbol of justice and as a democrat.[8] The argumentative orientation of Khalid's recall of early Islamic history is that "Islam is democratic and that democracy is Islam."[9] Underlying the articulations of democracy within the Arab-Islamic model is the desire to prove its compatibility with the ideas of government associated with Western civilization. The task of Khalid and 'Imara, in this regard, responds to some imperative that guided turn-of-the-century Arab-Muslim reformers such as Muhammad 'Abduh.

Theoretical Constraints

As mentioned above, in treating the subject of democracy in their countries, Arab intellectuals have attempted to begin from an analysis of objective social conditions rather than from a theoretical outline of what defines democracy. Grounding the discussion in an empirical approach while deriving the theoretical basis of the conception of democracy from the Western experience underlies much of the tensions that characterize the discourse. In adopting the Western model as a frame of reference, the theoretical and philosophical principles that undergird that experience have to be dealt with not only in their context of emergence but also in relation to the sociohistorical conditions of the Arab world today. In other words, underlying parliamentary democracy, electoral systems, and divisions of power are visions of the polity and the citizen's position in it, notions of freedom, and definitions of the social that cannot be isolated from the institutions and forms that embody them. The question to be raised here is: What is the relevance of these principles to this particular juncture of Arab history? The comparative frames referred to earlier have as their focus institutions and processes, but their underlying social, political, and philosophical principles reveal inherent theoretical constraints that reappear in the debates.

A related tension is located in the evaluative statement that there is no democracy in the Arab world. This conclusion, which also serves as the premise for much of the debates and discussions, presupposes a knowledge of what democracy is. Indicators of its absence constitute the elements of a negative definition, that is of nondemocracy. The components of this negative definition give us some idea of what the concerns of Arab intellectuals are when talking about democracy. Nonrepresentativeness and nonaccountability, authoritarian style of rule, and repressive practices are characteristics of Arab government that signal their undemocratic nature. What is involved here are two interrelated issues: the organization of the polity and the rules governing it, and the values ascribed primacy in human society. In our investigation of the concept of democracy in Arab thought, we find that the second issue is of primary importance and it is the driving force behind the attempt to grapple with the question of state and government.

Proceeding from an investigation of the current situation in the Arab world we find that values such as freedom and liberty are not accorded their position of primacy in society. The investigations reveal an absence of freedom and of institutions representing the idea itself. The concern with freedom and liberty arises in relation to the awareness of state practices, such as human rights violations, that are perceived as total negations of these values. This, in turn, is related to the association of the concept of democracy with the question of human rights. Democratic institutions in this respect are seen as the instrument in charge of embodying and protecting the values that ensure the respect of human rights.

Now, if we turn to the conceptualization of these values in the discourse, we find that they acquire a sense of universality that is used to suspend debates regarding their field of meaning and relevance in the Arab experience. According to one intellectual, certain principles such as freedom of expression and the humanity of the individual are independent values which need not be tied to a particular goal, because they exist as self-contained values in social life.[10]

Yet we are still confronted with the issue of the relation between the values on the one hand, and the forms and institutions that embody them on the other. In defining the essence of democracy as "respect for the humanity of the individual,"[11] it becomes necessary to address the institutional side of the equation. This gives rise to debates on forms of government, political participation, and legitimacy. Thus, we find competing notions of freedom and equality (political vs. social) seeping into the examination of questions such as the merits of a multiparty system with Western-style democracy as opposed to a socialist system based on single-party rule.

In his 1983 conference presentation on the evolution of the concept of democracy in political thought, 'Ali al-Din Hilal traced the rise of tensions between freedom and equality with the articulation of democracy and liberalism.[12] Hilal identifies equality as the essence of the concept of democracy as it developed historically. He also proposes to effect a separation between democracy as a historical concept and liberal democracy, which arose with bourgeois capitalism. It is not clear how Hilal conceives of political democracy since the political liberties it implies are part of the concept of liberal democracy he is proposing to cast aside. What we find in Hilal's position, and in similar discussions, is the attempt to deal with the different articulations of liberty and equality as made by Western liberals and social democrats. The former view egalitarian politics as incursions on individual liberty, while the latter point to the threats economic inequalities pose for freedom.

Indeed, in the Arab context, the debate over the nature of democracy crystallizes the tension between individual liberty and political rights on the one hand, and equality on the other. In a 1979 seminar, Husam 'Isa presented a view of democracy emphasizing its social aspects and pointed to the limitation placed on equality by two of the fundamental ideas of equal liberty: the rule of law and equality before the law. Drawing from President Nasser's discourse, 'Isa used the example of the equality of the landlord and the tenant before the law and argued that this was a formal equality that would result in real inequalities. 'Isa also presented an associational version of participatory democracy in which syndicates and unions, not political parties, are the organs of representation.[13] The underlying vision here is that in a setting characterized by socioeconomic inequalities, and because of the limitations imposed on the exercise of liberty by poverty and the lack of education, some would be at a disadvantage in relation to others in their exercise of civil and political liberty. Equality in this context requires interventionist policies and trade-offs between liberty and primary social goods. The need for such trade-offs is not accepted by some intellectuals.[14] However, the articulation of political democracy with social democracy poses the questions of the economic logic of society and the nature of the state. The crux of the matter here has to do with the relation between rights and social justice, and the basis on which a prioritization of values is made.

While the concern for human and civil rights focuses on the demands for individual freedoms, the discourse of democracy develops within the wider problematic of *nahda* or of development. In Samir Amin's terms it is the project of social democratic development. In this regard, the rights and freedoms that come under the rubric of liberal democracy must be situated in relation to the social needs and wants of the people at this particular juncture in Arab history. Given the centrality of the role of the state in the goal of social transformation, the interplay between state and society represents a key element in the conceptualization of democracy. We shall now examine how the discussions on state and society elucidate the principles on which the envisioned democratic community is to be based.

Rethinking the Principles
of the Democratic Political Community

Democracy and the Politics of Authenticity

The various articulations of the discourse of *nahda* are guided by two different philosophical traditions, one searching for universality of civilization and the other emphasizing the historical specificity of culture. One espouses a progressivist philosophy of history, the other expresses an organic perspective on history. The first position advances a view of history as the accumulation of human development. In some cases it bears resemblance to the Western experience of development and the West's production of that experience as best represented in the developmentalist paradigm whose conventional narrative of the story of the Western transition from the Middle Ages into the modernity of the present is taken to represent the march of progress and the process of civilization itself.

The critique of that position, in contrast, holds that there exists in history a structure inherent to a certain culture and that carries within it the continuity of the "Self." It follows that any project for social transformation must be authentic, in so far as it is derived or based on this defining essence. This view is clearly expressed in 'Adil Hussein's construction of a model for democracy in the Arab world.[15] Working within the framework of historical specificity, Hussein articulates a novel concept of democracy. He defines it as guided policy and as a feature of all civilizations. Democracy here is understood as good government or the government that achieves the good of the people. The form of government capable of doing this is one shaped by the historical specificity of a country and that carries within it the inherited elements of its past. Looking at Arab-Islamic history and drawing heavily on the Muhammad 'Ali era in Egypt, Hussein finds the central state as the key institution that defines the nation. The democratic nature of politics is associated with an elite group composed of intellectuals, technocrats, bureaucrats, and so on, who act as an advisory body to the ruler and who represent the national good.

Absent from this formulation is an active population. The people's role in this model is that of receiver, and it is rarely an actor. Its consent appears to depend on an "inspiring ideology," which, in Hussein's terms, forms the basis of state-society relations. Hussein, however, does not rule out the use of coercion by the state, nor does he see it as undesirable. Rather, it exists as a last resort. Commentators on Hussein's model have criticized its elitist vision, which excludes meaningful popular participation.

Hussein's reductionist view of history and essentialist conception of politics present an additional problem. In positing the central state as the basic structure embodying the historical essence of the nation, there is a risk of reverting everything back to that single principle. Furthermore, the investment of this essentialism in politics conflates the political with the policy of the state.

Secularism Versus the Islamic State

The Islamists' demand for the establishment of an Islamic state has elicited various reactions, ranging from approval with qualification to complete rejection. Rejection of the Islamists' proposals—often in the name of safeguarding the values of democracy and rationality—has been accompanied by a defense of secularism, itself conceived as a corollary of these values. This association of secularism with democracy is questioned by some Arab intellectuals, as will be shown below. In one interpretation, the opposition between secularists and Islamists is construed as a false issue.[16] Muhammad 'Abid al-Jabiri argues that the opposing banners of secularism and the Islamic state were carried at the turn of the century *nahda* and subsequently to express the position of different forces vis-à-vis democracy. In a sense, Jabiri sees the banners as a cover for other concerns. He contends that the *ulama* (religious scholars), fearing exclusion from modern systems of government, have clung to a vision of government they termed Islamic and that allowed them continued participation. On the other hand, thinkers and activists originating from minority groups, who were and are apprehensive about the majority rule that characterizes a democratic system, have sought guarantees of their rights in the secular state. This, in Jabiri's opinion, was nothing more than formulating the concept of democracy in mistaken and artificial terms.

Today's confrontation between the supporters of the secular state and the proponents of the Islamic state is not without its links to the protagonists' hopes and fears regarding democracy. The secularists view the religious state as an absolutist repressive institution that, in principle as well as in practice, offers no guarantees for the protection of civil and human rights. Proceeding from a reading of the historical record of the caliphate, Farag Fawdah argued for the comparative merit of the secular state. In *al-Haqiqa al-gha'iba*, secularism is pronounced synonymous with democracy, while the religious state is associated with absolutism.[17]

According to Fu'ad Zakariyya, the religious state, by virtue of its metaphysical foundation (that is, upholding divine sovereignty) cannot guarantee the protection of civil rights, while the secular state can, since it posits the human being at the center of the organization of human society. The primacy of human sovereignty permits the establishment of a system of checks and limitations on abuses of power.[18] It should be noted that the idea of secularism is articulated here within the problematic of *nahda*, itself framed by the Western experience. Democracy, secularism, and the rule of reason are understood as interrelated elements of a higher stage of civilizational development. With the progress of science and the separation of knowledge from the field of belief, a secular rational approach to nature and society emerges. Zakariyya associates democracy with the rule of reason and the decline of absolutist authority characteristic of religion.[19] A degree of rationality thus appears as a prerequisite for freedom of choice and thought. What we find in this formulation is a reproduction of the schism between the cognitive universe of knowledge based on reason and that of religion based on faith. The former mode of thinking is democratic, while the latter is absolutist and dogmatic.

The interpretation of divine sovereignty, however, is not agreed on among the various thinkers of the Islamist movement. In some Islamist writings the divinity of government seems to flow from the divinity of the law (the *shari'a*). This concept is well articulated by Sayyid Qutb's notion of *hakimiyya* (God's governance) and its adoption by the jihad militants in Egypt and their spiritual leader Shaikh 'Umar 'Abd al-Rahman. In other writings, such as those of Rashid al-Ghannushi (leader of the Tunisian Islamist party, al-Nahda), sovereignty is derived from the people. What we have here are two positions with respect to the *shari'a*: In one the application of the *shari'a* is tied to a particular form of government (*hakimiyya*), though it is not well defined; and in the other, the application of the *shari'a* is separate from the political arena. Al-Ghannushi, in fact, distinguishes between legal legitimacy and religious legitimacy.[20]

The positions taken by the various Islamist movements vis-à-vis liberalization in the political field represent different strategies for bringing about change, that is the establishment of the Islamic state. While jihad's ideology conceives of change as a result of the war waged against state and society by the "few believers," al-Ghannushi sees change as the outcome of the democratic process of elections. It must also be noted that the adoption of one position does not exclude the use of means associated with the other. Thus, the Islamists in Egypt voice and extend their support during elections to parties sympathetic to their demands, as was the case with their endorsement of the Labour Party. This occurs despite Shaikh 'Abd al-Rahman's declared opposition to democracy, which he identifies as fallible rule of the people and as the negation of *hakimiyya,* which is the infallible rule of God.[21]

A similar distrust of the people is articulated by 'Ali Belhadj and 'Abassi Madani, the leaders of the Front Islamique du Salut (FIS) in Algeria. While the movement sought power through legal channels, its leaders expressed their willingness to oppose a non-Islamic state even if it is a representative one. Belhadj stated the necessity of war against the infidels in the case where the people deviate from the "Islamic frame": "If the people vote against the law of God, this is but a blasphemy. Ulemas order [sic] this case to kill the infidels because the latter want to substitute their authority for God's."[22] The charter of the FIS proposes a political system based on *shura*, which is set in opposition to the political despotism of the actual system.

In Egypt, the conception of society and the polity that emerges in the radical Islamist discourse is derived from the construction of the Muslim as a juridical subject—that is, as a subject whose status is defined according to a legal grid that determines his or her conformity to the *shari'a*. This grid governs all aspects of the subject's life, including his/her relation to all institutions and rules that govern social practices. The individual's position in the polity is defined in terms of *ta'a* (obedience) to the Muslim ruler, and jihad against the infidel ruler. Yet by interpellating the subject as the believer and not as a member of a Muslim community, the discourse allows no place for political activity on the part of the collectivity of which the Muslim is a member.

Secularism and Democracy

The association between secularism and democracy is challenged by a number of Arab intellectuals. Thinkers like Hasan Hanafi, Muhammad 'Abid al-Jabiri, and Burhan Ghalyun contend that secularism is a nonissue. In Ghalyun's terms secularism has been transcended as a problematic and has been replaced by democracy.[23] For Jabiri, it is a false issue and should be substituted by the demand for rationalism and democracy.[24] According to Hanafi, the term is alien to Arab culture and civilization and represents no real need; what is at stake, rather, are the values of freedom and equality.[25] The logic of the arguments each of these thinkers put forward is the dissociation of secularism from democracy in Arab thought. In this section we shall discuss briefly the import of these arguments and the extent to which they succeed in effecting the separation between secularism and democracy.

Ghalyun conceives of democracy as a "theoretical and practical frame for the realization of the values of reason, freedom and political revolution"; as such it has gone beyond secularism.[26] It has done this by creating the institutional system invested with legal powers to regulate the exercise of liberty on the one hand and legal and ethical equality on the other.[27] Ghalyun provides a stagelike account of the history of secularism and the evolution of values of intellectual and political freedom. In this account, secularism appears as a transitional theory that is subsequently superseded by democracy. First, secularism contributed to the rise of the modern state, liberated from the domination of the Church, and based on values of freedom. However, secularism was not sufficient for the regulation of the state. Democracy thus developed to be a model for the crystallization of the principles regulating the state.[28] With this development, Ghalyun declares that the era of the religious state has passed and that the model of the democratic state accords more with the values common to all cultures and civilizations.

Ghalyun's history of secularism incorporates the Soviet experience in order to support his argument that secularism has become an ideology and a tool in the hands of power and that it no longer guarantees freedom of belief or political liberty.[29] In this context, secularism is incapable of allowing for the plurality of beliefs and hence stands in opposition to democracy. It should be noted that Ghalyun's view of religion and the evolution of its role in society enters into his critique of secularism. Following the separation of religion and politics in the West, religion gradually regained its natural position in society as a source of values that interacts with other realms like politics and science.[30] It is as a source of values and as an element of the expression of the plurality of beliefs that religion has a role to play in politics as guaranteed by democratic values. In Ghalyun's schema, politics draws on the values of society; religion is a source of values and, therefore, is an actor in politics. This also follows from his formulation that democracy allows for the correspondence between the values and goals guiding official politics and the authority of the state on the one hand, and those of society on the other.[31]

Jabiri's rejection of the problematic of secularism in favor of that of democracy and rationality begins with the formal definitional content of secularism. He points out that secularism is identified with the separation of church and politics, however, Islam has no church—that is, it has no religious institution. At the same time, Jabiri asserts that Islam is both religion and state, a claim that, according to him, does not justify the call for secularism. In Islam, religion was separate from politics as indicated by the separation of the *ulama* from the *umara* (princes). The Islamic state appears as the historical state, which, following the period of the four Rightly Guided Caliphs, became political government (*mulk siyasi*).[32] In other words, the Islamic state is a political entity that, in its historical development, was not a religious state. Jabiri believes that in such a formulation, the issue of secularism versus the religious state is displaced, while the real issue continues to be democracy.

Critics of Jabiri's argument contend that the fact that the *ulama* in Islam serve as the body of religious authority warrants the call for the separation between religion and politics.[33] This separation represents the logic of the opposition between religious reasoning and human rationality realized in secularism.[34] While the critiques point to a lack of precision in Jabiri's terms, they reveal the existence of common ground on the issue of the separation of religious authority from politics. For Jabiri as it is for Ghalyun, the religious state remains an unacceptable formula in politics.

The State and Democracy

In the developmental model adopted by many Third World thinkers—including a number of Arab thinkers—the strong state was espoused as the agent of nation building and reconstruction. Thinkers working within a Marxist framework also carved out a role for the state in the struggle for economic independence. But in dealing with the issue of democracy, the state's position in the national project is not as secure as it used to be. The assessment by some that the revolutionary project has failed is accompanied by a rethinking of the role of the state and proposals on how to limit its powers. Moreover, the growing contention is that the state is retreating in the face of the rising tide of civil society. The validity of such a claim depends on empirical analysis indicating the retrenchment of the state. Nonetheless, it is safe to argue that, in theoretical terms, the state's central role is questioned.

The new state, as articulated in Ghalyun's recent work (1991), is not the national state but the democratic state. In Ghalyun's formulation it is a procedural institution, separate from authority and distinct from politics. To understand Ghalyun's vision of the state, we must look at his analysis of the state in the Arab world and the reasons for what he terms the crisis of state and authority. This crisis has its origins in the identification of the state with the national project of modernity conceived as the ideology of the state and actualized in a policy of oppression and control.[35] This reflects an absence of a concept of politics and of its structure understood as social practice and of its civil and ethical bases.[36] These bases are the sources of authority and the guarantee of legitimacy. The present-day struggle between the Islamists and the state has to do with determining the values and principles on which to construct the state and to base authority.[37] Ghalyun situates the struggle in the context of the bankruptcy of the national state and in its inability to achieve and offer what accords with the structure of values and beliefs (the source of authority and legitimacy).[38]

Confronting the crisis requires renewal of political thought and reexamination of the concept of the state and its relation to civil society.[39] Ghalyun's proposals for the resolution of the crisis outline the need to distinguish between state and politics—that is, between state and regime. Politics is produced by society, while the state is a procedural means for the development of consensus and crystallization of the majority.[40] The state regulates the authority that is in charge of the implementation of policies representing the will of the society. In this regard, it does not devise policies nor does it determine goals; rather, it is society that constitutes the source of values and politics.[41] Politics in this sense represents a social and collective activity whose roots extend into civil society, drawing on its values and beliefs.[42] The democratic state is the political frame in which a dialogue between competing views and the practice of freedoms as well as the sustenance of the collective will can take place.[43]

Ghalyun's notion of the state as a procedural institution and as the political frame separate from politics postulates a number of principles that require further scrutiny. In the first instance, the state is advanced as a neutral overseer of competing interests and as an arbiter in charge of sorting out the majority position. This postulate presupposes that power can be restricted to certain realms and can thus be left out of the institution of the state. On this basis Ghalyun effects a separation between state and regime for the purpose of limiting power to the latter. Drawing on Foucault's ideas on the systematization of power and its embodiment in techniques and institutions, in practices of discipline and normalization, one can argue that the rational state with its procedures is a locus of power and that, therefore, it constitutes an arena of struggle and contestation.

Second, Ghalyun's notion of the state suggests that it is a form empty of content. However, a closer look at the idea of the state identified as a political frame reveals otherwise. If one understands the principles of political activity Ghalyun invested in the state to be the rules of conduct of political association—that is, the mode by which individuals relate to one another in the political community and according to which they identify as members of that community—then it becomes imperative to define the substantive content of these principles. The qualification of the frame as democratic invests the principles of association with the content of equality and freedom, a content that is subject to different interpretations. The point to be made here is that the frame is as much about politics as the politics Ghalyun wants to leave in the hands of society and its representative regime.

Democracy and Intellectual Freedom

The demands for the Islamic state and the application of the *shari'a* have focused the debates on the need for the protection of certain liberties such as freedom of thought and speech that are seen as threatened by the Islamists' attempt at reclaiming a traditional authority in the domains of culture, art, and thought. The use of the Islamic juridical concepts of the permissible and the forbidden (*mubah* and *muharram*) and its association with the rulings of *takfir* (declaring someone an apostate) are among the primary ideological weapons used by the Islamists against their opponents. The danger to intellectual freedom this represents has not been lost on Arab intellectuals—particularly when accusations of *riddah* (apostasy), leveled against those who do not conform to the Islamist interpretation, constitute a criminal charge carrying the death sentence in countries where the *shari'a* is applied. It is in this context that one intellectual argues that of the many problems facing democracy, the most dangerous is the project of the Islamic state.[44]

These apprehensions must be understood in relation to the Islamists' attempt to eliminate opposing discourses. As Zakariyya points out, the *takfir* charges are supported by a claim to monopoly over the truth. At issue in this discussion is the ethic of action embodied in *takfir* and in its terms of legitimation. Following the 1992 assassination of Egyptian intellectual Farag Fawdah by members of a militant Islamist group, much of the intellectual response dealt with the implication of *takfir* charges for society and the polity, and with the frame of political action necessary for the functioning and protection of democracy.[45] For some, the assassination of Fawdah signaled the interruption of the dialogue between the militant Islamists and their opponents.[46] This meant that the boundaries of acceptable performances had been transgressed and, in doing this, the militants had forsaken their membership in the political community. The assassination, and the reaction it unleashed, highlight the confrontation between two conceptions of community and their underlying principles. In their efforts to make the community of believers coterminous with the political community, the Islamists seem to follow an ethic of action whose justification is articulated in terms of an overriding idea or an absolute truth. The opposing view of community is inspired by the principles of democracy as a guiding ethic of interaction in the polity.

One reading of this confrontation views it in terms of the opposition between a communal vision of the good and the individualist views of rights.[47] I wish to raise a number of reservations in regard to this way of framing the debates. First, in their struggle for power, the Islamists' discourse and strategies aim at bringing about closure by fixing meanings. This effort does not mean that there is consensus in Arab and Islamic society over the good. Rather, what exists is a plurality of discourses. Second, the dichotomy between individualism and communitarianism that is posited in this reading excludes the concern for community as an important element of the defense of certain democratic principles. In other words, the rights that are asserted in the struggle for intellectual freedom are to be seen as necessary conditions for the proper functioning of a specific kind of association among citizens—the democratic community.

It is precisely the ethic of action that finds justification in *hakimiyya* that is found to be incompatible with democracy.[48] It should be added that the totalizing tendency of a single governing doctrine such as that imputed to *hakimiyya* is a charge made against other ideological currents. In fact, Ghali Shukri argues that it is symptomatic of thought and politics in the Arab world.[49] In a sense, the critique of the referential authority of the Arab Islamic heritage is representative of a stand against all attempts at homogenizing the intellect and in turn undermining freedom of thought.[50]

Conclusion

The debates and discussions among Arab intellectuals about the nature of democracy reflect a paramount concern with the principles that ought to be constitutive of the political community. In this sense, the definition of democracy in terms of equality and freedom expresses normative principles guiding association and action in the polity. The different interpretations of these principles advance varying views of the individual, society, and their interrelation. The tension between equality and freedom expressed in these interpretations is not merely an echo of the ongoing debates between Western neoliberals and social democrats. Rather, it points to the need for thinking about the relevance, for the Arab context, of the underlying philosophical and social principles of democratic institutions and the values they embody. In other words, questions of liberty and equality acquire a special importance within the discourse of *nahda*. In the search for a civilizational project, the question is raised as to how a rights-based notion of the individual can be reconciled with the imperatives of collective social action and responsibility such a project entails. Arab intellectuals must contend with the need to institute mechanisms for safeguarding individual freedoms in the face of state practices that betray a disregard for human rights. At the same time, the merits of formal equality found in liberal democracies are put into question in reference to the Arab social order, which is marked by vast economic and social inequalities. In this context, egalitarian politics are viewed as essential for addressing the inequities of the social order.

In the approach to *nahda* as a societal project that involves the Arab citizen as a member of a democratic community, the role of the state is undergoing revision. The limitation of state power through the expansion of societal involvement in politics is put forward in proposals for reforming the polity. This connects with current discussions about civil association and the rising interest in what is seen as a budding civil society in Arab countries.

Several issues that arise in thinking about the principles of the political community are dictated by the present conjuncture of Arab history. The challenge posed by the Islamists, and the climate of violence in which the state and the militant Islamist groups are engaged, have highlighted the need for the protection of civil and political liberties and the necessity of the separation of religious authority from politics. Thus, while the relation between secularism and democracy remains a contentious issue, the opposition to the idea of the religious state forms a common ground for the proponents of the secular state as well as for those intellectuals who wish to displace secularism from the debate. At the same time, the Islamist movement is acknowledged as a political force, thereby underlining the importance of reaching consensus on the mode of relations in the political community. Essential to this consensus are rules of action that safeguard the plurality of positions against the threats of absolutism.

Notes

1. On the problematic of renaissance in Arab thought see Muhammad 'Abid al-Jabiri, *Fi al-khitab al-'arabi al-mu'asir* [On Contemporary Arab Discourse] (Beirut: al-Tali'a, 1982). For a discussion of the ideas of the early *nahda* see Albert Hourani, *Arabic Thought in the Liberal Age: 1798–1939* (London: Oxford University Press, 1976).

2. Muhammad 'Abduh, *al-Islam wa al-nusraniyya* [Islam and Christianity] (Cairo: Matba'at al-Manar: 1350h) quoted in Sa'id Bin-Sa'id, *al-Iydiyulujiya wa al-hadatha* [Ideology and Modernity] (Beirut: al-Markaz al-thaqafi al-'arabi, 1987), p. 11.

3. Muhammad 'Abid al-Jabiri, *Fi al-khitab al-'arabi al-mu'asir* [On Contemporary Arab Discourse] (Beirut: Dar al-tali'a, 1982).

4. A number of seminars and conferences were dedicated to the study of the crisis of democracy in the Arab world. The discussion in this section draws on a 1979 seminar entitled "Azmat al-dimuqratiyya fi al-watan al-'arabi" [The Crisis of Democracy in the Arab Nation], and a 1984 collection entitled *Azmat al-dimuqratiyya fi al-watan al-'arabi* (Beirut: Center for Arab Unity Studies, 1984).

5. Khalid al-Nasr, "Azmat al-dimuqratiyya fi al-watan al-'arabiy" [The Crisis of Democracy in the Arab Nation], in *al-Dimuqratiyya wa huquq al-insan fi al-watan al-'arabi* [Democracy and Human Rights in the Arab Nation] (Beirut: Markaz dirasat al-wihda al 'arabiyya, 1983), pp. 25–61.

6. In *al-Hiwar al-qawmi al-dini* [The National/Religious Dialogue] (Beirut: Markaz dirasat al-wihda al-'arabiyya, 1989), pp. 254–256.

7. Khalid Muhammad Khalid, *Difa' 'an al-dimuqratiyya* [In Defense of Democracy] (Cairo: Dar thabit lil-nashr wa al-tawzi', 1985), pp. 201–202.

8. Khalid, *Difa' 'an al-dimuqratiyya*, pp. 206–211.

9. Khalid, *Difa' 'an al-dimuqratiyya*, p. 213.

10. "Nadwat azmat al-dimuqratiyya fi al-watan al-'arabi" [Seminar on the Crisis of Democracy in the Arab Nation], in *al-Dimuqratiyya wa huquq al-insan fi al-watan al-'arabi* [Democracy and Human Rights in the Arab Nation] (Beirut: Markaz dirasat al-wihda al-'arabiyya, 1983), p. 101.

11. "Nadwat azmat al-dimuqratiyya fi al-watan al-'arabi," p. 101.

12. 'Ali al-Din Hilal, "Mafahim al-dimuqratiyya fi al-fikr al-siyasi al-hadith" [Concepts of Democracy in Modern Political Thought], in *Azmat al-dimuqratiyya fi al-watan al-'arabi* [The Crisis of Democracy in the Arab Nation] (Beirut: Markaz dirasat al-wihda al-'arabiyya, 1984), pp. 35–49.

13. "Nadwat azmat al-dimuqratiyya fi al-watan al-'arabi" [Seminar on the Crisis of Democracy in the Arab Nation], in *al-Dimuqratiyya wa huquq al-insan fi al-watan al-'arabi* [Democracy and Human Rights in the Arab Nation] (Beirut: Markaz dirasat al-wihda al-'arabiyya, 1983).

14. "Nadwat azmat al-dimuqratiyya fi al-watan al-'arabi."

15. 'Adil Hussein, "al-Muhaddidat al-tarikhiyya wa al-ijtima'iyya lil-dimuqratiyya fi al-watan al-'arabi" [The Historical and Social Determinants of Democracy in the Arab Nation], in *al-Dimuqratiyya wa huquq al-insan fi al-watan*

al'arabi [Democracy and Human Rights in the Arab Nation] (Beirut: Markaz dirasat al-wihda al-'arabiyya, 1983), pp. 199–242.

16. Muhammad 'Abid al-Jabiri, *Ishkaliyyat al-fikr al-'arabi al-mu'asir* [The Problematics of Contemporary Arab Thought] (Beirut: Markaz dirasat al-wihda al-'arabiyya, 1990).

17. Farag Fawdah, *al-Haqiqa al-gha'iba* [The Missing Truth] (Cairo: Dar al-fikr lil-nashr wa al tawzi', 1988), p. 100. Fawdah was later assassinated by militant Islamists.

18. Fu'ad Zakariyya, "al-Falsafa wa al-din fi al-'alam al-'arabi" [Philosophy and Religion in the Contemporary Arab World], in *al-Sahwa al-islamiyya fi mizan al-'aql* [The Islamic Resurgence on the Scale of Reason] (Cairo: Dar al-fikr al-mu'asir, 1987), pp. 151–183.

19. Zakariyya, "al-Falsafa wa al-din fi al-'alam al-'arabi," p. 168.

20. Rashid al-Ghannushi and Hasan al-Turabi, *al-Haraka al-islamiyya wa al-tahdith* [The Islamic Movement and Modernization] (n.p., 1981), pp. 33–34.

21. 'Umar 'Abd al-Rahman, *Kalimat haq* [A Word of Truth] (Cairo: Dar al-'itisam, 1987).

22. Translated from "Les mots du FIS," *Algérie Actualité*, 4–10 January 1990, p. 9. See also "Interview Abassi Madani à Algérie Actualité: Les prochaines élections seront déterminantes . . . ," *Algérie Actualité*, 4–10 January 1990, pp. 8–9.

23. Burhan Ghalyun, *Naqd al-siyasa: al-dawla wa al-din* [Critique of Politics: The State and Religion] (Beirut: al-mu'assasa al-'arabiyya lil-dirasat wa al-nashr, 1991).

24. Muhammad 'Abid al-Jabiri, "al-Islam laysa kanisa kay nafsilahu 'an al-dawla" [Islam Is Not a Church to Separate from the State], in Hasan Hanafi and Muhammad 'Abid al-Jabiri, *Hiwar al-mashriq wa al-maghrib* [The Dialogue of the East and the West] (Cairo: Maktabat Madbuli, 1990), pp. 45–49.

25. Hasan Hanafi, "al-Islam la yahtaj ila 'ilmaniyya gharbiyya" [Islam Does Not Need Western Secularism], in Hasan Hanafi and Muhammad 'Abid al-Jabiri, *Hiwar al-mashriq wa al-maghrib* [The Dialogue of the East and the West], pp. 42–45.

26. Ghalyun, *Naqd al-siyasa*, p. 402.

27. Ghalyun, *Naqd al-siyasa*, p. 402.

28. Ghalyun, *Naqd al-siyasa*, p. 403.

29. Ghalyun, *Naqd al-siyasa*, p. 406.

30. Ghalyun, *Naqd al-siyasa*, p. 415.

31. Ghalyun, *Naqd al-siyasa*, p. 441.

32. Jabiri, "al-Islam laysa kanisa," pp. 47–49.

33. See Jurj al-Tarabishi, "al-Intelijentsiya al-'arabiyya wal-idrab 'an al-tafkir" [The Intelligentsia and the Strike of Thought], in *Hiwar al-mashriq wa al-maghrib* [The Dialogue of the East and the West], Hasan Hanafi and Muhammad 'Abid al-Jabiri (Cairo: Maktabat Madbuli, 1990), p. 138, and 'Abd-allah Bunfur, "Bayna fikr al-dawla wa al-fikr al-hur" [Between State Thought and Free Thought], in *Hiwar al-mashriq*, p. 165.

34. Bunfur, "Bayna fikr al-dawlah wa al-fikr al-hur," p. 167.

35. Ghalyun, *Naqd al-siyasa*, p. 425.

36. Ghalyun, *Naqd al-siyasa*, p. 427.

37. Ghalyun, *Naqd al-siyasa*, p. 431.

38. Ghalyun, *Naqd al-siyasa*, p. 432.

39. Ghalyun, *Naqd al-siyasa*, p. 433.

40. Ghalyun, *Naqd al-siyasa*, pp. 438–439.

41. Ghalyun, *Naqd al-siyasa*, p. 439.

42. Ghalyun, *Naqd al-siyasa*, p. 440.

43. Ghalyun, *Naqd al-siyasa*, p. 451.

44. Muhammad Ahmad Mahmud, "Huriyyat al-fikr bayna al-siyaq al-islamiy wa al-siyaq al-mu'asir" [Freedom of Thought between the Religious Context and the Contemporary Context], *Mawaqif* 65 (Autumn 1991), p. 98.

45. See *al-Ahram* from 12 June to 30 June 1993, and particularly the issues of 17, 20, and 30 June 1993. Of the many pertinent analyses dealing with the signification of the assassination, see Ghali Shukri, "al-Dhakira wa al-hawiyya wa surat al-'alam" [Memory and Identity and the Vision of the World], *al-Ahram*, 17 June 1992, p. 11.

46. Shukri, "al-Dhakira wa al-hawiyya." In subsequent analyses, others argued that entering into a dialogue with "extremist religious groups" was futile. See Hussein Ahmad Amin, "'Ala masharif al-qarn al-wahid wa al-'ishrin" [On the Threshold of the Twenty-First Century], *al-Ahali*, 3 February 1993, p. 8.

47. These are the terms adopted by Kevin Dwyer in his attempt to frame the confrontation between the Western-based human rights movement and indigenous claims to authenticity in many Third World countries. Dwyer uses the Salman Rushdie case as an example of the opposition between communal sensibilities and the universal claims of the human rights advocates. Kevin Dwyer, "Universal Visions, Communal Visions: Human Rights and Traditions," *Peuples Méditerranéens* 58–59 (January–June 1992), pp. 205–220.

48. Zakariyya, "al-Falsafa wa al din."

49. Shukri, "al-Dhakira wa al-hawiyya."

50. Although limited in scope, 'Aziz al-'Azma articulates a critique of absolutist thought that he sees as characteristic of the heritage's referential authority. 'Aziz al-'Azma, *al-Turath bayna al-sultan wa al-tarikh* [The Heritage between Authority and History] (Beirut: Dar al-tali'a, 1990), pp. 11–40.

6

Islam and Pluralism

Gudrun Krämer

The activism of sociopolitical groups claiming the mantle of Islam and the movement toward a liberalization of economic and political life in certain countries of the Muslim Arab world have engendered an animated and often polemical debate about Islam, the state, and democracy—a debate that is not only laden with methodological problems but also highly politicized. One need only follow the discussions about human rights "in Islam," about the status of non-Muslim minorities or women, or about Islamic concepts of liberty or equality to see the intrinsic problems, emotions, and interests involved. Does political democracy presuppose not just economic, but also intellectual, liberalism? Can Islam allow for liberal thought without losing its true essence, and what constitutes this essence, if it exists?[1] Can liberal democracy be considered a set of political techniques of which some elements can be adopted without abandoning one's cultural identity or "authenticity" (but again, what is authenticity and what is its status compared to other values such as equality, social justice, and modernity)?[2]

For better or worse, one finds oneself in the midst of the old and heated debate about the essence of Islam, about authenticity and Orientalism, a debate which, as inevitable as it may seem, runs the risk of blocking certain paths of research even before these have actually been tried. If here the discussion is on Islam and pluralism,[3] it is in order to limit the study to one of the constitutive elements of any liberal, democratic order and to avoid, as much as possible, the general debate about identity, structure, and history. At the same time, it is quite clear that this debate cannot be altogether avoided. The larger themes are implicit in the distinction made here between a theoretical level, seeking to present "the position of Islam" on pluralism, and a "practical" level constituted by the actual positions and actions taken by Islamist activists. On both levels, one is faced with a wide range of opinions, from the categorical rejection of any opinion or political organization outside of the (ill-defined) framework of

Islam, such as is put forth by Taqi al-Din al-Nabhani, founder of the Islamic Liberation Party (*Hizb al-tahrir al-islami*),[4] to the ambiguous formulations of Yusuf al-Qaradawi, prominent professor of Islamic law and
Muslim Brother, to the nuanced and strikingly liberal reflections of Rashid
al-Ghannushi, intellectual head of the Tunisian Renaissance Party (*Hizb
al-nahda*). For practical reasons, this study will largely be based on the
Egyptian and Tunisian cases.

Theoretical Positions

On a theoretical level, two opposing theses compete. The first and largely
dominant one, in a kind of political *tawhid*, stresses the unity of the community, an ideal strongly emphasized in the Quran and the Sunna of the
Prophet. In the juridical theory of the sources of Islamic jurisprudence
(*usul al-fiqh*), it corresponds to the concept of *ijma'*, that is, to the consensus of the Muslim community expressed, according to majority opinion, by its religious scholars (*ulama*).[5] Pushed to its logical conclusion, the
emphasis on unity can imply the refusal of all divergence of opinions, of
all criticism or opposition to the dominant doctrines and practices, which
are denounced as *fitna*, a menace to, and a crime against, the all-important
value of Muslim unity. If there is one single truth, and if it can be unmis-
takably identified, there is no room for one crucial element of political and
intellectual liberalism: free debate.

Opposing this unitarian thesis is another, albeit minority, view which,
based on a well-known quranic verse (Sura 49:13), underscores the elements of diversity or pluralism in the legal and historical heritage of the
community. Here, the concept of *ijma'* is contrasted to the notions of personal opinion in legal matters (*ra'y*) and of local customary law (*'urf*),
which historically led to the creation of the four recognized Sunni schools
of law (*madhhab*, plural *madhahib*).[6] Even though there is only one text
(the Quran) and one truth (Islam), this does not necessarily mean that hu-
mankind is capable of reading the former correctly and of finding the truth
with infallible certainty. The foundations of the faith established by the
consensus of the Prophet's companions (*salaf salih*) excepted, there is
hence no human infallibility, whether one considers the *umma* in its entirety, the caliphs, the *ulama* or those holding authority (*ulu al-amr*) in
general. No Muslim has the right to claim a monopoly on truth or the interpretation of the text of which several readings exist.

It should be noted that, in reality, the two theses are often combined.
One will therefore quite often find an intermediate position, based on the
type of argument, "yes, but . . . ":[7] Yes, there do exist elements of diversity
between people, and even between Muslims, and yes, it is possible to have

diverging interpretations of the sacred texts, but these should not exceed certain limits, more or less narrowly defined. It is these limits that make for the difference between the theoretical positions.

The first thing one notices about the extreme positions is that they derive from the same type of reasoning. In all cases, the obligatory references to the sources held to be sacred are made—to the Quran in the first place, and to the Sunna of the Prophet in the second, but in order to arrive at diverging, if not contradictory, conclusions. In addition, reference is made to juridical theory, whose logic and terms are then identified with political theory and practice: Diversity of opinions in legal matters (*ikhtilaf*) is compared to political contest, schools of law are equated with political parties, and so forth. There is, in fact, no reason to be surprised by this: It is the traditional, and generally accepted, mode of philosophical, social, and political reasoning in Muslim and Islamist circles. Even authors in favor of separating religion and politics, such as 'Ali 'Abd al-Raziq, Farag Fawdah, or Muhammad Sa'id al-'Ashmawi, have referred to these sources and to the pious ancestors, the *salaf* (using their own selection of sources and of ancestors), to justify their revisionist interpretation of the Islamic heritage. They have been fighting their adversaries on their own turf and with their own arms.[8]

The political interpretation of sacred texts and juridical concepts so characteristic of modern Islamist discourse—be it reformist, radical, or revolutionary—does not constitute a new phenomenon: The ideologization of Islam did not begin in the nineteenth century but rather, when, at the battle of Siffin in A.D. 657, under the rallying cry of "*la hukma illa li-llah*" ("all decisions belong to God"), certain followers of the caliph 'Ali turned against him in the name of divine sovereignty. Already at this stage we see the ambiguity in terms that may have a juridical, moral, or political meaning, such as *hukm* (legal decision/rule), *shura* (consultation), or *umma* (community), that were to give rise to so much political strife and academic controversy.

Here, as with respect to many other questions that, in the past, have divided Muslims from the createdness of the Quran, the divine attributes, or the intercession of the Prophet to the relation between free will and predestination, it is not the issue of whether this or that reading of the texts can be justified or not. It is also not the question, in the present case, whether the quranic verse mentioned above (Sura 49:13—"Lo! We have created you male and female, and have made you nations and tribes that ye may know one another") can really serve as a basis for political pluralism or whether legitimate divergence of opinions (*ikhtilaf*) or the plurality of law schools can be used to legitimize political debate and the formation of political parties. In a pragmatic approach, we will simply state that, following the example of the most distinguished scholars of the classical age, contemporary authors refer to the sources in order to legitimize their own approach to current social and political questions.

Even if, according to a hadith attributed to the Prophet but classified as weak, divergence of opinions can actually be considered a divine grace (*ikhtilaf ummati rahma*),[9] diversity has its limits. In order to be tolerated, it must concern the details of religion (*furu'*) only, without encroaching on its foundations (*usul*). Debate must fall short of any radical revision of the axioms of the faith. This does not answer the question of who has the right and the obligation to define what constitutes the foundations of the faith (*usul al-din, al-ma'lum min al-din bil-darura*), that, according to modern terminology, constitute the unchanging essence of Islam (*al-thabit*), and what constitutes the details derived by human reason from this unchanging base by adopting its guiding principles to the incessant changes of time and place (*al-mutaghayyir*). It does not address the problem of legitimate authority and effective power in an Islamic society. The issue of excommunication of Muslims (*takfir*), which the advocates of God's exclusive sovereignty (*hakimiyyat Allah*) use so freely, demonstrates very well the high stakes involved in the politico-religious realm. The risks were recognized by the great scholars of the past very early and very clearly as a grave menace to the unity and strength of the community.[10]

There is another important point to be made: In order to stay legitimate, the debate must not reflect private interest, which is commonly identified with the moral category of personal whims, passions, and desires (*ahwa'*), so strongly condemned in the Quran and almost universally rejected as destructive and illegitimate.[11] According to this point of view, which can be considered predominant, there exists only one single legitimate interest, and that is the interest of the *umma* in its entirety (*al-maslaha al-'amma*), which by and large corresponds to the Western notion of public interest. Public interest has not been uniformly defined by the masters, from Imam Malik to al-Shafi'i and al-Shatibi, whose comments and theories remain the reference point for contemporary authors. It is, however, largely acknowledged as one of the secondary sources of law and, in the framework of *siyasa shar'iyya*, as one of the main principles of political organization.[12]

It is true that the existence of various social groups within Muslim society is generally acknowledged. There are Muslims and non-Muslims, Sunnis, Shi'ites and other "sects" (scrupulously listed and classified in a specialized type of literature); there are also various social strata and diverse ethnic groups. However, they must not be divided by particular interests, let alone antagonistic ones. Muslim society has indeed been characterized as being "plural" but not "pluralist."[13] Differing opinions and interests, if they exist, should be balanced and rendered compatible within a harmonious whole, reflecting the ideal of equilibrium (*tawazun*), that can justly be considered the junior counterpart to the ideal of unity.[14] The horror of *fitna* (strife, disunity within the community) translates into an aversion toward all conflict, even of a nonviolent nature.

The conclusion drawn by many activists and theoreticians who reject particular interests takes us back to the unitarian thesis: There can be only one party in Islam, and that is the party of God (*hizballah*), which is opposed by only one other party, that of the devil (*hizb al-shaytan*).[15] It follows that there is no legitimate role for political associations and parties representing particular interests which, by definition, serve only to divide—that is, weaken, the one and undivided community.

One may speculate at length about this preoccupation, if not obsession, with unity, a preoccupation closely linked to dreams of self-sufficiency and power. There are those who trace this unitarian tendency to the very essence of the Islamic faith, explaining the concern for political unity by the oneness of God, political *tawhid* by religious *tawhid*. They are, of course, engaged in the same political interpretation of religious dogma and ethical norms that characterizes the Islamists. "One God, one law, one community, and one leader" sounds impressive enough. The unitarian logic serves to enhance a totalitarian vision of Islam and the political order founded on it, even if the Quran as its only uncontested source does not easily lend itself to this totalitarian interpretation. Even if the Quran does, of course, insist on the absolute oneness of God (*tawhid*) and the unity of the community (*wahda*), it does not do the same with respect to political leadership. In fact, the Quran says notoriously little about the subject, and when it commands obedience to the legitimate authorities, it names them in the plural: "*Obey God, and obey the Prophet and those among you who are in command (ulu al-amr)*" (Sura 4:59). It is therefore not the faith that demands unified and single leadership. It was specific historical circumstance that caused the *umma* to choose one single leader to guide it. Its rationale was well expressed in a phrase attributed to the first successor of the Prophet, the Caliph Abu Bakr: "This community needs a leader" ("*la budda li-hadhihi al-umma mimman yaqumu biha*").[16]

There is no need, therefore, to refer to the metaphysical in order to understand the seductive appeal of the unitarian dream: History itself is greatly sufficient for explaining the continuing search for unity and unanimity. The weakness of the young community against superior forces made it an urgent priority to preserve unity among Muslim ranks. The need for unity was part and parcel of the anticolonialist struggle and rhetoric. It continues to be upheld by Islamic activists who consider the West's current "intellectual aggression" (*al-ghazw al-fikri*) to be as dangerous as the politico-military aggression of the past. One should note in passing that this historical heritage largely explains one notable gap in the expression of liberty of conscience. At the same time that the principle "no compulsion in religion" (*la ikraha fi al-din*) is maintained, the conversion of a Muslim to another religion (apostasy, *riddah*) is not recognized. By linking these conversions to the revolt of certain Arab tribes after the death of the Prophet (the *riddah*), which led to the first division of the community, they are viewed as inciting a revolt against Islam and all Muslims. An apostate is therefore regarded as a traitor and should be punished as such. Any religious conversion, however individual or quiet, is or can be perceived as an aggressive political act.[17]

To summarize, one finds that, side by side with the unitarian/totalitarian vision of Islam and of the Muslim *umma*, largely considered the only authoritative one, there is another tradition that accepts the divergence of opinions as a normal and natural phenomenon, desired by God who, in His wisdom, chose to create different beings, living in differing circumstances of time and place. Some proponents of this second tradition go as far as to suggest that this diversity of nature and opinion is beneficial for the community as a whole. It must, however, be noted that even for the supporters of a pluralist vision, legitimate controversy finds its limits when it touches upon the bases of the faith (*al-usul al-thabit*), that cannot be questioned. They, too, recognize the dichotomy between truth and falsehood (*haqq* and *batil*), the licit and the illicit (*halal* and *haram*), and the accepted and the rejected (*ma'ruf* and *munkar*). As long as this dichotomy is upheld, any political decision can or might be turned into an article of faith.

In fact, the real test of pluralism and democracy arises when the "Islamic framework" (*itar al-islam*), which is always invoked but rarely defined with precision, is exceeded. What, then, is the status of those who, by birth and/or by personal choice, put themselves outside this framework or outside the pale—non-Muslims on the one hand, but also free-thinking Muslims, atheists, Marxists, and perhaps even liberals on the other? Would Christians, Communists, and liberals have the right of free expression and free association in an "Islamic order" (*nizam islami*)? Would an Islamic state permit the formation of a Christian or a communist party?

On this point, the response of the theoreticians is clear and nearly unanimous: There must be no criticism of the religion or attacks against it, and no freedom of expression for the enemies of Islam—not only apostates, renegades, atheists, and Communists, but also Christians, Jews, or Baha'i (the latter considered to be apostates). This implies a serious (and arbitrary) restriction of the pluralist principle that presupposes liberty of conscience, of faith, and of opinion. In the vast literature on the subject there certainly are nuances, stricter or more lenient formulations, and there is a diversity of sanctions to be imposed on those who transgress the more or less rigidly defined limits of the law, but the position basically stays the same. The debate about conversion or apostasy and the excommunication of Muslims (*riddah* and *takfir*) already mentioned above, reflects the stakes involved in the issue, and the cases of Mahmud Taha, former head of the Sudanese Republican Brothers, executed in 1985 for heresy[18] and of the author Salman Rushdie, threatened with execution for blasphemy by the Iranian authorities, illustrate the problem.

The only possible breach in this front of refusal is based on the legal principles of public interest (*maslaha*) and necessity (*darura*), which, following the rule *"la darar wa-la dirar,"* permit that, in exceptional cases, the divine commandments may be suspended in order to avoid the major damage their application might cause to the community. It is by this means that Yusuf al-Qaradawi, who does not oppose the existence of political parties as such, conceives the possibility that a communist party could be tolerated on the territory of Islam:[19] Communism, he argues, is against Islam as it is against all religion.[20] There is hence no place in an Islamic state for a communist party (and he does not forget to mention that many states considered democratic do not tolerate communist activity either). But, he continues, there are situations where the interest of the Muslims (*maslaha*) is better served if communists are allowed to act openly rather than being pushed underground, where they may pose a much greater danger to the community. The decision falls to the "men who loosen and bind" (*ahl al-hall wa-al-'aqd*) under their political and administrative authority (*siyasa shar'iyya*). It should be noted in passing that al-Qaradawi is using the same arguments as many critics of the Islamic movement in government circles and the opposition who suggest recognizing the Islamists as legitimate participants in the political contest rather than denying them recognition and forcing them into clandestine, violent action. If overt activity allows them to disseminate their program, it will also show their weaknesses, and deprive them of their aura of martyrdom. Yet, for al-Qaradawi, toleration remains based on considerations of interest and necessity, and it could be withdrawn once circumstances change. He does not advocate the acceptance of free competition between ideologies and political parties.

Political Practice: The Egyptian Case

Theory, and even more so practice, do not stop here: It is the very process of liberalization (or, to be more precise, the limits of this process) that have led certain Islamists to modify, or even revise, their position concerning ideological and political pluralism.[21] The example of the Egyptian Muslim Brothers serves to illustrate this evolution of thought and practice that, in the course of the 1980s, gradually distanced them, little by little, from the unconditional condemnation of party politics or partisanship (*hizbiyya*) that the founder-leader of the movement, Hasan al-Banna

(1909–1949) stood for. His negative attitude to party politics and pluralism is well known. In fact, it is little more than the traditional discourse on the subject:[22] There is but one legitimate party in Islam, and that is the party of God; political parties such as existed under the Egyptian monarchy were nothing but cliques of large landowners pursuing their own egotistical interests; political parties merely serve to divide and weaken the Egyptian nation as well as the Islamic *umma,* which against colonial aggression must have one goal—to maintain unity within its ranks. For this reason, the Muslim Brotherhood is not a political party, but rather an association (*jama'a*). Its mission (*da'wa*) consists basically of religious, moral, physical, and political education. This requires social, economic, cultural, and political activities that go far beyond the narrow political concerns of political parties.[23] The rejection of *hizbiyya*, involving unconditional loyalty to the party, its leaders, and its program, has not prevented the Association of the Muslim Brothers from developing many traits of a political party (at least of the Egyptian model),[24] to the point that it is precisely the members' partisan spirit and their blind allegiance to the group and its leaders (*hizbiyya, asabiyyah*) for which critics within and without the movement reproach it.[25]

Political liberalization under Anwar Sadat (1918–1981), and the establishment, after 1976, of a multiparty system, albeit limited and tightly controlled by the state,[26] produced a gradual change in the strategy and political thinking of the Egyptian Muslim Brothers, which, however, was not fully expressed until the 1980s, under the government of Husni Mubarak.[27] Even in the era of Hasan al-Banna, the Muslim Brothers had recognized the parliamentary system as the legal framework of their activities, in which politics played an integral role. In the 1940s, al-Banna and 'Umar al-Tilmisani, who was to become the movement's supreme guide in 1972, had even put forth their own candidatures in national elections.[28] Under Sadat, the Muslim Brothers cooperated, on an individual basis, in the committees for the defense of liberty and for solidarity with the Palestinian people, the two causes uniting all opposition groups in the Arab world, from Marxists to liberals to Islamists. In the 1976 elections, the Islamist current was represented by independent candidates, of which a sizable number were elected to Parliament.[29]

All the while, the regime continued (and continues) to refuse to grant the Muslim Brothers official status as a religious, social, or political association, trying to exclude them, as a religious movement, from political competition: The 1977 law on political parties, amended in 1979, does not admit parties based on a principle of exclusivity, be it religious, ethnic, or racial.[30] The only way to recognize the Brotherhood as a legal political party would therefore be to reinterpret this law (for example, by underscoring the fact that it does not exclude non-Muslims from its ranks). The

Brotherhood's position, between actual tolerance and the denial of official status, continues to be ambiguous, and its legal field of action remains entirely at the discretion of the authorities—a situation deemed most favorable by the majority of Arab regimes. In this situation full of ambiguities, be they intended or not, the Muslim Brothers have found a loophole in the form of electoral alliances (*tahaluf*) with officially recognized parties, exchanging the Neo-Wafd party, its partner for the May 1984 elections, with the Socialist Labor and Liberal parties for the April 1987 elections.[31]

There was one important exception, though: The Tagammu' (*hizb al-tajammu' al-watani al-taqaddumi al-wahdawi*), uniting a large part of the Egyptian left, was not included in the negotiations, held in the spring of 1987, about the formation of a united opposition front. According to several participants, including Khalid Muhyi al-Din, general secretary of the Tajammu', the Muslim Brothers stipulated that if it wanted to be part of the planned front, it first had to separate itself from its atheist members— the Communists and Marxists.[32] This fact is important because it offers one of the few occasions for observing how the declared principles of pluralism and tolerance are applied in practical politics. It appears that cooperation or even toleration do not include the Marxist left. This position can hardly surprise, considering the frequent assertions that, except in the case of necessity or higher interest, Communist or atheist activity cannot be admitted in an Islamic society.[33]

Parallel to their electoral activities, the Muslim Brothers continued their efforts to obtain official recognition that would guarantee their legal and autonomous existence,[34] without actually transforming themselves into a political party.[35] By 1986, this transition had been made, too: Muhammad Hamid Abu al-Nasr, the new supreme guide (*murshid 'amm*), elected after the death of 'Umar al-Tilmisani in April 1986, announced that statutes and a program were being prepared, and that his association would ask to be registered as a political party. When they formally handed in an application in 1990 to be registered as a political party, it was rejected by the government.[36] In any case, participation in Egyptian parliamentary life remained contentious within the Brotherhood and was strongly criticized by its rivals in the radical Islamist camp.[37] Political participation was all the more disputed because the electoral alliance of 1987 included parties who, in the very recent past, still placed themselves in the Arab socialist current. They did, of course, try to erase as quickly as possible the traces of this legacy, removing the embarrassing qualifier "socialist" from their party's name, growing beards, and cultivating a religious discourse. They were subsequently more or less taken over by their Islamist allies. Iman Farag, in a telling metaphor, speaks about "party squatting."[38] Along with most other opposition forces, they boycotted the parliamentary elections of 1990 to protest continued government interference and manipulation.[39]

It is not in the purview of this chapter to evaluate the ongoing experience of political participation or integration. Interesting as it may be, it has not yet produced a definitive result.[40] The purpose here was rather to point to the way Islamist thought and practice have evolved over time resulting, to a large extent, from interaction with society and the government in power.

The Tunisian Case

In the 1980s, the Tunisian Islamists grouped around the Islamic Tendency Movement (MTI, *harakat al-ittijah al-islami*), which transformed itself in 1989 into the Nahda Party, showed the clearest acceptance of pluralism. Here, as with the Muslim Brothers, historical experience, giving rise to criticism and self-criticism, was crucial in the evolution of thought and practice.[41] In the 1970s, the Tunisian Islamists had still been content to repeat, more or less faithfully, the themes of the radical discourse based on a reading, often rather simplistic, of the masters:[42] Abu al-A'la al-Mawdudi, Hasan al-Banna, and Sayyid Qutb above all, followed by the Iraqi Muhammad Baqir al-Sadr and the Iranian 'Ali Shari'ati, but also the Indian Abu al-Hasan al-Nadwi who, for his part, was quite critical of political Islam.[43] Like them, Tunisian Islamists condemned contemporary society as "impious" (*kafir*) and "ignorant (of Islam)" (*jahili*). They rejected all that was not Islam, proclaimed the sole sovereignty of God (*hakimiyyat Allah*), and called for the overthrowing of all despots and idols (*taghut*). Democracy, like socialism, was among these idols of foreign, non-Islamic origins: Both were therefore to be rejected and fought.

Toward the end of the 1970s, a combination of new factors—the Islamic revolution in Iran on the one hand, the severe socioeconomic crisis and mounting protest, followed by limited liberalization within the country on the other—led the movement to reevaluate its positions. Reevaluation and self-criticism sealed the fragmentation of the movement,[44] leading to the secession, in 1980, of a group of progressive intellectuals (*harakat al-islamiyyin al-taqaddumiyyin*) around Salah al-Din al-Jurshi and Ahmida al-Nayfar.[45] At the same time, the majority faction, grouped around Rashid al-Ghannushi and 'Abd al-Fattah Muru, came to the conclusion that they, too, had to adopt the democratic option. Newly organized as the Islamic Tendency Movement, they proclaimed their support for democracy and pluralism in their founding manifesto of June 1981. At a news conference, they also declared that they were renouncing all monopoly and guardianship (*wisaya*) over Islam, the truth, and the popular will, a formula that has been repeated ever since by their leaders.[46] However, they were unable to dispel the doubts of their critics and opponents, who continued to question their democratic credentials: Was the option for democracy simply a tactical move designed to take advantage of the democratic game, or was it a definitive ("strategic") decision that would hold, even if the Islamic movement were to take power, one way or another?[47] Countering these doubts, Ghannushi, like Muru, insisted that for him, the choice of liberty, pluralism, and democracy was definitive (strategic) and not conjunctural.[48]

This does not mean that a stage has been reached at which such reflections are irreversible, nor that there isn't the possibility of a return to the hard positions refusing pluralism. We are dealing with a debate in progress, and much will depend on the balance of forces within the various societies, and the strategy of different state elites toward the opposition in general and the Islamic movement in particular. By and large, it seems to be the regime's strategy toward the Islamists, pragmatics as well as militants, that determines, in large measure, the political strategy of the latter. Be that as it may, the internal dynamic, theory, and practice of the Islamic movement, so heterogeneous and diversified, is closely linked to political experience, and merits close study in order to end the often sterile abstractions about the relationship between Islam, the state, and politics.

Notes

An earlier version of this chapter appeared in French in *Démocratie et démocratisation dans le monde arabe* (Cairo: Dossiers du Centre d'Études et de Documentation Économique, Juridique et Sociale, 1992). The editors wish to thank CEDEJ for permission to include it in this book.

1. This is the question Leonard Binder raised in his stimulating study, *Islamic Liberalism, a Critique of Development Ideologies* (Chicago: University of Chicago Press, 1988), without, however, giving a conclusive response. See also Yahya Sadowski, "The New Orientalism and the Democracy Debate," *Middle East Report* 183 (July–August 1993), pp. 14–21, 40.

2. The discussion on religion, culture, and authenticity (*asala*), which, concentrating on the relationship of Islam, Arabism, and local tradition(s), has produced an enormous and ever-growing corpus of literature, will not be considered here. For the question of cultural transfer, see Bertrand Badie, "Le transfert de technologie politique dans le monde arabe, de l'importation à l'innovation," *Bulletin du CEDEJ* 23 (1988), pp. 109–123.

3. See, for example, Saad Eddin Ibrahim, ed., *Al-ta'addudiyya al-siyasiyya wa al-dimuqratiyya fi al-watan al-'arabi* [Political Pluralism and Democracy in the Arab World] (Amman: Arab Thought Forum, 1989); Muhammad Ahmad Khalafallah, "Al-islam baina wahdat al-iman wa-ta'addud al-qira'at wa al-mumarasat," in Saad Eddin Ibrahim, ed., *Al-sahwa al-islamiyya wa-humum al-watan al-arabi* [The Islamic Awakening and the Concerns of the Arab World] (Amman: Arab Thought Forum, 1988), pp. 147–164. For theoretical studies, see Ahmad Jalal Hammad, *Hurriyyat al-ra'y fi al-midan al-siyasi fi zill mabda' al-mashru'iyya, bahth muqaran fi al-dimuqratiyya al-gharbiyya wa al-islam* [Freedom of Opinion in the Political Sphere in Light of the Principle of *Mashru'iyya*] (Mansura: Dar al-wafa',

1987); Ahmad Shawqi al-Fanjari, *Al-hurriyya al-siyasiyya fi al-islam* [Political Liberties in Islam] (Kuwait: 1983). For a critical approach, see also 'Ali Umlil, *Fi shar'iyyat al-ikhtilaf* [On the Legality of Divergence] (Rabat: Al-majlis al-qawmi lil-thaqafa al-'arabiyya).

4. Andreas Meier, *Taqi al-Din al-Nabhani's Entwurf einer islamischen Verfassung* (Hamburg: unpublished Master's thesis, University of Hamburg, 1986); for the Tunisian activists of Hizb al-Tahrir, see *al-Mawqif* 42, 2 March 1985, and *Maghreb/Al-Maghrib*, 23 January 1989.

5. This discussion will not deal with the controversy over the nature, objective, and foundations of the *ijma'*, a controversy in which Islamic scholars have engaged since the earliest days of Islam. If, in the juridical theory of *usul al-fiqh*, the *ijma'* is almost universally accepted as one of the principal sources of law, there is no consensus on what constitutes the consensus itself: Is it a temporal element (the consensus of the *ulama*, or of all the Muslims of the same generation), or a local element (the consensus of the *ulama*, or of all the Muslims of the same region), or a combination of both (the consensus of the *ulama* of one generation and region)? If the second is the case, local custom and law (*'urf*) is being integrated into building consensus, adding one more element of diversity or pluralism to the legal heritage. For a detailed analysis, see Camille Mansur, *L'Autorité dans la pensée musulmane. Le concept d'Ijma' (Consensus) et la problematique de l'autorité* (Paris: J. Vrin, 1975).

6. The importance of the local factor in Islamic law and Islamist activism, which is supposed to develop its specific strategies in permanent interaction (*tafa'ul*) with its own society, is underscored by the leaders of the Sudanese and Tunisian Islamist movements, Hasan al-Turabi and Rashid al-Ghannushi. The last makes direct reference to local custom and law (*'urf*) recognized by the *ulama* of the Classical age: "Al-fikr al-islami bayn al-mithaliyya wa al-waqi'iyya," written in 1982, cited in *Mahawir islamiyya* [Islamic Axes] (Cairo: Bayt al-ma'rifa 1989), pp. 23–29; Hasan al-Turabi, "Al-sahwa al-islamiyya wa al-dawla al-qutriyya fi al-watan al-'arabi," in Ibrahim, ed., *Al-sahwa al-islamiyya*, pp. 307–341; al-Turabi, "Al-bu'd al-'alami lil-haraka al-islamiyya, al-tajriba al-sudaniyya," in 'Abdallah Fahd al-Nafisi, ed., *Al-haraka al-islamiyya: ru'ya mustaqbaliyya, awraq fi al-naqd al-dhati* [The Islamic Movement: A Futuristic Vision] (Cairo: Maktabat Madbuli, 1989), pp. 75–98. For the Jordanian Muslim Brothers, see *Liwa' al-Islam*, 30 December 1989, pp. 44 and 60. For a wider perspective, see James P. Piscatori, *Islam in a World of Nation-States* (Cambridge, UK: Cambridge University Press, 1986).

7. See, for example, Yusuf al-Qaradawi, *Al-sahwa al-islamiyya bayn al-ikhtilaf al-mashru' wa al-tafarruq al-madhmum, dirasa fi fiqh al-ikhtilaf fi daw' al-nusus wa al-maqasid al-shar'iyya* [The Islamic Awakening between Legitimate Diversity and Reprehensible Division] (Cairo: Dar al-sahwa, 1990).

8. 'Ali 'Abd al-Raziq, *Al-islam wa-usul al-hukm* [Islam and the Foundations of Governance] (Cairo: 1985); Farag Fawdah, *Qabl al-suqut* [Before the Fall] (Cairo: Dar al-bayda, 1987); Fawdah, *Hiwar hawl al-'almaniyya* [A Dialogue over Secularism] (Cairo: Mahrusa lil-nashr, 1987); Muhammad Sa'id al-'Ashmawi, *Usul al-shari'a* [Fundamentals of the Law] (Cairo: Maktabat Madbuli, 1978); *Al-shari'a al-islamiyya wa al-qanun al-misri (dirasa muqarana)* [The Islamic Shari'a and Egyptian Law] (Cairo: Maktabat Madbuli, 1988); *Al-khilafa al-islamiyya* [The Islamic Caliphate] (Cairo: Sina lil-nashr, 1990).

9. Cited from Malik b. Anas by al Ghazali, S. D. Goitein, *Studies in Islamic History and Institutions*, Vol. 1 (Leiden: E. J. Brill, 1966), p. 164. See also N. J. Coulson, *A History of Islamic Law* (Edinburgh: Edinburgh University Press, 1964), p. 101.

10. For apostasy and *takfir* in the classical tradition, see Rudolph Peters and Gert J. J. De Vries, "Apostasy in Islam," *Die Welt des Islams* 17 (1976–77), pp. 1–25; Joel L. Kraemer, "Apostates, Rebels and Brigands," in Ilai Alon, ed., *Religion and Government in the World of Islam* (Tel Aviv: Tel Aviv University, 1983); Werner Schwartz, *Gihad unter Muslimen* (Bonn: Orientalisches Seminar, 1980). For a concise contemporary statement, see Yusuf al-Qaradawi, in Yasir Farahat, *Humum al-muslim al-mu'asir fi fikr al-da'iyya al-islami al-duktur Yusuf al-Qaradawi* [The Concerns of the Modern Muslim in the Thought of Muslim Thinker Yusuf al-Qaradawi] (Cairo: 1988), pp. 99–102. For modern Egypt, see Salim 'Ali al-Bahnasawi, *Al-Hukm wa-qadiyyat takfir al-muslim* [Power and the Issue of Excommunicating Muslims] (Cairo: 1977).

11. Hasan al-Banna, "Da'watuna," in *Majmu'at rasa'il al-imam al-shahid Hasan al-Banna* [The Collected Letters of the Martyred Imam Hasan al-Banna] (Dar al-Shihab), pp. 23–25. To cite but one other example: 'Adnan 'Ali Rida al-Nahwi, *Malamih al-shura fi al-da'wa al-islamiyya* [The Features of Shura in the Islamic Call] (Riyadh: 1984), presents, in 685 pages, the most conservative and orthodox viewpoint possible with respect to political organization in general and *shura* in particular. For a notable exception, reflecting practical rather than theoretical considerations, see the Tunisian Rashid al-Ghannushi, who explicitly recognizes particular interests not only in the interpretation of reality, but also of the sacred texts: *Mahawir islamiyya*, pp. 25–29, 41–43, 143.

12. "Maslaha," in *Encyclopedia of Islam*, new edition. Contemporary authors refer notably to the *Muwafaqat fi usul al-shari'a* [Agreed Bases of the Law] ('Abdallah Daraz, ed., 4 Vols., Beirut, n.d.) by Abu Ishaq al-Shatibi, an *'alim* from Andalusia (died in 1388), representing the Malikite school, which today is popular in North Africa and Sudan. See Fahmi Huwaidi, *Al-Qur'an wa al-sultan* [The Quran and the Power] (Beirut; Cairo: Dar al-shuruq, 1981), and Khalid Muhammad Khalid, *Difa' 'an al-dimuqratiyya* [In Defense of Democracy] (Cairo: Dar Thabit, 1985).

13. Benjamin Braude, Bernard Lewis, eds., *Christians and Jews in the Ottoman Empire: The Functioning of a Plural Society*, 2 Vols. (New York: Holmes and Meier, 1982).

14. Al-Nahwi, *Malamih al-shura*, serves as a perfect example of this harmonizing approach, which denies the very possibility of conflict (obviously dictated by egotistical interests) between true believers.

15. Martin Kramer, "The Moral Logic of Hizballah," *Occasional Papers* 101 (Tel Aviv: The Dayan Center for Middle Eastern and African Studies, 1987), p. 2.

16. For a critical analysis of the unitarian view, which emphasizes the doctrinal and practical need for Muslim unity, see Ridwan al-Sayyid, *Al-umma wal-jama'a wal-sulta, dirasat fi al-fikr al-siyasi al-'arabi al-islami* [Community, Group, and Power: A Study in Arab Islamic Political Thought] (Beirut: 1984).

17. Peters and De Vries, "Apostasy in Islam."

18. Rif'at Sayyid Ahmad, *Li-madha a'damani Numayri? Qira'a fi awraq al-shaykh Mahmud Taha* [Why Did Numayri Execute Me?: A Reading in the Papers of Shaikh Mahmud Taha] (Cairo: Dar al-alif, 1985).

19. Farahat, *Humum al-muslim al-mu'asir*, pp. 79–81, 90–94.

20. See the famous *fatwas* against the Communists by the Shaikh al-Azhar, 'Abd al-Halim Mahmud: *Fatawa 'an al-shuyu'iyya* [Fatwas on Communism] (Cairo: Dar al-ma'arif, 1976).

21. For the viewpoint of a Syrian activist, see Munir Muhammad al-Ghudban (pseud.), *Al-tahaluf al-siyasi fi al-islam* [Political Alliances in Islam] (al-Zarqa': 1982).

22. *Majmu'at rasa'il*, in particular "Da'watuna," pp. 9–28, "Risalat al-mu'ta-mar al-khamis" (pp. 147–187), and "Nizam al-hukm" (pp. 209–227); see also Jabir Rizq, *Al-dawla wa al-siyasa fi fikr Hasan al-Banna* [The State and Politics in the Thought of Hasan al-Banna] (Mansura: Dar al-wafa', 1985).

23. Hasan al-Banna, "Risalat al-mu'tamar al-khamis," in *Majmu'at rasa'il*, pp. 157f.

24. The Brotherhood is included, as *hizb al-ikhwan al-muslimin*, in a study by Mahmud Mutawalli, *Misr wa al-hayat al-hizbiyya wa al-niyabiyya qabla sanat 1952* [Egypt, Political and Syndical Life before 1952] (Cairo: Dar al-thaqafa lil-tiba'a wa al-nashr, 1980), pp. 319–337. See also Richard P. Mitchell, *The Society of the Muslim Brothers* (London: 1969), pp. 232–294; Tariq al-Bishri, *Al-haraka al-siyasiyya fi misr, 1945–1952* [Political Activity in Egypt, 1945–1952], 2nd ed. (Beirut; Cairo: Dar al-shuruq, 1983); Ridwan al-Sayyid, *Al-islam al-mu'asir, nazarat fi al-hadir wa al-mustaqbal* [Contemporary Islam, Opinions on the Present and the Future] (Beirut: Dar al-'ulum al-'arabiyya, 1986), p. 24.

25. For internal criticism, see 'Abdallah al-Nafisi, "Introduction," *Al-haraka al-islamiyya*, pp. 11–32 (esp. pp. 24–31); and "Al-ikhwan al-muslimun fi misr: Al-tajriba wa al-khata'," *Al-haraka al-islamiyya*, pp. 203–268; Farid 'Abd al-Khaliq, "Nahwa muraja'at al-maqulat wa al-aliyat," *Al-haraka al-islamiyya*, pp. 311–321; Khalis Jalabi, *Fi al-naqd al-dhati, Darurat al-naqd al-dhati lil-haraka al-islamiyya* [On Self-Criticism: The Necessity of Self-Criticism in the Islamic Movement], 3rd ed. (Beirut: Mu'assasat al-risala, 1985). For the Tunisian movement, see Rashid al-Ghannushi, *Mahawir islamiyya*, p. 144, but also, *Qadat al-haraka al-islamiyya al-mu'asira, al-Banna-al-Mawdudi-al-Khumayni* [The Leaders of the Contemporary Islamic Movement: Al-Banna, al-Mawdudi, al-Khumayni] written in 1979, cited in *Maqalat*, I, 2nd ed. (Tunis: Matba 'at Tunis Qartaj, 1988), pp. 87–105; and Ahmida al-Nayfar, cited by François Burgat, *L'islamisme au Maghreb. La voix du Sud* (Paris: Karthala, 1988), pp. 244–247. For a general critique of the Islamist move-ment, see the Lebanese activist Fathi Yakan, *Ihdharu al-AIDS al-haraki? Zahirat tamazzuq al-buna al-tanzimiyya wa-kaifa nasun bunyatana?* [Beware the Organi-zational AIDS] (Beirut: 1990); and *Mushkilat al-da'wa wa al-da'iyya* [The Prob-lem of the Call and the Caller], 4th ed. (Beirut: 1968); Yusuf al-Qaradawi, *Al-sahwa al-islamiyya bayn al-juhud wa al-tatarruf* [The Islamic Awakening between Rejection and Extremism], 2nd ed. (Cairo: Dar al-shurug, 1984). See also my paper, "Die Korrektur der Irrtümer: Innerislamische Debatten um Theorie und Praxis der islamischen Bewegungen," in Cornelia Wunsch, ed., *XXV. Deutscher Orientalistentag, Vorträge* (Stuttgart: 1994), pp. 183–191.

26. Raymond Hinnebusch, *Egyptian Politics under Sadat: The Post-Populist Development of an Authoritarian-Modernizing State* (Cambridge, UK: Cambridge University Press, 1985).

27. Al-Nafisi, *Al-ikhwan al-muslimun fi misr*; Gudrun Krämer, *Ägypten unter Mubarak, Identität und nationales Interesse* (Baden-Baden: Nomos, 1986); and Krämer, *Die Wahl zur ägyptischen Volksversammlung vom April 1987* (Eben-hausen: Siftung Wissenschaft und Politik, 1987); Martin Forstner, "Auf dem legalen Weg zur Macht? Zur politischen Entwicklung der Muslimbruderschaft Ägyptens," *Orient* (Hamburg) 29, 3 (September 1988), pp. 386–422; Olaf Far-schid, "Hizbiyya: Die Neuorientierung der Muslimbruderschaft Ägyptens in den Jahren 1984 bis 1989," *Orient* (Hamburg) 30, 1 (March 1989), pp. 53–72.

28. Mahmud 'Abd al-Halim, *Al-ikhwan al-muslimun, ahdath sana'at al-tarikh* [The Muslim Brotherhood: Events which Made History], I (Alexandria: Dar al-da'wa, 1979), pp. 294–298, 324–329; for Tilmisani, see *al-Sharq al-Awsat*, 26 July 1984.

29. For an analysis of the elections see Mark N. Cooper, *The Transformation of Egypt* (Baltimore: Johns Hopkins University Press, 1982), pp. 204–234.

30. Gamal al-'Utaifi, *Al-tariq ila al-dimuqratiyya* [The Road to Democracy] (Cairo: 1978), pp. 37–41.

31. There is no room here for a detailed discussion of the history, implications, and perspectives of these political alliances. For the 1984 elections and the alliance with the Neo-Wafd, see 'Ali al-Din Hilal, ed., *Intikhabat majlis al-sha'b 1984* [The Parliamentary Elections, 1984] (Cairo: Markaz al-dirasat al-siyasiyya wa al-istratijiyya bi al-Ahram, 1986) and the polemical study by Zuhair Marwini, *Al-ladudan, al-wafd wa al-ikhwan* [Bad Boys: The Wafd and the Ikhwan] (Beirut: Dar Iqra', 1984); for 1987, see Gudrun Krämer, *Die Wahl*; Mona Makram Ebeid, "Political Opposition in Egypt: Democratic Myth or Reality," *Middle East Journal* 43, 3 (Summer 1989), pp. 423–436; for a very hostile view of the alliance, see Gamal 'Abd al-Sami', *Al-Kitab al-aswad li-ahzab misr, I. Al-tahaluf al-marhun* [The Black Book of Egyptian Parties, I. The Mortgaged Alliance] (Cairo: al-Matabi' Brissdan, 1989). For 1990, see Iman Farag, "La politique à l'égyptienne, lecture des élections législatives," *Monde Arabe. Maghreb-Machrek* 133 (July–September 1991), pp. 19–33.

32. *Uktubar*, 22 March 1987; for the Muslim Brotherhood, Hamid Abu al-Nasr, in *al-Sharq al-Awsat*, 8 March 1987; Krämer, *Die Wahl*, pp. 19–23.

33. See above notes 19 and 20.

34. *Al-Wafd*, 19 April 1984; *al-Sharq al-awsat*, 17 April 1987.

35. Interview with 'Umar al-Tilmisani in *al-Ahrar*, 7 November 1983; see also *al-Sha'b*, 25 March 1986; *al-Nur*, 9 April 1986.

36. *Al-Nur*, 26 November 1986; similar declarations by his predecessor, 'Umar al-Tilmisani, in *Akhir sa'a*, 6 February 1985 and *al-Sha'b*, 18 March 1986; also Ahmad Saif al-Islam, Hasan al-Banna, *al-Jumhuriyya*, 19 March 1987; Ma'-mun al-Hudaibi, *The Middle East*, May 1990, p. 22; see also *Liwa' al-Islam*, 26 February and 28 March 1990.

37. *Al-Sharq al-awsat*, 20 and 22 February 1987; *al-Jumhuriyya*, 19 March 1987; *Ruz al-Yusuf*, 20 April 1987. For the radical associations competing with the Muslim Brotherhood for control of the university, see *Al-taqrir al-istratiji al-'arabi 1988* [The Arab Strategic Bulletin 1988], (Cairo: Al-Ahram Center for Political and Strategic Studies, 1989), pp. 510–526; for a specific example, an incident at the University of Sohag, see *al-Musawwar*, 8 December 1988; *al-Ahrar*, 12 December 1988.

38. "Le politique à l'égyptienne," p. 24.

39. "Le politique à l'égyptienne," p. 24.

40. For a more detailed analysis see my paper, "The Integration of the Integrists: A Comparative Study of Egypt, Jordan and Tunisia," in Ghassan Salamé, ed., *Democracy Without Democrats? The Renewal of Politics in the Muslim World* (London: I. B. Taurus, 1994), pp. 200–226; and Azzam Tamimi, ed., *Power-Sharing Islam?* (London: Liberty/Muslim World Publications, 1993).

41. For the historical evolution of the MTI's discourse, see 'Abd al-Latif al-Harmasi, *Al-haraka al-islamiyya fi tunis* [The Islamic Movement in Tunisia] (Tunis: 1985), pp. 59–68, 73, 100–141; and Muhammad 'Abd al-Baqi al-Harmasi, "Al-Islam al-ihtijaji fi tunis," in *Al-harakat al-islamiyya al-mu'asira fi al-watan al-'arabi* [The Contemporary Islamic Movements in the Arab World] (Beirut: Center for Arab Unity Studies, 1987), pp. 247–299.

42. See 'Abd al-Latif al-Harmasi, *Al-haraka*, pp. 60f, 92; 'Abd al-Baqi al-Harmasi, "Al-Islam," pp. 256–258; *Realités*, 9 March 1984; *Maghreb/Al-Maghrib* 150, 5 May 1989.

43. Above all in "Urid an-atahaddath ila al-ikhwan," conference held in Cairo in 1951; see notably his *Al-tafsir al-siyasi al-islami fi mir'at kitabat al-ustadh Abi al-'Ala' al-Mawdudi, wa al-shahid Sayyid Qutb* [The Political Interpretation of Islam in the Writings of Abu al-'Ala' al-Mawdudi and the Martyr Sayyid Qutb], 2nd ed. (Cairo: 1980).

44. For al-Ghannushi's point of view, see his commentary on the paper of 'Abd al-Baqi al-Harmasi, in *Al-harakat al-islamiyya al-mu'asira*, pp. 300–308. For a critical analysis of the internal conflicts about the political strategy, 'Abd al-Hayy Bul'aras and Hisham al-Haji, "Al-ittijah al-islami: khilafat tuhaddid bil-inqisam," *al-Mawqif* 27, 17 November 1984.

45. The positions of this group, very interesting intellectually, albeit limited in their immediate impact, are presented in their journal *15/21*, published since 1982, and in a brochure written by Salah al-Din al Jurshi, Muhammad al-Qumani, and 'Abd al-Aziz al-Tamimi, *Al-muqaddimat al-nazariyya lil-islamiyyin al-taqaddu-miyyin, li-madha al-Islam? Kaifa nafhamuh?* [Theoretical Introduction for Progressive Islamists] (Tunis: Dar al-Buraq lil-Nashr, 1989). According to the journal *Realités* 184, 24 February–2 March 1989, they proposed at that time to form an Islamic association by the name of *al-tanwir wa al-tahrir* [Enlightenment and Liberation]. Note, in passing, the connections between this group and the Egyptian philosopher Hasan Hanafi, and the debates taking place in intellectual journals such as *al-Muslim al-mu'asir* (Beirut), *Fikr* (Cairo), *al-Hiwar* (Beirut), and *Ijtihad* (Beirut). See also Muhsin al-Mili, *Zahirat "al-yasar al-islami" (qira'a tahliliyya naqdiyya)* [The Phenomenon of the Islamic Left] (Tunis: 1983).

46. *Al-bayan al-ta'sisi li-harakat al-ittijah al-islami*, in al-Ghannushi, *Mahawir islamiyya*, pp. 157–160; for the press conference, *Maghreb/Al-Maghrib* 150, 5 May 1989.

47. This question divides, for example, the two Tunisian researchers, 'Abd al-Latif and 'Abd al-Baqi al-Harmasi: Whereas the first saw it as tactics that would be abandoned the moment the movement took power (*Al-haraka al-islamiyya fi tunis*, pp. 94, 130–136; article in *al-Mawqif*, 9 February 1985), the latter believed it to be a strategic decision by the leaders that might, however, be reversed by the militant rank-and-file of the movement, if the moderate line was not rewarded by the authorities (*al-Islam al-ihtijaji fi tunis*, pp. 283f.; *Realités* 189, 2–8 June 1989). For skeptical voices, see also *al-Mawqif* 62, 27 July 1985. Skepticism is based notably on a secret strategic paper of the MTI (*Ru'ya fi al-khatta al-marhaliyya lil-'amal al-siyasi*) [An Opinion on the Phased Plan for Political Action] circulated in late 1983 (French translation in *Soual* 5, April 1985, pp. 179–200); see *Realités*, 7 July and 17 November 1984; Bul'aras, al-Haji, "Al-ittijah al-islami." For a virulent criticism of the movement, see Hamma al-Hammami, *Didd al-zallamiyya. "Al-itti-jah al-islami" harakat nahda . . . am harakat inhitat?* [Against Oppression: "The Islamic Tendency Movement"], 3rd ed. (Tunis: Hamid lil nashr, 1989).

48. "Al-haraka al-islamiyya wa al-tahdith," conference held at the University of Khartum in 1979/1980, cited in al-Ghannushi, *Mahawir islamiyya*, pp. 31–44 (40f.); interview with the newspaper *al-Mujtama'*, in *Mahawir Islamiyya*, pp. 141–147, with an explicit criticism of the Egyptian Brotherhood, which arrogated to itself the role of guardian over its society (p. 145); commentary on the paper of 'Abd al-Baqi al-Harmasi, in *al-Harakat al-islamiyya al-mu'asira*, pp. 300–308. Al-Ghannushi has since published his thoughts in a book-length study, *Al-hurriyat al-'amma fi al-dawla al-islamiyya* [Public Liberties in the Islamic State] (Beirut: Center for Arab Unity Studies, 1993). See also *Realités/Haqa'iq* 37, 13 July 1984; interview with 'Abd al-Fattah Mourou, *Realités* 12, 19, and 26 April 1985; analyses, *Realités* 180, 27 January–2 February 1989, and *al-Mawqif* 150, 5 May 1989.

2

Civil Society:
Actors and Activism,
Empowerment
and Peripheralization

7

The Concept of
Civil Society and the Arab World

Mustapha Kamel al-Sayyid

Despite the current use of the term "civil society" in scholarly debates on transitions from authoritarianism in countries of Eastern Europe and parts of the South, social scientists are not in agreement either on the usefulness of the concept or its precise definition. This debate divides academics not only of the North but also of the South, some of whom see in the concept yet another example of an ideological product exported by the now postindustrial center to intellectuals of the periphery to perpetuate its dependency. It is true that very few concepts of social science enjoy consensus among its practitioners. However, this fact alone is no consolation to those willing to use the concept. For the debate in this particular case is not limited to its contours; rather it extends, more seriously, to the appropriateness of the concept as a tool for the understanding of social and political processes presumably taking place in non-Western societies.

Arab intellectuals, espousing different ideological causes, have engaged their theoretical arsenals in this battle, which has taken place in scientific conferences and on the pages of Arab periodicals. Without denying the lack of autonomy of theoretical production in the Arab world, the debate on this concept in Arab countries did not simply echo similar debates in the center. Arab intellectuals of various ideological and scientific camps had preoccupations of their own, stemming from particular features of their societies and polities. The arguments each camp marshaled in support of its position have therefore enriched the debate about civil society worldwide, both in scope and in content.

This chapter discusses very briefly some of the theoretical issues raised by Arab intellectuals engaged in this debate, including the scientific status of the concept, the universality of any of its definitions, premodern origins of civil society in the Arab world, the actors qualified to be among its collective members at present, the distribution of power within civil society and, finally, deciding which Arab countries come closest to an acceptable definition of civil society.

Scientific Status of the Concept

Why has the concept of civil society so suddenly become a coin of wide circulation since the 1980s, nearly five decades after the death of the latest prominent philosopher who accorded it a central place in his theoretical apparatus? Is resurgence of interest in this concept a manifest indication of the realization by social scientists that, in using it, they could illuminate certain aspects of concrete changes that took place in some regions, changes referred to by Samuel Huntington as democracy's "third wave"? Or is it simply an ideological tool, used by some intellectuals and politicians in order to propagate a certain model of society that had been presented under different labels many times before?

Those who are skeptical about the scientific status of this concept have formulated three arguments in favor of their call for its rejection. They would argue, first, that it is nearly impossible to come to a commonly accepted definition of the civil society concept, as a close examination of its history would suggest only one conclusion, namely that it has meant different things to different people. Adam Ferguson, John Locke, Friedrich Hegel, Karl Marx, and Antonio Gramsci, to name but the most prominent among those who had recourse to that term, each employed the concept to denote certain aspects of social reality at variance with what was meant by any of the others. While Adam Ferguson did not distinguish between civil society and the state, John Locke considered it the only foundation for a legitimate constitutional order. Hegel had stressed the conflictual nature of "civil society," which needs the state to acquire a sense of purpose and unity. Marx added that such a conflictual nature, rooted in the social division of labor, would disappear only in a communist society, which would put an end to both the division of labor and the state. The Italian political philosopher and leader Antonio Gramsci was concerned about demonstrating how institutions of civil society could play a dynamic role in perpetuating the hegemony of one class or in enabling a dominated class to establish its counterhegemony.[1] Critics of the civil society concept would find no possible common ground among these philosophers on which an acceptable definition of this concept could be established.[2]

They would add, second, that the sudden resurgence of the concept in the 1980s owes much to the wishes of conservative scholars and politicians in the advanced capitalist countries. These pursue their ideological crusade against those scholars and leaders who are not convinced that capitalism is the only solution to all problems of underdevelopment as well as authoritarianism. Such conservative scholars assert that a civil society is inseparable from a capitalist economy. In their writings, civil society is a value-laden term, uncritically offered as a panacea for all problems of those societies that have not yet acceded to the stage of capitalist nirvana.[3]

Finally, these critics would argue that talk about civil society is only old wine in new bottles. This concept is merely a new device to repeat often-heard discourses about civilized nations, development, modernization, and so on. According to them, conservative scholars strive to rescue discredited notions of modernization by reformulating their essential arguments, largely of an ideological nature, using the older terminology of civil society. Such critics hold that the new discourse is no different from the old talk about structural differentiation, subsystem autonomy, and secularization of political culture, echoed in books about political development in the 1960s.[4]

The critics are correct in their account of the difficulties of disentangling a commonly accepted definition of that concept out of the voluminous ideological discourse of which it has been recently a part. However, societal actors in different parts of the world, notably in Eastern Europe and countries of the South, have recently become not only more assertive but also have displaced regimes that seemed to be very well entrenched. Earlier social scientists did use the concept of social movements in different contexts—to characterize those social groups and actors of a new type who made their presence temporarily felt on the political scene. However, the social movements concept might not be adequate to describe what could become in future a new balance of forces between the state and society. If the concept of civil society could be reformulated instead to suggest this balance of forces, without linking it necessarily to a particular economic system, or at least considering its association with capitalism as a research hypothesis, that concept might prove useful indeed.

Definition of Civil Society

In a similar manner to the international debate about the concept of civil society, the Arab debate gave rise to basic disagreements among intellectuals on both the scientific status of the concept and on its applicability to Arab conditions. Some of the arguments formulated on the pages of international academic journals were echoed by Arab intellectuals, while some new issues have been raised by other participants in the debate. The debate itself reached its climax in early 1992, at the time of the symposium on civil society in the Arab world organized by the Center of Arab Unity

Studies in Beirut[5] and the publication of the first issue of the *Civil Society Newsbulletin* by the Ibn Khaldoun Center for Development Studies in Cairo. Since not all participants in that debate enjoy access to the contributions of foreign scholars not widely available in the Arab world or in Arabic, the interest shown by Arab commentators in such issues reflects specific concerns of Arab intellectuals and are not simply an echo of theoretical and ideological discourses in the North.

Any observer of that debate could discern divisions similar to those that characterized the debate in the North. Some Arab commentators categorically reject the concept; others suggest alternative terms more appropriate to the Arab context; a third group calls for enlarging the concept to include certain groups not usually considered within civil society in its European definitions; a fourth group prefers to maintain one variant or another of the concept in its classic formulations.

Those who reject the concept express the conviction that what Arab countries needed for the time being was to strengthen the Arab state, which at this stage was incapable of carrying out its developmental task and was subject to penetration by foreign powers. A strong society, in their view, would first require a strong state. Arab historical experience suggested, according to them, that it was usually the state, under Muhammad 'Ali in Egypt, for example, that initiated and carried out social reform. The discourse on civil society at present would only serve to undermine a weakened Arab state. It accords very well with the interests of foreign powers, but not those of Arab peoples. This statist position was advocated particularly by certain Nasserite intellectuals, but might not reflect the point of view of all Arab nationalists.[6]

Some Islamist intellectuals have assumed a form of apologist stand in that debate, expressing the belief that Islamic states did not try to dominate society and that the practice in such states accorded a considerable measure of autonomy to several societal actors, which they found to be a useful precedent for Muslim countries at present. The term *mujtama' madani*, the usual Arab translation of "civil society," smacks in their view of its Western origins, which stress membership in a particular community qualified as civil, as distinct from any other community, particularly one based on religion. These intellectuals prefer, therefore, another term that could reflect particular features of Arab culture. For one, an alternative term was *al-mujtama' al-ahli* or the "unofficial society,"[7] while another has favored *mu'assasat al-'umma* or the "nation's institutions," guided by *maqasid islamiyya* or "Islamic goals."[8]

The Islamists' stance on this issue was no different from that of some liberal nationalists who have called for maintaining the concept of civil society while adapting it to reflect specific conditions of Arab culture. Thus, without using the term "unofficial society," advocates of this view came closest to identifying civil society institutions with all those economic, cultural, or religious institutions that are not subject to a single uniform regime imposed by public authorities and that act under conditions allowing them to expand, renovate, compete with each other, and innovate in their activities.[9]

Finally, a minority of Arab intellectuals found that the analytical power of the concept of civil society would be diluted if it were to be given a different meaning in the Arab context. The analytical power of the concept resides, in their view, in its distinction between a civil society and all other types of society that are judged to be uncivil. Such a distinction would lose much of its theoretical and political importance if it were to be diluted by including, under its umbrella, organizations based on primordial loyalties or that are not founded on the free consent of their members. However, those who adopt this view disagree on the particular variant of the European definition of civil society that should serve as the point of reference. The Ibn Khaldoun Center opts for a Lockean approach, while publications of the Arab Research Center in Cairo favor a Marxian perspective.[10]

One should not blame Arab intellectuals for this lack of agreement on a commonly accepted definition of the concept, for it is not in the nature of social science debates—in the Arab world or elsewhere—to produce a consensus. In fact, more could be gained through a dialectical process of intellectual exchange of argument and counterargument. It is more useful for such a debate to decide about the criteria to use in evaluating different approaches to this problem.

Does this discourse refer to an ongoing process in the Arab world, or at least in some of its countries, similar to what has happened in other parts of the world at an earlier date, namely a higher degree of assertiveness on the part of certain societal actors, of a modern nature, vis-à-vis the state? If such a process does indeed take place, then it would be meaningful to analyze it using the same concepts that have been used elsewhere. The specific features of that process could be gauged only if they were to be analyzed using a common yardstick to compare the process to what happened in other parts of the world. On the other hand, if there are no indications that such a process is taking place in the Arab world, then it would be reasonable to look for other concepts that could come to terms with unique features of the Arab situation.

One could already find several indications of the assertiveness of societal actors in many Arab countries (e.g., in Mauritania, Morocco, Algeria, Tunisia, Egypt, Jordan, Lebanon, the Occupied Territories, Yemen, and Kuwait). One could see also stirrings of such societal forces in other countries—in Syria, for example, or even in Saudi Arabia. The concept of civil society could be used to shed light on this process, without claiming that a civil society in the full sense does exist in any of these countries.

A synthesis of both Lockean and Marxian discourses could be useful, not as an eclectic list of the features of civil society, but as a meaningful framework of analysis of both the structure and process of civil society. The principal propositions in this framework are the following:

1. A civil society would exist only in countries in which class divisions are becoming increasingly important as a basis of social organization and in shaping citizens' perceptions of their own situations.
2. In a civil society, the state abides by certain rules in dealing with societal actors, recognizing in particular their autonomy.
3. Citizens relate voluntarily to each other on the basis of shared interests that do not exclusively replicate primordial ties.
4. State and society accept and protect the exercise of the right to dissent by citizens, including expressing views at variance with those of the majority, provided that dissenting minorities do not use force in persuading others to adopt their views.
5. Civil society does not necessarily encompass the whole of society in any country.
6. The presence of a civil society in any country does not necessarily entail that groups forming this civil society are equal in terms of political resources, including their relative access to state authorities.[11]

Components of Civil Society

What collective actors constitute civil society in Arab countries? Obviously the answer depends on the definition of civil society as well as on the social structure and political system prevailing in any particular country. Some collective actors are, nevertheless, the object of consensus among Arab intellectuals. They unanimously consider them part and parcel of any civil society, but they disagree on the status of other actors, excluded by some commentators while included in that society by others. The dividing line is the definition adopted for civil society by these intellectuals. However, in all cases, some actors are definitely more influential than others and some large social groups do not find any place in civil society, either directly or indirectly.

Political parties and secondary associations of all types are unanimously accepted by Arab commentators as the backbone of civil society. Indeed, the discourse on the subject gives the impression that civil society in Arab countries is limited to such associations. It is usually understood in Arab debates that such organizations are meant when that term is invoked by a speaker in a public meeting or in an article in a newspaper or scholarly journal. Thus, political parties, professional associations, business groups, trade unions, private societies—*jam'iyyat*, that is, social clubs, literary and scientific societies—all are accepted as part of civil society. Some authors would exclude political parties from civil society, however, as they have more to do with the state. Yet the fact that most opposition political parties have no chance of forming the government in nearly all Arab countries would give credence to the view that they act more as interest groups than as political parties intent on the exercise of power.

Neotraditional institutions that combine both primordial ties and a modern formal organization would also fit easily in a commonly acceptable definition of civil society. Purely religious associations established by Muslims or Christians, such as Young Muslim or Young Christian associations in Egypt, the Shi'ites' Amal or Hizballah in Lebanon, as well as organizations in the capital city that bring together people who came originally from a certain province, could be examples of this category. Thus people who came from upper Egypt, or Sharqiyya, Gharbiyya, and other governorates of the Nile Delta could find in Cairo associations at their service. Country people who moved to Aden in the late 1930s and early 1940s established social clubs founded on ties of common birthplace, such as Nadi Dhabman and Nadi al-Qubeita, through which they carried out their political struggle against the monarchy in Yemen.[12]

More problematic in this respect would be traditional groups that have not yet acquired a formal organization. Islamist writers point to a long-established tradition in Islamic states in the past of respect for the autonomy of various types of groups ranging from the *ulama*, or men of religion, and other religious orders of Christians and Jews, to guilds as well as the charitable *waqf*-based institutions.[13] They comment extensively on the role of *waqf* institutions in providing educational, health, and welfare services in Islamic societies as a good example of a powerful spirit of private voluntary action under Islamic civilization. As they enlarge the concept of civil society to encompass all nonofficial bodies, they would like to include all institutions of a traditional nature under the umbrella of this society, regardless of their possession of a formal organization. Thus, both Wajih Kuthrani and Burhan Ghalyun would include tribal, communal, and familial formations. A Yemeni intellectual argued that tribes in his country, with their customs, traditional and electoral arrangements, and division of labor practices, are the oldest institutions of civil society in Yemen.[14] Although at present these formations in Arab countries are no longer purely traditional institutions—they have some modern features such as involvement in a cash economy and the use of modern means of communication and mobilization—their inclusion within the concept of civil society is bound to dilute the civil nature of that society. Membership of such formations is not based on consent and hence they cannot be considered voluntary associations. Moreover, what would be the dividing line between a civil society and a "natural society" if formations founded on primordial ties are considered part of the former? A state-society framework for the analysis of politics must consider the role such formations play in politics, but their political involvement alone is not a sufficient basis for including them in a civil society or even of labeling a society in which they are politically active as civil in character.

Such considerations do not apply to politico-religious movements in the Arab world like the Islamic Salvation Front (FIS) in Algeria, the Nahda Party in Tunisia, the Muslim Brotherhood in Egypt, and a host of other organizations in nearly all Arab countries. For such movements are based on voluntary membership and do possess formal organization, though not always recognized by Arab states. Islamists claim that they are a prominent component of civil society since they enjoy the support of large numbers of citizens and are active in various areas of social action, thus reflecting the vitality and innovative disposition of wide strata of the population who had hitherto been excluded from politics.[15] Their opponents counter that such movements espouse totalitarian ideologies and are committed to a model of society in which those who hold different beliefs or even views have no place. Some statements of FIS leaders during the legislative election campaign in 1991 confirmed suspicions of opponents of the Islamic movement that intellectual dissent, diversity of views, freedom of expression and association—all basic features of a civil society—have no place in a country ruled by an Islamist movement.[16] Such suspicions were heightened by the statements of Shaikh Muhammad al-Ghazali, a prominent figure in the Muslim Brotherhood in Egypt, who testified at the recent trial of the assassins of the secularist writer Farag Fawdah that the penalty for apostasy in Islam is murder, to be carried out by any Muslim.[17] Practices of ruling groups in countries claiming to be guided by principles of Islamic *shari'a*, such as the Sudan since June 1989 and Iran since the revolution, did not allay fears that the exercise of power by any of these movements that raise the banner of political Islam would be equivalent, in the view of their critics, to the death of a civil society.[18] Leaders of Islamic movements, with the exception of the more radical groups in each of these countries, struggle to convince other political forces that such suspicions are unfounded. Their endeavor in this respect is enormously difficult, given some of their practices in the past and many of their statements at present.

Another important observation flows from this account of all possible candidates for membership in civil society, namely that the civil society likely to emerge in Arab countries has favored private business groups in countries such as Morocco, Tunisia, Egypt, and Kuwait. The pro-monarchy parties, with close links to business groups, have been the backbone of nearly all Moroccan governments since the late 1960s, a position that has been maintained despite the limited successes of the leftist Socialist Union of Popular Forces and the nationalist Istiqlal in the most recent legislative election in the country, in the spring and summer of 1993. Privatization measures in Tunisia have reinforced the position of the country's business groups, well represented within the ruling Democratic Constitutionalist Rally.[19]

In Egypt, the strong ties between government officials on the one hand and private and foreign enterprises on the other hand are illustrated by lists of membership in businessmen's associations, and the post-cabinet careers of several ministers as well as their family connections. The major lobbies of businessmen in the country, such as the Egyptian-American Business Council, the American Chamber of Commerce in Egypt, and the Egyptian Businessmen's Society, include among their members many former ministers and senior officials of the government. Cabinet members since the 1970s aspire to lead private firms once they quit the cabinet. Several of them became major bankers or heads of powerful joint-ventures in the country immediately after they were dropped from the cabinet under Presidents Sadat and Mubarak. That was the case of Dr. 'Abd al-'Aziz Hijazi, president of one bank and a joint venture, the late Kamal Hassan 'Ali, who headed the Egyptian-Gulf Bank, Mustapha Khalil, and many other former ministers. President Husni Mubarak, when asked about the business activities of ministers' sons and relatives who win lucrative government contracts, did not find anything wrong with such activities, since his government should not discriminate in this respect against sons of ministers.[20] Finally, in Kuwait the last legislative election brought the head of the country's powerful Chamber of Commerce to the post of speaker of the National Assembly.

The Islamic movement has benefited from this development, but its most important factions are outlawed in Algeria, Tunisia, and Egypt. There are also indications that leaders of the mainstream faction of the Islamic movement in countries such as Egypt, Jordan, and Kuwait have strong business interests.[21]

On the other hand, under conditions of both economic and political liberalization, which stimulate the emergence of civil society in some Arab countries at present, two groups face the risk of marginalization, with one likely to be marginalized within civil society, while the second faces the prospect of marginalization outside civil society. Organized labor, definitely a component of civil society, has witnessed an erosion of both its political power and living conditions in countries that have pursued economic liberalization. Former authoritarian systems ruled by a single party based their legitimacy on an implicit social contract with labor and the urban and rural masses, as well as the middle classes. With the demise of such regimes, organized labor could not compete successfully with business groups either in postpopulist regimes or in regimes committed to a liberal model of development since independence, such as Morocco and Lebanon. Organized labor resorted to collective protest actions in Morocco, Tunisia, Lebanon, and Yemen, but did not succeed in regaining better access to state authorities in any of these countries. Nor is it likely to improve its position in this respect with the mounting pressures of international financial institutions or governments of donor countries to pursue policies of structural adjustment, whose burden falls squarely on organized labor as well as on the salaried middle class.

Organized labor's loss of power was vividly demonstrated in many Arab countries in the last decade by the forced resignation of its former influential leaders, the imprisonment of recalcitrant unionists, and the lack of response to workers' demands for protection against the galloping cost of living, which led trade unions to engage in widespread collective protest actions. Thus Habib Bin 'Ashur in Tunisia and Sa'd Muhammad Ahmad in Egypt had to withdraw from the trade union scene under government pressures in the two countries. A powerful leader of one of Morocco's federations of trade unions spent nearly two years in prison for his opposition to the government. It is no wonder, under such conditions of lack of responsiveness by the government to trade unionists' demands, that workers engage in collective protest actions on a wide scale, resorting to strikes, marches, and demonstrations, which gave rise to bloody clashes with security forces, who do not accept this method of expressing workers' demands. Such protest actions took place recently in Morocco, Algeria, Lebanon, and Yemen, and on a local scale in Egypt.[22]

As for the urban poor and the peasants, who do not possess organizations acting on their behalf, they find no place for themselves in an emerging civil society. Growing numbers of urban and rural poor in Arab countries that are not wealthy petroleum exporters have not prompted any attempt to establish proper mediating mechanisms between these groups and organizations of civil society. It is not certain that Islamic movements do reflect aspirations of these groups for decent survival, as they stress the importance of issues that are not of immediate concern to them.

Could an emergent civil society survive with the majority of the population condemned to a situation of marginality in every sense of the word, either within or outside civil society?

Civil Society and Arab Political Systems

Despite many disagreements among Arab intellectuals they seem to concur on one thing, namely that a genuine civil society, no matter how it is defined, does not exist in any Arab country. None of them could seriously question this claim, for civil society involves for all of them an ideal to which no Arab country has come close. Civil society evokes an image of a political order respecting the civil and political rights of citizens, leaving free space for a wide variety of their activities, and responding to their deeply held wishes and aspirations for personal dignity and decent living. Arab political systems are short of all these qualities.

However, applying some of the criteria mentioned in the previous section of this chapter, Arab political systems would differ with respect to the extent to which civil society associations have evolved. Of all the five criteria, the line of demarcation among many Arab countries in this respect coincides with the extent to which freedom of association is respected. On the basis of this criterion, three groups of countries can be discerned:

1. Countries that allow a reasonable measure of freedom of association, authorizing political parties and permitting the establishment of various types of professional associations, class-based organizations, and private societies. These are the countries that embarked on the path of political liberalization (e.g., Mauritania, Morocco, Algeria between 1988 and 1991, Tunisia, Egypt, Jordan, and Yemen). Kuwait comes close to this group, although political parties have not been legally authorized, but different political groupings are known to exist and have openly contested legislative elections.

2. Countries where associations of various types do exist but are subject to heavy controls by a dominant party, a single party, or a mass organization. This is the case in regimes that used to be considered the radical regimes of the Arab world, namely Libya, Syria, Iraq, and Sudan.

3. Finally, countries where freedom of association is not recognized, whether for political parties, professional associations, or trade unions. This is the situation notably in countries that are members of the Gulf Cooperation Council, with the exception of Kuwait.

Following this classification, one could identify three types of regimes with respect to the presence of features of civil society. The first group of countries is those characterized by an emergent civil society, while the second consists of regimes suppressing it and the third group offers weak signs of its presence. This classification suggests that civil society is absent in societies in which class divisions are of recent origin and still largely overshadowed by ethnic and tribal loyalties. However, such a criterion is not sufficient to explain the absence of civil society and should be combined with the nature of the political system. This classification also demonstrates the close link between political liberalization and the emergence of civil society. No other criterion could bring together countries that are as far apart in terms of their social structures and history of state formation as Egypt and Jordan or Yemen, or, for that matter, Tunisia and Kuwait.

Some observers of Arab politics have expressed the hope that the presence even of an emergent civil society could be an early step toward full democratization of Arab political systems.[23] However, the opposition of sections of ruling groups in some Arab countries, particularly Tunisia and Egypt, to a recognition of the presence of the Islamist movement as an autonomous political actor, especially after the aborted electoral victory of the FIS in Algeria, dampened such hopes. There are no signs that other countries in this category are about to make a leap forward toward full democratization of their political systems. Ruling groups in such countries do keep various mechanisms of control that they do not hesitate to use when the vitality of the nascent civil society threatens to exceed the limits they have fixed to guarantee their continued monopoly over national structures of decisionmaking.

Recent practices of ruling groups in Tunisia, Egypt, and Kuwait illustrate how control of such mechanisms could be used to delay the emergence of a powerful civil society. In the three countries, laws on freedom of association were introduced or amended with the deliberate intention of excluding certain groups or personalities from associations altogether or preventing them from occupying any leading positions in them. The Tunisian government issued a law on associations that bans leaders of political parties from membership of the highest organs in the associations. The ban was aimed at the Tunisian League of Human Rights (TLHR), whose secretary-general happened to be a leader of the Social Democrats' Movement. Prominent members of the TLHR were divided on this issue, with some of them arguing that the law constituted a flagrant violation of freedom of association and amounted to a grave interference in the internal affairs of their association, while other members were willing to abide by its provisions. Dispute over this law has not enabled the association so far to resume its activities[24]—a situation with which the Tunisian government does not feel unhappy, particularly since its human rights violations, including torture, were condemned in reports of international human rights organizations.[25]

The Egyptian government, taking advantage of its near-monopoly of representation in the People's Council (the country's national assembly), pushed through the adoption of a law on elections in professional associations, claiming that it aims at encouraging members' participation. The law was adopted without any consultation with leaders of the country's 21 professional associations. Seventeen professional associations rejected the law, arguing that it violated the constitutional right of associations to adopt their internal regulations. The law required participation of at least 50 percent of members of professional syndicates in elections of their leading organs; failing that, members would be called on to participate in a second election, and a quorum of one third of them would be sufficient. If such a condition is not met, the syndicate in question would be run by an administrative council, made up of the oldest members of the association and headed by a senior judge. Leaders of syndicates argued that it would be difficult to get this relatively high quorum in large syndicates with a heterogeneous membership, such as the lawyers, doctors, and graduates of faculties of commerce. The fine provided for in the law was not, in their view, a practical way to encourage participation, since it was too low and difficult to collect. Moreover, they found it incomprehensible that a law claiming to aim at enhancing members' involvement in the affairs of their syndicates bans the holding of elections in the syndicates on weekends or during official holidays.[26]

Similarly, the Kuwaiti government has recently joined those Arab governments that restrict freedom of association by issuing a decree declaring that all associations established since the Iraqi invasion of the country were illegal. Thus, all human rights organizations in the country, including the popular Committee for the Care of Kuwait's War Prisoners, were outlawed. The government claimed that all such organizations were not officially authorized, but many observers believed that the government was concerned that their example would be followed by others. It also wanted, in their view, to appropriate exclusively for itself any credit for progress in the release of Kuwaiti prisoners of war believed to be still in Iraq.[27]

As for the second category of Arab countries, where associations of various types exist but are subject to heavy controls exercised by the government through a dominant, single party or a mass organization, there are no signs that the grip of the state on associational life is loosening. In these countries—including Iraq, Syria, Sudan, and Libya—the government's tight controls were maintained despite the release of hundreds of political prisoners in Syria, for instance, some of whom had spent more than 20 years in prison.

Nor are there indications that any of the countries in the third category are about to move up to the second category. Some middle-class associations—for example, lawyers or teachers—and social and sports clubs have come into being in some of these countries, particularly Bahrain and the United Arab Emirates; but trade unions are banned in all of them, whether for foreigners or nationals. The limited attempt by some forward-looking members of the elite to promote the human rights cause, while using the symbolic language of Islam together with the regime, was aborted. Thus, Saudi authorities reacted very harshly to the announcement that a society for the defense of *shari'a* rights had started its activities. It banned the society, arresting some of the founders, and dismissed other members from their posts. The government obtained the help it wanted from the College of Ulama, which issued a statement condemning the establishment of such an association as unnecessary, since in the *ulama*'s view, the rights of people under the Islamic *shari'a* are well protected in the country.[28] This incident suggests that the ruling monarchy in Saudi Arabia is adamantly opposed to any attempts by any other group to share with it the legitimating use of Islamic concepts. An association suggesting that the rights of citizens under the Islamic *shari'a* are in need of protection in Saudi Arabia would cast doubts on the claim of spokesmen of the monarchy and its allies in the religious establishment that they alone are capable of guaranteeing such rights.

Conclusion

Despite much debate about ideological uses of the civil society concept, it might be possible to arrive at a definition of civil society that would make it a useful tool in analyzing processes of empowerment of certain societal actors and their assertiveness vis-à-vis the state.

Some Arab intellectuals have suggested either expanding the concept of civil society to include traditional groups or replacing it by other concepts they consider more appropriate for Arab culture. However, such alternative formulations would dilute the concept and render the comparison with other regions rather difficult.

According to the criteria of civil society suggested in this chapter, an emergent civil society could be said to exist in some Arab countries that have embarked on a process of political liberalization. It is not a general feature of all Arab political systems. Components of civil society are suppressed or controlled by the state in another category of Arab countries and are not allowed to exist in a third category. However, even where an emergent civil society is said to exist, it is rather elitist in nature, since large masses of the people are either marginalized within civil society—for example, organized labor—or excluded from it—for example, the urban and rural poor.

The march toward a full-fledged civil society is often interrupted by the restrictive measures on associational life several Arab states are accustomed to introducing whenever they perceive a challenge to their power by any organizations of civil society. Recent examples of such practices are found in Egypt, Tunisia, and Kuwait. Similarly strict censorship was imposed on the media by the Lebanese government, which threatened to stifle expression of views critical to the government in a country that prided itself in the Arab world on the freedom of its media.

Governments in Arab countries are not solely to blame for the sluggish emergence of civil society in the Arab world. Certain factions of the Islamicist movement in Algeria and Egypt have demonstrated intolerance toward ideas and people who dare to think differently about their country's affairs. Some prominent Algerian intellectuals have been assassinated, probably by militants of the Islamic Salvation Front, because they disagreed with some of its views on Algerian society. Followers of the Islamist movement in Egypt have also found it convenient to describe anyone who disagrees with their movement on any issue to be an apostate, and hence, presumably, liable to murder according to Shaikh Muhammad al-Ghazali's views. This Islamist discourse led their followers to assassinate the secularist writer Farag Fawdah in June 1992 and to attempt, unsuccessfully, to murder the novelist and Nobel laureate Naguib Mahfouz in October 1994.

As the Islamist movement has gained a prominent place in society and politics in several Arab countries where a civil society has made large strides, such as Egypt, Jordan, Yemen, and Kuwait, one wonders whether actions of alleged assassins of intellectuals in Algeria and Egypt and attitudes toward freedom of thought and expression revealed by some leaders of the Islamist movement in the two countries are typical of all Islamist movements or are simply individual, isolated cases.

Some Arab intellectuals have come to the conclusion that, on such issues, there are no differences between the "radicals" and the "moderates" within the Islamist movement. The two factions are all ready to identify anyone who disagrees with their views to be an apostate who should be murdered. This writer is of the view that such differences do indeed exist within the Islamicist movement. Thus, although Islamist figures who spoke on this issue showed solidarity with Shaikh Muhammad al-Ghazali, it was clear they felt embarrassed when forced to do so.

The future of civil society in Arab countries is therefore uncertain. The process of political liberalization, which allowed its organizations autonomy and freedom of action, stopped short of full democratization of political systems in some countries where it has taken place, like Egypt and Tunisia, and was reversed in others, namely the Sudan and Algeria. On the other hand, some important organizations of civil society that could come to power in a situation of full democratization have totalitarian claims that might endanger the survival of civil society itself.

Are such difficulties in the emergence of civil society in Arab countries due to Arab political culture or to the present economic and social crisis in many of them? As the debates in Part I of this volume suggest, this is a question for which, at present, there is no clear answer.

Notes

1. Norberto Bobbio, "Gramsci and the Conception of Civil Society," in Chantal Mouffe, ed., *Gramsci and Marxist Theory* (London: Routledge and Kegan Paul, 1979).

2. Saif al-Din 'Abd al-Fattah, "Al-mujtama' al-madani wa al-dawla fi al-fikr wa al-mumarasa al-islamiyya al-mu'assira" [Civil Society and Contemporary Islamic Thought and Practice], in *Al-Mujtama' al-madani fi al-watan al-Arabi wa dawruhu fi tahqiq al-dimuqratiyya* [Civil Society in the Arab World and Its Role in Establishing Democracy] (Beirut: Center of Arab Unity Studies [CAUS], 1992).

3. Abd al-Kader Zghal, "Le concept de société civile et la transition vers la democratie," in Michel Camau, ed., *Changements Politiques au Maghreb* (Paris: Éditions du CNRS, 1991).

4. Burhan Ghalyun, "Bina' al-mujtama' al-madani al-'arabi, dawr al-'awamil al-dakhiliyya wa al-kharijiyya" [Establishing Arab Civil Society: The Role of Internal and External Factors], in CAUS, *Al-mujtama' al-madani*.

5. CAUS, *Al-mujtama' al-madani*.

6. Hussam 'Isa, "Commentary," in CAUS, *Al-mujtama' al-madani*.

7. Wajih Kuthrani, "Al-mujtama' wa al-dawla fi al-tarikh al-arabi" [Society and State in Arab History], in CAUS, *Al-mujtama' al-madani*.

8. Seif al-Din 'Abd al-Fattah, "Al-Mujatama' al madani."

9. Ghalyun, "Bina' al-mujtama'," p. 738.

10. For the definition of civil society adopted by the Ibn Khaldoun Center, see Saad Eddin Ibrahim, *Civil Society*; Center of Arab Research, *Qadaya al-mujtama' al-madani al-'arabi fi daw' utruhat Gramsci* [Questions of Arab Civil Society in the Light of Gramsci's Theses] (Cairo: Center of Arab Research and Eibal Foundation for Studies and Publishing, 1992).

11. Mustapha K. al-Sayyid, "A Civil Society in Egypt?" *Middle East Journal* 97, 2 (Spring 1993).

12. See the comments of Muhammad 'Abd al-Malik al-Mutawakkil in CAUS, *Al-Mujtama' al-madani*, p. 589.

13. Bernard Lewis, *The Political Language of Islam* (Chicago: University of Chicago Press, 1988), ch. 2.

14. Ghalyun, "Bina' al-mujtama'"; Kuthrani, "Al-mujtama' wa al-dawla"; and the comments by al-Mutawakkil.

15. See the comments by 'Issam al-'Iriyan in CAUS, *Al-mujtama' al-madani*, pp. 319–321.

16. 'Ali al-Kinz, "Min al-i'jab bi al-dawla ila iktishaf al-mumarasa al-ijtima'iyya" [From Adulation of the State to the Discovery of Social Praxis], in CAUS, *Al-mujtama' al-madani*.

17. Amnesty International, *Amnesty International Report 1992* (London: Amnesty International Publications, 1992).

18. Al-Kinz, "Min al-i'jab."

19. On business involvement in politics in Tunisia, see Eva Bellin, "Tunisian Industrialists and the State," in I. William Zartman, ed., *Tunisia: The Political Economy of Reform* (Boulder and London: Lynne Rienner Publishers, 1991), pp. 59–63. On Morocco, see Mark Tessler, "Image and Reality in Moroccan Political Economy," in I. William Zartman, ed., *The Political Economy of Morocco* (New York and London: Praeger, 1987), pp. 50–52.

20. See the interview with President Mubarak in *al-Mussawar* (Cairo), 24 September 1993.

21. Alain Roussillon, "Secteur publique ou sociétés islamiques de placement de fonds: la recomposition du système redistributif en Egypt," in *Bulletin du Cedej* (Cairo) 17, 23 (1988).

22. René Gallisot, "Les émeutes, phénomènes cycliques au Maghreb: rupture ou reconduction du système politique," in Camau, *Changements Politiques*, pp. 41–50.

23. Muhammad 'Abid al-Jabiri, "Ishkaliyyat al-dimuqratiyya wa al-mujtama' al-madani fi al-watan al-'arabi" [Problematic of Democracy and Civil Society in the Arab Motherland], *Al-Mustaqbal al-'arabi* (January 1993).

24. Arab Human Rights Organization, *Newsbulletin* 60–61 (January–February 1993), p. 8.

25. Amnesty International, *Amnesty International Report 1992*, pp. 255–257.

26. See, on Egypt, "Parliament Pushes Union Law Through," in *Civil Society and Democratic Transformation in the Arab World,* newsletter (March 1993), pp. 3–6.

27. *Middle East Watch* 5, 6 (September 1993).

28. *Arab Human Rights Organization Newsbulletin* 64 (May 1993), p. 15; 65 (June 1993), p. 10.

8

The Press and Democratic Transition in Arab Societies: The Algerian Case

Lise Garon

Democracy, in the modern sense of the term,[1] assumes a society with a public space in which contending debates and peaceful struggles are waged between state and societal actors in pursuit or in defense of power. The evolution of an authoritarian or totalitarian state toward "democracy" thus involves the development of a civil society, gradually escaping the control of the state apparatus so as to acquire the means for its autonomous public expression. This evolution is driven by the power relationships between involved actors, and by the strategies they use to influence and improve their position vis-à-vis one another. In this context, there is much to say about the role of the press in Arab transitions; most Arab societies are indeed undergoing, at the end of the twentieth century, a period of transition many observers have hastily characterized as democratic.

At the outset of transition, state and societal actors will often claim that an integral democratic system has been effectively constructed.[2] Yet several necessary conditions must exist for the stable functioning of "democracy"; first and foremost is freedom of expression and a free flow of information. Indeed, how can free elections ensure changes in government if messages from the opposition are unable to reach the electorate? How can public debates be sustained if information does not flow freely? How can the courts' independence and integrity be protected if the press cannot disclose the abuses of central authorities? Transition periods are, therefore, particular, for the pluralism of state and civil institutions cannot guarantee the proper functioning of democratic institutions (especially the defeat of incumbents) if the public diffusion of information is obstructed. To use Alfred Sauvy's felicitous phrase, information is the keystone of "democracy";[3] the media, and especially the press, are themselves an essential part of this foundation. Unfortunately, barely two or three monographs[4] have focused on the press as part and parcel of transition analysis;[5] thus little is known on the role of the press in democratic transition.

This chapter will use the Algerian case, as well as references from other Arab countries, to theorize on the role of the press at various stages of political evolution.[6] The importance of Algeria stems from its recent experience with societal transformation. Two initial phases of evolution (social vacuum, until the October 1988 riots, and social explosion, until the 1992 coup) reflected the decay and disappearance of a totalitarian state.[7] Since 1992, a third phase, that of eroding pluralism, is emulating the experience of most of Algeria's Arab neighbors. Algerian society was thus subjected, very quickly, to a variety of transformations rich in theoretical insights about the role of the press—the forgotten actor in transition analysis.

The chapter is structured as follows: The first part will focus on the Arab (and Algerian) press's lack of leadership in the building of civil society, witnessed at all stages of transition. The second part will discuss factors explaining the vulnerability and passivity of the press. Underdevelopment is ruled out as an explanation, as the emphasis shifts to civil society and its influence on conflicts and associations between the press and transition actors; in a climate of uncertainty, the press's survival strategy seeks to benefit from favorable decisions of other actors and avoid the alienation of dominant actors. In the third part I will explain how, nonetheless, a vulnerable and passive press may well accidentally trigger key developments in a transition. This said, the press can also deliberately and effectively challenge established authorities; this is a paradox that will be addressed in the last part of the chapter.

The Press as Actor: Passivity and Vulnerability

The rise of civil society in Arab countries is a prerequisite of the pluralism of the press and the free flow of information. In other words, the press, seemingly the most vulnerable actor in the transition process, did not catalyze any changes in power relationships within political society. It merely reacted to the changes induced by other actors[8] at different phases of the transition, from the period of social vacuum to pluralism.

The Social Vacuum Phase

This initial phase is associated with the decay of the totalitarian state: It was experienced in socialist Algeria, Nasserite Egypt, and in the People's Democratic Republic of Yemen (PDRY); it currently characterizes Libya, Iraq, and Syria. While in sole control of the public sphere, the totalitarian state monopolizes political power, and can only do so by utterly crushing all societal and individual initiative.[9] This entails a total ban of opposition, official or officious censorship, compulsory supervision of all public functions by the single party or a similar control structure,[10] the selective application of the law, court abuses, and police terror. It becomes inconceivable that a society may construct a differentiated political status, organized outside the symbiotic framework that currently binds it to the state.

Civil society here lacks autonomous structures of expression and action. The press has no bearing on policies of liberalization, fully designed and controlled by the state in search of renewed legitimacy. The press itself is controlled through reaffectations, new nominations, sanctions, lower distribution, or obstructed circulation. A newspaper that dares trespass the narrow boundaries set by the state will likely face severe retributions. Criticizing the regime, giving editorial access to the opposition, or revealing "strategic" secrets are particularly punishable infractions—eliciting layoffs and expulsions (such as in socialist Algeria)[11] or, worse, abduction, torture, and the death penalty (Syria and Iraq).[12]

In this phase of totalitarian decay, the press will often adopt a critical or polemical tone. Such criticism, however, is fully in line with governmental or presidential directives, echoing official attacks against pseudo-adversaries of the "Arab nation" (Zionism, neocolonialism, the plotting West, etc.) or recently dismissed leaders. The press thus restates elite debates and, through official criticism, pledges faithfulness to the People, the president, or the Revolution. Such illusory freedom of expression does not replace the ideological jargon, more suitable to censorship and propaganda than actual information, which still dominates the press. Polemics and critiques amount to another form of rhetoric aimed at protecting the credibility of a mobilization press,[13] forever the transmission belt of state propaganda.

The Phase of Social Explosion

The political evolution of a country will follow one of two scenarios upon the crumbling of the totalitarian state: The state will either control (with uneven success) the rhythm and the forms through which civil society emerges or, more bluntly, it will have lost much of its authority. The first scenario unfolded in post-Nasserist Egypt, as the boundaries on democratic transition set by Sadat controlled the emergence of political parties and the press; opposition parties waited until 1977 for the right to publish their newspapers. Unable to freely express itself, the Egyptian press could not act as a driving force in the transition process.

The second scenario, social explosion, has been characteristic of Algeria and Yemen. In the latter case, South Yemen's brutal one-party system was cast aside after the fusion, as the new country experienced the sudden appearance of a fragmented opposition (over 40 parties). The Yemeni press then started to operate amid legal guarantees for freedom of expression and an open climate of critique and contestation. Through extensive financial support from the state, over 160 newspapers and magazines were started up.

In Algeria, the totalitarian state was dismantled following the 1988 riots. Civil society awoke through an explosion of social forces (associations, parties, newspapers, etc.), most of which carried very little weight in the struggle for power.[14] The June 1990 municipal elections underscored the extreme fragmentation of the "democratic" opposition and the discrediting of the former single party, the National Liberation Front (FLN).[15] The press was similarly affected. New publications suddenly flourished, and a serious split within the journalists, writers, and translators union—once fully controlled by the FLN—rocked the profession; this first experience with dissension was consecrated in the February 1988 founding of the Algerian Journalists' Movement, quickly followed by new, rival groups, whose proliferation fractured the movement and halted its push.

Algeria and Yemen share both a phase of social explosion and a concomitant erosion of state authority, both absent in Egypt. Is there a cause-and-effect relationship between the decline of state power and the explosive awakening of civil society and the press? This should be investigated, for it may soon characterize other countries in the Arab world (Syria, Libya, Iraq) or elsewhere (the former Soviet Union). In all certainty, the thundering roar of freedom emanating from the burgeoning civil society, in the social explosion phase, will conceal the vulnerability of civil actors and of the press especially.

Indeed, the Algerian case underscores the questionable character of such nascent freedom. Consider, for instance, the presidential "blessing" of the new papers, which included working space, equipment, distribution services, and a three-year salary pay to those journalists willing to leave the public sector to the benefit of the young independent press. While pluralism and contestation became the new mottoes of an Algerian press now ready to report and reflect on once forbidden issues, the extent of its powers is undoubtedly circumscribed. The Algerian press has little informative capacity: Nothing pertaining to individual leaders or high-level debates is divulged.[16] Yet is it a critical press? Not quite. Few dared criticize a self-proclaimed pluralist-leaning president who still held on to all levers of power, yet most lashed out at him as his authority weakened after the 1990 municipal elections; this unanimous critique is hardly different in meaning from the unanimous consensus around the single-party rule before 1988.

Since the 1988 riots, the press's strong denunciations of the state have been continuously accompanied by references to democracy. However, such pervasiveness of democratic themes is not a function of press power, and rather reflects a general societal acceptance of the concept. Democracy is now the war horse of both civil and state actors: No political demand or decision may now be considered or legitimized without uttering the magic word.

This is, by all means, a new language, which emerged from the sensational settling of accounts among the elite following the riots.[17] Like any other actor, the press seized the buzz words, consolidating its influence by advocating the new values. Above all, unrestrained by a state whose authority had collapsed, it fired full force on all conceivable targets at the top. Its strategy for influence, on the eve of the 1992 coup, was simply to go with the flow.[18]

The Phase of Selective Pluralism

The Islamic Salvation Front (FIS) was heading straight to a majority vote after one round of legislative elections in December 1991. The president had agreed to work with an FIS parliament. However, the military elite, publicly targeted by FIS rhetoric and prompted by the press, easily yielded to pressures from the "democratic"-leaning Socialist Forces Front, unions, and the Human Rights League, all of which had just created a Salvation Committee for Algeria. Elections were suspended in early 1992, and the military forced the president's resignation. Thus began an exclusionary regime, controlled behind the scenes by the military. The FIS was dissolved, its publications banned.

A relationship of mutual dependence thus arose between the regime and civil society. On the one hand, the "democratic" opinion in society has called on the military to cancel the elections, deflect the Islamist attack, and save the Republic. On the other hand, while the military has forcibly secured more latitude to display its authority than at any other time since the 1988 riots, it must also exercise restraint, lest it destroy pluralism and alienate all support from society (which facilitated the coup) in its own struggle against the Islamists. Most civil actors, therefore, are free to debate publicly and to criticize the leadership.

Still, freedom of information and expression is not risk free. Four dailies were suspended in 1992 (the lengths of the suspensions varied).[19] In all cases, the government claimed that they had endorsed a campaign of destabilization and manipulation against national unity and state security by spreading "false information" or divulging "strategic economic secrets." This said, the press in Algeria does not know precisely how much latitude it may enjoy: The boundaries of censorship are not formally defined, but must be ascertained by trial and error. It is indeed a perilous exercise, for the vagueness of formal rules elicit their arbitrary application by the state, at whatever time deemed appropriate.[20] As the official discourse likens press critiques to the Islamist cause, the lingering impression remains of a government regulating the printed media with nebulous and arbitrary rules.

Therefore, the usual forbidden territory remains untrodden. For instance, *Le Matin* was suspended for disclosing the freezing of Algerian credit by Italian banks. *La Nation* was similarly punished for announcing the arrest of the Tuareg's spiritual leader. In other words, "strategic" secrets, the purview of a small group within the leadership, are simply not part of the information game.

Consider also a prime ministerial directive to all ministries and state enterprises, which specified that all media inserts were to be handled by the National Editing and Publishing Agency (NEPA)—the official agency in charge of editing and publishing. Likewise, the prime minister announced that publicity inserts would not exceed 30 percent of newspaper space. Profitability schemes would rather have called on NEPA to examine the various degrees of newspaper exposure, using such marketing tools as "gross exposure points" or "cost per thousand exposures." Such logic, however, was not to be considered. Through the 30 percent norm, the state's objective was to maintain control over the development of the press, its quality, and mission—although there is little evidence that the state will use the norm for political ends.

In sum, the Algerian press, totally free to express its opinions for a short period, soon regressed to the more strictly controlled position of its Arab peers. It is a vulnerable actor, learning to follow opaque (thus unarguable) guidelines. Furthermore, it still does not have access to a privileged (but also poorly defined) type of information, prerogative of the ruling elite. Fellow journalists in Morocco, Kuwait, and Lebanon need not be envious anymore.

Transition and the Press

Third World ideology usually attributes the press's vulnerability and lack of independence to a financial weakness inherent in underdevelopment. Lacking financial autonomy and harassed by the courts (suspensions, arrests, trials, etc.), the press can scarcely conduct its own surveys and reports; its only sources of information are the state and the opposition parties. Therefore, according to the argument, economic development is a necessary and sufficient condition for freedom of the press. The case would appear especially solid in Algeria, as many newspapers are owned by journalist collectives, sponsored since 1989 by the Algerian state (providing salaries, workspace, etc.); no large press enterprise exists in the country.[21] Underdevelopment, then, would stand as an unsurmountable barrier to press freedom and influence.

Nonetheless, this broad hypothesis, however popular, can be rebutted. Moncef Ben M'Rad,[22] editor of the Tunisian weekly *Haqa'iq* (Réalités), concludes from his analysis of financial obstacles: "All those negative elements may have come together to oppose us, yet we have pursued our struggle; after all, publishers from the American Far West did eventually found the *Washington Post.*"[23]

Empirical data support Ben M'Rad's opinion; underdeveloped Costa Rica does display an independent and influential press. Similarly, the Lebanese press has developed an international reputation and circulation. In contrast, economic prosperity cannot guarantee freedom of the press, as witnessed with many Third World dictatorships. In the Arab world, for instance, Rugh has noted how the increasingly wealthy Saudi press, in the late 1970s, was no less influenced by state pressure.[24] Jac-Kyong Lee has made similar comments[25] about Asia's four "tigers,"[26] where prosperity extended to the press industry without the accompanying freedom of information and expression. The root of the paradox, he says, stems from a weak civil society—indeed the essential factor affecting the role of the press; such weakness greatly enhances the risks that individual liberties and "democratic" principles be arbitrarily defined by the prince. Freedom of the press, especially, will hinge on the ruling elite's "benevolence."

One might object that the high economic growth experienced by the "tigers," Saudi Arabia, and also Algeria, did not eliminate illiteracy; presumably, little revenue can be derived from general readership. Thus, the economic variable would remain essential in analyzing the Third World press: financial survival seems contingent on pleasing the ruling elite. However, such deference is not merely the purview of dictatorships with high illiteracy rates. As Willnat explains,[27] the East German press, through the transition years, ran against the current of liberalization and *glasnost* by clinging to journalistic practices of the totalitarian era. Acknowledging that readership in the GDR was among the widest in Europe (1.5 dailies and 1.4 weeklies read per 1,000 inhabitants), one must conclude that literacy does not guarantee press independence.

In sum, the cases described above ought to temper the economistic hypothesis (prosperity, growth) in explaining the rise of press freedom; economic variables may be merely contingent factors. We should consider, then, another hypothesis: The direction of transition might ultimately be affected by actors' perceptions of the situation. Here economic considerations shape the various options offered to social actors; they may slow down (but not immobilize) transitions, or play a useful role (though never essential) therein.

As a general rule, the independent press in the Third World relies neither on large financial resources nor on any tradition of independence vis-à-vis the state; what matter are the existing power relationships. The Algerian case, again, demonstrates how the press positions itself vis-à-vis other transition actors, seeking possible—or impossible—alliances that, ultimately, will shape its role; targeted groups may include the opposition, parliament, the executive, the ruling elite, and so on.

The Press and Opposition Parties

Should the implementation of multipartyism in Algeria have prompted an information "opening" from opposition papers? Admittedly, the latter could not escape party discipline; as an official opposition party press, their role was to transmit the new political message. In principle, however, party competition should have improved the flow of information, with the various parties (including the FLN) seeking to uncover their opponents' secrets.

Yet, old habits do seem to die hard. As in the past, parties may be striking agreements, as one big "family," which would curtail the spread of information. For instance, in the Gulf crisis, in September 1990, the president and two opposition leaders, Muhammad Abbassi Madani (FIS) and Sa'id Sa'adi (the Gathering for Culture and Democracy), jointly defined the limits of public disagreements. After their meeting, Sa'adi declared that "all Algerians must speak the same language in foreign policy."

Parliament and the Press Agenda

In contrast with the old European and American "democracies," the Algerian parliament occupies only a marginal place on the press agenda. On the issue of public financial management, for instance, the usual stories pertain to the personal fortunes of leaders from socialist Algeria (these are often rumor based) or to old corruption inquests and trials. One particular case, on that latter note, is that of General Ben Loucif, released in 1986; indeed, the press learned only in 1992 that he had been investigated for embezzlement. Significantly, the press relied on a leak from the army, and not on any parliamentary debate. Obviously, a problem exists if six years are needed to reopen the books: Clearly, the controls on public funds management have no preventive effect. Even the expression "taxpayer" is absent from public debate.

As the press claims to be the witness and the torchbearer of democracy, it is necessarily dealing with a problem if parliament is so poorly entrenched in its agenda. This question is missing from the agenda because of the executive strategy of bypassing the parliament and controlling the agenda through the policies and reforms it announces. Unsurprisingly, the executive shows little diligence and imagination in creating parliamentary controls over public spending;[28] the real power, rooted in neopatrimonialism, is still based on networks of "clients." Monopartyism in parliament thus deprives the press of an alliance that would reinforce its influence in the transition process; under such circumstances, the development of the press can only be delayed.

Jousting with the ruling elite without the support of a multiparty parliament and of a strong "democratic" opposition, the Algerian press has no choice but to seek protection among this ruling elite—or, at the very least, to refrain from enticing excessive hostility on their part. No doubt the executive and the military can punish undue temerity from newspapers.

The Press and the Executive

Without reviewing the rules of the game set by the 1989 constitution and the 1990 Information Act, the new executive never hesitates to repress the media, so as to contain them within specific boundaries. Three mechanisms of support are at its disposal:

1. The judiciary: The 1990 Act, while revoking state ownership of the press, curtailed the free flow of information by forbidding (a) the diffusion of "false information" or "libel"; (b) attempts to jeopardize national unity and state security; and (c) criticisms of Islam and other revealed religions. The Act was invoked to justify suspensions of papers as well as other administrative measures that proliferated after the coup.

Continued recourse to this mechanism could become delicate. For instance, in Yemen not only have administrative decisions been overruled by the courts, but the government has often retreated in view of the sheer delays and costs attached to judiciary processes.[29] Similar success, though, could occur in Algeria only if judges are granted necessary autonomy (for instance, if they cannot be removed from the bench).

2. Publicity: Through NEPA,[30] the state has remained the press's most important client.[31] In principle, then, the executive could use its advertising power to blackmail "offensive" newspapers.

3. Logistics: State monopolies over paper and printing are a latent threat against those newspapers that may have stepped out of line. Harassment measures may include paper shortages (arbitrarily limiting circulation) and publishing delays (explained away by technical problems).

The state needs no recourse to strong-arm tactics so as to expose the weakness of the press. The perpetual sword of Damocles is wielded from its position as regulator, client, and supplier—all at once.

The Press and the Ruling Elite

The Algerian army has never tolerated threats or challenges to its authority, and the press has basically respected this informal rule in Algerian politics. While the press has violently attacked the president since June 1990, the historical rulers of Algeria—the military—were left unquestioned. In fact, this is part of a pattern in the Arab world, where attacks on the ruling elite (Saudi royal family, 'Alawi clan in Syria, military in Algeria or Egypt, etc.) are met with immediate response: suspensions or trials in milder cases of criticism, definitive bans for more serious assaults. The ultimate taboo thus remains unshaken: Only "official" information (including high-level debates about main policy orientations), watered down through censorship and ideological jargon, can be released about the ruling elite.

In sum, an essential lesson may be drawn from the Algerian experience: When the press cannot muster any support from a developed and differentiated civil society, a credible opposition, a legitimate parliament, and an independent judiciary that would defend it against power abuses, then it is bound to adopt a low and prudent profile in dealing with the ruling elite—that actor that can decide its fate. The press's lack of leadership in transition is easily understood in light of the above.

Accidents Tipping the Course of History

Sanders has argued that the East European, Soviet, and Chinese media unwittingly triggered the collapse of the socialist bloc by creating an informational environment that would inevitably stir popular riots.[32] In Algeria,[33] there is no doubt that the public press's analysis of the economic crisis and social problems helped weaken the regime. Faithfully responding to calls from the head of state, the press plastered headlines about the economic crisis, the general sense of utter dissatisfaction in society, and the incompetence and power abuses of bureaucrats. Along the way, it admitted to self-censorship, thus discrediting the very information it was releasing. Tame as always, it repeatedly transmitted presidential directives, never to be followed. It alluded to foreign reports on the sporadic riots, strikes, and underground opposition in the country. Gradually it shaped the picture of a decadent, halting state, thus establishing a necessary informational environment for popular uprising. Ultimately, it would also provide the trigger for freeing such popular anger.

On the eve of the 1988 riots, with the continuing deterioration of the economy, social tensions were still running high and dividing a ruling elite in search of solutions. President Chadli Bin Jadid, preparing for the sixth FLN Congress, turned popular attention to completely different matters in a speech in which he accused unidentified members of the ruling elite of irresponsibility and of undermining the reform of public enterprises. The press, traditionally favorable to the president, copiously reported the speech, which Bin Jadid concluded by calling for the resignation of those individuals who had not performed according to expectations.[34]

The president could not have revealed more clearly the extent of his isolation and of the divisions among elites. This uncommon admission, reported by all newspapers, fueled the rumor of impending riots. This rumor must have been quite plausible to the general population, which had witnessed more and more strikes and riots in recent years. Indeed, at the very time, strikes were plaguing the PTT (postal and telecommunication services) and the public enterprises. Moreover, a general strike had just been called for 5 October.[35]

Factors leading to the consensus breakdown had existed for a long time,[36] yet general popular outburst was delayed until October 1988. It took place as a self-fulfilling prophecy, after the high tension permeating the country had undoubtedly actualized the rumor of riots.[37] The rumor had modified the informational milieu from which social actors could frame their judgments. A sequence of close events thus probably acted as trigger for the riots:

- The head of state's misguided admission of failure in his late-September speech
- The press's magnifying of that mistake through regular headlines about the speech
- Popular rumors hinting at imminent troubles of great magnitude

Though a subordinate actor, the press thus played a noticeable role in the collapse of the FLN state, and would manifest its presence again soon after, in the three-week period between 5 October and the announcement of "democratic reforms." This was a time of uncertainty in which the army, the FLN, and the president remained noncommittal. The Algerian Human Rights League filled the void by summoning some 500 journalists to its commission of inquiry on human rights abuses and information deficiencies in the October riots. The event was duly covered by the public press. The concerted action between the League and the journalists against censorship and torture—if not tipping the scale—at the very least created a conducive climate for the upcoming declaration on "democratic reforms." For the third time in a short period, the press merged with a coalition of actors to (involuntarily) influence the course of events.

Examples from Algeria and the socialist bloc thus illustrate a long-standing idea in social science:[38] Social evolution is not merely a function of actors' strategies, but also of the unforeseen consequences of their actions. The press, then, while unable to anticipate its own impact, does act as a trigger for impending crises; this, indeed, might well constitute its essential role in the process of social change.

Moderating Authoritarian Rule?

Several Algerian papers composed of journalist collectives, including *Al-Watan*, have adopted an aggressive denunciation strategy vis-à-vis the executive. Does this reflect press power or executive weakness? A look at the careers of Bin Jadid, Boudiaf,[39] and 'Abd al-Salam[40] would suggest the latter: A leadership void has coincided with the rise of the press as opposition power.

In the phase of selective pluralism, the press has maintained its ability to criticize the government, as witnessed by the clash between Prime Minister 'Abd al-Salam and *Al-Watan*. Though not boundless, the power of critique is now a given.[41] The prince may not order the press at will.

Paradoxically, the pluralist press's own development has sensitized it to the precariousness of "democracy." Democratic pretensions are then disappearing from its discourse. Instead, there appears an obsessive preoccupation with anything that might threaten the "freedom" of information. Authoritarian velleities, similar to those of the past, are perceived in instances of television censorship, the firing of the justice minister, or government accusations against the independent press. The arrest of a journalist or the suspension of a newspaper guarantees a headline and a response; meanwhile, the press circulates petitions and organizes manifestations calling for the enhanced freedom of the profession.

In Morocco, party newspapers have circumvented royal directives and have survived the ensuing repression. In Kuwait, *Al-Qabas*, owned by a handful of rich trading families, has criticized the government and denounced human rights violations despite censure, court harassment, and expulsions. In Lebanon the pluralist press, similarly dodging censure and judicial accusations, has developed an international reputation. Such fragmentary democracies, to use Sklar's expression,[42] are emerging, if embryonic in the Arab world.

These authoritarian regimes, despite differences in political culture and history, do share a common concern: Namely, to control the press's quest for space, for the right to overcome its isolation and speak about its weakness and the grave risks it unceasingly faces. The independent press in transitional societies may not prevent the display of authoritarian measures, but it does complicate any attempt to strengthen authoritarian practices.

Conclusion: Lessons from the Algerian Experience

The picture of the Algerian press in the transition process is one of vulnerability to power relationships, as it follows the various phases of development. Channeling the official discourse in the phase of social vacuum, newspapers evolved according to the subsequent changes in civil society: Initially, they too exploded; then, in the phase of selective pluralism, a private press has developed. This press, independent from the state and political parties, witnessed firsthand the threats to a burgeoning democracy, and did take several risks in spite of its precarious position. Basically, the Algerian press was much more reactive than proactive in the movement, benefiting from both the "democratic reforms" initiated by the state and the demands from the "democratic" line in civil society. As well, concertation with other actors influenced the transition process in unexpected ways.

This model of political change may be applied only to those countries that have experienced, or are experiencing, a complete shutdown of civil society—with a qualifier, however: The transition process does not necessarily involve a three-stage evolution toward "democracy." Egypt, for instance, did not—following Nasser's death—witness a social explosion similar to Algeria's. As for Yemen and Algeria, social explosion and state collapse understandably produced an environment favorable to press freedom that was unprecedented in the Arab world, and allowed for journalistic practices that had to be tolerated by the ruling elite—in each case, the self-discovered legitimacy of the exercise may dissuade the ruling elite from imposing a return to authoritarian rule. It is a potentially stabilizing factor for pluralism that does not exist in Egypt or Tunisia.

In spite of this unique advantage, Yemen and Algeria have undoubtedly not proceeded beyond Dahl's phase of unstable polyarchy. Transition may still be reversed, as suggested in the postindependence cases of Syria, Iraq, and Sudan. In Syria, the period between independence and the union with Egypt generated many new publications, most linked to a political party, a group, a family, or even another country. Iraqi independence also announced an era of party pluralism and of concomitant press freedom, by which party newspapers openly displayed opposition viewpoints; in both countries, this came to an end with the Ba'thist takeover. In Sudan, the string of military regimes was nonetheless interspersed with pluralist jolts, at the level of both press and party.

In all three cases, social and press pluralism were insufficiently entrenched to prevent a drift toward totalitarianism. They typified the problem of new states, where "openness" hinges more on a leadership's individual decisions than on established institutional rules and, therefore, where the status of the independent press is precarious. If, in each case, a brief, unstable period of pluralism gave way to totalitarianism, then by no means is the scenario inapplicable to the new pluralist societies in Algeria, Tunisia, Egypt, Jordan, and Yemen. Totalitarianism may well emerge, for example, from Islamist or praetorian rule.

The risk of totalitarian rule, however, seems less salient for those societies with a long pluralist tradition and stable civil institutions: Morocco, Kuwait, Lebanon. Such underpinnings allowed, in each case, a pluralist (i.e., "diverse")[43] press to prosper and survive either the hand of the *amir* (Morocco, Kuwait) or a civil war (Lebanon). In all three countries, newspapers are owned by wealthy businessmen, influential families, or major parties, all of which use the print media to buttress their economic or political power. The case is different in Algeria and Yemen; there, private publishing is handled by journalist collectives.

For a time, Algeria and Yemen met the conditions that spurred the development of a pluralist press in Lebanon, Kuwait, and Morocco.[44] These include the decline of state repression,[45] party pluralism, readership, as well as support from the state and civil actors, and the state's relatively tame approach to repression. Still, the development of a pluralist society in Algeria and Yemen cannot yet compare to that in Morocco, Kuwait, or Lebanon. Uncomfortably situated amidst civil conflict, the Algerian and Yemeni press both now stand on decidedly shakier ground.[46]

Notwithstanding these differences between posttotalitarian and post-authoritarian democratization or stable and unstable pluralism, four provisional conclusions can be inferred from the Algerian case concerning the role of the press in the democratic transition in general:

1. The press is not a driving force in this process but a vulnerable actor trying to follow the flow.
2. Financial weakness does not explain the vulnerability and the lack of leadership exhibited by the press. The decisive factor, rather, consists in the actual power relationships between the actors of the transition.
3. In spite of its exposed position in the transition process, the press acts, unintentionally, as a trigger to crisis, tipping the course of the game by disclosing new opportunities to the other actors.
4. Although a return to authoritarian practices by state actors is more costly when the press challenges authoritarian state behavior and critically assesses the state of democratization, the press alone—as the Algerian case shows—cannot prevent the erosion of pluralism.

Notes

The author wishes to thank Dr. Boucetta Allouche for his bibliographical research and critical comments.

1. Dahl prefers the term "polyarchy." See Robert A. Dahl, *Polyarchy: Participation and Opposition* (New Haven and London: Yale University Press, 1971).

2. Lise Garon, "Les médias algériens et la crise d'octobre 1988," in Wolfgang Slim Freund, ed., *L'information au Maghreb* (Cérès Productions: Tunis, 1992); and *L'obsession unitaire et la Nation trompée: la fin de l'Algérie socialiste* (Quebec: Presses de l'université Laval, 1993).

3. Alfred Sauvy, "L'information, clé de la démocratie," *Revue française de science politique* 1, 1/2 (May 1951), pp. 26–39.

4. See Jac-Kyoung Lee, "Press Freedom and National Development: Toward a Reconceptualization," *Gazette/International Journal for Mass Communications Studies* 48, 3 (1991), pp. 149–163; Robert E. Sanders, "The Role of Mass Communication Processes in Producing Upheavals in the Soviet Union, Eastern Europe, and China," in Sarah Sanderson King and Donald P. Cushman, eds., *Political Communication* (Albany: State University of New York Press, 1992); and Lars Willnat, "The German Press during the Political Transformation of East Germany," *Gazette/International Journal for Mass Communications Studies* 48, 3 (1991), pp. 193–208.

5. The literature on democratic transition includes Robert Dahl, *Polyarchy: Participation and Opposition*; Guillermo O'Donnell, Philip C. Schmitter, and Laurence Whitehead, eds., *Transition from Authoritarian Rule: Prospects for Democracy* (Baltimore: Johns Hopkins University Press, 1991); Terry Lynn Karl and Philippe Schmitter, "Les modes de transition en Amérique latine, en Europe du Sud et de l'Est," *Revue internationale des sciences sociales* 128 (special issue: *Le temps de la démocratie*) (May 1991), pp. 285–302; Jacques Mariel Nzouankeu, "L'Afrique devant l'idée de la démocratie," *Revue internationale des sciences sociales* 128 (May 1991), pp. 397–409; Ghassan Salamé, "Sur la causalité d'un manque: pourquoi le monde arabe n'est-il donc pas démocratique?," *Revue française de science politique* 41, 3 (June 1991), pp. 307–340.

6. In the Arab world, the press contrasts with radio and television, which are usually state property and act as mouthpiece for the official discourse. Quite to the contrary, the press explicitly expresses opinions and, in permissible political contexts, is a vehicle of opposition and contestation to state authority. More likely to influence the transition process, the press therefore becomes the exclusive focus of this essay. (Film and literature also seem to influence transition, and would be worthy of analysis in a separate paper; so is, for that matter, the political rumor—an often neglected mass medium.)

7. Not all scientists agree on the use of the concept. Following Hannah Arendt (1972), the concept of totalitarianism is targeted to revolutionary movements and some religious sects. Such restrictive interpretation effectively rules out its use in the USSR, Algeria, Nazi Germany, and Fascist Italy (yet Mussolini originally defined the notion, and applied it to his regime). Indeed, the phase of conquest and consolidation eventually yields to softened state control and dampened fervor and mobilization. Thus construed, the totalitarian state cannot exist but temporarily. A dynamic approach to the concept should solve this puzzle. Totalitarianism is best understood not as an ideal type, but as an evolving phenomenon encompassing phases of revolution, postrevolution, and decay. In this latter phase, administrative paralysis and social pressures force a gradual removal of the state from the public sphere.

8. This is not peculiar to the Arab world. The passivity of the press in transition was noted in Asia (Lee, 1991) and in the German Democratic Republic (Willnat, 1991). The story is altogether different in stable democracies, where the press can trigger major crises: Consider the breakdown of the Italian political elite during the winter of 1993, the Watergate scandal in the United States, the natural gas scandal in Quebec in the 1950s, etc.

9. "L'écrasement absolu du ressort de la société et des individus face à l'autorité centrale," Bertrand Badie and Guy Hermet, *Politique comparée* (Paris: PUF, Collection "Thémis," 1990), p. 181.

10. For example, Libya's revolutionay committees.

11. Garon, *L'obsession unitaire et la Nation trompée.*

12. For Syria, see Middle East Watch, *Syria Unmasked: The Suppression of Human Rights by the Assad Regime* (New Haven and London: Yale University Press, 1991); for Iraq, see Middle East Watch, *Human Rights in Iraq* (New Haven and London: Yale University Press, 1990).

13. The term is Rugh's. See William A. Rugh, *The Arab Press: News Media and the Political Process in the Arab World* (Syracuse: Syracuse University Press, 1979).

14. Dahl refers to the "unstable polyarchy" in this context. See Robert A. Dahl, *Democracy and Its Critics* (New Haven and London: Yale University Press, 1989).

15. The main opposition party, the Islamic Salvation Front (ISF), still won about 35 percent of ballots cast.

16. Garon, *L'obsession unitaire et la Nation trompée.*

17. The president's political opponents were effectively deprived of their top-ranking positions and branded the "stakeholders of socialist orthodoxy" (a pejorative term indeed to anyone familiar with the media code in Algeria).

18. See Garon, *L'obsession unitaire et la Nation trompée,* for details on the role of the press in the phase of social explosion.

19. These are: *Le Matin, La Nation, Al-Jaza'ir al-Youm, Al-Watan.*

20. This observation is valid for the Arab world as a whole.

21. Similar observations hold for Morocco and Tunisia. The major publications come from the Middle East.

22. Moncef Ben M'Rad, "Réalités—Éditer un magazine hebdomadaire en Tunisie: contraintes et ouvertures," in Wolfgang Slim Freund, ed., *L'information au Maghreb.*

23. Editor's translation.

24. Rugh, *The Arab Press.*

25. Lee, "Press Freedom and National Development," pp. 149–163.

26. South Korea, Taiwan, Hong Kong, and Singapore.

27. Willnat, "The German Press during the Political Transformation of East Germany."

28. Prime Minister 'Abd al-Salam claimed to be "powerless" on this issue.

29. Middle East Watch, "Yemen Toward Civil Society," *Middle East Watch* 4, 10 (November 1992).

30. In 1992, the prime minister called upon managers within the various ministries and public enterprises to channel their publicity through ANEP. See "La publicité contrôlée: une arme politique?" *Al-Watan,* 27 December 1992, p. 1.

31. According to *Al-Watan* (30 January 1993, p.1), the public sector accounts for 70 percent of advertising.

32. Sanders, "The Role of Mass Communication Processes in Producing Upheavals."

33. Garon, *L'obsession unitaire et la Nation trompée.*

34. As usual, the speech was printed verbatim in *Al-Mujahid.* See *Al-Mujahid,* 21 September 1988, pp. 11–14.

35. Riots broke out in Algiers on precisely that day.

36. For details on the lengthy agony of the FLN state, see Garon, *L'obsession unitaire et la Nation trompée.*

37. A rival hypothesis has also been suggested: Riots would have followed a plot within the ruling elite aimed at the overthrow of the regime. This thesis is based on facts uncovered by journalist Frédéric Fritscher of *Le Monde* (1988). However, it does not withstand scrutiny. The plot leaders were never identified, the risk incurred by either the president or his opponents would have seemed far too great, and the scheme simply did not fit with the styles involved—the president was known for his prudence and even his hesitance, the head of the FLN (Messaadia) had always favored consensus building so as to avoid uncontrollable upheaval, and the army would opt for a coup, rather than subversion, to overthrow the regime. Abed Charef (1990) also refers to this hypothesis, but remains noncommittal.

38. For a background on that idea see André Gosselin, "L'analyse des effets pervers en sciences des communications," *Canadian Journal of Communication* 17 (1992), pp. 379–388.

39. Immediate successor to Bin Jadid, Boudiaf was assassinated a few months after his nomination.

40. Prime minister in 1992–1993.

41. This is indeed exceptional in the Arab world.

42. Richard L. Sklar, "Development Democracy," *Comparative Studies in Society and History* 29, 4 (October 1987), pp. 686–714.

43. The term is Rugh's. See Rugh, *The Arab Press*.

44. Rugh, *The Arab Press*.

45. Colonialism in Morocco, Kuwait, and Lebanon; totalitarianism in socialist Algeria.

46. In Algeria, this has been manifest in both government pressure on the press (in June 1995, for example, the authorities ordered the temporary closure of three newspapers for simply printing the acronym of the FIS) and attacks by Islamic militants against secular journalists (also in June 1995, the thirty-sixth such journalist was assassinated). *Reuters World Report,* 8 June 1995; *Associated Press,* 18 June 1995.

9

Democratization and Social Islam: A Case Study of the Islamic Health Clinics in Cairo

Janine Astrid Clark

This chapter addresses the question of Islam and democracy by taking what can be termed a "bottom-up" or "grassroots" approach to democratization, one that focuses on the significance of civil society in the transition to democracy. Choosing Islamic health clinics in Cairo as representative of these grassroots activities, it examines four major themes from the mainstream Sunni literature on democracy in order to provide a framework with which to analyze these clinics and the role they are playing in determining political change in Egypt. Specifically, this chapter looks at: (1) the sovereignty of the community in determining its head or popular participation; (2) *shura* (consultation), and its informal or formal institutionalization; (3) the conception of pluralism; and (4) the inclusion or exclusion of non-Muslims, women, and secularists.

It will be argued that Islamic clinics, at the grassroots level, are playing a limited but positive role in the process of democratization in Egypt. In other words, these clinics are fostering greater informal participation than their non-Islamic counterparts. However, while they can be seen as conducive to democratization, they are not providing the building blocks for a democratic conception of state or society. Islamic clinics are not actively or consciously engaged in establishing any form of an alternative conception of state and society at the grassroots or national levels.

The essence of the civil society approach examines the role of civil associations in the transition to democracy as well as their role in laying the foundations or building blocks for a future democratic state and society.[1] The former involves the types of policy changes for which civil associations are pressuring: Are civil associations limiting the prevailing authoritarianism through pressing for policy changes that would increase the differentiation between the state and civil society? The latter questions whether civil society itself is democratic. Grassroots or voluntary associations are understood to be microcosms of a future alternative vision and organization of society. Hence, to what degree are decisions made in a democratic and participatory manner, and is this reflected in the organizational structure? Questions regarding the democratic nature of civil society furthermore encompass the relationship between civil associations and other groups and individuals within society: What degree of "civility" or tolerance is displayed toward groups with differing ideologies or social bases? What is the relationship between the association and the surrounding community? To what degree is the neighborhood able to participate in the management—or the negotiation of management—of its interests?[2] While authors differ as to the significance of the above-mentioned variables in the process of political change, the two aspects of the civil society approach are not unrelated. Stated simply, an association that operates along democratic lines fosters participatory experience, leadership skills, and democratic values, to name just a few, which prepare people for democratic political activity and urge them to demand change in all facets of their personal and public life. It is in this manner that the democratic ideal spreads, roots itself, and ultimately brings about political change.

When examining the question of Islam and civil society, the analysis of civil society becomes further complicated. The primary issue is the degree to which the Islamic political "project" or its ideological vision of politics and society is democratic. Greater elements of democratic thought have been noted in Islamic thinking and ideology in recent years; however, the majority of academics and intellectuals have greeted this development with skepticism.[3] They argue that Islamists are only adopting the language of democracy and pressuring for full democratization in Egypt as a political ploy. Once in power, democratic institutions would be dismantled and an authoritarian Islamic state structure would be put into place. When examining Islamic grassroots activities, this unresolved debate raises not only the question of the democratic nature of Islamic thought but also the role or weight of ideology as opposed to practice. To what degree are the clinics ideologically influenced by mainstream Islamic political thought, and does it matter?[4]

A second issue involves the relationship between Islamic civil associations, such as Islamic health clinics, and organized Islamic political groups. Are the clinics tied to or directed by Islamic groups? The professional syndicates, in particular the more "sensitive" syndicates such as the doctors', are seen by Roussillon, for example, as providing a fertile terrain for the (re)islamization of social practices and as constituting the site of the most significant advances of the Islamic wave in Egypt.[5] It is through the medical clinics, among other institutions, Roussillon argues, that the Islamists, within the syndicate and without, have been able to operationalize

what he sees as their essentially undemocratic message and gradually substitute their control over institutions and neighborhoods in place of that of
the state and of the traditional elites.[6] An examination of democratization
and Islamic clinics must therefore address the issues of the inspiration and
leadership of the clinics, whether or not the clinics are attempting to create
an Islamic model for state and society, and whether they are in fact engaged
in a battle against the state for grassroots institutions and popular sentiments.

Islamic medical clinics as a case study are therefore highly representative of the debate concerning the role of civil society in democratization
and the debate concerning Islam and democracy within Egypt. Furthermore, the medical syndicate elections draw greater attention than those of
the national assembly.[7] For some observers in the press the medical syndicate, within which the Islamic list dominates, represents a seedbed of
democracy, the results of its elections consolidating the emerging democratic movement in Egypt.[8]

Very little data, however, have been published to date on Islamic clinics. In addition, the majority of the studies that do exist are outdated.[9] To
this author's knowledge, only two current studies exist involving in-depth
field research in Islamic clinics in Cairo. Neither of these studies, however, examines the question of democracy.[10] Hence the political meaning
of the Islamic medical clinics has become a hotly debated, although un-
derresearched, topic in Egypt.

In order to assess the clinics' relationship to Islamic ideology and
groups, the clinics must first be situated within the debate concerning
Islam and democracy. This chapter will therefore begin with an analysis of
the bases of political power in Islam and the changes that have taken place
in mainstream Sunni thought as regards democracy today. After a discussion of the activities of mainstream Islam in Egypt, this chapter will focus
on the case study of Islamic clinics and, using four themes from the Islamic literature on democracy as guidelines, will examine the significance
of the clinics for political change in Egypt. In particular, it will focus on
democratic change, within the framework of Islam and without.

The Bases of Political Power in Islam

On Muhammad's last pilgrimage to Mecca, he made an address containing
all the basic ingredients of his legacy for the future political life of the
Muslim community: the Quran, the family of Muhammad, and the example of Muhammad.[11] Yet the correct mix of these ingredients has remained
a subject of active disagreement.

Two principles emerged after Muhammad's death as the basis for political power in Islam: *bay'a* (oath of allegiance) and *shura* (consultation).

As Hourani explains, while some of the earlier rulers were designated by their predecessors, others were chosen by an "election committee," a group of community leaders. This element of choice was theoretically symbolized by the ceremony of *bay'a*, the formal acknowledgment of a new caliph, and pledge of loyalty to him by the notables of the *umma* (community). While the *bay'a* clearly did not represent choice or election in the full sense, but rather recognition and the community's acquiescence to authority, it was not understood as passive obedience to the ruler.[12] According to the generally held theory, the ruler should consult the leaders of the community (*shura*) and they should give him moral advice and exhortation (*nasiha*).[13]

True sovereignty of the community rested with God. Rulers were not independent agents but the channels through which God worked. Hence, as Hourani states, the *shari'a*, the statement of God's will, was supreme in society. Technically the whole sphere of legislation was therefore removed from the competence and responsibility of the ruler.

In theory, therefore, the caliphs possessed neither God's power of making laws nor the Prophet's function of proclaiming them. It was the task of the *ulama*, the learned class of religious and legal scholars, to translate God's will into a more detailed law that could apply to new and changing aspects of life. Despite this, rulers were by no means weak. In addition to the judicial and executive power, the early caliphs exercised direct military and fiscal control of the Muslim community. As the Muslim community expanded, the rulers appointed judges, governors—basically all offices. There was no formal or informal separation of powers.

Islamic law, *shari'a*, the basis of legislation, evolved from two sources. The first is the Quran, the literal word of God as revealed through the Prophet Muhammad. The second most important source of guidance in Islam is the hadith, the traditions (*sunna*) of what Muhammad said and did. When a situation arose in which the Quran and hadith were not able to provide clear guidance as to legislation, Islamic jurisprudence relied on personal opinions of Muslim jurists, analogical reasoning, independent legal reasoning, and consensus of the learned.[14] Hence, no legal reasoning or decisionmaking occurred at the popular level.

Several themes forming the bases of Islamic political theory were clearly developed early in Islamic history. Essentially it was a highly centralized leadership with no separation of powers. Any form of "popular participation" was limited to a small elite that was consulted on matters of decisionmaking. This consultation, however, was not necessarily binding, nor was it specified who should be consulted and how. Islamic law was the law of the state, and on issues not directly covered by the religious sources, decisions were reached by the *ulama*. The question that remains is whether Islamic political thought has become more participatory and democratic and, if so, whether these changes are reaching the grassroots level and being put into practice.

The Ideological Debate over Democracy Today

As Esposito and Piscatori state, essentially three main positions can be found concerning the subject of democracy within Islamic literature today. The first is a full acceptance of democracy: Islam and democracy are compatible because of the "need of rulers to consult widely and to govern on the basis of consensus."[15] The second wholly rejects democracy as being incompatible with Islam. Popular sovereignty usurps God's sovereignty; the recognition of the primacy of the people's will amounts to substituting the human-made law for divine law. In addition, some Muslim radicals reject any form of parliamentary democracy as a form of Westernization, incompatible with local traditions.[16] The third position, the mainstream opinion, argues in favor of what can be termed a limited democracy, one with a limited form of popular sovereignty that is restricted and directed by God's law.[17]

While large areas are still being debated, mainstream Sunni opinion within Egypt shares several basic assumptions.[18] The first of these is that Islam provides a comprehensive system of life—individual, political, and social. While Islam is religion and state, this does not mean that no distinction is made, as Gudrun Krämer states, between the spheres of religion proper and of worldly affairs. This distinction, Krämer explains, is

> . . . reflected in Islamic legal theory . . . , which distinguishes between the *'ibadat*, involving a person's relation with his or her creator (essentially the five pillars of Islam—the profession of faith, prayer, fasting, almsgiving and the pilgrimage), and the *mu'amalat*, covering all other aspects of economic, political and family life. While the *'ibadat* are eternal and immutable, the *mu'amalat* can be adapted to the changing requirements of time and locality, provided the results conform to the word (*nass*) and spirit (*maqasid*) of the shari'a.[19]

Islam is therefore flexible. It is generally agreed that for Islam to flourish a strong state is needed, but the form this state takes is secondary. What matters "is the purpose of the state and the principles it rests upon."[20] Hence, while *shari'a* must be applied, there is no specific form of organization through which it must be applied.[21] One finds, therefore, in the literature a discussion of what is *shari'a* and what is not, what is untouchable and binding and what is not, and the degree to which there is room for human interpretation.

Finally, as stated above, it is felt that there is no such thing as popular sovereignty if it means that people may do as they wish; God alone is sovereign. However, the community does have sovereignty in that the political head of the community is entrusted with the organization of the community. Hence, the authority to apply God's law has been transferred, as Krämer states, to the community as a whole. The head of the community or state,

> . . . no matter whether he . . . be called imam, caliph or president, is the mere representative, agent or employee of the community that elects, supervises and if necessary deposes him, either directly or via its representatives.[22]

There is thus a greater acceptance of the need for a separation of political powers in which there is a system of checks on the legislature and executive.[23]

As a consequence, in modern political thinking there has also been an increased emphasis on *shura* and a greater awareness of the necessity to formulate and institutionalize it.[24] *Shura* is furthermore presented as the functional equivalent of Western parliamentary rule.[25] According to Krämer,

> [m]ost authors tend to regard *shura* as both required and binding . . . , to accept the principle of majority decision, and to see it as a formal process and an institution—that is, a *shura* council made up of elected members, who ought to include specialists in Islamic law as well as in other fields. What they have in mind, then, is a council of experts deciding on the grounds of "objective" (Islamically valid) right and wrong, and not a political assembly representing conflicting opinion and interest. The ideal amounts to an expertocracy headed by the Just Ruler.[26]

In terms of the debate concerning pluralism, there is a general acceptance of differences in opinion. This is provided that these opinions remain within the framework of Islam. While freedom of the press, opinion, and belief are guaranteed, these are guaranteed provided that they do not violate Islam. Atheists, communists, and Marxists, and possibly even Nasserrists and Christians, could be excluded from political participation or even free expression of views. Political debate would therefore be restricted to matters of detail and implementation of *shari'a* without touching the foundations of Islam and the Islamic order. Topics considered as contrary to the *shari'a* or the essence and spirit of Islam would be excluded. Hence, intellectual pluralism is limited. In addition, the rights of non-Muslim minorities clearly remain as those of a second-class citizen. Women's rights, for example, would be limited under an Islamic state, the area of personal law—specifically questions of polygamy, divorce, and veiling—being particularly problematic.

Mainstream thought therefore argues in support of a limited democracy—not a religious state but a democracy with free elections, multipartyism, and decisionmaking based on consultation. Sovereignty is in the hands of the people or community. It is a democracy, however, that limits itself to ideologies and peoples supportive of an Islamic order. In addition, despite the much greater emphasis on *shura*, it is also one of limited participation, as the conception of *shura*—who is to be consulted, to what degree it is obligatory, and how it is to be institutionalized—is not fully defined. It is these four themes, therefore—popular participation, consultation, ideological pluralism, and minority rights—that will form the bases of the analysis of Islamic clinics and the degree to which they can be said to encourage democracy.

Mainstream Islam in Practice in Egypt Today

According to Ibrahim, Islamic groups or "activist Islam" within Egypt can be

> . . . divided into four broad tendencies, all of them activists and committed to the cause of an Islamic socio-political order, but widely differing on issues of strategy, tactics, and internal organisation. These four tendencies [are] the apolitical Muslim Brotherhood; the mainstream Muslim Brotherhood; the anti-regime Muslim groups; and the anti-society Muslim groups.[27]

For the purposes of this chapter, mainstream Islam in Egypt is therefore understood as the first two of these tendencies: those that do not condone violence against the state and can be said to represent a "social Islam," one that is not isolationist and does not shun society.

After a long history of political violence and repression under both Nasser and Sadat (which resulted in the splintering of the Muslim Brotherhood of Hasan al-Banna into a broader Islamic "movement" composed of the four tendencies mentioned above), the mainstream Muslim Brotherhood renounced violence in the 1970s under the leadership of 'Umar al-Tilminsani. Once referring to the corruption, factionalism, and personal interests of political parties, today the oft-quoted word *hizbiyya* ("partyism") refers to the recognition of a pluralistic multiparty political system, the decision to take part in elections, parliament, coalitions with other parties, and to strive to be constituted as a legal political party.[28] Since the mid-1980s, at the very latest, the Brotherhood has supported democracy and a free competitive party system in which an Islamic party would participate. With campaign slogans such as "Islam is the solution," "Islam is a holy book and a sword," and "Muhammad is our leader and the Quran is our constitution," their political goal is the establishment of an Islamic order.[29]

Hence the Brotherhood has not only come to accept pluralism in the form of different parties but, more importantly, has accepted the multiparty system as a legitimate form of the *shura* principle adapted to modern realities.[30] Furthermore, it has demonstrated its willingness to cooperate and form coalitions with political parties. While still legally banned both as an organization and a political party, the Brotherhood participated in the 1984 elections in an alliance with the New Wafd Party and again in the 1987 elections in a coalition with the Socialist Labor Party and the Liberal Party.[31] Published figures show that of the 448 seats in parliament, opposition parties won 108 in 1987—the largest number since the advent of the parliamentary system in 1924. The alliance list of the Socialist Labor Party, the Liberal Party, and the Muslim Brotherhood won 17 percent of the vote and 56 seats.[32] This was the highest number of seats obtained by any opposition party. Furthermore, 38 of these seats can be estimated as won by the Brotherhood, an increase of 30 seats from 1984.[33] This alone is still larger than the second largest opposition party, the New Wafd, which won only 35 seats in 1987.[34]

While the mainstream Muslim Brotherhood has adopted the political activism of the original Brotherhood, its social activities have come under the realm of what Ibrahim calls the apolitical Muslim Brotherhood. Still loyal to the mission of the Muslim Brotherhood, this tendency, smaller in number and composed of "mostly middle-aged professionals . . . has decided to devote its time and energy to religious teaching, moral reinforcement, and setting up modern economic and service institutions along 'Islamic lines.'"[35] This includes the establishment of economic enterprises, including Islamic banks, investment companies, factories, large-scale farming and agribusiness, as well as social and educational services such as Islamic medical clinics and welfare organizations. It is this tendency within mainstream Sunni Islam, and in particular Islamic medical clinics, with which this chapter is specifically concerned.

The Case Study: Islamic Clinics

Islamic clinics vary greatly in terms of their size and facilities. They include clinics with two doctors and one nurse as well as clinics with 200 doctors and 200 nurses and clerks. The majority of the clinics, however, range between staffs of 10 to 25 doctors. Other than the smallest clinics, the services offered by the clinics are quite extensive and impressive and often include surgery, cardiology, ophthalmology, detoxification programs, gynecology, dentistry, X-ray facilities, and laboratories for tests, to name a few. Most of the clinics are located above mosques with entrances at the side of the mosque building; the larger facilities, however, are located in separate buildings attached to the mosques.

The majority of Islamic clinics in Cairo are located in the poor, crowded central areas as well as the newer outlying areas of the city. No precise data are publicly available as to the exact number of the clinics; however, Morsy's study roughly estimates the number of Islamic clinics in Cairo between 300 and 350.[36] A total of 10 clinics and 25 interviews with the directors, doctors, and nurses within Islamic clinics were used in this chapter's analysis. In addition, 20 interviews were conducted with shop-keepers neighboring the clinics. While not representative in number, an attempt was made to make the case studies representative in terms of both size and geographic location.

Before analyzing the clinics, it must be noted that voluntary associations in Egypt are regulated by Law 32 of 1964. In terms of their organizational structures, several points must be mentioned. First, all associations must have a general assembly, which meets regularly and elects the board of administration or board of directors. The board must also have specified regular meetings and all its decisions must be taken by majority vote. However, the associations lay down the conditions for membership in the general assembly and, in addition, the board may appoint a manager from among or outside its membership to be empowered with the disposal of any matters entering within its competence.[37] Therefore, the elections conducted in the associations that run the clinics and the separation of powers within them cannot be seen as influenced in any way by activist Islamic and/or democratic thought.

Sovereignty of the Community in Determining the Leadership: Popular Participation

In more than half the case studies—seven out of 10—the founding of the clinics was a local neighborhood initiative, one in which a group of neighbors approached the mosque concerning the possibility of establishing an association in order to open a clinic. Furthermore, for nine of the clinics in the case study, funding was primarily a local initiative, based on donations from the neighboring community. In one case, the foundation of the clinic became a community event in which neighbors donated *everything* from cement, iron pillars, and money to physical labor in order to facilitate the building of the clinic. Furthermore, this same clinic's association (as well as one other's) established a condition that only people from the neighborhood may be members in the association.

A similar situation was found in another clinic, where the association appealed to wealthy merchants to contribute to the building of the clinic.

These merchants usually had some tie to the mosque and in the majority of cases were in fact people who had grown up in the neighborhood and, upon raising their financial and social statuses, moved elsewhere. These merchants consequently acquired seats on the clinic committee/association board. In another case, the clinic was able to call upon donations from previous members of the neighborhood who had migrated to the Gulf.

The integration of the clinics into the respective neighborhoods is also well established. In the smaller clinics, scenes were regularly witnessed in which association members and others from the neighborhood gathered in the office of the medical director or the association director to discuss events and the clinic. While performing a medical role, these clinics also appear to be performing a social role in the community and through this social role are also able to better ascertain the needs of the neighborhood.

When shopkeepers were questioned, however, as to their involvement in the clinic, there were no positive responses that community members approach the clinic to make suggestions, and in only two cases had shopkeepers been approached by the clinic concerning advice. The responses by the shopkeepers did not reflect a sense of representation or participation within the associations.

The clinics can therefore be said to be built at the communities' initiative and essentially by the communities. Neighborhoods surrounding the clinics are wholly integrated into its establishment. While there is a great deal of community participation in initiation and fundraising, however, participation appears to be limited to this initial phase of the clinics' establishment. While two clinics actively encourage community members, including the poor and illiterate, to become involved in the general assemblies of their respective clinics, general assemblies tend to be composed of the original founders and major donors. Fees are required for membership in the associations; however, the major stumbling block to greater community participation does not appear to be the fee but rather a lack of encouragement. Therefore, while associations are on the whole composed of people from the neighborhood, the poor—the very people the clinics are serving—are not directly represented and do not take part in the management or the negotiations of the management of their interests.

For essentially the same lack of encouragement, the bulk of doctors are also not in their general assemblies nor consequently on their boards of directors. In only one clinic are there doctors in the general assembly and in only three clinics are doctors on the boards of directors. In two of these, doctors were selected by members of the boards to be on it while in the third case the doctors were elected by the general assembly. None of the clinics had nurses either in the general assemblies or on the boards. While six of the 10 clinics did have technical or medical directors to represent the doctors' and the clinics' concerns, in only two of the cases were the technical directors on the board of directors. In the other four clinics the technical directors are occasionally invited to attend the boards' meetings if the doctors' opinions are needed on a medical issue. The bulk of the doctors are therefore not in their general assemblies, nor on their board of directors, nor on a medical committee.

While on the one hand doctors themselves feel that they are too busy for such extra responsibilities, on the other, the associations regard doctors as employees and not necessarily as joint participants. In one clinic, however, doctors were restricted from membership in the assembly and board in order to prevent tension among doctors and to ensure that all decisions taken were for the benefit of the clinic and the patients and not for the benefit of one or a few doctors. As employees of the associations, doctors on the whole are not formally involved in determining the leadership of the associations and consequently the clinics.

As the right to vote in Islamic clinics is dependent upon membership in the general assembly, the majority of doctors, nurses, technical directors, and patients are unable to use voting as a method either of determining the head of the board and committees or of popular control. As stated above, while consultation is widely practiced, it is not binding and the solicited advice need not be heeded. Hence, once the general assembly has elected members to the board, only the board exerts any formal control over decisions.

Neither the community of the patients, those living in the neighborhoods surrounding the clinic, nor the community of the doctors, therefore, determines the head of the associations in a formal, institutionalized manner. Membership in the associations is open, however, to doctors, patients, and community members should they choose to join. In addition, open channels are available in the clinics for doctors and community members to make suggestions.

Social Islam as represented in the Islamic clinics is participatory, albeit in a limited sense. The community participates in the funding and early establishment of the clinic and in this sense can be argued to reflect a degree of emphasis upon the *umma* as the source of authority. However, beyond the communities' donating of money, material, and time, their role is limited to suggesting services to the clinic at its own initiative. It is important to note, though, that in general this lack of encouragement also seems to reflect the fact that there appears to be no conscious attempt at creating an alternative organizational structure or vision within the clinics.

Shura: *Consultation*

While doctors and nurses are not included in the formal decisionmaking process, much decisionmaking in the clinics is less formal and more participatory than the structure of the clinics would imply. Due to both the smallness of the clinics as well as the desire to serve the poor and make the clinic as successful as possible, decisions in the clinics generally involve a large degree of consultation with staff not directly on the boards.

In fact, when doctors were asked whether they participate more or less in decisionmaking in an Islamic clinic as compared to their non-Islamic counterparts, 16 stated that they definitely participate more in decisionmaking, while only two (both from the same clinic) felt they participate less in decisionmaking. Five respondents were unsure and two felt that the degree of participation was the same as elsewhere. In most cases doctors have complete control over the daily running of a clinic in terms of medical issues and daily problems, and usually have the decisionmaking authority to reduce the fees for an especially poor patient or even charge nothing. In some cases, this includes decisions relating to small repairs, renovations, problems concerning electricity, water, furniture, and the cleaning staff.

In most cases, doctors are clearly aware of the high degree of consultation within their clinics and are very supportive of it. One example is particularly representative of the smaller clinics. In this clinic doctors are consulted regularly via the technical director on both administrative and technical issues, albeit more so on technical issues for obvious reasons. In addition, medical meetings among the doctors are called regularly and combined meetings with both the doctors and the board are held concerning larger decisions, such as the hiring of a new doctor. Thus, the doctors are wholly integrated in the decisionmaking process, albeit in an informal way.

Finally, in the case of one of the largest and most famous clinics in the city of Cairo, where senior doctors are appointed to the board, junior doctors are encouraged to express their views and concerns regarding medical issues to these doctors so that they may be presented at the board. Through the system of submanagers (who are not doctors but administrators), doctors deal with nonmedical issues. Each medical unit of the clinic is therefore run very independently from the others and consequently decisionmaking within the clinic is decentralized and based on a large degree of consultation.

In addition, it must be noted that in the majority of clinics visited, doctors and nurses are able to approach board members on a daily basis, as they pray regularly in the mosque. For example, one nurse, while wholly excluded from any formal decisionmaking process, noted that she regularly sees members from the administration praying on Fridays and freely approaches them on these days with her requests or comments.

In all the clinics the technical directors are easily found and approached (as the interviewer learned firsthand), since they are present each evening working in their capacity as doctors. The interviewer often saw patients approach the technical directors with questions and suggestions, and doctors were able to do the same. One of the clinics also has an "open-door" policy to the director of the association. In this case, the association director is available to the public and the doctors every evening in his office at the clinic.

To summarize, through regular consultation the majority of the clinics operate in a highly participatory and consultative manner, one that is more participatory than in non-Islamic clinics. Doctors are regularly consulted on their opinions and patients have open avenues to the directors (or in some cases even their friends before or after prayer) to give suggestions. This participation is not formalized, however, in any organizational structure. Consultation is not required and is not binding. The common goal and desire to ensure the success of the clinic in terms of helping the poor results in most cases in an informal, ongoing consultation system. However, while the associations are able to appoint doctors and/or managers to their boards, this only occurred in three clinics. Hence, while an increased emphasis on *shura* is clearly evident in the Islamic clinics, it is not as yet *formally* established into a more democratic structure, explicitly Islamic or otherwise. Furthermore, the participation and experience in the clinics does not appear to be "transferable." When asked if they had gained any leadership experience working at the clinic, 22 out of 25 doctors/nurses said they had gained none. Hence while the doctors participate more in decisionmaking, they are not gaining leadership skills that could be applied to other aspects of their personal lives or within civil society.

The Concept of a Limited Pluralism

When doctors were questioned as to their voting habits within the medical syndicate, it was found that of the 18 doctors interviewed, eight voted in the 1992 syndicate elections. Of these, five voted for the Islamic List, two chose candidates from both the Islamic List and the National Democratic Party (the government party), and one voted solely for the NDP. A similar diversity of opinions was evident when doctors and directors were asked about their voting patterns in the national elections. Of the 25 respondents questioned, 10 vote on a regular basis: five for the NDP, two for the Labor Party/ Islamic List coalition, one for Tagammu' (the leftist party), one selected candidates from all the parties, and one would not divulge for which party he votes.

Clearly, participants within the clinics are not limited only to those who support the Islamic List and the implementation of *shari'a*. This same diversity of thought was witnessed when the respondents were asked about their political views concerning the slogan "Islam is the solution." Out of

the 25 interviewees, only six supported the slogan with its political impli-
cations; among the other responses were even those that were antagonistic:
"When they explain their slogan, then I'll be able to give an opinion. But
I feel that these are the right words being used for the wrong purposes."

In addition, only three clinics specify certain religious-ideological beliefs as conditions for membership in their general assemblies. The remaining seven clinics have no ideological criteria other than a willingness to do
charity work in service of the poor. This pluralism, however, must be seen
as a reflection of the lack of political ideology within the clinics. Health
care, not Islam or democracy, is the goal of the clinics, and as such pluralism is encouraged when hiring in order to obtain the best health-care givers.

The Inclusion/Exclusion of Women and Minorities

In order to determine the status of women and Christians within Islamic
clinics, interviewees were questioned as to whether female doctors work at
the clinic, whether or not women have to wear a veil, and whether Christians were able to work at the clinics. In terms of the former, no clinic
stated any policy against employing female doctors, and female doctors
were witnessed at work in nine of the 10 clinics. In addition, only two
clinics specify that all female staff must don veils. Furthermore, women
are not limited to the role of gynecologists or to treating women only. Female doctors practice all fields of medicine, and male gynecologists are
also present in the clinics. Women on the whole are therefore not discrim-
inated against in any way according to their religious observance.

While none of the clinics currently have Christian doctors on staff,
three had had Christians working for them in the past. None of the clinics
have a policy against hiring non-Muslims. In addition, many of the clinics indicated a desire to have Christians on staff. While three of the clinics have
ideological criteria for their association members, this does not apply to
the doctors they hire. Certainly the majority of the Islamic clinics indicated that they want the best doctors they can get, Muslim, Christian, or
otherwise. Ideological and religious beliefs in general do not seem to interfere with the practice of medicine. In addition, all of the clinics receive
Christian patients. In fact, up to 25 or even 35 percent of the cases treated
in some Islamic clinics are Christian.[38] While the number of Christians
working in the clinics is not overly encouraging, it appears that, as with
the issue of ideological pluralism, the majority of clinics seem to be solely
concerned with caring for the sick, regardless of who is doing the caring.

Implications for the State/Civil Society Differentiation

Having examined the functioning of the clinics and argued for the lack of
a political agenda within them, it is important to look at the actual political

policies participants within the clinics are espousing. Are these demands consistent with democratic change? This section will therefore review the specific demands of the medical staff concerning the role of the government in providing health care in Egypt, as well as the desired relationship between the Islamic clinics and the government.

Of the 25 respondents interviewed, 20 clearly feel that the relationship between the Islamic clinics and the government should be one of increased cooperation. This cooperation should be in the form of monetary funding or loans for buying equipment in particular, the elimination of taxes for the clinics, as well as increased supervision in order to increase or maintain the medical standards of the clinics. Three interviewees stated that the government is either doing its best or is too economically burdened to assist the clinics. Only two respondents argued that the government should not interfere with the clinics, primarily because of what they feel is the ineptitude of the government.

Hence, the majority of the participants are not demanding a greater differentiation between state and society but rather the opposite. This is confirmed by a study conducted by *al-Wafd,* which found that the doctors interviewed within Islamic clinics would like the establishment of a system in which the syndicate is the third side in a ratified work contract between the associations and the doctors. Furthermore, they would like some sort of network or association established that would enable the clinics to better coordinate their activities and resources.[39] As noted above, in addition to pressuring for an increase in government aid, the study found that doctors would also like to have medical work exempt from taxation.[40]

On the whole, therefore, the clinics are not objecting to government supervision over the clinics with respect to medical practice and the objectives of the clinics' expenditures. Rather, *al-Wafd*'s study found that they would like only the cessation of government control over the association and interference in the administration. This appears to be based on the doctors' fear that the situation in the clinics will become like that of the government hospitals: overbureaucratized and inefficient.[41] Far from challenging the state in the field of health care, Morsy agrees that

> . . . the charitable health services offered by Islamist groups help maintain an indispensable component of the social welfare package and therefore simultaneously help such groups gain legitimacy *in,* and affirm the legitimacy *of,* the social system (cf. Jacobsen 1986: 131).[42]

Furthermore, interviews with the 25 directors and doctors as well as with the shopkeepers, confirm Morsy's assertion that the clinics are not viewed by the respondents in terms of a protest against the state or in terms of any political statement. As Morsy states, "far from representing an alternative health care strategy that challenges state authority, Islamist medicine is considered as a vehicle for power sharing."[43] In other words, Islamic clinics are not seen in the sense of a struggle for liberation, as an example of "power for the powerless." Both doctors and patients alike view them specifically in terms of the medical services they offer. Furthermore, they view the clinics and their work within them as complementary extensions of, or partnerships with, the government health services. In general, they seek greater cooperation between the two. These demands do not, on the whole, reflect a desire for a greater separation of state and society.

Conclusion

In all the clinics studied, the doctors and directors use the words *shura* (consultation) and democracy freely and frequently when describing their clinic. Without a doubt, the doctors are clearly aware of the greater participation they enjoy in the Islamic clinics, and are highly supportive of it. On the other hand, the interviewer did not find any evidence of a conscious effort to create an alternative conception of decisionmaking nor a strong consciousness of empowerment. The clinics are seen in a purely medical sense and the greater participation seems to be influenced by the strong desire to make the clinic as successful as possible. In addition, however, this participation may also be seen as part of a vague attempt to run the clinics along "Islamic lines." While no clinic directly expressed the conscious application of *shura* as part of an overall Islamic "model" that they are trying to establish, *shura* is clearly evident and is valued and seen as an important element in the functioning of the clinics.

As indicated above, despite the presence of *shura*, the interviewer could not find any indication that the clinics are attempting to create a new Islamic conception of state and society either. When asked about the Islamic principles that are applied in the clinics, the vast majority of respondents mentioned such criteria as charity and helping the poor. While charity is important in Islam, it is not exclusive to Islam and does not make something necessarily Islamic. There appears to be no attempt to apply any Islamic laws per se, as evidenced by the fact that in eight of the 10 clinics women do not have to be veiled. In addition (while male doctors may treat female patients according to Islam), many of the clinics do not have female gynecologists, a service many of the patients at the clinics expect from an Islamic clinic.

Islamic clinics are clearly influenced by mainstream Islamic thought, as evidenced both by the literature doctors claim to read and their emphasis on *shura*. Field research did not, however, reveal the implementation of an Islamic model, nor any evidence of institutional links or ties between the clinics and politically active and organized Islamic groups. Nor did the researcher find any form of political battle against the state at the grass-roots level. This conclusion is based on the inspirational and financial sources of the clinics, which are usually local and community based, the lack of religious and/or political propaganda within the clinics, as well as the clear distinction interviewees made between "us" and "them" when discussing Islamic groups.

The researcher also did not find any evidence that the clinics are con-tributing to the appeal and expansion of the Islamic "movement" and thereby strengthening the latter's ability to force the regime to undertake political openings. The people who come to the clinics do so because of the availability of better health care, but this does not translate into support for Islamic groups. The inspiration, establishment, and funding for the clinics comes primarily from community sources, people from the sur-rounding neighborhood. Patients often know and visit the members of the board of directors or the director himself. Hence, when speaking, as stated above, about the Islamic movement in Egypt, interviewees made clear both directly and indirectly the distinction between the Islamic "movement," which is beyond the community and active at a different and "higher" level within society, and the grassroots, community-based clinics. Inter-viewees were furthermore often critical of individual members they knew personally in the associations or of the clinic as a whole, and some even expressed their preference for private clinics or a different Islamic clinic. Hence the clinics are not seen as a model of what Islam can do; rather, they are judged in terms of the performance of a particular group of indi-viduals. The clinics are therefore not gaining adherents to Islam, but to a particular clinic alone.

The greater degree of participation and *shura* within the clinics is con-ducive both to democratization and to the changes within Islamic thought. Beyond this point, however, there appears to be no spirit, experience, or activities that would imply a grassroots consciousness of change. While their mere presence may have political significance, the clinics themselves are concentrating solely on providing good and inexpensive health care. In the course of doing so they are giving their members, as well as their sur-rounding communities, more involvement and participation. This is lim-ited, however, to donations on behalf of the neighborhoods and sugges-tions on behalf of the medical staff. While Islamic medical clinics are creating a more active civil society through the creation of a form of com-petition among neighborhoods to establish their own clinics, this "compe-tition" is limited to a relatively small segment of society and, more impor-tantly, it is understood in terms of charity or volunteer work, not in terms of self-help and the need to be autonomous from the state.

In conclusion, the underlying issue that remains to be addressed is the importance of ideology and the democratic functioning of associations in the process of democratization. Certainly authoritarian associations can contribute to the development of civil society and the creation of sufficient pressure to force political openings. They cannot, however, contribute to the establishment or institutionalization of a democracy. A functioning democracy requires more than democratic rules and procedures; it requires an understanding and internalization of the values of democracy—values that can only be fully inculcated through both education and democratic experience. Associations that provide these lessons contribute to the creation of a citizenry that will operate both at home and in public life, as well as in the workplace, in a democratic manner. It is also a citizenry that will be vigilant to incursions against democracy. While the democratic practices at the micro level are not necessarily a valid test of the likely practices of the leadership at the state level, they do provide at a very minimum a picture of the practices of the vast numbers of citizens working within the state machinery and related institutions and how they choose to execute or not execute state policies.

Notes

I am greatly indebted to the editors of this volume, as well as to Dr. Saad Eddin Ibrahim, Dr. Raymond Baker, 'Abd al-Rahman Hillel, Salah Taha, and Daniel Gabriel for their insights, support, guidance, and assistance in researching and writing this chapter.
    1. See, for example, John Keane, *Democracy and Civil Society* (London: Verso, 1988); Michael Bratton, "Beyond the State," *World Politics* 41 3 (1989), pp. 407–430.
    2. Mohammed El-Sayyid Said, "Métamorphoses du champ sociétal à partir du renforcement des mouvements à référence religieuse," *Dossiers du CEDEJ: Modernisation et Nouvelles Formes de Mobilisation Sociale* (Cairo, 1991), p. 79.
    3. For example, Sami Zubaida, "Islam, the State and Democracy," *Middle East Report* 170 (November–December 1992), pp. 2–10.
    4. See, for example, Judith Miller, "The Challenge of Radical Islam," *Foreign Affairs* 72, 2 (Spring 1993), pp. 43–56; Leon T. Hadar, "What Green Peril?" *Foreign Affairs* 72, 2 (Spring 1993), pp. 27–42; Gudrun Krämer, "Islamist Notions of Democracy," *Middle East Report* 183 (July–August 1993), pp. 2–13; Gudrun Krämer, "Islam et Pluralisme," *Démocratie et démocratisation dans le monde arabe* (Cairo: Dossiers du CEDEJ, 1992), pp. 339–351; Hala Mustafa, "Les forces Islamistes et l'expérience démocratique en Egypte," *Démocratie et démocratisation dans le monde arabe* (Cairo: Dossiers du CEDEJ, 1992), pp. 379–395; John Esposito and James Piscatori, "Democratization and Islam," *Middle East Journal* 45, 3 (Summer 1991), pp. 427–440; William Zartman, "Democracy and Islam: The Cultural Dialectic," *Annals* 524 (November 1992), pp. 181–191.
    5. Alain Roussillon, "Entre Al-Jihad et Al-Rayyan: Phénomenologie de l'islamisme égyptien," *Dossiers du CEDEJ: Modernisation et Nouvelles Formes de Mobilisation Sociale* (Cairo, 1991), p. 50.

6. Roussillon, "Entre Al-Jihad et Al-Rayyan," p. 45.

7. *Al-Sha'ab*, 7 April 1992. The importance laid on the medical syndicate elections, especially for the more educated sectors of society, can be explained by a variety of reasons. First, the elections are conducted in a fair environment with the votes being sorted and counted in the presence of representatives of all the candidates. Second, under the present situation of limited democratic freedoms and elections that are deemed unrepresentative, professional syndicates and nongovernmental associations have come to substitute for the expression of opinions. Finally, because of local, Arab, and international interest in the operation and political attitude of the Islamist movement, attention has recently been focused on the Medical Syndicate's election. "The Elections of the Medical Syndicate," *Civil Society* 5 (May 1992), pp. 5–6.

8. "The Elections of the Medical Syndicate," p. 5.

9. Morroe Berger, *Islam in Egypt Today* (Cambridge: Cambridge University Press, 1970). For other examples, review the literature review in Sarah Ben Nefissa-Paris, "Le mouvement associatif egyptien et l'islam," *Maghreb-Machrek* 135 (January–March 1992), pp. 19–36. Two of the few current studies are those of Ben Nefissa-Paris, who looks at the spread of Islamic associations in Egypt, and Roussillon's study of Islamic banking. See Sarah Ben Nefissa-Paris, "Le mouvement associatif egyptien et l'islam," and Alain Roussillon, *Sociétés islamiques de placement de fonds et ouverture économique* (Cairo: CEDEJ, 1988). Numerous studies do exist, however, on the Islamic groups' activities within the professional syndicates in Egypt. Here one can find the type of policy changes the Islamists are pressuring to enact. See Amani Qandil, "Études des groupes d'interêt en Egypte: aspect international et aspect particulier," *Dossiers du CEDEJ: Études Politiques du Monde Arabe* (1991), pp. 85–98.

10. See Soheir Morsy, "Islamic Clinics in Egypt: The Cultural Elaboration of Biomedical Hegemony," *Medical Anthropology Quarterly* 2, 4 (December 1988), pp. 355–369; Iman Roushdy Hammady, "Religious Medical Clinics in Cairo," Master's thesis no. 885, American University of Cairo, 1990.

11. According to one source, Muhammad stated: "God has given two safeguards to the world: His Book [the Quran] and the *sunna* [the example] of His Prophet [Muhammad]." According to another source: "God has given two safeguards to the world: His Book and the family of His Prophet." Roy P. Mottahedeh, "The Foundations of State and Society," in Marjorie Kelly, ed., *Islam: The Religious and Political Life of a World Community* (New York: Praeger Publishers, 1984), pp. 55–56.

12. Albert Hourani, *Arabic Thought in the Liberal Age, 1798–1939* (London: Oxford University Press, 1962), pp. 5–6.

13. Hourani, *Arabic Thought in the Liberal Age*, p. 6.

14. Frederick Mathewson Denny, *An Introduction to Islam* (New York: Macmillan Publishing Company, 1985), pp. 217–220.

15. John Esposito and James Piscatori, "Democratization and Islam," *Middle East Journal* 45, 3 (Summer 1991), p. 434.

16. Esposito and Piscatori, "Democratization and Islam," p. 428.

17. Esposito and Piscatori, "Democratization and Islam," pp. 436–437.

18. Gudrun Krämer, "Islam and Democracy: The Contemporary Sunni Debate," paper presented at the 1992 Annual BRISMES Conference, St. Andrew's, Scotland, July 1992. Mainstream Sunni opinion within Egypt includes the Muslim Brotherhood from Hassan al-Banna to individual thinkers committed to the Islamic awakening, such as Muhammad Salim al-'Awwa and Fahmi Huwaidi.

19. Krämer, "Islamist Notions of Democracy," p. 4.

20. Krämer, "Islamist Notions of Democracy," p. 4.
21. Krämer, "Islamist Notions of Democracy," p. 4.
22. Krämer, "Islamist Notions of Democracy," p. 6.
23. Krämer, "Islamist Notions of Democracy," p. 7.
24. Krämer, "Islam and Democracy," p. 7. See also Ann Elizabeth Mayer, "Islamic Law," in Kelly, *Islam*, p. 232.
25. Krämer, "Islamist Notions of Democracy," p. 7.
26. Krämer, "Islamist Notions of Democracy," p. 7.
27. Saad Eddin Ibrahim, "Egypt's Islamic Activism in the 1980s," *Third World Quarterly* 10, 2 (1988), pp. 640–641.
28. Richard Mitchell, *The Society of Muslim Brothers* (London: Oxford University Press, 1969), p. 54. For an excellent discussion of the Muslim Brotherhood's changing and divided attitude toward political parties, see Olaf Farschid, "*Hizbiya*: Die Neuorientierung der Muslimbruderschaft Agyptens in den Jahren 1984 bis 1989," *Orient* 30, 1 (1989), pp. 59–73.
29. Martin Forstner, "Auf dem legalen Weg zur Macht? Zur politischen Entwicklung der Muslimbruderschaft Agyptens," *Orient* 29, 3 (1988), p. 400.
30. Gudrun Krämer, "The Change of Paradigm," *Peuples Mediterranéens* 42–43 (October 1987–March 1988), pp. 295–296.
31. Farschid, "*Hizbiya*," pp. 55–56.
32. Mona Makram-Ebeid, "Political Opposition in Egypt: Democratic Myth or Reality?" *Middle East Journal* 43, 3 (Summer 1989), p. 432.
33. Mona Makram-Ebeid, "The Role of the Official Opposition," in Charles Tripp and Roger Owen, eds., *Egypt under Mubarak* (London: Routledge, 1989), p. 42.
34. Makram-Ebeid, "Political Opposition in Egypt," p. 432.
35. Ibrahim, "Egypt's Islamic Activism," p. 641.
36. Morsy, "Islamic Clinics in Egypt," p. 356.
37. Law 32/1964 of the Ministry of Social Affairs. English text provided by the Legal Research and Resource Center for Human Rights, Cairo.
38. *Al-Ahram*, 4 April 1990. In some Christian clinics, the percentage of Muslim patients may even be as high as 70 percent. According to *Al-Ahram* these clinics represent an example of national unity. Furthermore, the percentage of Muslim patients in Christian clinics does not decrease with the establishment of Islamic clinics in the same area.
39. *Al-Wafd*, 12 April 1987.
40. *Al-Wafd*, 12 April 1987.
41. *Al-Wafd*, 12 April 1987.
42. Morsy, "Islamic Clinics in Cairo," p. 360.
43. Morsy, "Islamic Clinics in Cairo," p. 355.

10

Political Liberalization, Gender, and the State

Mervat F. Hatem

Political liberalization in the Arab world has been characterized by state ambivalence toward women. This has represented a dramatic change in what had been a "friendly" relationship between women and the state under bureaucratic authoritarian regimes. Up until 1976, when Egypt began the regional move toward political liberalization, many states of both the *mashriq* and the *maghreb* (Iraq, Syria, Egypt, Sudan, Libya, Tunisia, Algeria, and South Yemen) recognized women's formal rights to education, work, and political participation.[1] In Tunisia, Syria, and Iraq, the state took the added step of introducing important changes in the personal status laws (regulating marriage, divorce, and the custody of children), which enhanced women's right to divorce and outlawed or placed numerous restrictions on polygamy.[2] This form of state feminism (i.e., the sympathy of the state to some feminist demands) contributed to the emergence of middle class women as active actors in these societies and enhanced their modernist credentials. Middle class women joined the state sector in large numbers and became instrumental in the successful provision of important social services like education, social work, and health care, and participated in running the systems of local and national administration. Their economic dependence on the state contributed to their loss of political autonomy. Official women's organizations set women's social and political agendas and subordinated them to state policies.

The developmental crisis of these bureaucratic authoritarian regimes contributed to the general collapse of Arab state feminism in the 1980s. The move toward political liberalization was characterized by the developmental and the political retreat of the state, the emergence of a limited power-sharing arrangement among the state, private capital, and the upper segments of the middle class, represented to some extent by the new multiparty systems. A polarized and sometimes violent struggle between the secular-ist states and their Islamist challengers also frequently emerged.

There is little theoretical discussion of how this limited liberalization has affected women's citizenship rights and roles. This suggests a double ambivalence—of liberal states toward women and their associations, and of liberal political theories vis-à-vis gender.

Liberalism, Liberalization, and Gender

The majority of the liberal and eclectic/leftist scholars of Arab societies do not extensively discuss gender and/or women's associations in the debate on Arab political liberalization. When passing references are made to gen-der, it is as an issue or a cultural artifact that distinguishes the Islamist from the secularist players.[3] Even more infrequently, there are some references to women's associations and their activities[4] whose operation and activities are not integrated in the discussion of civil society. The above provide, however, glimpses of their respective assumptions regarding the role of women's associations in the new societies. The liberals assume that all the institutions of civil society (including those of women) will play the same role.[5] In contrast, eclectic/leftist scholars single out women's associations and human rights groups as having a pivotal role to play in deepening de-mocratization by functioning as "critical agents vis à vis the regime."[6] The former suggest that women's associations will acquire political recognition by virtue of their assertion of "fundamental moral claims namely the dig-nity of the person and the equality of the individual."[7] The latter disagree, suggesting that they will "confront greater state opposition."[8] This they at-tribute to either the continued political authoritarianism of the state or "government's indulgence to the demands of the militant Islamists,"[9] but not to liberal politics. In short, while disagreeing on the role of women's as-sociations and their relationship to the state, both liberal and eclectic/left-ist scholars view women's rights as compatible with liberal politics.[10]

What these views ignore is the extensive feminist debate on how the organization and history of liberal societies provided new bases for gender inequality.[11] According to this view, liberal society is divided into the "public (social, political and history) and the private (the personal, do-mestic and the familial)" spheres, which represent the division of the sexes.[12] The former gains its meaning and significance from its opposition to the latter, which serves as its natural foundation.[13] The emphasis on women's domestic roles has contributed to their exclusion from the public arenas and associated benefits.[14]

Does liberal discrimination against women end when they leave the private arena and start their associational drive in the public/civil arenas?

Are the liberal public rules "gender neutral" in the way they deal with women as citizens and as organized groups? Again, feminist theorists are skeptical of these claims to neutrality. They argue that they serve as an institutional cover for liberal acceptance of the continued male domination of the political arena and identification of that arena with masculinity. Rationality within liberalism is, historically, a masculine quality synonymous with universalist political practices and discourses. Not only did it exclude women, but it refused to acknowledge that its universalism was an expression of sexual difference. When classical liberal theorists discussed femininity, they used it to question women's rationality. For John Stuart Mill, the stress of narrow-minded special interests disqualified women from participation.[15] Immanuel Kant viewed their lack of individual autonomy as another reason for their exclusion.[16] For these reasons, the political arena was not "gender neutral." The hierarchical relationship between the civil and the domestic, and the presumed difference between the two as representatives of the genders, serve as important bases of liberalism as a "modern fraternal patriarchy."[17]

The above concepts and assumptions are not questioned in the debate on Arab political liberalization. The public arenas are discussed as the more appropriately civil.[18] In contrast, the private arena is described as a part of "natural society,"[19] which includes "primordial organizations."[20] The former, dominated by men, occupies center stage and the latter, where women are active, is located outside the definition of politics. Intellectually, the exclusion is justified on the grounds that civil society includes modern associations organized voluntarily[21] and whose membership is based on consent.[22] This idealization of the institutions of civil society, as a basis for excluding women and/or the private sphere from discussion, needs to be put in question because it does not describe the behavior of either public or private associations. For instance, membership in Arab professional associations is a condition for one's practice of the profession, which negates the elements of consent and volunteerism as key distinguishing features of "modern" versus "traditional" institutions. Equally important, families have increasingly become the target of public policy and are, consequently, no longer just private.[23] If the theoretical justifications for declaring familial and domestic formations outside civil society no longer hold, then the decision to remain faithful to them is largely arbitrary and/or political.

In considering familial and domestic social groups as part of "natural society" and as "primordial" structures, the political concerns of women are marginalized in two different ways. First, if they belong to "natural society" then their position, their relationship to men, and the roles they play in society are declared unproblematic. They are not part of the social order whose change is negotiated. Second, while other public institutions legitimately pursue their "particular" interests, the label "primordial" applied to gender actors establishes their devalued status in an ideal typical "universalist" male discourse.

Given the above biases, the liberal options offered to women's associations are limited and limiting. If they accept their "secondary status," women are secured a limited political presence. The minority associations that take on an overtly political tone (whether Islamist or feminist) that question the bases of this arrangement (i.e., gender as nonpolitical or the political as gender-neutral) are likely to meet opposition.

From this perspective, Arab political liberalization does not represent an aberration from a liberal ideal. Both show little sympathy for women's equal rights and/or their questioning of existing rules. In this chapter, I will examine how the emerging Arab liberal systems have exhibited political ambivalence regarding gender, women, and their associations. While in some instances the state has loosened its institutional grip on women by recognizing their nongovernmental associations, it has in others used its formal or informal power to influence their operation. In some cases, it has sacrificed women's rights to appease its opponents. In others, it has defended their rights and used them as a weapon against challengers. Middle class women's associations have exhibited similar ambivalence vis-à-vis political liberalization. While most benefited from it by organizing themselves and experimenting with new discourses, they were not committed to the rights of other associations to exist and/or to political liberalization itself. The result is a renewed dependence on the state, its political opponents, or international donors.

In an attempt to explore the above conjectures, this chapter will focus on the cases of Sudan, Tunisia, and Egypt. In each case, an examination of the changing relationship between women (their associations) and the state will precede discussion of the resulting perspectives and discourses available on women.

Sudan: Gender and Regime Change

The regime of Ja'far al-Numayri used state feminism in the 1970s to give itself a progressive facade. It quickly abandoned it in the face of the political and economic crises of the early 1980s. The regime resorted to Islamization in 1983 to cement a new alliance it formed with the Islamists. The mass revolt of 1985, which brought about the fall of the regime, contributed a short, liberal experiment in which feminist, technocratic, and Islamist women's organizations coexisted. The 1989 coups brought to power a new Islamist regime that sought to depoliticize gender by demobilizing feminist associations and accommodating academic/technocratic ones. As part of that strategy, it mobilized Islamist associations around the goal of socializing gender.

During its early years, the Numayri regime (1969–1985) acted as a champion of women's rights. It responded positively to the demands put forward by the Sudanese Women's Union, an independent leftist organization.[24] After co-opting its agenda, the regime turned against it in 1971 and replaced it with its own Sudan Women's Union. The latter became the women's wing of the regime's only political party, the Sudanese Socialist Union.[25]

Sudanese state feminism boasted the following achievements:

- In the economic arena, the 1973 Labor Act gave women the right to equal pay for equal work. It also gave them the right to two months' paid maternity leave and the right to one hour per day to feed their infant children.
- Women were given the right to inherit the pensions of their male kin.
- In the political arena, women were given 25 percent of the total number of seats on the People's Local Councils and also the right to compete for open seats. In addition, they were allocated seats in the People's National Council and represented at every political level within the ruling party.[26]

These accomplishments gave the regime a progressive image. With state feminism serving as a source of legitimacy, the regime was unwilling to tolerate independent nongovernmental women's associations with competing political visions and agendas. Exceptions were made, however, with regard to technocratic and academic nongovernmental associations. The case of the Babiker Badri Scientific Association for Women Studies (which was established and recognized by the regime in 1979 and continues to operate today) is instructive.

The association was formed following a national symposium on "The Changing Status of Sudanese Women," held to celebrate the seventy-fifth anniversary of the *Ahfad* (descendants) schools that played a special role in women's education.[27] The first *Ahfad* school was established in 1903 by Babiker Badri to provide elementary education for boys and girls.[28] They eventually were expanded to provide women with education at all levels. The establishment of Ahfad University College in 1966 to provide for "the education of women in the areas of child psychology, pre-school education, family sciences (nutrition, pre- and post-natal care and child care), management, organization, rural extension education and development"[29] was their crowning achievement. The naming of the association after Badri and the institutional links it maintained with the college, its students, and its faculty were a tribute to the "founder of Sudanese education for girls."[30]

The association's goal was "to carry out research on the status of Sudanese women and . . . projects suggested by that research, to encourage research workers in the field of women studies and to join efforts with similar national and international societies."[31] It gave priority to the training of rural women and the eradication of female circumcision in its activities.[32] Without significant economic or political support from the state, the association, its publication *Women* (*al-Nisa'*), and 11 out of its 15 projects were funded by international donors. The Soroptimist International funded the publication of its magazine, which was to serve as a "newsletter and an awareness bulletin worldwide."[33] As a result, the magazine was divided into a large English section that targeted the international audience and a very modest Arabic one that addressed the national one. UNICEF, the Ford Foundation, Oxfam, the Norwegian Action Group, and the Swedish Housewives Association funded many of its training projects.[34] This heavy dependence on international donors raised the issue of who set the agenda for the association and the extent to which its projects reflected national priorities.

Because of the association's research goals, membership was open to educated women, with the level of education not specified. Men and international women with similar academic interests could become affiliated members. This special membership determined the discourse the association produced on the relations between the women researchers of Ahfad College (who were urban middle class), the rural working class women they studied, and the state. The secretary-general of the association explained that because 1 percent of the female population in the Sudan went to the university, the members recognized themselves as socially privileged.[35]

> It becomes the civic duty of university educated women to *share* with their rural sisters this privilege. The traditional acceptance and suitability of women to work with other women gives a good opportunity for university women to *help* their rural sisters[36] (emphasis added).

The above summarized the contradictory politics of the "women and development" discourse that the association developed. It presented itself in two contrasting ways. On the one hand, there was the "egalitarian rhetoric of sharing" and on the other, there was the "condescending view of rural women as needing the help of their educated sisters." In this so-called woman-to-woman approach, college women claimed to be sharing their privilege (knowledge, education, and training) with rural women, but in fact, they established their professional (and class) authority over the personal and work lives of these women. The following was how the magazine explained the thinking of the association and Ahfad University on helping rural women.

It is considered that *a minimum of social development* is a precondition for economic development; not merely a consequence to it. And that women, housewives in particular, should be given special attention because their roles as mothers and housekeepers are *of high value to society and not only to their families*. The status of and aspirations of housewives should be raised. They should be *encouraged* to participate more in raising the economic *standard of living of their families* and given alternative ways of doing this outside family work by motivating them *to be* trained in other economic activities by *raising* their organizational abilities and leadership *skills*[37] (emphasis added).

According to the developmental discourse, rural women represented a problem to their societies. They lacked the minimum social development that made economic growth possible. They were not citizens entitled to rights, but objects of change that "had value" for societal goals. In this enterprise, the association coordinated its work with state agencies and local councils.[38] To improve the prospects of rural families, women's obligations were multiplied. Through training in health care and home economics, they became rough copies of "professional women." The acquisition of these skills was presumed to be the solution to their subordination. Paradoxically, the members of the association indicated in their magazine articles that their professional training had not ended discrimination against them.[39] In other words, in spite of the rhetoric of empowerment, training offered rural women new types of subordinate roles.

Middle class women participated in and benefited from this emphasis on training. For example, when Ahfad College's "Extension Agents in Rural Development for Women" program stated that it was committed to learning from rural women, it was referring to the use of rural women in surveys and interviews conducted by university women for college credit.[40] When the program declared its interest in involving women in the planning of projects, it interpreted this as having college women learn about the needs of rural women so that they can "represent them." Finally, the program's claim to involve rural women in the implementation of projects was nothing more than an expectation that they would submit to the application of the research results to their personal and domestic lives. In these experiments at social engineering, women researchers intervened in the minute details of family (e.g., nutrition, family and reproductive health, home management, and sexual practices) and work (what to produce, how to produce it, time management, and business management) lives of rural women. To ensure their continued control of the change, they trained rural leaders at the villages and at Ahfad College whose task was to monitor other villagers.[41]

In short, the Babiker Badri Scientific Association for Women Studies did not challenge the power relations that connected different classes, international and national actors, state, and women. They added new ones that put the family and work lives of rural women under their professional control. This explained why the different regimes could easily accommodate them.

State feminism did not survive the economic and political crises of the 1980s. During its last years, the Numayri regime formed an alliance with Hasan al-Turabi's Muslim Brotherhood that it hoped would give it a new basis of legitimacy. The result was the adoption of a restrictive form of Islamization in 1983. While the alliance gave the regime two more years in office, it turned the secularists and the African and Christian South against it. Islamization Sudanese style sought to establish the hegemony of the *shari'a* over secular and customary laws.[42] In seeking to create a homogeneous legal system, it eliminated the expanded maneuverability women enjoyed by the availability of the different legal and ethnic traditions.[43]

A mass revolt assisted by support from the military in April 1985 led to the overthrow of the Numayri regime. The new regime suspended the Islamist laws, but did not dismantle them.[44] Like the previous brief liberal experiments, the one in 1985 witnessed the reemergence of the religiously based Umma Party, representing the Ansar sect, and the Democratic Unionist Party of the *Khatimiyya* order. In addition, the Muslim Brotherhood/National Islamic Front emerged as a large source of opposition to the major parties. It capitalized on their equivocation regarding the principle of an Islamic state[45] to attract some of their followers.

This represented a further politicization of religion as a basis of political legitimacy for the liberal state, which had its impact on the public debate on gender. The reemergence of the Sudanese Women's Union in 1985 as a secular and leftist voice, and its embrace of the improvement of women's rights—especially in the area of personal status—did not have a marked effect on the debate. The public discussions of the law were largely focused on the extent to which the *shari'a* guaranteed women's equality.[46] Here, the Islamist women activists were on more comfortable ground and the secularists were forced to argue their case in Islamic terms.

The ideological division of Sudanese women became institutionalized in the elections that followed. Each political party co-opted active middle and upper class women to its side. Two women from the National Islamic Front were elected to the Constituent Assembly in 1986. The government of Sadiq al-Mahdi, the leader of the Umma Party, selected, for the first time, a woman to a cabinet position.[47]

A military coup led by General Umar al-Bashir put an end to this short liberal experiment. The new military regime in alliance with Hasan al-Turabi's National Islamic Front established a new Islamist state in the Sudan. Judging from the statements made by Hasan al-Turabi, the leader of the National Islamic Front, on the gender concerns of his government and the institutional strategy that was used to implement them, the new regime contemplated a two-pronged approach. There was the short-term use of state power to use gender as a means to give the society an Islamic character and direction. Al-Turabi suggested that this approach was largely dictated by the nature of the transitional period and the weakness of the civil society inherited from the totalitarian state of Ja'far al-Numayri.[48] In the long run, the regime intended to rely on social institutions to define women's roles and to sanction their content. In the Islamist approach to gender, the "government cannot give women's rights by decree as in the case of Tunisia. It has to come from the bottom of society—from the people."[49]

Given the above perspective, the regime halted the secular women's activities and associations (excepting the technocratic ones)[50] as part of the effort to point the society in an Islamic direction. It also explained the use of state authority to instruct women to wear the Islamic dress. According to al-Turabi, the state was reluctant, however, to use the penal code to punish those who do not adhere to it, as is the case in Saudi Arabia.[51] This step would have gone too far in the opposite direction of the Islamist goal to rely on "society [as] a form of control."[52]

With regard to the content of its gender program, the new government held a conference on Women and National Salvation in January 1990 whose purpose was to discuss the role that women would play in the Islamist state. The conference adopted a very specialized and an academic approach to women's issues[53] whose effect would depoliticize their concerns. At the same time, it recommended the establishment of its own official women's organization to be called the "General Union of Sudanese Women" to articulate the regime's views regarding women and to contribute to their development at home and at work.[54]

In other words, the new state strategy was to socialize gender issues; that is, to define them narrowly as those that relate to women's interests and roles in the home and the workplace. In establishing the nonpolitical character of these concerns, the regime proposed a return to the older Islamic definitions of women's citizenship that restricted their activities and interests in the political arena. With gender as a secondary social concern of the state, these issues can legitimately be put back in the hands of individual patriarchs and the family.

Tunisia: Bureaucratic Control of the Gender Agenda

At first glance, the rise of nongovernmental women's associations in Tunisia during the last 14 years seems paradoxical. Most analysts (whether Tunisian, Arab, or international) had hailed the personal status code, adopted by the regime of Habib Bourguiba in 1956, as establishing "modern legal" bases for women's equality. The emergence of an independent women's club in 1979 represented a different feminist consciousness for a new generation that, while proud of the accomplishments of state feminism, was dissatisfied with the authoritarian state and its gendered policies. The state was very suspicious of and unsympathetic to the club, which challenged its feminist credentials. It politicized the personal status code as a means of excluding the Islamists from the liberal process and co-opting the new feminists. The contraction of the liberal rules and the use of state repression against the Islamists identified state feminism with that of the authoritarian secular state.

In 1979 a women's club was formed within the Tahir al-Haddad Cultural Center in Tunis. In the absence of political freedoms, then, the cultural arena emerged as the only place where activists (including feminists) could organize. The state viewed these middle class feminists with suspicion. It excluded them from its discussion of gender issues (like family planning) for fear of their criticism of its programs, which did not treat women well and/or did not provide them with real choices.[55] Worse, local authorities aggressively went after them in an effort to tarnish their reputations and discredit their agendas.[56]

The Tahir al-Haddad Cultural Center, named after one of the early nationalist supporters of women's rights and the only center in the country run by a woman, provided a safe haven for the group.[57] At the beginning, the members described themselves as both political and leftist. In the club's platform, they stated that the struggles of women were "tied to the struggle against imperialism, to the Arab world's and the Third World's struggle for liberation."[58] Their discussions of the gendered identities and commitments of the club contributed a different discourse. The club was identified as a women's club whose membership was open only to women, even though men could be invited to its debates. It was devoted to the "reflection and the study of the conditions of women in Tunisia . . . [and the pursuit of these goals] *democratically*."[59] Included in this new democratic practice was a conscious discussion of which language and rules to adopt and how to reject all forms of hierarchy.[60]

Toward that goal, they divided themselves into small study groups, where members could be actively involved in small, safe settings. There, different perspectives coexisted and there was no pressure to select one to represent the group. Members explored issues such as women and the family, women and feminism, women and sexuality, and women and power. Out of these studies, there emerged a feminist critique of patriarchal power institutionalized in different arenas of society and internalized by women —for example, the patriarchal character of the 1956 code, women's unequal status in politics, and the denial of rights to abandoned children. The following is a brief summary of some of their reflections, published in their journal *Nisa'*.

Because the 1956 code outlawed "polygamy, repudiation and *le droit de djeber*, a provision under which women's consent was not required at marriage,"[61] its progressive character was assumed. There were no studies that show how widespread polygamous marriages were in Tunisia in the 1950s and the extent to which this was the *major* problem facing women of different classes. There was no discussion of how the code substituted one type of patriarchal marriage with another: monogamy in place of polygamy. Within monogamous families, the code recognized the husband as the head of the household. The law also recognized the need to consider social customs in resolving issues related to marriage. As a result, the decision of who to marry remained subject to social pressure. Guardianship of children was defined as a male right from which women were excluded unless the husband died or lost eligibility.[62] Finally, while women had an equal right to divorce, the expenses of filing for divorce and women's continued economic dependence on men made this a right that most were unable to freely exercise.[63]

Next, the club addressed itself to the state's requirement that women be elected to a certain quota in municipal elections. In its view, the provision implied that women were incompetent in the political arena and hence in need of state intervention. Moreover, the allocation of a quota for women did not solve the problem of underrepresentation. In effect, it abandoned the right to political equality. Finally, the club came out in support of the rights of abandoned children. The state had resisted pressure from human rights and feminist groups to extend them equal rights because the Islamists claimed that legal rights to children born out of wedlock was an "assault on the integrity of the family."[64]

The above views put the club and its journal in an unenviable position between the state and the Islamists. Since 1984, the Islamic Tendancy Movement had begun to challenge the modernist credentials of the 1956 code and its legal break with some Islamic traditions and interpretations. They argued that the code has contributed to the "disintegration of society."[65] Rashid al-Ghannushi explicitly criticized those "who dared liken the banning of polygamy to a 'liberating asset.'"[66] He called for a public referendum on the code to "reexamine the situation of the Tunisian family and a study of the effects of the law on the family. . . . Has the Tunisian family become more harmonious as a result of this law or not?"[67]

The state viewed the above attack as an indirect challenge to its legitimacy and responded by strongly defending the code. This put *Nisa'* in an awkward position. Their feminist views simultaneously put them in opposition to the Islamists and the state. While they were critical of the code's limitations, unlike the Islamists, they did not want it repealed; rather, they were demanding its radicalization. They feared the state, which could use their critiques as an excuse to close down the journal.[68]

The attempt to avoid hierarchical organizational rules and the fight against the emergence of dominant perspectives was undermined by the need to distribute editorial and legal responsibilities in publishing *Nisa'*. Because the membership was unable to agree on a unified strategy in dealing with the state and tolerate the existence of "major differences" among their ranks on the relationship between feminism and politics, the group broke down into competing factions and the defection of those members committed to the development of a new democratic feminist practice.[69] Financially, the journal suffered from the unwillingness of the Ministry of Cultural Affairs to extend it normal support: The ministry bought 10 subscriptions instead of the 1,000 it usually bought from other cultural journals. As a result, the journal ceased publication in 1987.[70]

The defecting members formed their own independent association titled *Nisa' Dimuqratiyyat* (Democratic Women) to distinguish themselves from the National Union of Tunisian Women, one of the organs of the ruling party. This met with official disapproval. While they remained active in the debate on national issues, the state denied them legal recognition until 1989, when liberal rules were formally declared.[71]

The advent of the regime of Zein al-'Abidin Bin 'Ali on 7 November 1987 contributed to the further politicization of the personal status code by formally using it as a test of Islamist acceptance of the liberal legality.[72] In addition to renouncing the use of violence, adopting a democratic approach, and a commitment not to organize within the army, al-Ghannushi declared that the personal status code is "a body of choices and decisions which are part of different schools of Islamist thought," that is, an example of *ijtihad* (interpretation).[73] He added, however, that it should not be considered something sacred since, like other human accomplishments, it may need to be reevaluated from time to time without its essence being called into question.[74]

Despite these important concessions, in addition to the change of the movement's name to *al-Nahda* (Renaissance) to comply with the requirement that no reference be made to religion in party platforms, *al-Nahda*'s inclusion in the National Pact did not signal its effective incorporation in the political process. There were new state demands in 1989 that used gender issues as a means to politically expel the party. In the words of the president: "Nothing justifies the creation of a group as long as it has not defined the type of society it commends, clarified its position towards a certain number of civilizational issues and committed itself to respect the equality of rights and duties of citizens, men and women as well as the principles of tolerance and of the liberty of conscience."[75] That statement elevated gender equality to new political heights. In it, the ruling party implied that it adhered to that principle and that others who did not should be excluded. So instead of forging a new consensus, the state imposed one over a divided population. While on the surface the regime's commitment to gender equality was highlighted, the use of extensive state repression against *al-Nahda* identified the state and women's rights with political authoritarianism.

To improve its seriously tarnished liberal image, the regime celebrated the twenty-sixth anniversary of its personal status code on 13 August 1992 by passing a "package of measures to consolidate women's gains."[76] The posts of secretary of state to the prime minister in charge of women and family affairs and secretary of state in charge of social promotion were created to give special attention to women's issues. The identification of gender rights with family and social development adhered to old patriarchal assumptions regarding women's role in society and the policies needed to solve their problems. The changes introduced in the personal status code included:

- A woman's status as a minor ended with her marriage at the age of 17, giving her immediate control of her affairs.
- A mother's consent became a legal requirement along with that of the father in the marriage of a daughter who is under 20.
- A state fund was created to guarantee the legal payment of alimony to divorced women.
- Tunisian women married to nonnationals had the right to pass on their nationality to their children, just as men did, but with the father's consent.[77]

The above showed how the 1956 code and the new changes, which had been hailed as liberating women, enshrined patriarchal control in numerous practices. It gave fathers or husbands formal authority over women until the age of 20. A father's consent was legally required for the marriage of his daughter, but not for that of his son. More seriously, alimony went uncollected in many cases. This made the right to divorce economically cumbersome to women and children, who found themselves without an immediate source of income. Finally, even when the new law attempted to secure the right of Tunisian women who are married to foreigners to pass on their nationality to their children, the consent of their husbands was required.

In the wake of these changes, Tunisian femocrats (feminist bureaucrats) mounted a campaign to persuade the women's nongovernmental associations to join in a formal united front against the Islamists in defense of the regime against international audiences critical of its repressiveness.

As a result, the regime regained its bureaucratic control of the feminist agenda. In an attempt to minimize the importance of their relations with the state, the Tunisian femocrats argued that the official women's union now operated as a nongovernmental association.[78] This was very difficult to accept when the state continued to appoint the president of the union and expected both to represent it.

In conclusion, bureaucratic state feminism has been resurrected by the authoritarian regime of Bin 'Ali to give it a liberal facade. There are major political differences between the state-sponsored legal reforms of 1956 and 1992. While those passed in 1956 represented the basis for an emerging national consensus on a new role for women in independent Tunisia, the 1992 legal changes appeal only to the secularist segments of the population and as such represent a divided society and the modest appeal of the regime. In using women's rights to exclude the Islamists, the regime has dangerously politicized gender and guaranteed that it will be used in the future against secularist and feminist women.

Egypt: The Abandonment of State Feminism

Egyptian political liberalization has now been in place for almost two decades. During this period, the debate on the role that women should play in the new political system was shaped by both the secularists (represented by the state under presidents Anwar Sadat and Husni Mubarak) and by the Islamists (represented by the Muslim Brotherhood, the only organization that allowed limited participation). The secularist state pursued two strategies that reflected its changing attitude to women. In the 1970s, the state emphasized women's gendered difference and their dependence on the protective arm of the state to secure their rights. In the 1980s it abandoned this strategy in favor of a formal one that defined political equality as having the same rights as men and ignoring the problem of underrepresentation. The Islamist view of liberalization emphasized how women had a choice between the secularist and Islamist views of women's roles and rights. The Muslim Brotherhood viewed women's sexual and gendered difference as a basis for underlining their familial roles as a means of direct and indirect political participation.

Political liberalization began in 1976 with the establishment of a multiparty system, freer elections, and a less controlled press. The Sadat regime allied itself with the Islamist groups to distinguish itself from the secularist views of its predecessor. It also used them to politically dislodge the Nasserists from important institutions of civil society (the universities and professional associations). Islamist success in this task encouraged the more radical elements among them to pursue their own political agenda.

The kidnapping and murder of Shaikh al-Dahabi, the minister of religious affairs, ended the friendly relations between the regime and these groups.

As if to signal that break, the regime used the issue of women's rights to rally the secularist public behind it. In 1979, the regime passed two presidential decrees that addressed some of the legal and political disadvantages associated with gender difference. The first decree added 30 seats earmarked for women to the Egyptian parliament and specified that 20 percent of the seats in the 26 local governorate councils would be for women.[79] The second decree introduced some reforms in the personal status laws by arguing that the first wife of a man who takes a second wife was entitled to file for a divorce on the grounds that this constituted harm. It also guaranteed a divorced mother the right to the family home until her children grew up.[80]

Both decrees recognized the fact that gender difference contributed to legal and political inequalities. The strategy used by the state to correct these asymmetries was to give women some new electoral and legal rights that do not diminish or impinge on existing male privilege. For instance, the parliamentary seats earmarked for women were added to the original number, instead of being subtracted from those for male members. In contrast, the stipulation that 20 percent of all local council seats be given to women did take away seats from male candidates, but it recognized, in violation of the constitutional principle of political equality, the legitimacy of giving 80 percent of the seats to men.

As far as the personal status law was concerned, the amendments did not presume to give women the equal (unconditional) right to divorce, they just added polygamy to the list of conditions that entitled women to file for a divorce. Considering the small incidence of polygamous marriages in contemporary Egypt, this was not a major legal or symbolic advance. What was a real privilege was giving divorced mothers the right to the family home. Given housing shortages and the expense involved in securing housing, this was an important right.

The use of presidential decrees to introduce these changes reflected on their political legitimacy. In choosing to bypass an unsympathetic parliament, the regime was breaking its own rules. As a result, the public viewed the new measures augmenting state feminism as undemocratic creations of the regime. The high constitutional court reversed both of these decrees in the 1980s on procedural grounds. In 1985, the court argued that there was no national emergency that justified the use of a presidential decree to pass the personal status law while parliament was in session. In 1987 it struck down the reserved seats for women on the grounds that special treatment for women contradicted the constitutional commitment to equality. While the court came out in favor of formal political rights for women, it opposed state strategies to deepen them.

The Mubarak regime did not challenge these legal reversals. It used them as part of a calculated strategy to politically appease the Islamists and to draw them into the system. In both the 1984 and the 1987 elections, the regime gave its official blessing to the electoral alliances between the Muslim Brotherhood, considered to be a moderate representative of the Islamist trend, and the New Wafd Party and then the Labor Party. It was hoped that these electoral strategies would divide the Islamist groups and encourage the Brotherhood to work through the political system. The Mubarak regime also used the legal reversals of its successor's gendered agenda to underline its own socially conservative credentials. The new personal status law it passed in 1985 retreated from the previous legal recognition of a divorced mother's right to the family residence and a woman's automatic right to divorce in case her husband took a second wife.[81] Then, President Mubarak publicly applauded the cancellation of the reserved parliamentary seats for women on the grounds that it was a measure of Egyptian women's political maturity and ability to run for elections without state support.

These actions amounted to a rejection of state feminism. One of their consequences was to free secularist women to organize around gender issues. Islamist women had already begun their mobilizing in the 1970s. When the Muslim Brotherhood was allowed to resume publishing its journal, *al-Da'wa* (the Islamic Call), Zaynab al-Ghazali was among its prominently featured writers. Secularist women began by forming women's committees within the existing institutions in civil society, especially professional associations (like the Journalists' Syndicate and the Arab Lawyers Federation) and the workers' unions. In addition, they have created numerous nongovernmental advocacy associations for women.[82] *Jam'iyyat tadamun al-mar'at al-'arabiyya* (The Arab Women's Solidarity Association), led by Nawal El-Saadawi, claimed for itself the feminist mantle.

Thus a major ideological split was solidified among active middle class women, largely around the old Islamist and secularist positions. Contrasting the organizational views and the gendered perspectives produced by al-Ghazali's Muslim Brotherhood and El-Saadawi's *Tadamun al-mar'at al-'arabiyya* serves as a means of analyzing the discourses produced by women of this class.

Both al-Ghazali and El-Saadawi emerged as the prominent Islamist and secularist stars of the 1980s.[83] They defined the views of their associations.[84] Both had independent foreign audiences and supporters (Arab and international) and hence were independent operators. The idea that their associations were to be committed to a different practice and/or to give women associational channels of expanded participation was more rhetorical than real. Finally, both El-Saadawi and al-Ghazali have emerged as partisan spokeswomen for the secularist and Islamist views on women.

In her published works, al-Ghazali adhered to dichotomous definitions of masculinity and femininity. She argued that men and women had different "temperaments" (*tabi'a*) that led them to engage in distinct activities.[85] She emphasized the important roles women played in the development of a dynamic family. Public work could only be considered in the case of economic need, and by encouraging women to take on public roles outside of the home the secular state and the secularist feminists had created serious problems in the home, workplace, in the streets, and in production.[86] Al-Ghazali suggested that women's citizenship should be rooted in the family while that of men should be premised on their work outside it.[87]

More recently, al-Ghazali has taken on the issue of gender equality. She argues that women did not have a "special status in Islam," citing the hadith that declared "women were siblings of men" (*al-nisa' shaqa'iq al-rijal*).[88] She pointed out that while some argued that men were superior to women because only the former were prophets, all of these prophets were raised by women. Both men and women were to contribute in different ways to overcoming the "underdevelopment of the Islamic nation." More recently, al-Ghazali adopted the position that "Muslim women should play a role outside of the home if the interest of the Islamic state required it . . . provided she is dressed modestly and is able to juggle both the private and public tasks."[89]

In contrast, El-Saadawi defended the formal rights of women as public actors. While recognizing how capitalist development was behind the more conservative social climate, she blamed the women who have taken up the veil for not understanding the connotation of their actions and how the veil was a metaphor for giving up reason in the name of religion.[90] She accused them of not distinguishing between what was and was not important in Islam. El-Saadawi even described them as suffering from false consciousness.[91] The definition of feminism that the association's journal espoused was decidedly upper middle class. For the most part, it put emphasis on individual needs for creative self-expression, autonomy, and independence.

Given these views, the association and its journal did not pose a serious social or political threat to the state in the gender arena. The state suspended the association only when it criticized its position on the Gulf War, citing the association's law (no. 32) that forbids discussion of politics. Given the limited following of the association and its failure to build bridges with other active women's groups, the state's actions were met with a national lack of concern. Instead, there was a wave of protest from El-Saadawi's international supporters.

Conclusion

The theoretical view of political liberalization as "woman friendly" is problematic. Liberal political debates do not usually pay much attention to women. When they do, they accept the modern definition of the sexual division of labor, which relegates men and women to opposite arenas: the public versus the private. Movement toward the public incorporation of women does not necessarily translate into the freedom to represent their familial/private concerns. It presents them with a public arena that seeks to subordinate them and their agendas to broader political concerns.

In the cases discussed in this chapter, the joint legacy of the bureaucratic authoritarian state and the liberal ones seems to be a state willingness to use gender for its political ends. While the Sadat regime and that of Bin 'Ali used women's rights to fight their Islamist opponents, the Mubarak regime offered it to them as a concession. What this suggests is that, despite the exaggerated importance given to gender in the polemics between the secularists and the Islamists, it was in fact a safe political card. The minor changes that the regimes of Numayri, Sadat, Bin 'Ali, and al-Turabi introduced in the personal status laws were effective in needling one's opponent without spending valuable political capital. In contrast, the use of economic and political policies to spell out differences with one's opponents could have more serious consequences.

Loosening the state's grip on the gender agenda and women's associational drive proved to be a mixed blessing. In the Egyptian case, loss of state support coincided with loss of new and old rights for women throughout the 1980s. While it gave Islamist and feminist associations a certain degree of autonomy, it also had the effect of forcing them to search for national and international allies to depend on. The result was to substitute one form of political dependence with another. Instead of reliance on the state, the Babiker Badri association and the Tadamun association developed economic and political dependence on international donors and audiences. The political cost of that strategy was seen in how the state could move against Tadamun without risking its support among secular middle class women. Neither the feminists nor the Islamists developed novel perspectives on gender. A good part of their creative energy was spent on attacking each other as surrogates of larger groups.

The resurgence of state feminism in Tunisia had its own problems. In exchange for renewed state control of the gender agenda, modest new rights were offered to women at the cost of inhibiting the creative gendered perspectives on new forms of democratization. The use of gender as a means of excluding the Islamists sets women up as a political target in the next round. The use of this strategy by the Sadat regime in 1979 backfired against women in the 1980s.

What kinds of changes would an Islamist triumph in the very unstable liberal systems of Egypt and Tunisia bring about? If the policies of the Islamist state in the Sudan are any indication, then one would expect the socialization of gender issues. This represents a conservative Islamist definition of women's citizenship. It narrowly defines women's interests as social and locates them back in the family and/or workplace. As such, it is a marked retreat from the postcolonial national discourses on gender that aimed at the integration of women and their concerns into the economic and political agendas of the secular state. Ideology aside, it represents another state response to the existing political economic crises. In abandoning one more of its public occupations (an expanded public gender agenda), the Islamist state chooses the less expensive private roles for women. By handing state power over women to individual patriarchs in the family, it also hopes to cement its solidarity with many patriarchs, whom it cannot reward in any other way. The emphasis on the social nature of gender thus devalues it as a basis for a conservative consensus.

Notes

1. Suad Joseph, "Elite Strategies for State Building: Women, Family, Religion and State in Iraq and Lebanon," in Deniz Kandiyoti, ed., *Women, Islam and the State* (Philadelphia: Temple University Press, 1991), pp. 181–187; Layla Abu Sha'r, "Al-mar'at wa al-tanmiya," *Al-'arabiyya al-suriyya: 1975–1985* (Damascus: Matba'at al-Qiyada al-Qutriyya, 1987), pp. 83–128; Mervat Hatem, "The Paradoxes of State Feminism in Egypt," and Magda al-Sanousi and Nafisa al-Amin, "The Political Engagement of Sudanese Women," in Najma Chaudhuri and Barbara Nelson, eds., *Women and Politics Worldwide* (New Haven: Yale University Press, forthcoming); Mustafa O. Attar, "Ideology, Value Changes and Women's Social Position in Libyan Society," in Elizabeth Warnock Fernea, ed., *Women and the Family in the Middle East* (Austin: University of Texas Press, 1985), pp. 121–133; Tunisian External Communication Agency and the National Union of Tunisian Women, *Women in Tunisia: Their Struggles and Their Gains* (Tunis: Tunisian External Communication Agency, 1993), pp. 40–44; Abdel Qadir Jaghlul, ed., *Al-mar'at al-jaza'iriyya* [Algerian Woman] (Beirut: Dar al-Hadatha, 1983); Maxine Molyneux, "The Law, the State and Socialist Policies with Regard to Women: The Case of People's Democratic Republic of Yemen 1967–90," in Kandiyoti, ed., *Women, Islam and the State*, pp. 252–260.

2. *Women in Tunisia*, pp. 18–21; *Al-murshid fi qanun al-ahwal al-shakhsiyya* [Guide to the Personal Status Law] (Damascus: Dar al-'Awar lil Tiba'a, 1985), ch. 2; Joseph, "Elite Strategies for State Building," p. 184; Molyneux, "The Law, the State and Socialist Policies," pp. 258–259.

3. AbdelKader Zghal, "The New Strategy of the Movement of the Islamic Way: Manipulation or Expression of Political Culture?," and ElBaki Hermassi, "The Islamicist Movement and November 7," in William Zartman, ed., *Tunisia: The Political Economy of Reform* (Boulder: Westview Press, 1991).

4. Mary Ann Tetreault, "Civil Society in Kuwait: Protected Spaces and Women's Rights," *Middle East Journal* 47, 2 (Spring 1993), p. 288; Augustus Richard Norton, "The Future of Civil Society in the Middle East," *Middle East Journal* 47, 2 (Spring 1993), p. 214; Julie Peteet and Barbara Harlow, "Gender and Political Change," *Middle East Report* 173 (November–December 1991), p. 6.

5. Muhammed Muslih and Augustus Richard Norton, "The Need for Arab Democracy," *Foreign Policy* 83 (Summer 1991), pp. 6–7.

6. The Editors, "The Democracy Agenda in the Arab World," *Middle East Report* 174 (January–February 1992), p. 2.

7. Norton, "The Future of Civil Society," p. 214.

8. Peteet and Harlow, "Gender and Political Change," p. 6.

9. Peteet and Harlow, "Gender and Political Change," p. 6.

10. Peteet and Harlow, "Gender and Political Change," p. 7; Norton, "The Future of Civil Society," p. 214.

11. Carole Pateman and Elizabeth Gross, eds., *Feminist Challenges: Social and Political Theory* (Boston: Northeastern University Press, 1986); Gisela Bock and Susan James, eds., *Beyond Equality and Difference: Citizenship, Feminist Politics and Female Subjectivity* (London: Routledge, 1992); Carole Pateman, *The Sexual Contract* (Stanford: Stanford University Press, 1988).

12. Carole Pateman, "Introduction: The Theoretical Subversiveness of Feminism," in Pateman and Gross, eds., *Feminist Challenges*, p. 6.

13. Pateman, "Introduction," p. 6.

14. Jane Flax, "Beyond Equality: Gender, Justice and Difference," in Bock and James, eds., *Beyond Equality and Difference* (London: Routledge, 1992), pp. 195–196.

15. Janna Tompson, "Women and Political Rationality," in Pateman and Gross, eds., *Feminist Challenges*, p. 103.

16. Jane Flax, "Is Enlightenment Emancipatory?" unpublished manuscript, pp. 4–7.

17. Pateman, *The Sexual Contract*, ch. 1.

18. Mustapha Kamel al-Sayyid, "The Civil Society Concept and the Arab World," paper presented to the conference on Political Liberalization and Democratization in the Arab World, Montreal, 7–8 May 1993, p. 14.

19. Al-Sayyid, "The Civil Society Concept."

20. Sami Zubaida, "Islam, the State and Democracy: Contrasting Conceptions of Society in Egypt," *Middle East Report* 179 (November–December 1992), p. 4.

21. Zubaida, "Islam, the State and Democracy."

22. Al-Sayyid, "The Civil Society Concept," p. 14.

23. Peter Gran, "'Private' Rather than 'Public': No More New Possibilities for the Family in Middle East Studies," unpublished manuscript, 1993.

24. Sondra Hale, "The Wing of the Patriarch: Sudanese Women and Revolutionary Parties," *Middle East Report* 16, 1 (January–February 1988), pp. 27–28.

25. Hale, "The Wing of the Patriarch," pp. 27–28.

26. El-Sanousi and al-Amin, "The Political Engagement of Sudanese Women," pp. 28–29.

27. "Babiker Badri Scientific Association: The Establishment and the First Decade," *Women* 4 (March 1990), p. 18.

28. "Babiker Badri Scientific Association," p. 18.

29. "Babiker Badri Scientific Association," p. 18.

30. "Babiker Badri Scientific Association," p. 18.

31. Iman Ahmed, "Report on the Seminar: Grass Root Activities Related to Women in Eastern and Southern Africa," *Women* 3 (November 1988), p. 22.

32. "Babiker Badri Scientific Association," p. 18.

33. Asia Maccawi Ahmed, "Women in Public Administration and Management," *Women* 2 (December 1986), pp. 22–23.

34. "Babiker Badri Scientific Association," p. 22.

35. Amna A. Badri, "University Women as Extension Agents: A Woman to Woman Approach," *Women* 2 (December 1986), p. 5.

36. Badri, "University Women as Extension Agents," p. 6.

37. "Babiker Badri Scientific Association," p. 18.

38. "Babiker Badri Scientific Association," pp. 19, 21.

39. Ahmed, "Women in Public Administration and Management," p. 17.

40. Badri, "University Women as Extension Agents," p. 6.

41. Badri, "University Women as Extension Agents," p. 6.

42. Interview with Dina Sheikh El-Din Osman (chair of the Department of Commercial Law, University of Khartoum).

43. Interview with Dina Sheikh El-Din Osman.

44. Eric Rouleau, "Sudan's Revolutionary Spring," *Middle East Report* (September 1985), p. 4.

45. John Esposito, "Islamic Revivalism in the Sudan," in Shireen Hunter, ed., *The Politics of Islamic Revivalism* (Indianapolis: Indiana University Press, 1988), p. 201.

46. Sondra Hale, "Women's Activists of the National Islamic Front—Sudan," paper read at the Middle East Studies' Association annual meeting, Portland, Oregon, 28–29 October 1992.

47. El-Sanousi and al-Amin, "The Political Engagement of Sudanese Women," p. 30.

48. "Hiwar ma'a Dr. Hasan al-Turabi," *Qira'at Siyasiyya* 2, 3 (Summer 1992), p. 10.

49. "Hiwar ma'a Dr. Hasan al-Turabi," p. 10.

50. El-Sanousi and al-Amin, "The Political Engagement of Sudanese Women," pp. 31, 32.

51. El-Sanousi and al-Amin, "The Political Engagement of Sudanese Women," pp. 31, 32.

52. Aminah Hajara, "A Roundtable Discussion with Dr. Hasan al-Turabi," *Inquiry* 1, 4 (August 1992), p. 44.

53. El-Sanousi and al-Amin, "The Political Engagement of Sudanese Women," pp. 32–33.

54. El-Sanousi and al-Amin, "The Political Engagement of Sudanese Women," p. 33.

55. Kevin Dwyer, *Arab Voices: The Human Rights Debate in the Middle East* (London: Routledge, 1991), p. 184.

56. Dwyer, *Arab Voices*, p. 184.

57. Dwyer, *Arab Voices*, p. 184.

58. Dwyer, *Arab Voices*, p. 184.

59. Dwyer, *Arab Voices*, p. 195.

60. Dwyer, *Arab Voices*, p. 195.

61. Leila Hessini, "The Tunisian Family Code: A Historical Perspective," *AMEWS Newsletter* (March 1993), p. 1.

62. 'Aicha al-Tarabulsi, "Majallat al-ahwal al-shakhsiyya: 'awamel muhaddada," *Nisa'* (April 1985), p. 13.

63. Al-Tarabulsi, "Majallat al-ahwal al-shakhsiyya," p. 13.

64. Dwyer, *Arab Voices*, p. 203.

65. Sassiya, "Huquq al-mar'at muhaddada," *Nisa'* (April 1985), p. 12.

66. Zghal, "The New Strategy of the Movement of the Islamic Way," p. 208.

67. Sassiya, "Huquq al-mar'at muhaddada," p. 12; Dwyer, *Arab Voices*, p. 43.

68. Dwyer, *Arab Voices*, p. 202.

69. Dwyer, *Arab Voices*, p. 207.

70. Dwyer, *Arab Voices*, p. 146.

71. Dwyer, *Arab Voices*, p. 200.

72. ElBaki Hermassi, "The Islamicist Movement and November 7," in Zartman, ed., *Tunisia*, p. 198.

73. Hermassi, "The Islamicist Movement and November 7," in Zartman, ed., *Tunisia*, p. 198.

74. Hermassi, "The Islamicist Movement and November 7," in Zartman, ed., *Tunisia*, p. 198.

75. Hermassi, "The Islamicist Movement and November 7," in Zartman, ed., *Tunisia*, p. 202.

76. The Tunisian External Communication Agency and the National Union of Tunisian Women, *Women of Tunisia*, p. 60.

77. The Tunisian External Communication Agency and the National Union of Tunisian Women, *Women of Tunisia*, p. 61.

78. Dr. Nebiha Gueddana, "The Role of Women in Modern Tunisian Society," presentation by the Secretary of State in Charge of Women and Family Affairs, Washington D.C., 18 March 1993, p. 4.

79. Jehan Sadat, *Woman of Egypt* (New York: Simon and Schuster, 1987), p. 364.

80. Sadat, *Woman of Egypt*, p. 364.

81. Mervat F. Hatem, "The Enduring Alliance of Nationalism and Patriarchy in the Muslim Personal Status Law: The Case of Modern Egypt," *Feminist Issue* 6, 1 (Spring 1986), p. 36.

82. There were the *Bint al-Ard* (Daughter of the Land) association, *Jami'yyat al-katibat al-misriyyat* (the Egyptian Women Writers' Association), and *Jami'yyat al-muhtammat bi Shu'un al-mar'at al-Misriyya* (the Communication Group for the Enhancement of the Status of Women in Egypt).

83. Both published numerous books and traveled widely. See Ibn al-Hashimi, ed., "Al-mar'at al-muslima ila ayn," in *Humum al-mar'at al-muslima wa al-da'iya zaynab al-ghazali* [The Concerns of the Muslim Woman and the Message of Zaynab al-Ghazali] (Cairo: Dar al-I'tisam, 1990), pp. 271–296, for a list of al-Ghazali's published writings and invitations to speak all over the world. For El-Saadawi, see her *Rehlati hawl al-'alam*, volumes 1 and 2 available in English translation *My Travels Around the World* (London: Minerva, 1992).

84. Valerie J. Hoffman, "An Islamic Activist: Zaynab al-Ghazali," in Fernea, ed., *Women and the Family in the Middle East*, pp. 236–237.

85. Al-Ghazali, "Hathihi al-tanzimat al-nisa'iyya tahdim wala tabni," in al-Hashimi, ed., *Humum al-mar'at al-muslima*, p. 55.

86. Al-Ghazali, "Hathihi al-tanzimat," p. 56.

87. Al-Ghazali, "Al-mar'at wal-'amal," in al-Hashimi, ed., *Humum al-mar'at al-muslima*, p. 39.

88. Al-Ghazali, "Al-mar'at al-muslima ila ayn?" in al-Hashimi, ed., *Humum al-mar'at al-muslima*, p. 58.

89. Al-Ghazali, "Al-mar'at al-muslima ila ayn?" in al-Hashimi, ed., *Humum al-mar'at al-muslima*, pp. 64–65.

90. Nawal El-Saadawi, "Raf'a al-hijab 'an al-'aql," *Nun* 3 (November 1989), pp. 4–5.

91. El-Saadawi, "Raf'a al-hijab 'an al-'aql," pp. 4–5.

3

Political Economy

11

Resources, Revenues, and Authoritarianism in the Arab World: Beyond the Rentier State?

Giacomo Luciani

Paradigms are necessary tools of analysis, yet they run the risk of freezing our discourse into rigid boxes, lacking the flexibility and multidimensionality that are needed to understand real life. The difficulty is exacerbated whenever discussing transitions: Paradigms always tend to appear immutable, while transitions can take so many different paths.

The rentier state paradigm is no exception.[1] It is by now widely accepted that oil rent is a key factor in understanding Arab economic and political realities. It is also widely accepted that access to such rent is a factor reinforcing the control on power of existing authoritarian regimes, independently of the fact that the latter differ greatly among themselves.

The correlation between the rentier foundations of the state and authoritarianism may be viewed as a corollary to the notion of autonomy of the state, but it adds an explanatory dimension to the existence of such autonomy. All states can be autonomous in the short run, but in the longer run their ability to act autonomously from society is linked to their revenue foundations.[2] A state that economically supports society and is the main source of private revenues through government expenditure, while in turn is supported by revenue accruing from abroad, does not need to respond to society. On the contrary, a state that is supported by society, through taxes levied in one form or another, will in the final analysis be obliged to respond to societal pressure.

However, the dynamic relationship between rent and political order is far from being automatic. In other words, the idea that changes in rent availability are *necessarily* linked to inverse changes in accountability, representation, and participation ("democratization") cannot be proven in general, and is in fact not supported by experience. A relationship does exist, but it is one that necessitates more complex historical and circumstantial analysis to be properly understood.

In view of the relative decline of the overall rent available to the Arab states, growing attention has been devoted to the question: What will come after the rentier state? That the rentier state will not last forever hardly needs to be argued. But how will the state evolve beyond rentierism? The question cannot be addressed in abstract terms—so many different paths are theoretically open for the transition to occur—but a discussion with reference to the recent experience of some Arab countries is possible. Not that rentierism will disappear soon—in fact, the contrary is true. But we can see what would be needed to overcome it, and why it is not done.

Specifically, the question that interests me is whether or not democratization is, or should be, part of an agenda to overcome rentierism. The answer is far from clear. On the one hand the existing authoritarian regimes —which have all been in power for a very long time, and which are inextricably tied to their rentier foundations—are most probably unable to reform from inside, and lack the credibility required to effectively pursue a different economic policy. On the other hand, the democratization option runs the risk of ushering into power forces that are neither democratic nor inclined to adopt the economic policies necessary for sustainable long-term development.

Arab (Political) Economies

As we look at the set of Arab countries, we are struck by their diversity. Indeed, there is greater variance in economic and demographic structures between Arab countries than there is in any other region of the world, a corollary to the fact that the Arab region is a land of extremes—extreme population density and dispersal, extreme land fertility and barrenness, extreme mineral wealth and scarcity, extreme personal money wealth and poverty. This is such an obvious statement that we tend to forget it: Only too often we find authors proposing generalizations about the Arab countries that are in fact valid for only one or two of them, albeit important. One should strenuously resist this temptation.

In particular, we should resist the temptation to describe all Arab states as rentier states—they are not. Government finance statistics clearly indicate that the oil rent is a primary (that is, consistently large) source of government revenue for only a few Arab governments—namely Kuwait, Abu Dhabi, Qatar, Saudi Arabia, and Libya. In the past, this was true of Algeria and, outside the Arab world, Iran as well; but today it is essentially no longer the case. The rest have had access to much smaller levels of rent,

Table 11.1 External Rents as a Share of Total State Revenue (%)

	1982	1983	1984	1985	1986	1987	1988	1989	1990	1991	1992
Algeria	n.a.	n.a.	n.a.	43.1	23.2	22.0	25.8	39.1	49.8	50.8	n.a.
Bahrain	73.4	67.4	68.4	70.2	62.7	61.0	56.8	58.9	65.0	61.8	63.0
Egypt	n.a.	n.a.	n.a.	n.a.	n.a.	20.8	20.4	18.0	39.5	33.5	n.a.
Iran	62.6	59.4	46.0	40.1	20.7	30.5	26.9	20.1	16.9	16.4	48.0
Jordan	36.6	34.3	21.2	31.3	23.5	21.7	24.6	33.7	18.8	n.a.	n.a.
Kuwait	93.8	93.6	93.6	94.6	95.8	n.a.	n.a.	85.9	91.2	80.5	90.2
Libya	n.a.	n.a.	n.a.	n.a.	65.2	66.8	58.2	47.2	61.6	n.a.	n.a.
Oman	89.4	85.7	81.0	82.2	73.6	82.2	79.7	81.2	85.1	79.7	82.6
Saudi Arabia	n.a.	n.a.	69.4	66.2	55.5	64.9	57.2	66.2	76.1	n.a.	n.a.
Tunisia	18.9	14.6	14.8	n.a.	n.a.	n.a.	n.a.	n.a.	n.a.	n.a.	n.a.
UAE	n.a.	n.a.	n.a.	n.a.	n.a.	82.3	74.2	86.1	86.4	82.4	n.a.
Yemen	n.a.	16.2	14.0	11.0	24.8	24.3	27.4	24.0	24.6	19.8	12.9

Note: This table attempts to capture the full extent of external sources of rent accruing directly to the government; thus it includes not just oil revenues, but also direct grants and other sources, such as the Suez Canal for Egypt or investment income for Kuwait. No single source exists for all countries and in some cases for one country for all years, hence data are not homogeneous. The most widely used sources have been those published by the International Monetary Fund and the Economist Intelligence Unit.

and the inflow has been far less reliable, especially if the source of the rent has been political (i.e., outside aid of one form or another).

Not all rent accrues to governments—some is captured by private individuals, mostly in connection with the process of government spending. Such rent may sometimes move across political boundaries in the form of migrants' remittances or private investment, yet it does not generate a rentier state in the receiving country. Hence it is, I believe, a mistake to mix genuine rentier states with those other states that rule over a society in which rent from abroad is an important component of private revenues, but not necessarily of state revenues.

At the same time, the importance of governmental as well as private rent generates a widespread attitude of rentierism (or rent-seeking) toward economic life. This is a common trait linking both genuine rentier states and states ruling rent-dominated economies, and it has an impact on the conduct of economic policy. The state in a rent-dominated economy is certainly much weaker and more vulnerable than a genuine rentier state, but it will be tempted to compete with its own citizens, and to position itself in order to capture a bigger share of the total rent circulating in the region. This strategy will be perceived as superior to devoting efforts to supporting the creation of economic productive capacity and genuine value added. The latter alternative cannot possibly yield such inordinately large and immediate return as rent seeking.

Rentierism and Structural Adjustment

The cyclical nature of the rent—be it direct or indirect—exposes actual or would-be rentier states to recurrent fiscal crises. Since 1986 practically all Arab states have been confronted with budget deficits of varying magnitude; indeed, some have lived through a fiscal crisis for much longer. Today, we pose the question of what comes beyond rentierism because the latter is increasingly manifesting its limitation as a solution for the long-run survival of the Arab state. If oil prices were high and growing, we would probably not even ask the question.

The theme of overcoming rentierism is thus closely connected with structural adjustment. The latter is often decried as an imposition on the part of the International Monetary Fund and the World Bank, or on the part of the United States, but it would be difficult to argue that the region has received less generous treatment (be it from God or from contemporary donors) than the rest of the world. The roots of the fiscal crisis of the Arab states are rather solidly planted in the unwillingness of Arab governments to face up to their problems in due course of time.

Structural adjustment policies are rejected because they are said to weigh more heavily on the poor. An immediate connection is established in the minds of most commentators between agreement with the IMF, higher bread prices, and riots in the streets. Yet the record of structural adjustment programs shows that they do not need to have a regressive impact on income distribution, and in the case of many Arab countries this finding would most certainly be confirmed.[3] Moreover, while specific austerity measures tied to structural adjustment can be linked to particular eruptions of mass protest, in general they do not usually result in fundamental political instability.[4]

Structural adjustment policies normally entail a cut in government spending. Usually too little attention is given to the nature of the expenditure that is cut; but it is clear that cuts in military spending and in prestige investment projects have a much smaller negative impact on income distribution than do cuts in personnel expenditure. The latter, in turn, are preferable to cuts in subsidies, which in turn are preferable to cuts in direct basic services such as education and health.

Many Arab countries maintain substantial military expenditures, which would make their task especially easy in devising a structural adjustment strategy with little or no negative impact on income distribution. The very magnitude of military spending as a share of total government spending as well as of GDP clearly indicates the scope for adjustment, had priority in the region ever been granted to genuine economic growth.

In fact, military spending has always been taboo, because many of the regimes have a military base or need the active support of their military. Moreover, military might has been used (particularly by governments that have little or no oil revenue) as a way of attracting foreign aid. Of course, one should not forget the realities of regional conflict. However, it is also a fact that military capability directly or indirectly justified by the Arab-Israeli conflict—and sometimes totally independent of it, as in the case of states that are geographically remote from Israel—has been used as the key instrument to redistribute rent within the Arab region.[5]

Structural adjustment also commonly entails reducing expenditure on government personnel. This may be achieved either by reducing salaries or by reducing the numbers employed in the public sector. The first solution may be appropriate in some of the richer oil producers, and may be tied to the question of adopting a competitive exchange rate policy.[6] It may not be appropriate in other countries, in which, to the contrary, civil servants' pay is so low that corruption is almost a foregone conclusion (the dismally low level of pay is itself the result of protracted, unresolved fiscal crisis).

Reducing the numbers employed in the public sector, on the other hand, is certainly appropriate in all Arab countries. The frequent policy of offering employment to all school graduates, independently of the actual need for them, has created bloated bureaucracies that are to this date a huge obstacle to liberalization and a production-oriented policy. The preoccupation

Table 11.2 **Military Expenditure as a Proportion of GNP and Total Expenditure**

	Military Expenditure/GNP (%)			Military Expenditure/Total Budget Expenditure		
	1970	1980	1990	1970	1980	1990
Algeria	2.1	2.1	1.5	8.1	13.8	9.5
Bahrain	n.a.	4.8	5.0	n.a.	41.4	40.7
Egypt	16.2	6.5	4.6	32.4	15.7	10.8
Iraq	11.2	6.3	20.0	37.6	26.9	n.a.
Jordan	17.8	13.8	10.9	41.0	35.8	32.7
Kuwait	3.9	3.5	6.5	7.6	11.0	19.9
Lebanon	2.8	4.1	n.a.	17.4	22.3	n.a.
Libya	4.1	10.0	8.6	9.9	26.6	29.2
Morocco	2.6	6.3	4.5	12.4	20.8	21.1
Oman	11.6	19.7	15.8	60.2	49.6	41.4
Saudi Arabia	11.8	16.6	17.7	27.5	26.7	38.5
Syria	11.9	17.3	13.0	37.6	35.8	69.8
Tunisia	1.6	2.2	3.2	5.4	11.1	7.4
UAE	n.a.	5.8	4.7	n.a.	41.4	40.7

Source: U.S. Arms Control and Disarmament Agency and Stockholm International Peace Research Institute.

of Arab governments is, and always has been, to keep potential opponents quiet. New graduate entrants in the workforce were not viewed as an asset that should be put to productive use, but as a potential source of trouble. The obvious consideration that every graduate employed in the public administration is a financial burden for his entire work life, while a graduate employed in the private sector is a potential taxpayer, never played a considerable role in the Arab government mind. A large bureaucracy is far from being a factor of egalitarian income distribution—quite to the contrary, it sits on the shoulders of the poorer strata of the population and exploits them legally and illegally. It is the same bureaucracy that consistently depicts structural adjustment as politically destabilizing, while in fact it only risks destabilizing their—overcrowded—rentier niche.

Structural adjustment also entails cutting expenditure on consumption subsidies, especially under conditions of rapidly increasing population. This has been, and in some cases still is, strenuously resisted by Arab governments, notwithstanding the fact that subsidies have to a considerable extent benefited the relatively well-off rather than the poorer sections of the population. The considerable implicit subsidy in the very low price of petroleum products is a classic example of this kind (how many who live in Cairo's "City of the Dead" own a car?). Subsidies generate distortions, and offer occasions for discrimination and favoritism. Hence they tend to encourage rent-seeking among all people.

If we take into account all the available alternatives, it is indeed difficult to argue that a structural adjustment policy ought necessarily to include cutting direct delivery of essential services such as health or primary education, or of subsidies on key consumer goods, such as bread. It is, therefore, certainly possible to initiate structural adjustment in most Arab countries while not worsening—and possibly even improving—the miserable standard of living of the poorest strata of the population.

Structural adjustment may also be achieved by increasing sources of government revenue, not just by cutting expenditure. Normally, revenue enhancement does not receive as much attention as expenditure cuts, because improvements require a much longer time to bring results, while the benefit of expenditure cuts may be immediate. However, it is indeed worthy of note that no Arab state, with the exception of Morocco and to a lesser extent Tunisia, has embarked on significant reform and expansion of its fiscal base for a period of over 20 years. The level of direct income tax collection is ludicrously low in most Arab states in which a personal income tax exists, and in a good number of them such a tax does not even exist. Surely there must be a political reason for this resistance to exploiting an obvious and unavoidable revenue source.

It must be recognized that direct tax revenue collection is more difficult in countries in which the economy is dominated by private rent accruing from abroad. Taxes on imports or indirect taxes are the usual response in this case. However, taxes on imports carry the negative consequence of easily creating distortions in the price signals to the domestic economy; even if they are designed to be neutral, they increase the equilibrium nominal exchange rate, and discourage exports. Governments should encourage remittances and investment from abroad by offering investment opportunities—for example, through the privatization of some government-owned enterprises and the development of a capital market— and encouraging the development of local productive enterprises that, once established, will offer a stable tax base. No Arab country has followed this path, as even the most "bourgeois" governments have resisted the privatization of such enterprises as the public utilities, which potentially offer the most interesting opportunities for the small private investor.

The only policy that is normally part of structural adjustment packages and was implemented by many Arab governments—at times, quite selectively—is trade liberalization. Import liberalization is considered an essential prerequisite to the development of nontraditional production and exports—yet export promotion received very little encouragement, with the exceptions of Morocco and Tunisia. Rather, imports were liberalized to improve the standard of living of the wealthiest part of the population and offer new opportunities for enrichment through foreign companies' representation. The allocation of licenses or government contracts allowed further creation of private positions of rent, rather than encouraging productive investment. Import liberalization took place in a context of continuing currency overvaluation, multiple exchange rates, and discriminatory access to credit, which did not encourage private agents to invest in nontraditional, potentially export-generating lines of production.

The Fiscal Crisis of the State and Rent-Seeking

If we examine the economic policies of rent-seeking (as opposed to truly rentier) states in the Middle East, we see that these were predominantly motivated by the desire to avoid adopting the set of measures that constitute a structural adjustment package. In several cases, the economic and fiscal crisis preceded rent-seeking, and whatever rent was captured was only used to postpone the day of reckoning. This is essential to understanding why moving beyond rentierism is so difficult: Structural problems have become much more unwieldy than they originally were.

Consider Egypt. The original developmental thrust that had been achieved under Gamal 'Abd al-Nasser was exhausted by the mid-1960s. Had a policy of structural adjustment been undertaken at that time—cut military spending and consumption subsidies, shift the domestic terms of trade in favor of agriculture by abolishing price and crop controls, encourage small private capital accumulation and avoid overstaffing in the public sector, allow equilibrium interest and exchange rates—it may have had an immediate positive impact on the Egyptian economy. The necessary ingredients of such a structural adjustment policy were clear already at that time, and Nasser certainly was in a position to revise the regime's economic strategy and vigorously promote growth. Instead, he tried to postpone the day when priority would need to go back to productive investment and employment, and sought an escape in regional activism. Egypt is still paying for that decision.

Nasser's approach was in essence never abandoned, notwithstanding its increasingly obvious shortcomings. Anwar Sadat announced a complete turnaround, but his liberalization was only very partial—it satisfied some of the rent-seeking instincts of the elite, but never seriously tackled the problem of promoting productive investment. A real shift in economic strategy may only have come in the early 1990s—and it is still only a possibility, not yet a foregone conclusion.

Structural adjustment, therefore, had to wait almost 25 years. In the intervening period, the problems and difficulties have increased enormously. First and foremost, population has grown, and it has gradually abandoned the countryside in the hope of capturing a few crumbs of the rent system in the cities. The original physical investment put in place in the initial industrialization drive has deteriorated, and is today in many cases beyond repair. Overstaffing in the public sector has become ever worse, and unemployment is almost a plague.

In these conditions, structural adjustment is bound to be a slow and painful process. Structural adjustment can only be a success if the private sector reacts by increasing investment in nontraditional export activities, and creates new jobs. Although some encouraging signs that this is happening are visible in Egypt, given the ever-increasing population pressure it is not clear that things are happening fast enough for a change to be felt by the Egyptian masses anytime soon.

Structural adjustment entails an initial cost and yields a political return—in terms of improved economic growth, employment, and income distribution—only in the longer run. The initial cost increases if adoption of a structural adjustment program is not timely. If it is delayed for as long as it was delayed in Egypt, the political return may not be there for several years; this may be too long a time for a regime that has clearly lost the respect of a large number of its people.

The speed of the response of the private sector depends on the credibility of the reform. It is difficult for private entrepreneurs to seriously believe that things have radically changed as long as the same individuals remain in power. Maybe, in fact, things have changed; but many entrepreneurs will want to carefully test the water before they take a jump. In this respect, while one cannot rule out a radical shift in economic strategy within a continuing regime, it is clear that a change in political leadership would underline the credibility of the shift in economic strategy. On the contrary, a shift in strategy undertaken by a president who has been in office for well over a decade, has resisted it so far, and is only accepting it now because he has no alternative (which is the case with Mubarak), is not bound to imbue private investors with great confidence.

One cannot rule out that under other historical circumstances an authoritarian regime may undertake policies of structural adjustment—this has happened in some countries in Asia (Taiwan, South Korea, Singapore) and Latin America (Chile). But in all these cases, the authoritarian regime inaugurated structural adjustment policies soon after its accession to power. What is not possible is to have structural adjustment under an authoritarian regime that has already been in power for decades, with no changes even in the top political personnel, and that has consistently followed policies aimed at maximizing rent generation and control rather than genuine economic growth.

What is true for Egypt is true for other Arab countries as well. Who is to believe the liberalizing instincts of Hafiz al-Asad in Syria or Saddam

Hussein in Iraq? One might say that the case of the Ba'thist regimes is extreme; consider, then, the case of Jordan. Ever since losing the West Bank in 1967, or at least since settling the issue of sovereignty through the expulsion of the PLO in 1970, Jordan could have followed a policy of aggressively developing production geared to the regional market. As a country deprived of mineral resources but surrounded by neighbors that are all rich in minerals, Jordan could have become the agricultural, industrial, and service center of the region, especially since Beirut became engulfed in civil war. Why has this not happened? Because the government of King Hussein paid foremost attention to capturing sources of rent through the constant underlining of Jordan's role as a front-line state in the conflict with Israel (probably more posture than reality, yet not exactly the right posture to attract industrial investment). Also, the government followed a suicidal "strong dinar" exchange rate policy that destroyed the competitiveness of the Jordanian economy and discouraged the localization of any economic activity there. The overvaluation of the currency was made possible by the huge influx of migrants' remittances, which could have supported a phase of rapid economic expansion and capital accumulation, but in fact was simply wasted in a housing boom. Not by chance, this economic strategy coincided with a long parenthesis in the life of Jordanian democratic institutions, and their revitalization only began when it became apparent that the sources of rent were rapidly drying up and a change of tack was inevitable.[7] Again, as in the case of Egypt, economic reform was initiated (all too timidly) almost 20 years too late, and its cost is bound to be much greater than it would normally have been.

Persistent Rentiers

Let us now consider the case of the genuine rentier states. Most of them, notably Kuwait and the other Gulf emirates, are too small to possibly develop a diversified economy: Their existence will always remain linked almost exclusively to the oil rent, with the possibility of partial downstream integration in refining, petrochemicals, and a few energy-intensive basic industries, such as aluminum smelting, which would allow some increase in the local generation of value added. However, it is dubious that such downstream activities could become a source of tax revenue, and the state is likely to remain essentially based on the oil rent.

The case of Saudi Arabia, however, is different both objectively, because the country is altogether of a different size, and subjectively, because it has followed the most determined policy to diversify its economic base and develop both its agriculture and its industry. The process of diversification of the Saudi economy is real enough. Notwithstanding government incentives and direct intervention in support of the private sector, positive value added is being created in most economic sectors. Therefore, the potential exists for the state to tap part of this value added, either by imposing higher user charges (i.e., reducing incentives) or by levying taxes. Yet for many years the Saudi government refused to consider taxes (indeed, in 1992 it actually *decreased* user charges) despite weakening oil prices and growing budget deficits. Only in its 1995 budget did the government announce small but significant reductions in consumer subsidies. Still it refrained from broadening its tax base, and directed many of its measures (for example, steep increases in visa and permit fees) against the expatriate labor force in an attempt to reduce the "export" of oil rents through remittances.[8]

This behavior is impossible to understand unless we take into account the fact that economic diversification was undertaken in an allocative spirit, in order to allow broader participation in the rent-circulation process. The drive toward economic diversification and industrialization is not an anomaly with respect to the allocative nature of the Saudi state, but is fully justified by the latter. Under Saudi circumstances, the demands of rent circulation and wealth redistribution motivate initiatives that end up creating a vested interest in favor of diversification, specifically industrialization.

Yet because of the allocative origin of the industrialization drive, it is likely that this will not be allowed to become a threat to the nature and stability of the regime. Industrialization will therefore be pursued, but not to the point of endangering the rentier order. The Saudi experience appears to prove that it is possible to pursue selective industrialization within an allocational order and as a tool promoting its stability. Industrialization will be cautious and controlled, and may in many respects appear to be suboptimal from a purely economic point of view. Faster industrialization, however, would require changes in economic policy and especially in social and cultural realities, which would inevitably also bring about political changes. There is widespread resistance to *all* of these changes, not just to the political ones on the part of an entrenched elite. Hence, the current cautious industrialization policy is perfectly justified from a political point of view.

It is sometimes said that the position of the Saudi government's finances is becoming increasingly tenuous.[9] The evidence is, primarily, the persistent budget deficits, expenditure cutbacks (including cuts of 19 percent and 6 percent in its 1994 and 1995 budgets, respectively), and the thinning of international reserves. But is this evidence enough? The government could easily cut much more expenditure (simply by eliminating some of the "fat," or reducing military spending and some subsidies) or increase revenue (by charging a price closer to cost for goods and services provided for by the government, or by resorting to a very modest devaluation of the riyal). The government does not care to do either because it can still easily finance the deficit through the sale of bonds on the domestic market. The latter remains very liquid, and money is constantly chasing investment opportunities, rather than the other way around.

Thus, fiscal imbalance is hardly a threat to the Saudi state in any sense except that there may be no limit to profligacy. The latter is not entirely new in Saudi history, and in the past it was successfully dealt with, without requiring a change of regime, yet requiring a change in the hands holding power (from Sa'ud to Faysal). Today, the situation may be similar in many respects. What threatens Saudi stability is not a fiscal crisis per se, but the grumbling of a private sector that complains of excessive defense expenditures and accuses the extended ruling family of monopolizing all profit opportunities (i.e., rent circulation) in the country.[10]

It is easier to solve the problem of the disgruntled business elite, excluding members of the royal family, than to address the problem of a growing population that has little skills and that refuses to compete for almost all available jobs because of status taboos. In the longer run, the existing wage segmentation according to nationality cannot but drive the Saudis—the relatively more expensive workers—out of the market. But this problem, too, can be solved incrementally, by devaluing the riyal and increasing the cost of employing expatriates. Both steps may have some political cost, but certainly not an unbearable one.

In short, it is certainly possible to envisage a scenario in which limited changes are introduced in Saudi economic policy that would effectively reabsorb the degree of discontent that may exist in the aftermath of the Gulf War. Such changes would mark a modest step in the direction of a more productive economy while, in fact, preserving the basic nature of the state as an autonomous rentier entity.

It is interesting to contrast the case of Saudi Arabia with that of Algeria, for which the same conclusion does not appear to hold. There is a major structural difference between the two—namely, the size of the rent available per capita. Algeria has at the same time a much larger population and a much smaller rent. What is a budding problem of Saudi unemployment (combined with the significant and persistent employment of expatriates) is a major, almost insoluble crisis in Algeria.

True, the fiscal crisis, which on the surface is Algeria's main problem, can and will be solved: Exports of gas will increase, and prices may somewhat improve, reconstituting a level of rent that would be sufficient to pay for government expenditure at its current level. But this would in no way support economic growth and the optimal utilization of available resources, including manpower.

The difference between Saudi Arabia and Algeria is that the former bred a sophisticated and wealthy private sector, and always kept the economy open to foreign competition. On the other hand, the private sector in

Algeria is very weak, and imports are tightly controlled. The beginnings of trade liberalization were reversed, and stringent new controls were imposed. As a consequence, the main activity of the private sector is busting controls, that is, contraband or *trabendo*. This implies, among other things, that the private sector prospers in illegality—something that is certainly not true in Saudi Arabia. The attitude to the government is therefore entirely different among private businessmen in the two countries: While the Saudi government can still count on a positive response on the part of the private sector, if appropriate policies are enforced, the Algerian government is unlikely to achieve the same.

Thus in Algeria the question of overcoming the rentier state is inescapable, while the same cannot be said for Saudi Arabia. And in Algeria, just as in Egypt or Syria, the transition to a production state requires a change in regime, while in Saudi Arabia a change at the helm may turn out to be sufficient.

The Evidence for Adjustment

That adjustment to a more productive and competitive economy is possible is proven, in the Arab context, by the cases of Morocco and Tunisia. Both countries accepted, after some protracted resistance, structural adjustment programs assisted by the IMF and the World Bank. Results in both cases have not been as spectacular as elsewhere in the world, but may nevertheless be rated as very satisfactory. Both countries have viable economies, with growing exports and declining external debt, and very small budget deficits. They could have done better, had they moved more promptly and boldly. In the case of Morocco, military expenditure continues to weigh as an excessive burden. Unemployment is still a problem, but the outlook for the future is not as desperate as elsewhere in the region.

Progress toward democratization has not been satisfactory in either country, and especially so in Tunisia. In Morocco, multiparty politics has been a reality for many years, and limited change has been allowed in forces participating in the government. Certainly, the king remains above criticism and continues to enjoy what many would regard as excessive power. Nevertheless, the influence of the Spanish transition is very clear, and so is the broad political support for progressive democratization. In Tunisia, President Bin 'Ali took power to overcome regime sclerosis, and has in a sense both suffered and benefited from opposing regional influences. These have, on the one hand, supported the formation and consolidation of the Islamic al-Nahda Party, and created conditions that enhanced its popular appeal (the second Gulf War). On the other hand, the experience of Algeria has certainly greatly reinforced the hand of the president in arguing in favor of only cautious and controlled movement (if any) toward further political opening. The limited nature of Tunisia's 1994 elections confirm the point.

Outside the Arab region, other countries prove that it is possible to transform the rentier state and engage in successful structural adjustment. Countries as diverse as Mexico and Indonesia prove that the transition is possible: In the case of the former, at the hands of a narrowly elected administration, which derived from its quasi-defeat the legitimacy to redefine its power base; and in the case of the latter, at the hands of an authoritarian government that cashed in on the flare-up of the oil rent, but very promptly understood that it was not going to last.

The Indonesian case also illustrates that the transition from rentier to production state *can* take place under authoritarian rule. The correlation between increased reliance on taxation of the domestic economy and democratization does not need to be immediate, and an authoritarian regime can maintain power by initiating and managing the transition. Progressively, the question of democratization will come to the fore, as the case of other Southeast Asian countries, such as Malaysia, illustrates. Yet the opening up of the political stage can, if adroitly managed, be very gradual indeed.

In fact, the standard argument in favor of the developmental role of authoritarian government is that it does not need to carefully balance private interest groups, and can afford to take a long-term view, because it is not subject to electoral cycles. In comparison, the least that can be said is that in Arab experience authoritarian governments have displayed no such farsightedness and attachment to the common good of the people. Quite to the contrary, they have displayed an extraordinary lack of vision, dragging their feet in order to avoid overdue policy changes that negatively affected the immediate interest of their supporters. They are, almost without exception, utterly discredited.

It is in this light that the question of democratization ought to be considered. Although the existing regimes obviously tend to perpetuate themselves in power, arguing that they should first achieve structural adjustment and only later democratize, it is increasingly evident that they cannot achieve what they say. The collapse of the communist regimes in Europe and the abandonment of central economic planning has exposed the "socialist" Arab regimes in key countries such as Egypt, Algeria, Syria, and Iraq, and made them appear increasingly anachronistic. In the rather desperate attempt to counter the perception of isolation, one hears frequent references to the "Chinese model" (the Cuban one being, presumably, not sufficiently promising). Is this a feasible alternative?

Quite clearly, it is not. China is a huge country, in which the vast majority of the people still live in the countryside and work in agriculture, while Arab countries are small, with populations that have mostly abandoned

agriculture and the countryside. China embarked on economic reform immediately following a change in political leadership, while all Arab leaders cling
to power. China started marketizing agriculture in the late 1970s, which is
what Egypt should already have done 10 years earlier, and failed to do. China
cracked down on a relatively small and isolated intellectual opposition, while
in Arab countries intellectuals have long ceased being the only opposition—
Islamic mobilization against regimes is a mass phenomenon.

It may, in the past, have been possible for the authoritarian Arab
regimes to embark on economic reform and consolidate themselves. But
they did not seize the opportunity, if they ever had one, and time is not
neutral.

As existing regimes cannot credibly undertake economic reform, a
way out will have to be provided either by a turn toward democratization
or by the advent of a different kind of authoritarian regime. That democratization may be conducive to economic reform, even in situations in
which the latter entails considerable cost in terms of living standards, is illustrated by the experience of the East and Central European countries.
Given the severity of the transformation they undertook, and the size of
the decline of GDP caused by the abandonment of central planning, it
would appear that democratization is a very powerful instrument to create
the needed consensus.

On the other hand, what possibility is there of some authoritarian government taking power that is more successful than the ones already in
charge? It is difficult to see what alternative power base could be found for
an authoritarian government that would receive the minimal consensus
necessary to pursue economic reform. A military strongman? But the military is part and parcel of the ruling regimes, and the only possibility of
one of them finding a new power base would be through an alliance with
the essential opposition force, that is, the Islamists (as in the Sudan).
Moreover, with opposition escalating into terrorism, and affecting key economic sectors, such as tourism for Egypt, it is increasingly clear that repression may not suffice to create a positive investment climate. It may, indeed, have the opposite effect, as the escalation of Algeria's bloody civil
war—and the concomitant flight of both expatriate workers and trade opportunities—has made clear.

Will Democracy Help?

There is, of course, no assurance that political liberalization will yield a
government willing and capable of engaging in economic reform. What
democracy does is establish the principle of governmental responsibility
and alternation in power. We may, for example, contrast the cases of

Argentina and Brazil: In the former democratization has, albeit not immediately, opened the door to economic reform; in the latter, it has not. In
Eastern and Central Europe, the path to economic reform in the new
democracies has been far from uniform.

In the Arab countries, the success of democratic institutions in promoting a viable economic strategy is made difficult by the relative lack of
attention to economic discourse in public opinion. Political forces do not
primarily differentiate themselves on the basis of economic policy preferences; they tend, rather, to polarize around issues such as the relationship
between religion and politics, or international alignments (pro- or anti-
Western). In particular, Islamic forces fall far short of proposing a coher-
ent economic policy program, and the question of which economic policies
may prevail under governments in which Islamic parties may be a key
component remains essentially quite open. The Iranian precedent is not
conclusive, as it displayed the coexistence of "radicals" and "moderates,"
proposing two quite opposed economic policy lines, and converging only
on a nationalistic distaste for foreign investment, multilateral organizations, and economic "dependence."

But neither the Iranian nor the Sudanese experiment is necessarily a
relevant precedent: The experience of other Arab countries may turn out to
be entirely different. Skepticism is warranted, of course: Most opposition
Islamist forces have been highly critical of even limited attempts at government economic reform. This is hardly surprising, however—oppositions, after all, tend to oppose government actions reflexively. Moreover,
it is not distaste for Islamist economic policy but rather fear of Islamist
popularity that has led regimes to be wary of political liberalization. However, the "Islamic threat" cannot be accepted as reason enough to postpone
democratization indefinitely.

Notes

1. For an overview of the concept of rentierism, see Hazem Beblawi and Giacomo Luciani, eds., *The Rentier State* (London: Croom Helm, 1987).

2. For a fuller discussion of this, see Giacomo Luciani, "Economic Foundations of Democracy and Authoritarianism: The Arab World in Comparative Perspective," *Arab Studies Quarterly* 10, 4 (Fall 1988).

3. Christian Morrisson, "Adjustment and Equity," OECD Development Center
Policy Brief 1 (1992).

4. Karen L. Remmer, "The Politics of Economic Stabilization: IMF Standby
Programs in Latin America, 1954–1984," *Comparative Politics* 19, 1 (October
1986), pp. 9–10; Henry Bienen and Mark Gersovitz, "Economic Stabilization,
Conditionality, and Political Stability," *International Organization* 39 (Autumn
1985), pp. 729–754; Henry Bienen and Mark Gersovitz, "Consumer Subsidy Cuts,
Violence, and Political Stability," *Comparative Politics* 19, 1 (October 1986), pp.

25–44; Mark Lindenberg and Shantayanan Derarajan, "Prescribing Strong Economic Medicine: Revising the Myths about Structural Adjustment, Democracy and Economic Performance in Developing Countries," *Comparative Politics* 25, 2 (1993), pp. 169–182.

5. Rex Brynen, "Palestine and the Arab State System: Permeability, State Consolidation, and the *Intifada*," *Canadian Journal of Political Science* 24, 3 (September 1991), pp. 607–610.

6. Overvalued currencies boost the purchasing power—and cost—of domestic wages.

7. Rex Brynen, "Economic Crisis and Post-Rentier Democratization in the Arab World: The Case of Jordan," *Canadian Journal of Political Science* 25, 1 (March 1992); Laurie Brand, "Economic and Political Liberalization in a Rentier Economy: The Case of the Hashemite Kingdom of Jordan," in Iliya Harik and Denis J. Sullivan, eds., *Privatization and Liberalization in the Middle East* (Bloomington: Indiana University Press, 1992).

8. Some efforts have also been made to increase the "Saudization" of the labor force; see *Los Angeles Times*, 17 January 1995.

9. *New York Times*, 22, 23 August 1993; Fareed Mohamedi, "The Saudi Economy: A Few More Years till Doomsday," *Middle East Report* 185 (November–December 1993).

10. Not all political dissatisfaction is economically generated of course—Islamists have, for example, been alienated by the kingdom's close political and military ties to the United States. However, both excessive defense spending and royal corruption are frequently cited. See, for example, the lengthy article in the *Los Angeles Times*, 3 January 1995.

12

Authoritarian Legacies and Reform Strategies in the Arab World

Daniel Brumberg

Some thirty years ago Samuel Huntington argued that, given their slender resource base, most Third World countries should limit the "disorderly" effect of democratic participation to generate the savings and institutions required for sustained economic growth.[1]

Recently Huntington's thesis has found new life, albeit in an altered conceptual form. Adam Przeworski and Guillermo O'Donnell, among others, have studied the efforts of reformers in Eastern Europe and Latin America to secure a "contingent" compromise that might mitigate the tension between economic efficiency and democratic participation. Such a pact entails an exchange by which ruling elites offer limited democratic reforms in return for a pledge by popular groups not to assert social demands that might undermine economic reform.[2]

Students of such pacts do not claim they are inevitable. They recognize, as recent events in Poland and Russia show, that contingent pacts can be reversed or watered down by the reassertion of leftist or nationalist forces. Yet despite such partial reversals, both Marxist and liberal scholars agree that while these postauthoritarian pacts are fragile, they will dominate the political landscape as we move into the twenty-first century.[3]

Where does the Arab world stand with respect to this conceptual consensus and empirical trend? Clearly outside it. For while a myriad of Arab states were shaken by economic and social crises during the 1980s, most Arab leaders successfully skirted the challenge of economic reform by using what I call "survival strategies" to minimally respond to the pressures for economic and political change without engaging in the risky game of power sharing.[4] This limited response to economic crisis was neither a reflection of a cultural proclivity for authoritarianism nor the manifestation of civil society's "resurgence." Instead, it mirrored the enduring legacies of "populist authoritarianism," and the strategies that elites used to reimpose their hegemony without undertaking major economic or politcal reforms.

To make the above case, I begin in this chapter by exploring the theory of "contingent democratic compromises." I then offer an alternative view, one that suggests the conditions that might promote or hinder the use of survival strategies. Subsequently I examine the fate of such strategies in Egypt, Tunisia, Algeria, and Syria. We shall see that after sustaining such strategies for a decade or more, Arab reformers were obliged to initiate wide-ranging market reforms. The recent demise of populist economics, however, has not brought about a shift to democracy. Instead, Arab leaders have tried to impose structural adjustment programs by authoritarian means. This development offers sobering lessons, not only about regime change in the Arab world, but also about the wider challenges of reform in Eastern Europe and the Third World.

Contingent Consent and the Forging of Democractic Bargains

The specter of democratic reform that in recent years has swept across many states might seem to confirm the linear theories advanced by Seymour Martin Lipset and Karl Deutsch;[5] in fact, however, this democratic "revolution" was less the product of inevitable historical forces than of a fortuitous convergence of events. These events included the 1982 debt crisis, the linking of debt relief to structural adjustment, and the breakdown of statist economies. These converging forces produced economic crises in no less than 17 authoritarian states.[6] Deprived of their ability to buy the political quiescence of their populations, authoritarian elites sought a "democratic" way out of their predicament.

I have referred to this solution as a "democratic bargain," an arrangement by which democratic reforms are used as a device to obtain economic reform. These bargains are "neither purely voluntary nor coercive enterprises; they are secured through political mechanisms . . . that facilitate the mobilization of winners in the economic reform contest and the marginalization of potential losers."[7]

Guillermo O'Donnell was the first to predict the conditions that might promote democratic bargains. He argued that the imposition of capital accumulation had so completely denuded authoritarian regimes of legitimacy that key coalition actors were tempted to seek support outside the regime by offering limited democratic reforms. O'Donnell and colleagues subsequently linked this structural analysis to a rational choice approach to create what Adam Przeworksi calls a "generic" theory of transitions. This theory holds that transitions are propelled by structural factors, in particular by the failure of authoritarian regimes to honor their promises of social justice. But this objective process assures no specific outcomes. Transitions are "uncertain" because they depend on a complex game by which actors anticipate the actions of others to produce a bandwagon effect that can force even hard-liners to jump on the democratic train.[8]

However, this quintessentially political game is not as undetermined as it seems. For while a transition requires rules that theoretically offer all groups the chance of winning, its success hinges on the ability of powerful elites to impose rules that assure that these elites will win more than others. Democratic transitions succeed, in Przeworski's words, because the "appearance of uncertainty" hides the reality that "actors know what is possible" at the outset of the game.[9]

Two propositions followed from the above analysis. First, transitions are most likely to succeed when soft-liners can show that popular groups accede to political procedures that secure the most valuable assets of dominant groups.[10] Any violation of this premise can stop a transition. Second, the more institutional and economic resources available to ruling elites relative to other groups, the more likely the former will obtain a measure of autonomy sufficient to advance onerous economic reforms while *maintaining* democratic credibility.

The Empirical Evidence

Ruling elites became aware of the instrumental benefits of democratic bargains following the 1982 debt crisis. Prior to that, they responded to the problems of hyperinflation and deficit spending by imposing stabilization measures via executive fiat. But when the IMF pressed for far-reaching structural reforms such as privatization, ruling elites were obliged to initiate political programs that linked private and state actors in complex coalitions.[11]

This process *did not* by itself require democracy. As Haggard and Kaufman have shown, the experience of Third World countries during the 1980s demonstrated that there was little correlation between regime type per se and successful economic reform. Rather, what counted was the openness of the ruling coalition to different social forces and the relative autonomy of state institutions vis-à-vis antireform groups. Where new democracies were based on a narrow coalition of proreform actors, and where this coalition forged institutions that insulated it from popular demands, reform succeeded. Conversely, where broad coalitions were penetrated by rent seekers, or where popular groups were organized and had access to antireform elements in the ruling coalition, reforms tended to fail.[12]

The Dominant Theory and Its Limitations

While events on the ground may have validated the dominant theory of "contingent" transitions, there were significant cases that defied its universal claims. For example, by creating strong authoritarian states that maintained discreet but effective links to key business groups in society, the "Asian tigers" promoted export-oriented market economies several decades prior to democratizing.[13] In the Arab world, reformers such as Husni Mubarak, Chadli Bin Jadid, and Zein al-'Abidin Bin 'Ali all tried to avoid the trials of economic and political reform despite the economic crises that were undermining their legitimacy.

These experiences suggest that the supposedly universal assumptions that inform the dominant theory of transitions must be reexamined. Two assumptions merit attention. It is assumed that regime transitions are propelled by what O'Donnell and Schmitter call the "resurrection of civil society," a process by which "agents of government control" are converted "into instruments for the expression of interests . . . against the regime" and new "grass-roots organizations" emerge.[14] Second, it is assumed that values and culture play no part in the forging of pacts. What counts, as Przeworski puts it, are "self-interested" (i.e., rational) "punishments" that spontaneously push all actors to comply with the rules of pact-making.[15]

Both assumptions are dubious. The premise that pact formation can be explained without addressing the role of values is belied by Przeworksi's own observations. He notes that the forging of democratic pacts in Eastern Europe was presaged by the death of a *belief* in "the very idea of rationally administering things to satisfy human needs. . . . "[16] However, while it may be true that social learning played a major part in creating the preconditions for democratic transitions in Eastern Europe, it does not follow that the discrediting of one belief system must automatically yield a "rational" universal ethos. Indeed, the revival of nationalist ideologies in Eastern Europe and Islamic fundamentalism in the Middle East demonstrates that indigenous cultural values can shape expectations in ways that can frustrate the forging of contingent compromises.

As for the assumption that pacts unfold via the "resurrection of civil society," it reflects a peculiarly Western notion that holds that civil society exists apart from the state and in a relation by which the first checks the power of the second. Where this relationship is violated, the argument goes, civil society will struggle to extract itself from the state's abnormal embrace.

Here again the fallacy of generalizing a universal law from a particular range of cases produces misleading conclusions. The state-society relationship that emerged in Western Europe was a product of particular social and intellectual forces. It does not follow that this same relationship must always replicate itself,[17] or that every entity that flowers under an authoritarian sun represents the rebirth of a civil society striving to undo the state's embrace.[18] On the contrary, for those who have grown accustomed to this embrace, it can become so institutionally and ideologically "natural" that the very idea of breaking it will seem foolish and even repugnant.

Imagining such a possibility demands the relinquishing of all teleological notions in favor of a historically grounded method that explains how the *legacies* of a specific state-society relationship make some transitions more likely than others. This approach not only accounts for diversity of transitions, but also illuminates those cases that the dominant paradigm treats as anomalous exceptions to the universal rule.[19]

In the particular cases of Egypt, Algeria, and Tunisia, their protracted and seemingly indefinite transitions can be accounted for by studying how reformers use the institutional, social, political, and ideological structures of "populist authoritarianism" to sustain their political survival.[20]

Historical Legacies and the Strategy of Survival

The populist authoritarian regimes emerged in Egypt, Tunisia, Algeria, and Syria during the 1960s.[21] They rested on a "ruling bargain" by which regimes promised their citizens social justice and economic security in return for the latter's political quiescence. While such bargains were not unique to the Arab world, the institutions, social coalitions, and ideologies that were used to secure them were to some degree distinctive to the Arab world.[22]

At the core, populist authoritarian regimes sought to provide an alternative to the brutal bureaucratic authoritarianism characteristic of Latin America, or the repressive Marxist-Leninism of Eastern Europe. Unwilling or unable to force accumulation through repression and/or mass mobilization, their leaders adopted halfway solutions to address the needs of as many social groups as possible within a context of state controls.[23]

Populist authoritarian rule entailed several key components.[24] The first was the creation of broad coalitions that embraced, to varying degrees, professionals, "national" capitalists, small independent farmers, workers, and the military. The junior members of this coalition—the workers, peasants, and professionals—were linked *and* subordinated to the state through clientelist, corporatist, and single-party mechanisms. To compensate for their subordination, popular groups obtained social benefits such as guaranteed public sector employment, subsidized food, and free higher education. This ruling bargain was given a philosophical gloss by official ideologies that celebrated the culturally "authentic" traditions of class unity and cooperation. In Egypt, Algeria, and Ba'thist Syria, this "Third Way" was enshrined in the language of "Arab socialism" and latently in the symbols of Islam.[25]

The Enduring Legacies of Populist Authoritarianism

Over time the above institutional, social, economic, and ideological structures created five overlapping legacies that bedeviled Arab leaders for
decades. First, because inefficient policies such as guaranteed state employment and import substitution could only be sustained by recourse to foreign
debt, loans, or rentier financing, the populist authoritarian state was tied to
an economic system that was digging its own grave. Second, far from being
"autonomous," this state was institutionally and ideologically intertwined
with key social groups whose loyalty flowed from the instrumental and thus
fragile calculations of a patron-client relationship. Any bid by the regime to
renege on the "ruling bargain" that sustained this relationship was bound to
provoke opposition from the popular groups whose livelihood depended on
the state. Third, while many of these organized groups had acquired sufficient autonomy to veto the state's economic reforms, they lacked the experience, leadership skills, and even ideology to constructively engage the
state in a negotiation over the bounds of such reform.[26]

Fourth, this situation of institutional dependency had an especially debilitating impact on professionals and businessmen—two groups that in
theory might cast a "swing vote" in favor of liberalization. During the
1960s Arab states virtually created the professional or "new middle class"
by expanding educational opportunities and by employing legions of graduates in state bureaucracies. As a result, professionals—and especially the
intellectual apparatchiks the state paid to speak on behalf of the former—
became forceful advocates of maintaining a strong state. A similar logic
applied to many businessmen, who obtained lucrative state contracts in return for their fealty. What remained of the Arab bourgeoisie was a small
and institutionally isolated sector that lacked sufficient allies to advance
market reform via a democratic bargain.

Finally, the implicit incorporation of Islamic concepts into populist
ideologies left an ideological time bomb ticking in the heart of Arab socialist doctrine. With their emphasis on the ideal of social justice and its
aversion to the notion of secular power sharing, these Islamic concepts
could be effectively mobilized against any regime that tried to impose the
hardships of economic reform through the morally dubious mechanisms of
a democratic pact.

In sum, the legacy of populist authoritarianism did not support the
forging of a democratic bargain. Arab reformers, like other Third World
leaders, would only pursue a democratic pact if they could impose enough
certainty to make the risk worth taking. But the organized reliance of
workers, professionals, students, and government employees on the state's
largesse deprived the state of a social base with which to advance these

reforms "democratically." For all concerned, economic reform was a zero-sum game—one whose only "certainty" was that it would very likely make losers out of those foolish enough to roll the dice in the first place.

Political and Economic Survival Strategies

If the legacies of populist authoritarianism hindered the creation of a democratic bargain, there was in theory the alternative of repression. However, exclusionary authoritarianism was precisely the kind of approach most Arab populist leaders had previously abjured. Moreover, as democratic forces from Warsaw to Santiago toppled authoritarian regimes, and as professionals in many Arab states began pressing for similar reforms during the 1980s,[27] the notion that social crises could be resolved by authoritarian means alone was discredited.

How could Arab leaders shape political openings that responded in a minimal way to the growing demands for political reform without unleashing forces that might bring the former crashing down? How could rulers play the transition game while minimizing or even precluding the possibility of losing? The answer lies in a combination of political and economic survival strategies.

Survival strategies have political and economic components. The goal of a political survival strategy is to open up the political arena to a degree of participation sufficient to attract support from groups with an interest in political reform, such as intellectuals and professionals, without at the same time creating conditions that might give these groups a means to undermine the hegemony of the ruling elites. This strategy works best when leaders can play one group against another and thus maintain the ability to strike at any group that "makes trouble." That is why those regimes that originally embraced a relatively wide coalition of social forces are better positioned to adopt such survival strategies than those that were based on a narrow coalition.

The goal of the economic survival strategies is to promote a degree of economic change sufficient to attract foreign investment, reduce debt payment, and raise foreign exchange without undermining the fundamental social and economic interests of those domestic groups and elites that are tied to the public sector. While the effectiveness of a particular survival strategy depends on the makeup of a given economy, this strategy usually includes a combination of two or more of the following:

1. Economic "compartmentalization" by which private actors assume tasks the state can no longer perform or that it is ready to delegate to others, such as the provision of credit by private banks

2. Limited stabilization or austerity measures such as minor reductions in subsidies, slight adjustment of interest rates, controlled devaluation, and selective import reductions
3. Selective trade reforms designed to raise foreign exchange and exports without exposing public sector producers to foreign or domestic competition. This approach often translates into a deregulation of the agricultural sector, a proreform constituency that often lacks the means to organize against the state
4. The provision of managerial "autonomy" without submitting industries to market competition or reducing the level of their subsidization by the state
5. The promotion of a "dualistic" approach by which joint ventures with private foreign and domestic actors are promoted in a coexistence with a subsidized public sector

It is vital to note what the above measures *do not* include. They do not include drastic cuts in government subsidies or privatization by either gradual or rapid means. On the contrary, the "dualistic" approach is designed to leave public sector industries completely or largely intact.[28]

The Paradoxical Dilemmas and Limits of Survival Strategies

The above economic and political strategies can buy ruling elites some time. But with few exceptions they eventually undermine themselves on both the economic and political terrains.

Politically, survival strategies pose risks for ruling elites. To begin with, even opposition groups that "play by the rules" can exploit openings to challenge regimes. Where rulers answer such defiance by reimposing authoritarian controls, they can polarize the political arena and undermine their legitimacy. The probability of such an outcome increases when political reform mobilizes groups—such as radical Islamists—who reject the very premise of power sharing. Under these conditions the space for regime-opposition accommodation can close almost as fast as it opens.

Economically, survival strategies can eventually aggravate rather than resolve crises. Minor increases in interest rates do not encourage investments since they are typically outpaced by high rates of inflation. Incremental devaluations fail to attract hard currency into the official banking system while they increase the costs of imports without making exports competitive. Where such incrementalist policies prevail, it is likely that hard currency will continue to flow out of the country, domestic investments will be funneled into unregulated investment schemes, and locally based import-substituting businesses will be squeezed while exporters are unable to compete abroad.

Most important, where public sector industries comprise a significant proportion of the national economy, a "dualistic" approach can drain the economy while undermining the growth of the private sector. This double blow occurs because the state must bail out inefficient, import-substituting industries by recourse to foreign debt or through printing more money. This results in high inflation—which punishes popular classes dependent on government wages or subsidies—and rising foreign debt. On the other hand, where scarce government funds are used to sustain state enter-prises—as in Tunisia, where capital transfers and subsidies to the state sec-tor increased from 10 to 52 percent from 1970 to 1980—there are fewer private or official funds to invest in the private sector. Moreover, the pri-vate sector takes a second hit insofar as the legal and bureaucratic controls that are retained to protect the public sector often constrain investment in private sector industries as well.

In short, economic survival strategies often produce two paradoxical effects. First, they can create a "lose-lose" game by imposing social and economic costs *without* creating the market incentives that promote pro-duction—thus alienating both losers and potential winners in the reform process. Second, unless regimes have external financial resources in the form of loans or grants to prop up this failing strategy, the only effective long-term solution is to adopt structural measures that address the root cause of economic stagnation. Ironically, by aggravating the economic sit-uation, survival strategies can leave governments with little choice but to adopt the very measures they wanted to avoid in the first place through adopting such strategies.

While noting the limitations of survival strategies, we should not con-clude that all populist authoritarian regimes are equally vulnerable to these limitations. Syria adopted an economic survival strategy that preserved "'national' economic sectors" without undermining the economy, at least for a time.[29] (However, for reasons discussed below, the curtailing of these reforms in 1991 suggests that Syria is the exception that proves the self-limiting rule of survival strategies.) Nor does the above analysis warrant the conclusion that the exhaustion of survival strategies *must* lead to democra-tization. All it implies is that when these strategies falter and regimes are obliged to adapt to structural adjustment measures, these steps will be com-plemented by a process of "political adjustment," which is designed to do precisely what survival strategies avoid: mobilize supporters of economic reform and isolate opponents. If suitable conditions exist, political adjust-ment might take the form of a democratic bargain. If these conditions are wanting, some version of exclusionary authoritarianism becomes likely.

Conditions That Favor or Hinder Survival Strategies:
Some Initial Propositions

The adoption and sustaining of survival strategies is a function of the regime's ability to do two things: First, to pacify as many groups as possible

without taking measures that would undermine the basic interests of any
one group. Second, to play one group against another in a way that allows
the state to check any group that violates the "rules of the game."

I would propose that the ability to sustain this juggling act depends on
the relative homogeneity/heterogeneity of the original ruling coalition. The
more this coalition embraced a wide spectrum of social groups in a mal-
leable system of interest representation and ideological expression, the
easier it is to play one group off against another. Paradoxically, a legacy of
relative pluralism makes it easier for elites to use survival strategies. Conversely, where the original coalition was tied by the state to only a few
popular social groups, and where these groups lacked alternative means of
organizing other than through state-controlled organizations, it becomes
harder for the state to disengage from these groups, to find allies for reform, and finally to play the various groups against each other in a manner
that enhances the state's room to maneuver against any one group.

Yet while a choice in favor of survival strategies depends partly on the
relative homogeneity/heterogeneity of the founding coalition, I would propose that two other factors play a crucial role in underpinning these strategies. The first is the commitment of both ruling *and* opposition elites to
the principle of limiting political and economic reforms. Where such commitment is absent or begins to wane, it becomes very difficult to translate
objective opportunities for survival strategies into reality. The second condition is the provision of external financial resources in the form of foreign
loans, grants, or rents. Such funds are critical because survival strategies
not only fail to remedy the root causes of economic reform but, as we have
seen, can aggravate economic problems. Thus when external resources
begin running out and ruling elites must make the tough choices required
by substantive market reforms, a moment arrives when it becomes proba-
ble that survival strategies will be abandoned in favor of democratic bargains or policies of exclusionary authoritarianism.

Egypt, Tunisia, Algeria, and Syria Compared

By and large, the poor Arab states did not suffer from the dilemmas created by populist authoritarianism until the early 1980s. Before that, Arab
leaders sustained their economies by relying on rents obtained directly or
indirectly from oil sales. For example, in 1982, 90 percent of the GDP in
Algeria derived from oil sales, while in Egypt the percentage of GDP represented by rents climbed from 15 percent in 1975 to 40 percent in 1983.[30]
Thus the very survival of the ruling bargain had become dependent on rentier financing.

The oil glut dealt a sharp blow to this house of cards. In one fell swoop oil output dropped from a 1979 high of 31 million barrels per day to 18 million in 1982, while the price of oil fell 50 percent. Loath to cut expenditures, Arab states took on more debt. In 1985 they owed $80 billion U.S., a debt whose servicing cost $11 billion a year. By the close of 1986 debt reached $144 billion—a 21 percent increase over the previous two years. To make matters worse, all this occurred as the IMF was linking debt rescheduling to structural adjustment measures. Under these trying conditions, poor Arab states had little choice but to forge an alternative to the ruling bargain.[31]

While the above developments had a differential impact on Egypt, Algeria, Tunisia, and Syria, their responses were similar: Unwilling to alienate key constituencies, ruling elites devised survival strategies as a way of avoiding the dangers of substantive reform. Where such strategies were effective—in Egypt and Tunisia—the legacies of populist authoritarians were relatively heterogeneous as measured by the breadth of social groups participating in the ruling coalition, the flexibility of interest representation, and the malleability of the ruling ideology. The existence of a relatively unified political elite and ample external funds also played a critical part in sustaining survival strategies. In contrast, where the above social, political, economic, and institutional resources were in short supply, the strategies failed—as in Algeria—or were abandoned to an uncertain future, as in Syria.

Egypt

Egypt's leaders pursued a political and economic survival strategy from 1974, when President Sadat began his *infitah*, to May 1991, when President Mubarak began a structural adjustment program.[32] The eclectic brand of populist authoritarianism Sadat inherited from Nasser helped make this 16-year record possible. Nasser's "alliance of working forces" embraced middle class peasants, workers, "productive" capitalists, urban professionals, and the military. Nasser imposed a different mix of corporatist and clientalist controls on each of these groups in an effort to contain them.[33] Furthermore, he tried to legitimate this "unruly" arrangement by promoting "Arab Socialism," a nebulous doctrine that invited as many views of socialism as there were interests represented in the ruling coalition.[34]

Sadat cleverly manipulated this eclectic legacy. In his *October Working Paper* on the one hand he asserted that protecting the social goals gains of the Revolution required limitations on democratic practice, while on the other hand he claimed that Arab socialism demanded a revived role for "productive" capitalism.[35] He proved similarly adept at juggling the institutional and social legacies of Nasserism. Faced by demands for a multiparty system, Sadat tried to discredit the intelligentsia by galvanizing workers and students behind the slogan of "defending the Revolution." He crowned these measures by mobilizing the landed elite during the 1976 People's Assembly elections. After securing their hegemony "democratically," his allies passed laws that gave the regime the legal right to restrict political participation.

Sadat matched the above maneuvers with an economic survival strategy that called for retaining the public sector's leading role in conjunction with a revitalized private sector. The Egyptian Trade Union Federation endorsed this dualistic approach, providing that it left the public sector intact.[36] The resulting predominance of public sector industries and the accompanying bureaucratic impediments to private sector development encouraged investors to put their money in speculative rather than in productive private-public sector joint ventures. By the end of 1978 the regime had approved only 134 joint ventures that collectively employed no more than 14,000 Egyptians.

The inflationary pressures generated by these policies obliged the regime to raise subsidies to $1.28 billion, which represented 30 percent of government expenditures in 1976. This trend pushed the balance-of-payments deficit from $2.6 billion in 1975 to $4.7 billion by the close of 1976. The ensuing balance-of-payments crisis set the stage for the infamous subsidy cuts of January 1977. Yet these cuts *did not* signal a break with the regime's survival strategy. Cairo sought to trim a mere $123 million from commodity supports, only a quarter of which (some $28 million) affected food costs.[37] Nevertheless, after the riots the regime withdrew the cuts. Henceforth, it funded its survival strategy by relying on external financial support, most of which came from expatriate earnings and from American aid distributed in roughly equal measures between grants and loans.

During the first four years of his rule Mubarak did not dramatically alter the contours of Sadat's economic survival strategy. Following sharp criticism regarding the "consumerist" nature of *infitah*, he told workers on May Day 1983 that there would be no "diminution in and no sale of the public sector." Indeed, the state increased its stake in the economy, with public revenue as a percentage of GDP rising from 34 percent in 1975 to 43 percent in 1984, and total public employment jumping by a factor of four between 1970 and 1986.[38]

This system teetered along for about another year. But by early 1986, a drastic drop in revenues from remittances, oil sales, and Suez Canal receipts so exacerbated the economic situation that the Reagan administration threatened to delay further aid unless Cairo began economic reforms. The regime then began negotiations with the IMF, a development that prompted protests from opposition leaders. In an effort to mollify his critics,

Mubarak invited opposition leaders to a national conference. But when they demanded a government of national unity, the regime abandoned all pretense of forging a consensus over reforms. Two weeks after winning 70 percent of the seats during the April 1987 parliamentary elections, the regime announced a stabilization agreement with the IMF.

The May 1987 IMF agreement demonstrated the irresistible logic of survival strategies. It did not confront critical issues such as food subsidies and left interest rates far below annual inflation and energy costs at 20 percent of world prices. In the next three years the regime failed to meet its commitments to the IMF. By the spring of 1989, with arrears nearing $5 billion, the May 1987 IMF agreement was dead, and with it all hope of attaining further standby credits.

The IMF's hardball tactics, combined with a continuing drop in external rents, prompted Cairo in 1989 and 1990 to reduce energy and food subsidies, raise interest rates, and enforce a 1988 law to regulate the Islamic investment companies. The regime also continued to promote "back-door privatization," or public-private sector joint ventures.[39]

None of the above measures addressed the root cause of the country's economic malaise: the drain on the economy exacted by public sector enterprises. From 1980 through 1988 the net rate of return on these public assets amounted to 2.1 percent, while the financial deficit run up by public sector firms equaled 6 percent of the national fiscal deficit.[40] To finance this deficit, Egypt assumed more external debt, which climbed to a record $54 billion by the end of 1988.[41]

Against this background of poor economic performance and growing international pressure for structural adjustment measures, Cairo again made some tentative efforts to mobilize political support for economic reform. In sharp contrast to his May Day speech seven years earlier, Mubarak told workers on May Day 1990 that "we are in a critical stage in the history of the human race. . . . We must embark on reforms." But a democratic bargain was not to be. With the onset of the Gulf War, the assassination of house speaker Rif'at Mahgub in October 1990, and the growing saliency of the army, a new consensus in favor of imposing economic reforms began to take shape in Mubarak's government. The regime's subsequent rejection of calls by the opposition parties for electoral reform prompted almost all the opposition parties to boycott the November 1990 People's Assembly elections. Six months later, the regime reached the most ambitious reform agreement ever acceded to by Cairo. In return for the regime's promise to enact a package of stabilization measures designed to prepare the economy for privatization, the IMF forgave $10 billion in debts and rescheduled another $10 billion. Thus by May 1991 Egypt's leaders had abandoned limited economic steps in favor of comprehensive market reforms.

Tunisia

Tunisia began an economic survival strategy in 1970 when, in the wake of a poor harvest and fiscal crisis, the state began promoting the private sector. The regime widened the scope of economic reforms in 1985, following a severe foreign exchange crisis. However, it did not match these measures with a political reform that afforded society much room to breathe. In April 1989 the ruling party used a winner-take-all system to sweep parliamentary elections. Running unchallenged at the same time, Zein al-'Abidin Bin 'Ali was "elected" president in a vote that drew only 2.1 million participants.[42]

What explains the relative success of Bin 'Ali's economic survival strategy in comparison to the limited scope of his political reforms? To answer this question we must examine the political and economic legacies of populist authoritarianism in Tunisia.

Bin 'Ali's rigid political reforms grew out of Tunisia's particular experience of one-party rule. In contrast to Nasser's Arab Socialist Union (ASU), Tunisia developed a single-party machine that rigorously controlled all associational groups, including the once powerful General Union of Tunisian Workers. As the party became stronger, its leaders concluded that the only way they could afford to safely share power was through the party itself.[43] As a result, when Bin 'Ali took power in 1987 he was obliged to make the ruling party (now renamed the Democratic Constitutional Rally or RCD), the vehicle of his political opening. His government did this in three ways: First, it co-opted leaders of the Tunisian League for Human Rights and Ahmad Mistiri's Social Democrats' Movement into the government. Second, it cajoled opposition leaders into signing a bogus "national pact." This pact not only failed to define a power-sharing formula; it denuded its call for pluralistic democracy by insisting that Tunisians unite "around the same consensus."[44] Third, prior to the April 1989 elections, the regime proposed a common voting list that allocated only a limited number of seats to the opposition parties.

The socioeconomic legacies of Habib Bourguiba's ruling coalition proved more amenable to a survival strategy than the political legacies. To begin with, while many sectors of the economy were brought under the umbrella of the state during the 1960s, Bourguiba retained a small private sector. Moreover, the boundaries between the state on the one hand, and the public and private sectors on the other, were permeable. Many private enterprises received loans, tax breaks, subsidized credit, and tariff protection from the state, while many "public" sector enterprises were heavily subscribed to by private investors since by law any enterprise in which the state held 10 percent or more of paid-up capital was subject to public sector management.[45]

By the early 1970s the intrinsic inefficiencies of this hybrid system produced a fiscal crisis. In response, the state began a campaign to expand the size of the private sector. Three official agencies supervised the creation of 800 new enterprises between 1967 and 1978. However, the state not only indirectly subsidized these new businesses; it also created 110 new public sector enterprises between 1973 and 1984.

This legacy of state-private-public collaboration proved economically costly but politically advantageous. It was costly because from 1972 to 1987 the state transferred the equivalent of 45 percent of gross investments to cover the losses of public sector enterprises.[46] These policies fueled inflation, whose effect the regime tried to militate by increasing subsidies.[47] The resulting deficit spending pushed external debt to $5.1 billion by 1985, 46 percent of GDP. When a foreign exchange crisis ensued, the government negotiated a deal with the IMF in 1986.

The IMF asserted that the 1986 agreement embraced a "comprehensive set of structural reforms." But Bin 'Ali could not fully implement these reforms without harming the public sector and its private sector rentier cousin.[48] Yet if he failed to take action, he risked loosing the three-year funding facility that the IMF offered as a reward for pursuing reforms.

In a bid to extract himself from this dilemma Bin 'Ali tried to transform the legacy of public/private collaboration that he had inherited into a political asset. He did so in three ways. First, rather than hazard a loss of public support by assailing the public sector, the regime reaffirmed its populist credentials by highlighting the state's welfare role in the national pact.[49] Over the next two years Bin 'Ali honored this commitment. Second, the regime exploited the reliance of private sector actors on the distribution of government rents through clientelistic networks. By doling out favors such as tariff reductions in a selective manner, the regime divided private sector actors while appearing to comply with the IMF's demands. Third, Bin 'Ali's regime exploited the above-mentioned arrangement by which public sector control had been imposed on enterprises that had significant private investment. By raising the ceiling at which businesses were classified as "public" to 50 percent in 1989, the regime "privatized" a *small* number of firms without having to invest much political capital in the effort.[50]

These measures were not inconsequential. In comparison to its neighbors, Tunisia made headway on stabilization.[51] However, by defining most of the public sector as "strategic," the regime avoided the risky task of privatization. Between 1987 and 1991, only 33 out of 189 public enterprises were privatized, a figure that amounted to a little over 1 percent of the total book value of existing public enterprises.[52] As the public sector continued to drain the economy, the regime took on more foreign debt. From 1985 to 1990, external debt rose from $5 billion to $7.5 billion, while the current deficit account—which had dropped from $587 million in 1985 to $60 million in 1987—rose to $500 million in 1990.[53]

At some point in 1990, Tunisia's economic plight prompted a decision to shift from limited economic reforms to a structural adjustment program. The regime, however, postponed this decision in order to crush the Islamic al-Nahda Party, which the regime apparently feared would mobilize public support in opposition to reforms.[54] Having achieved this goal by the close of 1992, the regime began a far-reaching structural adjustment program backed by the fist of exclusionary authoritarianism.[55]

Algeria

Algeria's leaders adopted an economic survival strategy in 1978. In the ensuing 10 years, President Chadli Bin Jadid presided over a series of incoherent reforms that had the unintended effect of aggravating socioeconomic conditions. The result was a social crisis that exploded in October 1988 when youths took to the streets of Algiers, Constantine, and other cities to violently protest food shortages. Bin Jadid tried to respond to the riots by grafting a political opening onto his economic survival strategy. However, he lacked the preconditions for it to be successful. Bin Jadid inherited a legacy of populist authoritarianism so bereft of social, institutional, and political pluralism that he had little opportunity to play the "juggling game" that is a vital part of an effective survival strategy. Moreover, the oil glut deprived Algeria's hydrocarbon-dependent economy of external resources. Most importantly, Bin Jadid's regime lacked any semblance of unity. Indeed, internal divisions in the Front de Libéracion Nationale (FLN) opened the door to the Islamists in 1991, producing a coup that ended Algeria's political reforms.

While not preordained, this paradoxical turn of events had its structural roots in the social, institutional, and ideological legacies of FLN rule. As was the case with Tunisia's ruling party, the FLN's co-optation of almost all social forces left little room between it and society. However, in contrast to the RCD, the FLN did not represent a cohesive ruling elite; rather, it provided a vehicle for the *politique des clans*. These clans employed two resources to overcome their own divisions. The first was patronage that derived from a hydrocarbon industry that accounted for three quarters of all economic activity by the mid-1970s.[56] The second was the "socialist" ideology of the revolution. As in Egypt and Tunisia, this ideology was populist in its social orientation and corporatist in its institutional/political vision. But in contrast to the former, Algerian socialism was extremely hostile to the private sector.[57]

Algerian *dirigisme* was sustained by huge state subsidies that discouraged production. From 1980 to 1986, real earnings per employee in manufacturing fell 27 percent, while gross output per employee fell 19 percent.[58] These inefficiencies might have compelled the regime to begin reforms earlier had it not been for oil. Following Mexico's lead, Algeria's leaders not only used oil rents to avoid major economic reform; they also borrowed heavily from international lenders to expand the public sector. As a result, long-term debt jumped from $937 million to $15 billion between 1970 and 1980.[59]

It was in this context of growing exposure to international creditors that Algeria's new president, Chadli Bin Jadid, initiated an economic reform program in 1978. That program, as one scholar noted, was designed to be "deliberately slow."[60] Rather than disassemble the social, institutional, and ideological legacy of Algerian socialism, it aimed to *reform this edifice from within* in order to protect the economic and political prerogatives of the "iron triangle" of FLN politicians, army officers, and state bureaucrats. Algeria's leaders began by restructuring SONATRACH, the national oil company. This version of *perestroika* entailed a devolution of limited autonomy over production and pricing, without subjecting this paramount sector of the economy to market forces. It was followed by efforts to promote the barely visible private sector. The guiding principle of this effort was set out by the FLN's central committee, which held that the private sector was "complementary" to the public sector. This dualistic approach was enshrined in the 1982 Investment Code, which decreased taxes for private enterprises and, most significantly, legalized the creation of joint ventures with private foreign firms so long as the state retained majority control.[61]

The above measures had little positive impact on government spending. On the contrary, official consumption as a proportion of GDP rose from 14 percent in 1980 to 16 percent in 1983. In a bid to reduce these expenditures and the country's external debts, Algeria's leaders adopted a "self-imposed" stabilization program in late 1983. This program was taken independently of the IMF, allowing Bin Jadid to argue that he was upholding the ideology of the revolution. But in honoring this legacy, the regime robbed the program of its punch. Free from foreign interference, Bin Jadid did not substantially reduce subsidies, raise interest rates, or devalue the dinar. Instead his limited measures had the paradoxical effect of suppressing demand while allowing expenditures and debt to rocket from $13.8 billion in 1984 to a record $22.8 billion in 1986.[62]

Hydrocarbon earnings allowed the regime to cover this gap for a time. But when these earnings plummeted from $13 billion in 1985 to $7 billion in 1986, the regime was obliged to adopt incentive measures designed to increase domestic production and particularly exports.

The dualistic orientation of this program was set out in the 1986 *Charte Nationale*. It held that the "national private sector must be integrated . . . in the framework of a development plan . . . (that) . . . rigorously organizes this sector's orientation. . . . "[63] Toward that end, the regime in 1987 replaced the ministry of planning with the *conseil national de planification.* This body presided over the creation of holding companies, which were in theory required to apply market principles. In addition, the regime passed a law that made the central bank independent of the treasury, raised interest rates, and, most importantly, began privatizing agriculture in 1988.[64]

With the partial exception of agricultural reform, these measures did not improve economic performance. Enterprise "autonomy" was superficial because the directors of many holding companies were former government employees. In addition, interest rates remained high and subsidies were retained. Yet, as is often the case with economic survival strategies, limited reforms designed to avoid political controversy still antagonized key public sector workers, students, and hard-line FLN apparatchiks. The evidence suggests that the latter instigated the food shortages that led to the October 1988 riots.[65]

President Bin Jadid responded to these events by initiating a political opening, insisting that "one cannot proceed with economic reforms . . . without engaging in political reforms."[66] Despite their democratic pretensions, these reforms constituted a political survival strategy. Their aim— as Bin Jadid put it—was to "galvanize the majority to support one . . . political action program . . . and allows . . . groups to express themselves. . . . "[67] In an effort to apply this corporatist vision in practice, the regime enacted legislation giving it the statutory and constitutional right to ban any political party or interest group that had violated "fundamental liberties, national unity, the independence of the country etc." This authoritarian qualification *explicitly ruled out* the creation of parties based exclusively on religious or sectarian identities.[68]

Yet having forged the legal basis for a political survival strategy, and having secured the military's support, the regime defied the logic of economic survival strategies by taking several measures that provoked strikes from the General Union of Algerian Workers and other popular organizations.[69] Moreover, in contradiction to its own laws, the regime permitted the creation of the Islamic Salvation Front (FIS), a party whose leaders not only spurned the constitution's democratic provisions, but also assailed the military in vitriolic terms. Bin Jadid allowed the FIS to participate in the June 1990 municipal and provincial elections, even though he knew that the FLN was so weak that if legislative elections were to follow, the party might, as he put it, be "mis en minorité."[70] What explains this bizarre failure to pursue a survival strategy?

Part of the answer lies in the economic plight that Algeria faced by 1990. Wed to a hydrocarbon-dependent economy that was going broke, and mired in foreign debt, Prime Minister Mouloud Hamrouche had apparently concluded by the spring of 1990 that only drastic reforms would save the economy. But if this was true, why adopt political reforms that undermined the regime?

The answer lies in the limited political assets at the president's disposal. As we have seen, Bin Jadid inherited a political system that had few vestiges of organized pluralism. Most importantly, with the decline of oil revenues and the FLN's ideological legitimacy, the ruling elite split into several factions, including a hard-line contingent, many of whom were elected in November 1989 to the FLN's Central Committee. With a Tunisian-style "reform" of the FLN ruled out, Bin Jadid tried to resolve his predicament by inventing, *ex nihlio*, the socioinstitutional pluralism he needed to outflank his FLN rivals. He did this by legalizing the creation of new interest groups, and by *promoting* the FIS's fortunes—even as the party's leaders rejected the constitution's democratic principles.[71]

This risky approach worked for a time. But when FIS leader Abbasi Madani called in May 1991 for a national strike to back his demands for early presidential elections and the revision of an election law that blatantly favored the FLN, Bin Jadid arrested him and 'Ali Belhadj on charges of sedition. Although the subsequent events are still murky, it seems that Bin Jadid believed that by depriving the FIS of its charismatic leaders, limiting proxy voting, and preventing a large number of ballots from reaching voters, he could reduce the FIS vote to manageable proportions. The military opposed this gamble, insisting that the FIS be banned. After Bin Jadid rejected this demand, Defense Minister Khalid Nezzar and his FLN allies let the first round of elections unfold in December 1991, in the apparent hope that an FIS victory would provide a pretext for a coup.

In an electoral system that rewarded larger parties, the failure of the FLN to mobilize the vote played into the FIS's hand. Although only 25 percent of the total registered electorate voted—one million fewer than in the June 1990 elections—the "winner-take-all" system allowed the FIS to obtain 188 out of 232 seats with just 48 percent of the actual votes cast. This put the Islamists on the verge of taking two thirds of the assembly seats in the next round of elections—thus giving Nezzar and company the pretext they probably wanted to halt Bin Jadid's chaotic political reforms.

During the first six months of 1992, a five-member Higher Council of State led by President Muhammad Boudiaf ruled Algeria. It suspended the elections, banned the FIS, and arrested at least 9,000 Islamists. Prime Minister Sid Ahmed Ghozali, who was also minister of the economy, at first tried to revive an economic survival strategy, insisting that the public sector was the heart of the economy.[72] But when industrial output fell by 5.5 percent in 1991, the regime announced a privatization program, a new commercial law, and subsidy cuts. These measures were followed by an IMF mission to Algeria in June.

The regime's shift in favor of far-reaching economic reforms was accompanied by Boudiaf's public attacks on corruption. It appears that Boudiaf paid with his life for these attacks. Within a month of his June 1992 assassination, FLN hard-liner Bel'aid 'Abd al-Salam forced Ghozali out.[73] A socialist who had presided over the nationalization program in the 1960s, 'Abd al-Salam rescinded almost all the measures taken by Ghozali. He ruled out privatization, reimposed government supervision over the public sector and central bank, and refused to reschedule Algeria's $25 billion debt with the IMF, preferring instead to enforce an austerity budget. This approach exacerbated the economic crisis, making the pressure for change irresistible. In September 1993 'Abd al-Salam was replaced by Redha Malek. The new prime minister appointed Mourad Benachenhou, an advocate of market reforms, as minister of the economy. By spring 1994 Algeria's leaders had recommitted the country to a structural adjustment program backed by military rule.[74]

Syria

President Hafiz al-Asad initiated an economic survival strategy in the mid-1980s, but backed away from it a few years later. His hesitancy was in part a product of the closed experiment in populist authoritarianism that the Ba'th Party began in 1963. Although he tried to breathe some social and political space into this experiment, Asad's room for maneuver was limited by the legacy he inherited in 1971.

Syria's Ba'thists built a Leninist party that consisted of a narrow alliance between a dominant core of military officers and intellectuals—most of whom by 1969 came from the 'Alawi community—and a subordinated peasantry and working class. Missing from this coalition was the bourgeoisie. By 1984 public sector industries employed one third of the labor force while producing 78 percent of gross industrial output.[75] What is more, public sector workers forged a privileged relationship with the Ba'th Party via the General Federation of Trade Unions. By the early 1980s the federation spoke for 31 percent of the economically active population.[76]

Assad's regime compensated for the inefficiencies of this command economy by relying on Arab aid. This aid financed nearly a quarter of total government expenditures by the early 1980s.[77] Oil money in turn promoted the growth of a parasitic alliance between an element of the bourgeoisie and state bureaucrats. As in much of the Arab world, this alliance promoted consumption rather than investment and growth. Moreover, a drop in Arab aid, from $1.8 billion in 1981 to $500 million in 1986, produced high deficit spending, trade deficits, and persistent foreign exchange crises.

To address this worsening economic situation the regime launched a series of economic reforms. From 1982 through 1984 it adopted limited measures that included banning imports of luxury goods, two devaluations, reductions of consumer goods subsidies, and the introduction of more flexible foreign exchange rules. In 1985 the regime adopted bolder measures. It raised prices between 7 and 144 percent on various consumer goods, allowed the import of goods for industrial production that had been available only to public sector firms, and facilitated access to credit for private sector importing. A year later it issued Legislative Decree Number Ten, which provided for joint-stock companies in agriculture and tourism. In addition it promoted tax breaks for agricultural production. Finally, in 1991 the regime passed a new investment code that reduced impediments to private sector investment and a new tax code that lowered private sector taxes.[78]

The above measures constituted a severely circumscribed economic survival strategy by comparison to the strategies of Egypt, Tunisia, and even Algeria. Having inherited a coalition beholden to a narrow band of interests, Asad's regime "carefully preserved the privileged position of 'national' economic sectors."[79] This dualistic approach was outlined during the eighth Regional Congress of the Ba'th in 1985. Following persistent opposition from the labor federation to economic reform, the Congress called for greater public sector efficiency and for continued state intervention in the economy.[80] Over the next five years, the regime not only ruled out privatization, it also opposed all private sector investment in heavy industry, as well as the introduction of private sector banking. Although the regime began a program to enhance public sector "capacity" in 1994, its modest economic reform program had stalled by that year, leaving the *Middle East Economic Digest* to lament that the regime is "taking an ultra-cautious approach to economic reform, and the business community is resigned to a long wait."[81]

What explains this short-lived survival strategy? Part of the answer may simply be that the regime had little social space in which to further such a strategy, and thus shut it down. Yet Syria's leaders not only sustained this strategy for six years, they did so in a manner that seemed to be economically efficient. In contrast to Egypt, Algeria, and Tunisia, where survival strategies eventually undercut aggregate economic growth and/or imposed high social costs, Syria's economy registered some gains. In 1989 it recorded its first trade surplus in 30 years, an event that was partly credited to joint-stock agricultural exports. In 1993 the GDP grew 10 percent, the private sector's contribution to GDP was 64 percent, inflation stood at 5.7 percent, and external debt remained at about $16.5 billion (30 percent of which was bilateral concessional debt from Russia). How did the regime achieve this level of growth without paying the costs that were shouldered by other Arab states?

One answer may be that Syria's leaders were loath to give their economic opening sufficient time to manifest these costs. Yet Syria's limited economic reforms *were* socially disruptive. The bloody 1982 Hama revolt was partly provoked by the vicissitudes of an economic opening that induced the urban petty bourgeoisie to challenge public sector privileges. Inflation repeatedly undercut public sector wages even though these wages were raised 47 percent between 1985 and 1987.[82] The resentment aroused by these policies was magnified by the flagrant corruption of officials and their cronies in public and rentier-private sectors.

However, if Asad's regime was not immune to the costs of an economic survival strategy, it had inherited a peculiar form of populist authoritarianism that helped it to mitigate these costs in a singularly authoritarian manner. In contrast to Egypt, Tunisia, and even Algeria—where to varying degrees legacies of limited pluralism helped rulers deflect the social costs of economic reform—Syria's military/sectarian (*'Alawi*) elite spurned the very principle of pluralism for reasons having to do as much with self-preservation as ideology. Thus, although the regime allowed two business leaders to run in controlled parliamentary elections in 1990, its inclination was to crush all dissent, imprisoning and even hanging businessmen who it accused of abusing reforms.[83] Had the regime pursued its economic opening, such abuses would probably have increased, leaving Asad with two equally bad choices: Open an ossified political system and risk an upheaval; or intensify political repression and loose legitimacy. By not enlarging the scope of economic reforms, he tried to evade this dilemma.

Syria's fortuitous economic circumstances also helped to minimize the scope of its survival strategy. Not only did oil sales boost the economy, private and official transfers furnished 60 percent of Syria's current account surplus in 1991.[84] Thus while not, strictly speaking, a rentier economy, Syria's economy depended on oil revenues, remittances, and Arab aid. After the Gulf War, inflows of Gulf aid eased Syria's foreign exchange crisis, leaving open the possibility that Syria's survival strategy was a "mere crisis-generated reaction to a temporary loss of foreign exchange."[85] If this is true, Asad's attempts to skirt economic reform may very well run out of steam.

The Rocky Road to Structural and "Political" Adjustment

The above review of survival strategies in four Arab states confirms several of the implicit predictions set out in the first part of this chapter. With the possible exception of Syria, limited economic reforms *did* spawn new socioeconomic problems that obliged reformists to adopt the very policies they had once deemed politically irrational. As suggested, this process was hastened by the depletion of external financial resources, a development that obliged reformists to adopt incentives to bolster economic efficiency and production. At each turn of this rocky road, it became harder to turn back. By the early 1990s, a revolution of sorts began to unfold, as the leaders of Egypt, Tunisia, and finally Algeria abandoned survival strategies in favor of structural adjustment programs.

A review of this trend shows that this shift has not come easily. In all three countries, reformists have encountered opposition from party apparatchiks, corporatist interest groups, and Islamists. What has distinguished the post-1990 period from the previous two decades, however, is the *resolve* of reformers to overcome these obstacles rather than yield to them.

These obstacles compelled Egypt's leaders to move slowly, out of concern that a rapid program would increase support for radical Islamists. In 1991, the regime entrusted the newly created Public Enterprise Office with the task of putting some $45 billion in state assets up for sale. In 1992 it enacted a new securities law and formed a Capital Markets Authority to raise investment funds. The following year saw the first sale of two major public sector enterprises, and significant moves to sell off at least 16 others.[86]

Tunisia, meanwhile, moved more quickly. Having broken the back of the Islamists, Bin 'Ali attempted to create an export-based economy by linking Tunisia to the European Community. In 1993, the regime lowered trade barriers, created two offshore zones, advanced privatization, eliminated almost all price controls, passed a new investment law designed to promote technology transfer and exports, created an International Cooperation and Investment Ministry and Industrial Promotion Agency, and moved toward full convertibility for commercial transactions.

By contrast, the efforts of Algeria's leaders to crush the Islamists absorbed nearly all the regime's energies. After Algeria fell into arrears on its $26 billion foreign debt in January 1994, the regime began negotiations with the IMF. In the spring it reached an agreement that provided for a $500 million standby loan and $300 million compensatory facility, in return for modified stabilization measures designed to minimize the social costs of economic reforms.[87]

The relative successes of Egypt and Tunisia by comparison to Algeria can be partly attributed to firm exe**u**tive leadership and to the exclusion of antireform elements from economic policymaking teams. As chairman of the investment authority, President Mubarak pushed for privatization. He was also probably responsible for the October 1993 cabinet reshuffle, which saw the forging of a proreform team under Minister 'Atif Sidqi. Similarly, President Bin 'Ali pushed for reforms, calling in 1994 for convertibility two years ahead of the official schedule. All of this stands in sharp contrast to Algeria, where disputes within the regime over the question of *political* reform diverted attention from the task of *economic* reform until spring 1994.

As the above efforts have unfolded, the leaders of Egypt, Tunisia, and even Algeria have recently turned to the task of forging a political base for their economic reforms. This shift was also anticipated in the first part of this chapter, in the suggestion that the adoption of structural adjustment measures is likely to be followed by efforts to create political mechanisms that empower the advocates of reform and isolate its opponents. Such "political adjustment" can take a democratic or exclusionary authoritarian form, depending on the institutional and ideological resources available to ruling elites and opposition groups.

In Egypt, Tunisia, and Algeria, political adjustment has taken an exclusionary form, in large measure because proreform forces lack institutional and ideological resources to advance structural adjustment democratically, while antireform forces have been mobilized by Islamic opposition groups. This does not mean that Islam is intrinsically anticapitalist. But moderate Islamists, who often advocate private property, have been outnumbered and outorganized by radicals who voice the despair of a new generation paying the bills of past leaders. These youths, and those who speak for them, are clinging to the ideological mantle of Arab populism at the very moment of its economic demise.

The exclusion of Islamists has come at great human cost. Yet the term "exclusionary authoritarianism" does not quite capture the political arrangements reformists have recently forged in their efforts to advance market reforms. Hesitant to forgo all semblance of legitimacy, reformists have tried to superficially integrate a variety of groups into the political process, while at the same time retaining sufficient autonomy to pursue economic reforms.

In Tunisia—as we might expect—this process has unfolded through the ruling party. Thus, prior to the March 1994 parliamentary elections, Bin 'Ali reserved 19 out of 163 seats for opposition parties by introducing a measure of proportional representation. Yet he did not hesitate to arrest journalists and opposition figures when they later challenged his policies.[88] Similarly, in January 1994 the rulers of Egypt and Algeria invited a variety of opposition parties, professional syndicates, and labor federations to participate in "national dialogues," the implicit purpose of which is to redefine (and limit) the boundaries of political participation.

Understandably wary of this effort, Egypt's New Wafd and Nasserist parties refused to begin a dialogue until the regime agreed to discuss political reform.[89] The regime's subsequent decision to meet this demand, at least in part, allowed the dialogue to begin in June 1994. However, the absences of the Muslim Brothers—who were excluded from the meeting—and of Wafd leaders—who rejected the regime's offer as insufficient—

placed the proceedings in some jeopardy. In Algeria, the attempt to hold a national conference failed, in part because the regime refused to talk with the FIS. In the ensuing months, hard-liners opposed all efforts by President Amin Zeroual to open talks with the Islamists. Although the appointment of a new prime minister and interior minister in April signaled a victory for regime moderates, escalating violence hindered the resumption of the conference.[90]

Conclusion: Kings Look East?

> How long can a regime have it both ways, conserving power and autonomy while selectively unloading economic decisionmaking onto a protected marketplace?[91]

It is too early to predict whether the above cautious measures to selectively open the field of political participation will succeed or fail. Much depends on the course of economic reforms. If they take root, even half-hearted efforts to build a political constituency for capitalism may develop a life of their own, compelling leaders to adopt genuine rather than spurious political reforms. Yet although this process might eventually resolve the trade-off between "conserving political power" and tolerating economic inefficiency, it will not necessarily do so by ushering in a liberal democratic dawn. On the contrary, capitalist development in the Arab world may eventually find an affinity for complex political systems that manage the tensions of markets through a combination of corporatist, pluralist, semidemocratic, and clientelist mechanisms.

This development would not be unprecedented. On the contrary, the "Asian tigers" used an ingenious mix of clientelist and bureaucratic devices to secure the collaboration of export-oriented business groups while systematically insulating the state from popular pressures or "rent-seeking" activities. Can this system of "embedded autonomy" be repeated outside the region?[92] This question has been raised in Eastern Europe; indeed it has been posed wherever the legacies of socialism have made a democratic approach to capitalism a risky venture.

While it is unlikely that the Asian approach can be replicated in the Arab world, certain aspects of it nevertheless find a resonance in some Arab countries. Indeed, it may be no mere coincidence that the Arab state that has registered the best record of structural adjustment is Morocco, a country in which clientelist links between the business community and the royal family apparently promoted rather than blocked privatization.[93] This fact raises an intriguing question: Do patrimonialist regimes such as those of King Hassan and King Hussein have advantages over populist regimes when it comes to promoting economic reforms?

One such advantage may be transparency. Because monarchs have not cloaked their rule in a progressive guise, they have been less vulnerable to the syndrome by which the masses become disillusioned with the illusory promises of leaders such as Gamal 'Abd al-Nasser. Moreover, by openly claiming the prerogatives and status derived from Islamic ancestry, monarchs such as Hassan and Hussein have not only been better positioned to arbitrate the painful transition to market economies, they have also found it easier to co-opt the Islamic opposition. Finally, as noted, clientelistic linkages between royal family and elements of the bourgeoisie have apparently facilitated rather than hindered the transition to market economies. In this sense the system of "embedded autonomy" may now be finding an echo in some quarters of the Arab world.

In time, Tunisia may be the most suitable postpopulist Arab candidate for an "Asian" approach. It has a relatively educated work force, a small population, new state organizations to promote exports, and privileged trade-links with the European Community. Moreover, as we have seen, clientelist links between the Tunisian bourgeoisie and the state go back several decades. These linkages have endured with the shift to structural adjustment. In fact, substantial financial donations by Tunisian businessmen to the ruling RCD suggest that clientelism may be adjusting to the "rational" demands of capitalism rather than giving way to the inexorable rise of a hegemonic bourgeoisie.[94]

President Bin 'Ali would be best served by presiding over this development rather than jumping into the fray. This may explain why he initially tried to enhance his status as "president" of all Tunisians rather than as leader of the ruling party. However, he could neither invent patriarchal legitimacy where such "reactionary" notions had been disavowed, nor could he separate himself from the ruling party lest he risk the fate of Algeria's Bin Jadid. Like other Arab leaders, Bin 'Ali found that the legacies of populist authoritarianism continue to exact a cost, long after these legacies had been repudiated in word if not in deed.

Notes

The author would like to express his gratitude to the following individuals for the insights they contributed to this study: Rex Brynen, Steve Heydemann, Bob King, Marcie Patton, Hugh Roberts, Lloyd and Susanne Rudolph, and Dirk Vandewalle.

    1. Samuel Huntington, *Political Order in Changing Societies* (New Haven: Yale University Press, 1968).

    2. Guillermo O'Donnell and Philippe Schmitter, eds., *Transitions from Authoritarian Rule: Tentative Conclusions about Uncertain Democracies* (Baltimore: Johns Hopkins University Press, 1986); Adam Przeworski, *Democracy and the Market Political and Economic Reforms in Eastern Europe and Latin America* (Cambridge, UK: Cambridge University Press, 1991).

3. See Larry Diamond, Juan Linz, and Seymour Martin Lipset, *Politics in Developing Countries: Comparing Experiences with Democracy* (Boulder: Lynne Rienner Publishers, 1990).

4. Daniel Brumberg, "Survival Strategies vs. Democratic Bargains: The Politics of Economic Reform in Contemporary Egypt," in Henri Barkey, ed., *The Politics of Economic Reform in the Middle East* (New York: St. Martin's Press, 1992), pp. 73–104.

5. Seymour Martin Lipset, "Economic Development and Democracy," in Lipset, ed., *Political Man: The Social Bases of Politics* (New York: Doubleday), pp. 46–76. Karl Deutsch, "Social Mobilization and Political Participation," in Jason Finkle and Richard Gable, eds., *Political Development and Social Change* (John Wiley: New York, 1966), pp. 384–402.

6. Stephan Haggard and Robert Kaufman, "Economic Adjustment and the Prospects for Democracy," in Haggard and Kaufman, eds., *The Politics of Economic Adjustment* (Princeton: Princeton University Press, 1992), pp. 319–350. The authors identify Argentina, Brazil, Bolivia, Uruguay, and the Philippines as countries where economic crisis preceded a transition to democracy. If we include in this list Eastern European cases, and those cases where economic crisis preceded political liberalization, we would add Zambia, Albania, Poland, the former USSR, Hungary, the Czech and Slovak Republics, Bulgaria, Egypt, Jordan, Algeria, and Tunisia, for a total of 17.

7. Brumberg, "Survival Strategies," pp. 75–76.

8. Guillermo O'Donnell, "Tensions in the Bureaucratic-Authoritarian State and the Question of Democracy," in David Collier, ed., *The New Authoritarianism in Latin America* (Princeton: Princeton University Press, 1981), pp. 285–331; O'Donnell and Schmitter, eds., *Transitions from Authoritarian Rule: Tentative Conclusions*; Adam Przeworski, "Some Problems in the Study of the Transition to Democracy," in Guillermo O'Donnell, Philippe Schmitter, and Laurence Whitehead, eds., *Transitions from Authoritarian Rule: Comparative Perspectives* (Baltimore: Johns Hopkins University Press, 1986), pp. 47–63; Przeworski, *Democracy and the Market*.

9. Przeworski, *Democracy and the Market*, pp. 12–13.

10. These assets can be economic or institutional. In the case of the military, for example, it may see democracy as a means of *securing* its institutional integrity.

11. Joan Nelson, "The Politics of Long-Haul Economic Reform," in Joan Nelson et al., eds., *Fragile Coalitions: The Politics of Economic Adjustment* (New Brunswick, NJ: Transaction Books, 1989), pp. 3–37.

12. Haggard and Kaufmann, "Economic Adjustment in New Democracies," in Nelson et al., *Fragile Coalitions*, pp. 57–77. Haggard and Kaufmann analyzed 10 "new democracies": Argentina, Bolivia, Brazil, the Dominican Republic, Ecuador, Peru, the Philippines, Thailand, Turkey, and Uruguay. There was little variation in macroeconomic performance between these new democracies and authoritarian regimes. But among the distinguishing factors that separated relatively successful new democracies—Turkey, Thailand, the Philippines, and South Korea—was institutionalization. Haggard and Kaufmann reached a similar conclusion in "Economic Adjustment and the Prospects for Democracy," in *The Politics of Economic Adjustment*, pp. 270–318.

13. See Peter Evans, "The State as Problem and Solution: Predation, Embedded Autonomy, and Structural Change," in Haggard and Kaufman, *The Politics of Economic Adjustment*, pp. 139–181.

14. O'Donnell and Schmitter, *Transitions from Authoritarian Rule: Tentative Conclusions*, p. 49.

15. Przeworski, *Democracy and the Market*, pp. 24–25.

16. Przeworski, *Democracy and the Market*, p. 7.

17. See Otto Hintze, "The Preconditions of Representative Government," in Hintze, *The Historical Essays of Otto Hintze* (Oxford: Oxford University Press, 1975), pp. 302–353; Adam Seligman, *The Idea of Civil Society* (New York: The Free Press, 1992). I am *not* arguing that the forces that molded Western Europe's civil society cannot emerge elsewhere. However, the Western European experience was not universal; other patterns of state-society relations have emerged that merit study.

18. For a good example of the universalist approach to studying civil society in the Arab world, see Augustus Richard Norton, "The Future of Civil Society in the Middle East," *Middle East Journal* 47, 2 (Spring 1993), pp. 205–216. For a dissenting view, see Iliya Harik, "Rethinking Civil Society: Pluralism in the Arab World," *Journal of Democracy* 5, 6, pp. 43–56.

19. For a similar critique as applied to Eastern European transitions, see Katherine Verdery and Gail Kligman, "Romania after Ceausescu: Post-Communist Communism?" in Ivo Banac, ed., *Eastern Europe in Revolution* (Ithaca: Cornell University Press, 1992), pp. 117–147.

20. Similarly, rather than attribute "post-Communist" Rumania's failure to advance democracy to some innate Rumanian proclivity for authoritarianism, we can explain the successful campaign by former apparatchiks to reimpose their hegemony to their skillful manipulation of institutional and ideological legacies bequeathed to them by Ceausescu. See Verdery and Kligman, "Romania after Ceausescu."

21. Variations of populist authoritarian states also emerged prior to this decade, particularly in Mexico under the PRI and, to some extent, in Brazil under the Estado Novo.

22. See Ronald Wintrobe, "The Tinpot and the Totalitarian: An Economic Theory of Dictatorship," *American Political Science Review* 84, 3 (September 1990), pp. 849–872. Also see Przeworski, who writes that what emerged in Eastern Europe was "an implicit social pact in which elites offered the prospect of material welfare in exchange for silence." Przeworski, *Democracy and the Market*, p. 2.

23. The populist authoritarian argument is implicitly set out in John Waterbury, *The Egypt of Nasser and Sadat: The Political Economy of Two Regimes* (Princeton: Princeton University Press, 1988), and explicitly in Robert Bianchi, *Unruly Corporatism: Associational Life in Twentieth Century Egypt* (New York: Oxford University Press, 1989).

24. Many of the dilemmas of the populist authoritarian state resemble those created by what Iliya Harik and Dennis Sullivan call the "patron state." However, whereas the patron state includes rentier, patrimonialist, and neopatrimonialist states, the populist authoritarian state is neopatrimonialist. See Iliya Harik and Dennis Sullivan, eds., *Privatization and Liberalization in the Middle East* (Bloomington: Indiana University Press, 1993), pp. 1–23.

25. See Egypt 1962, "Charter of National Action," in Nissim Rejwan, *Nasserist Ideology: Its Exponents and Its Critics* (New York: John Wiley and Sons, 1974). On Syria, see Sylvia G. Haim, *Arab Nationalism: An Anthology* (Berkeley: University of California Press, 1962). Tunisia under Bourguiba constitutes an exception.

26. Marsha Pripstein Posusney, "Irrational Workers: The Moral Economy of Labor Protest in Egypt," *World Politics* 46, 1 (October 1993), pp. 83–120.

27. See Saad Eddin Ibrahim's essay in this volume.

28. This should not be conflated with "gradualist" approaches to reform. Gradualist reforms may be more or less effective than shock therapy, but they aim

to achieve substantive structural changes. In contrast, the single long-term goal of survival strategies is to assure the political survival of the regime.

29. Steven Heydemann, "Taxation Without Representation," in Ellis Goldberg, Resat Kasaba, and Joel S. Migdal, eds., *Rules and Rights in the Middle East* (Seattle: University of Washington Press, 1993), p. 94.

30. This figure includes rents from oil sales, Gulf workers' remittances, and Suez Canal fees. See Brumberg, "Survival Strategies," p. 90.

31. "Putting the Brakes on Debt," *Middle East Economic Digest*, 12 December 1987, p. 16. These figures represent the total debt of 15 Arab states, including Saudi Arabia, whose debt had reached $14 billion by 1986. The crisis among the Arab oil producers was reflected in their current accounts, which dove from a $67 billion surplus in 1981 to a $12 billion deficit in 1983. See "Economic Upturn Forecast for 1984," *Middle East Economic Digest*, 24 February 1984, p. 31.

32. Unless indicated otherwise, the figures found in this section on Egypt are cited from Brumberg, "Survival Strategies."

33. Bianchi, *Unruly Corporatism*.

34. See the 1962 "Charter of National Action" in Nissim Rejwan, *Nasserist Ideology*.

35. Muhammad Anwar al-Sadat, *Waraqat Uktubar* (Cairo: Hay'at al-isti'lamat, jumhuriyyat misr al-'arabiyya, 1974).

36. Marsha Pripstein Posusney, "Labor as an Obstacle to Privatization: The Case of Egypt 1974–1987," in Harik and Sullivan, *Privatization and Liberalization in the Middle East*, pp. 85–105.

37. In addition, the regime planned to raise custom duties on imported electric household goods by 100 percent and duties on imported textiles by 50 percent.

38. Robert Springborg, "Egypt," in Tim Niblock and Emma Murphy, eds., *Economic and Political Liberalization in the Middle East* (London: British Academic Press, 1993), pp. 158–160.

39. Springborg, "Egypt," pp. 149–150.

40. Khaled Fouad Sherif and Regina M. Soos, "Egypt's Liberalization Experience and Its Impact on State-Owned Enterprises," in Harik and Sullivan, *Privatization and Liberalization in the Middle East*, p. 60.

41. *Middle East Economic Digest*, 2 February 1990, p. 14, and 3 August 1990, p. 13.

42. William Zartman, "The Conduct of Political Reform," in Zartman, ed., *Tunisia: The Political Economy of Reform* (Boulder: Lynne Rienner, 1991), p. 24.

43. Bourguiba's prime minister convinced him to hold multiparty elections in 1981. But the ruling party falsified the results after learning that some of its opponents had won seats. This event evidently influenced Bin 'Ali's views on political liberalization.

44. This consensus was defined by the regime. Am Al-Ahnaf, "Tunisie: un débat sur les rapports État/religion," *Maghreb-Machrek* 126 (October–December 1989), p. 105; Lisa Anderson, "Political Pacts, Liberalism and Democracy," *Government and Opposition* 25, 4.

45. Eva Bellin, "Tunisian Industrialists and the State," p. 49, and Abdelsetar Grissa, "The Tunisian State Enterprises and Privatization," in Zartman, *Tunisia*, p. 125.

46. Grissa, "The Tunisian State Enterprises and Privatization," p. 113.

47. David Hawley and Marcus Wright, "Tunisia: Riots Highlight National Tensions," *Middle East Economic Digest*, 6 January 1984, pp. 26–27; Grissa, "The Tunisian State Enterprises and Privatization," p. 112; Ridha Ferchiou, "The Social Pressure on Economic Development in Tunisia," in Zartman, *Tunisia*, pp. 101–108.

48. Jon Marks, "Tunisia," in Niblock and Murphy, *Economic and Political Liberalization in the Middle East*, p. 168.

49. In a speech prior to the signing of the pact, Bin 'Ali insisted that economic reforms could not proceed without political liberalization. Dirk Vandewalle, "Ben Ali's New Era: Pluralism and Economic Privatization in Tunisia," in Barkey, *The Politics of Economic Reform in the Middle East*, p. 119.

50. The threshold had already been raised to 34 percent in 1985.

51. Devaluation, price deregulation, and interest rate reform contributed to an average growth rate of 4.2 percent between 1987 and 1991. Corey Wright, "Tunisia: The Next Five Years," *Business America* 113, 24/25 (30 November 1992), p. 24.

52. Jamil Saghir, *Privatization in Tunisia* (Washington, DC: World Bank CFS Discussion Paper Series), p. 16.

53. Economist Intelligence Unit, *Country Profile* 1992–93. The Gulf War contributed to this trend, although there were underlying structural causes as well.

54. The regime tried to justify this policy by providing evidence of a "plot" to topple the government. See "The Military Court Examines the Case of the Plot Against Internal State Security" (Tunis: Tunisian External Communication Agency, 1992).

55. Nikki Keddie, "The Islamist Movement in Tunisia," *Maghreb Review* 2, 1 (1986), pp. 26–39; AbdelKader Zghal, "The New Strategy," in Zartman, *Tunisia*, pp. 205–220.

56. Dirk Vandewalle, "Breaking with Socialism: Economic Liberalization and Privatization in Algeria," in Harik and Sullivan, *Privatization and Liberalization in the Middle East*, p. 194.

57. Jean Leca and Jean-Claude Vatin, *L'Algérie Politique, Institutions et Régimes* (Paris: Presses de la Fondation Nationale des Sciences Politiques, 1975).

58. Karen Pfeifer, "Algeria's Implicit Stabilization Program," in Barkey, *The Politics of Economic Reform in the Middle East*, pp. 171–172.

59. Pfeifer, "Algeria's Implicit Stabilization Program," p. 161.

60. Vandewalle, "Breaking with Socialism," p. 191.

61. Vandewalle, "Breaking with Socialism," p. 194.

62. The regime devalued the dinar in 1985, letting it fall from $0.20 to $0.11. The devaluation's impact was limited by its incremental pace, and because Algeria's oil exports were denominated in dollars. Two subsidy reductions took place in 1985; the subsidy bill was not substantially reduced. As for interest rates, the government began to reduce them in 1987, three years into the stabilization program.

63. "La Charte Nationale," Article 3, "La Planification doit prendre en charge les activités du secteur national privé," *Maghreb-Machrek* 113 (July–September 1986), p. 115. Note that the 1976 charter unreservedly upheld the primacy of the public sector and socialism.

64. Vandewalle, "Breaking with Socialism," pp. 197–198.

65. Arun Kapil, *The Transition from Authoritarian Rule in Algeria: Phase 1, Toward Democracy or Democradure?* (unpublished manuscript, May 1991).

66. *Al-Moudjahid*, 11 October 1988; Arun Kapil, *The Transition from Authoritarian Rule in Algeria*, pp. 16–17.

67. FBIS-NES 88–206.

68. These qualifications were listed in Article 40 of the 1990 constitution. Similar provisions were spelled out in the 1989 "political party law" and the 1990 press code. See Kapil, *The Transition from Authoritarian Rule in Algeria*.

69. These measures included a new labor law that permitted the creation of independent labor unions and linked pay to production. See Jon Marks, "Algeria, the Monolith Cracks?" *Middle East Economic Digest*, 2 March 1990, p. 9; and "Algeria," *Middle East Economic Digest*, 6 April and 17 June 1990.

70. Hugh Roberts, "From Radical Mission to Equivocal Ambition: The Expansion and Manipulation of Algerian Islamism," a study prepared for the "Fundamentalism Project" of the American Academy of Arts and Sciences (1993), p. 50.

71. See Jon Marks, "Studying Algeria's Political Risk," *Middle East Economic Digest*, 9 March 1990, pp. 4–5; and Roberts, "From Radical Mission to Equivocal Ambition."

72. *Middle East Economic Digest*, 13 May 1992, p. 9.

73. *Middle East Economic Digest*, 7 August 1992, p. 7.

74. *Middle East Economic Digest*, 17 September 1993, p. 28.

75. See Raymond Hinnebush, "Syria," in Niblock and Murphy, *Economic and Political Liberalization in the Middle East*, pp. 180–182.

76. Fred Lawson, "Divergent Modes of Economic Liberalization in Syria and Iraq," in Harik and Sullivan, *Privatization and Liberalization in the Middle East*, p. 129.

77. Hinnebush, "Syria," p. 187.

78. Heydemann, "The Political Logic," in Harik and Sullivan, *Privatization and Liberalization in the Middle East*, pp. 25–26, 29.

79. Heydemann, "The Political Logic," p. 20.

80. Lawson, "Divergent Paths of Economic Liberalization," p. 132.

81. *Middle East Economic Digest*, 20 May 1994, pp. 2–3.

82. Heydemann, "The Political Logic," in Barkey, *The Politics of Economic Reform in the Middle East*, p. 26.

83. Lawson, "Divergent Modes of Economic Liberalization," p. 124.

84. *Middle East Economic Digest*, 8 October 1993, p. 3.

85. Heydemann, "The Political Logic," p. 30.

86. *Middle East Economic Digest*, 22 July 1994, pp. 2–4.

87. *Middle East Economic Digest*, 13 May 1994, pp. 2–3.

88. *Middle East International*, 15 April 1994, p. 11.

89. *Al-Ahram Weekly*, 9–15 June 1994, p. 2.

90. *Middle East Economic Digest*, 17 June 1994, p. 17.

91. Clement Henry Moore, cited in Vandewalle, "Breaking with Socialism," p. 207.

92. Peter Evans, "The State as Problem and Solution," pp. 139–181.

93. *Middle East Economic Digest*, 10 June 1994, pp. 2–3.

94. Bellin, "Tunisian Industrialists," p. 62.

13

Class, Economic Change, and Political Liberalization in the Arab World

Samih K. Farsoun and Christina Zacharia

An investigation into the relationship between social class and political liberalization cannot be fully developed unless four major interrelated issues are addressed: First, why has the question of political liberalization and democratization emerged so recently in the Arab world? Second, what is the origin of the ideology and policy of liberalization? Third, who or what social classes or political groups and institutions promote this policy and why? And fourth—and perhaps most relevant—what is the relationship between political and economic liberalization, and why are the two coupled and instituted together?

This latter question is the most significant because it is in terms of the intimate relationship between the economy and politics that we can begin to comprehend the impact of ongoing economic liberalization. Our thesis is that a privatized free market economy under a regimen of structural adjustment, integrated into the global market system, and undergirded by external political intervention is shaping the contemporary political dynamics of the Arab world.[1] More specifically, structural adjustment and economic reform is having a differential impact on varied social classes and sectors of Arab societies, and increasing social inequality while generating volatile political dynamics. Contrary to the assumptions of many liberal theorists, therefore, economic liberalization is thus undercutting the prospects of political democratization.

Economic Liberalization and Democracy

The success or failure of political liberalization depends on the resolution of the conflict between the Arab elites promoting free market economies, their regimes, and the authoritarian states they control, and subaltern and other social groups seeking democratic alternatives to, or nationalists and Islamists resisting, privatized free markets, client regimes, authoritarian states, and external intervention.[2] In short, the key question is why is this emergent liberalized order failing to gain the allegiance of the Arab masses and instead has (differentially) earned their enmity? The answer of a 26-year-old Algerian vendor is indicative: "I have lost every cent I had. . . . We have no work, no housing, and no freedom. Do they [the regime] wonder why we hate them? Do they wonder why so many young men join the militants?"[3]

Democracy is a process of empowerment, but if instituted and controlled from above to promote economic restructuring on behalf of domestic elites and foreign interests, it emerges more as a process of peripheralization for the already disadvantaged and downwardly mobile, thus creating resentment and both institutional and extra-institutional resistance. This is why electoral regimes (those who claim a semblance of Western-style representative democracy), especially in Egypt, Tunisia, and elsewhere, are being popularly opposed now.[4] However, the apparent smoother transition to electoral politics in Jordan and Morocco is in large part a consequence of a more sophisticated political management of structural economic adjustment and reform and of associated popular foreign policies on the part of the monarchs.[5]

The current deep economic crisis, the regimens of structural adjustment, the increased socioeconomic inequalities, and the feeling of alienation on the part of subaltern and other groups are undermining the basis for both a domestic and an Arab-wide consensus to establish and sustain *elite*-instituted political and economic liberalism and democracy. In an earlier work Farsoun argued that:

> The welfare (social service) programs of basic food subsidies that have been instituted by ruling elites to defuse popular discontent and to mobilize support for the regime will change over the years from being a grant of favor by the rulers to a political right of the citizen . . . that is the citizen's *political right* (not merely humanitarian right) to *economic security*. . . . This right may emerge in the early twenty-first century as the central issue of domestic Arab politics[6] (emphasis added).

Regimens of structural adjustment instituted by local elites—in response to external conditions and in the context of economic recession or crisis—have begun to curtail public investment, dismantle social services and basic food subsidy programs, and thus erode the "citizen's right to economic security." The political reactions to this have been different in varied Arab states. This is because not all structural adjustment programs are identical in actual implementation, although they share some common features: basic policies of austerity or deficit reduction through curtailment of public investment and social welfare, currency devaluation, "de-indexing" of wages and therefore reductions in real income, reductions in tariffs, opening of domestic markets, and privatization. Despite these commonalities, the phasing, severity, and mix of specific structural adjustment programs vary by country. For example, Egypt was able to extract remarkably soft terms from the International Monetary Fund, perhaps due to its strategic value to the United States and as a reward for supporting American policy during the 1990–1991 Gulf War. Similarly, Algeria has seen a relaxation of international financial pressure since the anti-Islamic military coup of 1992. And yet these two countries are experiencing the strongest, most widespread, and persistent antiregime popular movements in the Arab world.

Popular resentments—derived from the rise and then sharp decline in well being, that is, the increasing downward mobility, poverty, economic exploitation, and inequality; from disappointment in the failed promises of the regimes; from the perceived corruption of the regimes; from the cultural polarization between the elites and masses; and from frustration with regimes that are unable or unwilling to deal with the perceived humiliations perpetrated by foreign powers on the nation and faith—coalesced at this current conjuncture to ignite a movement for systemic political change among large sectors of the population. In short, the social, economic, and political impasse that had set in since the decline in oil revenues (mid-1980s), coupled with the social and political costs of structural adjustment, has triggered mass political alienation. Regime- or elite-instituted political liberalization at such a conjuncture is too little and too late. Opponents of liberalizing regimes are seeking more than democratization, they are seeking systemic change, perhaps a revolution.

Structural adjustment has another important consequence: a pattern of upward redistribution of resources and income. Our contention is that elite-instituted economic and political liberalism is incongruent or unsustainable in the context of socioeconomic polarization and mass political alienation and resentment. Apart from popular resistance by alienated social groups traditionally outside the dominant or governing political coalition (especially the peasantry and the urban underclasses) others within the coalition who perceive themselves as losers or potential losers may undermine policies of structural adjustment, economic, and even political liberalization.[7] Perhaps only if broad-based economic growth is coupled with political liberalism would elite-instituted democracy have a chance. That is, liberalization from above may succeed if a groundswell of popular support develops from below. In short, the manner and the concrete results of the political construction under regimens of structural adjustment of a privatized free market democracy in the face of social resistance will determine the dynamics of democratization of Arab states.

Political and Economic Transformation

In the past decade (1982–1992) several major interrelated developments have restructured the social, economic, political, and ideological orders of the Arab world. Compared to the previous decade, among the most significant are the sharp decline in oil revenues, the commensurate economic stagnation and deterioration of the "Arab oil economy" and the respective state economies linked to it, and the rise of the international Arab debt. Based on a report issued by the Arab League, in 1991 the "collective Arab debt" (presumably among the oil-poor countries) reached $250 billion.[8] The oil revenue boom of the 1970s and early 1980s created in the region an expansive (and expensive) social and physical infrastructure that in the "oil-bust" period (mid-1980s, and more so in the early 1990s), are burdens on the undiversified state economies, on the masses dependent on public investment and social welfare provided by the state, and even on those dependent on remittances from expatriate workers. Moreover, the financially weakened states have become simultaneously vulnerable to internal anti-systemic movements and to external economic and political pressures.

Economic decline led to structural economic crisis. For example, Egypt's debt increased from roughly $1.7 billion, or 22.5 percent of the GNP, in 1970 to $13.1 billion, or 51.7 percent of the GNP, in 1980[9] to $42.0 billion, or 123.4 percent of the GNP, in 1990.[10] Indicators of growth in productive sectors show stagnation and some decline from 1970–1980 to 1980–1988: GDP decreased 1.1 percent, growth rates in agriculture declined by 1.0 percent, in industry by 1.8 percent, and in services by 2.1 percent.

Inflation, however, rose during this same period from 7.3 percent to 10.6 percent.[11] In 1991 the inflation rate increased to 15.8 percent.[12] According to a special study by the World Bank, "inflation has been running at twenty five percent a year."[13] Indeed, according to the same report on Egypt, the economic situation is even more dire than presented above:

> Egypt is now experiencing a recession which has had adverse social consequences in terms of employment and standards of living. The growing budget deficit and the rising cost of external debts have placed new pressures on government expenditures. . . . The outcome has been a marked decline in the level of job creation in the public sector, a pattern of wage compression for civil service employees, diminishing public resources for the social sectors, and cutbacks in the food ration and subsidy system. The slowdown of investment and output in the private sector has had similar negative employment and income effects. Since the beginning of the recession in 1986, open unemployment, largely among youths, has risen rapidly, real wages have fallen in most economic sectors, and there are indications that the poorest groups in the population have been badly hurt.[14]

Since 1985, real wages have declined, in government dramatically, and also in the two other major economic sectors, private enterprise and public (see Figure 13.1). In addition, "total social expenditures have come down from a peak of 5.9 percent of GDP in 1984/85 to 4 percent in fiscal year 1990."[15] This decline affects most income groups; especially hardest hit are the rural and urban poor, women and children, public sector and lower-level governmental employees.[16] Accordingly, a process of wealth and income polarization has set in. These socioeconomic trends, coupled with a demographic explosion (in 1988, 40.4 percent of the Egyptian population was under 15 years of age),[17] underpin the current and future political, social, and economic crisis.

The differential impact of the crisis stems from the regimens of structural adjustment, privatization, and an upward shift of income and resources to the slim middle and upper class strata. Since the early 1980s, Egypt has become highly dependent on imported American food, machinery, and technology—not to feed its growing population, but to raise livestock and produce other luxury goods.[18] The main beneficiaries in the private and public sectors are the few who have access to the upper-level governmental and military positions, creating "an almost entirely autonomous enclave of middle-class modernity in an increasingly impoverished and marginalized Third World economy."[19]

Egypt is not an anomaly in the Arab region. Perhaps with the exception of the oil-exporting Gulf states, a deteriorating physical and social infrastructure, rising unemployment and inflation rates, and, especially in the urban centers, a rapidly increasing population and socioeconomic polarization characterize the social history of the past decade. All this is problematic for social peace and elite-inspired political liberalization.

This past decade was also punctuated by three major wars (the Israeli invasion of Lebanon, the Iran-Iraq war of 1980–1988, and the Gulf War of 1990–1991) that have had a significant impact politically, economically, and socially on the region and beyond.[20] Repressive Arab regimes that are unable or unwilling to solve the fundamental socioeconomic and political issues facing their respective countries and the region are also seen as dependent clients of the United States and thus increasingly delegitimized in the eyes of the disadvantaged groups. Collectively, these developments and perceptions led to increasing alienation and discontent among large sectors of the Arab peoples. With the promises of Arab socialism and oil wealth unfulfilled "the anger of disillusionment"[21] set in dramatically among the disadvantaged social classes.

These developments have become more dramatic as a result of the collapse of the Soviet Union both as a superpower of significant presence in the area and as a model of economic, political, and social organization. Coupled with the rejection of communism/socialism and the simultaneous

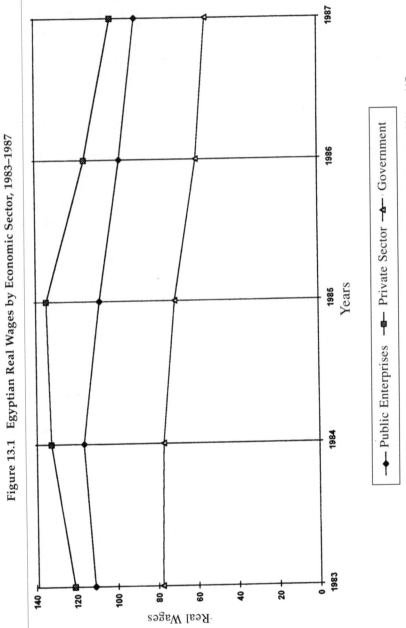

Figure 13.1 Egyptian Real Wages by Economic Sector, 1983–1987

Public Enterprises ◆ Private Sector △ Government

Source: World Bank, *Egypt: Alleviating Poverty During Structural Adjustment* (Washington, DC: The World Bank, 1991), p. 117.

rise of prodemocracy movements in Eastern Europe, Russia, and elsewhere, the position and ideology of the Arab left (the secular nationalist
regimes, parties, and social movements) are undermined. Moreover, neoliberal ideology and policy are actively promoted by the only remaining
superpower, the United States, by the international institutions—especially
the IMF, the World Bank, and the United Nations—that are under its influence, by some pivotal Arab regimes, some intellectuals, and most politicians. In short, the United States (with Israel's support) is attempting to restructure the region's political order in a manner that would sustain in the
long run both neoliberalism and regional American (and Israeli) hegemony.

While the promotion in the Arab world of neoliberal ideology and policy intensified since the late 1980s, it should be clear that Arab regimes instituted such measures differentially, unevenly, and haphazardly since
1973, when President Anwar Sadat of Egypt declared *infitah* (economic
and political opening to the West). Sadat, in his usual theatrical style, declared such a policy for the betterment of the Egyptian people and society. Other regimes followed suit quietly and unobtrusively, most recently
in response to IMF loan conditions of structural adjustment.[22]

The initiation of *infitah* was a consequence of the defeat of the self-
declared Arab socialist regimes at the hand of Israel in the 1967 and the
1973 wars, and the failure and consequent delegitimization of their state-
capitalist model of socioeconomic and political development. The brief
Arab revolutionary challenge (spearheaded by a resurgent Palestinian
movement) in the wake of the 1967 Arab defeat was quickly snuffed in
Jordan in 1970. After 1967, then Egyptian president Gamal al-Nasser, the
populist leader of Arab nationalism, opted for defusing the Arab cold war
with the oil-rich monarchies (and thus indirectly with the West), by abandoning the call for Arab unification, and for greater liberalization of the
economy instead of a war economy and mass revolutionary mobilization.
With these policies he actually prepared the ground[23] for his successor,
Sadat, who quickly proceeded to reverse everything that Nasserism stood
for: Arab unification, independence, and socialism.

What saved these discredited Arab socialist regimes (and others allied
with them) and blunted the revolutionary thrust was the rise of oil prices
starting in 1973. Vast oil revenues not only saved the regimes but also restructured the model of development of those economies and thus their
model of accumulation: A movement away from public national investment toward encouragement of private initiatives and more open markets.

In Arab intellectual discourse of the times, that new Arab order was
conceptualized as the victory of the *tharwa* (wealth) over *thawra* (revolution). This reconstituted the vectors of influence in the Arab state system.
Oil-based wealth of the high revenue era (1973–1983) launched a regionwide economic boom and rising standards of living, created new channels

of social mobility and enrichment, and promised power and influence in international relations. In consequence, a process of depoliticization set in and people accepted or ignored the authoritarian regimes under which they prospered.[24] The nationalist pan-Arab political culture disintegrated, and its liberationist ideology was abandoned by most sectors of the population.[25] Forgotten as well was the "social contract" between the sociopolitical movement ideologues (and intellectuals) and the authoritarian nationalist regimes for postponing the struggle for democracy until the nationalist struggle against Israel and its Western supporters was won. This "social contract" assumed that the struggle for national independence and development superseded democracy in priority.

The domestic and international political leverage of oil power lasted only briefly. The high oil revenues and the booming "Arab oil economy" that started in the mid-1970s collapsed by the mid-1980s. This was followed by a severe economic downturn and serious structural dilemmas: structural imbalances inherited from the boom period, problems of liquidity, international debt, debt service and balance of payments, rising unemployment, and social and economic disparities.[26] It was also followed by international debt and reduced diplomatic clout. Paradoxically, the rapid rise and then fall of economic well-being to a large extent triggered both liberalization from above and broad discontent and rising antiregime opposition from below, all of which intensified during the early 1990s.

The most sophisticated explanation for the initiation of elite political liberalization is proposed by Luciani. He points out that countries have "reverted to democratic rule" during times of economic crisis, including IMF-imposed structural adjustment.[27] The crux of Luciani's argument lies in the structure (sources) and balance (relative amounts of revenue and expenditure) of public finance (taxation and the expenditure of fiscal resources) as the latter relates to political institutions. To begin with:

> In states which derive a considerable part of their revenue from external sources (which we may call rentier or allocation states), it is the state that supports the domestic economy through public expenditure, rather than the economy supporting the state. . . . [P]ower in a rentier state is almost naturally vested in an authoritarian ruler.[28]

However, in states where public expenditures are financed by revenue from direct taxation that requires citizen compliance, regimes are responsive to citizen pressure and thus are also responsive to the demand for democracy. In other words, as authoritarian regimes lose external sources (or have little or no internal sources) of revenue and turn to taxing their citizens (asking them for economic sacrifices during times of crisis) either to repay international debt or to fund their restructured programs they liberalize the political institutions following the principle of "no taxation without representation." They typically seek, as in Sadat's and Mubarak's regimes, the voters' approval for the austerity policies. The controlled or limited nature of political liberalization from above is not systematically discussed by Luciani or others. That, however, is significant for the political and ideological response of the disadvantaged social classes who disproportionately suffer from the effects of structural adjustment and the economic crisis.

The Limits of Liberalization from Above

The ideology and policy of economic liberalization antedated the active promotion of political liberalization (especially democracy) by nearly two decades. Following Sadat's initiatives President Mubarak of Egypt introduced "democracy in doses."[29] Whatever halting efforts made during that period by indigenous movements in Arab states to promote civil and human rights were suppressed by both pro- and anti-Western Arab regimes while Israel intensified its violations of the human rights of the Palestinians.[30] In an article on contrasting conceptions of democracy and the state in Egypt Zubaida argues:

> The conditions for the development of spheres of social autonomy (political liberalism) are not only the "withdrawal" of the state, but also an active intervention of another kind: clear legislation and institutional mechanism which provide the framework of rights and obligations for these spheres. . . . [Ever since *infitah*, Egypt enacted] fragmentary and ambiguous legislation . . . resulting from *ad hoc* liberalization measures . . . in which the new spheres of activity are burdened with ambiguous regulation, or operate on the margin of the law.[31]

Egyptian civil associations are not operating under enabling laws of a "law-state"[32] but rather are subject to an electoral regime embedded in an authoritarian state bureaucracy that controls these associations in an arbitrary, rigid, and corrupt manner. As a consequence of corruption, Zubaida argues that the Egyptian bureaucracy favors the more "primordial" Islamic organizations over secular and modern civil associations—that is, traditional over modern civil society.[33]

In the past two decades, the social movements of political liberalization in the Arab world—the organizations of modern civil society—suffered not only internal state control and repression but also international isolation. Indeed, during the mid-1980s, the intensification of the socioeconomic and political crises triggered popular and civil associational opposition *and* increased regime repression and state terror. But such increased violations of human rights did not draw the serious attention of the

United States, the European Community, or the international NGOs, except minimally. That is, not until the prodemocracy revolutions of Eastern Europe, the collapse of the Soviet Union, the victory of the allies over Iraq in the 1990–1991 Gulf War, and the articulation in the United States of a triumphant neoliberal ideology. Since then an American ideology of a worldwide "democratic revolution," bonded with the idea of a privatized "free market economy," has been propounded in both the former Soviet bloc and the Third World.

Rather quickly in the 1990s, institutes for democracy (or civil society) were founded, foundations offered grants for research and writing on liberalization, conferences were organized, and intellectual discourse and production multiplied significantly. Over two dozen major and minor works addressed the question of democracy in tandem with free market economy in the Arab world.[34] Western liberal models of representative democracy, privatization, and free market economy, by both Western and Arab intellectuals alike, are posed as the long-sought panacea for all the social, economic, and political ills of the Arab world.[35] A subtext to this discourse in the West is that Islam and democracy are incompatible.[36] The old Orientalist mythology of the essential nature of Islam as despotic is resurrected and used to justify not only the nullification of the Algerian Islamic electoral victories but also the war against the Islamic militants in Egypt, the expulsion of 415 Palestinians by Israel, and Islam as the new enemy of Israel and the West. Acts of terrorism in New York in 1993 are held as another bit of evidence of the enmity of Islam. Islam has replaced Communism as the challenge facing the West.

This ideology has been coupled with a policy in which international institutions, private banks, and international governmental aid specified liberalized economic and political measures (or plans to institute such measures) as conditions for loans, loan guarantees, grants, and other aid protocols. These conditions "illustrate the contradictions for the [Mubarak electoral] regime: an authoritarian bureaucratic rigidity, but also a sensitivity to international public opinion, before which Egypt must appear liberal and moderate."[37]

An expression of this attempt is an advertisement the Egyptian government placed in the *Washington Post*.[38] This appearance of liberalism and moderation for Arab electoral regimes, which gives cover to and legitimizes authoritarian states, is common to all Middle Eastern states.[39] It is the current ideology of regimes whose ruling elites are actively promoting the twin policies of privatization and integration into international capital, as the Egyptian government proudly announces in the advertisement. Yet these policies bring with them the exploitation of Arab resources and labor by international capital and international lending institutions.

Political neoliberalism—whether in Latin America, the Arab world, or the rest of the Third World—is only for those indigenous elites, classes, or groups (and political parties) who are willing and able to support economic liberalism and the conditions of international lending institutions and core capitalist powers. All others face illegality and repression. In short, "[o]ne can question the long term viability of the new limited or exclusionary democracies of peripheral capitalism. They must continue to administer an austerity that polarizes rich and poor in the interests of external debt relationships."[40]

Structural Change

Arab economies underwent a series of basic structural changes over the past two decades, characterized by a rapid, intensified, and multifaceted integration of the oil-exporting economies of the peninsula into international capital and a dramatic shift from Arab socialism (state capitalism) to privatized, free market, and internationally linked economies. The latter is dramatic because it was a shift from a development strategy of national industrialization (largely import-substitution industrialization) and agrarian reform based on a mixed economy of public and private capital and regulated centrally by a nationalist elite to an export-oriented economy linked to domestic and foreign private capital but regulated, as Petras argued for Latin America, internationally by international institutions and the core capitalist states. Cox calls this global phenomenon "the internationalizing of the state":

> Its common feature is to convert the state into an agency for adjusting national economic practices and policies to the perceived exigencies of the global economy. The state becomes a transmission belt from the global to the national economy, where heretofore it had acted as the bulwark defending domestic welfare from external disturbances. . . . Through the financial mechanism, these debtor states are constrained to play the role of instruments of the global economy, opening their national economies more fully to external pressures.[41]

As in Latin America[42] and the rest of the Third World,[43] Arab governments *intervened* not to nationalize but to denationalize, to privatize, to invite international capital, to define the terms and set the conditions for foreign investments and takeovers of domestic enterprises. Governments intervened to control or restrain labor, especially in the export-oriented free zones. They intervened not to develop a diversified national industrial productive capacity and increased agricultural food productivity for the people, but rather to institute deregulation, which set these potentials back and helped shift food production toward elite consumer taste and export. They also intervened to transfer economic resources from public investment, from social services, and basic food subsidies to subsidies for export and foreign investors. States "socialized"[44] the repayment or compensation of private losses and debts, converting private to public debt, as in Kuwait (al-Manakh scandal).[45]

Finally, state monopolies are being put up for sale in Egypt and elsewhere. As in Latin America, multinationals are being offered equity in public firms or public resources (e.g., oil fields) as means for debt payment or for development investment.

In short, government intervention under the ideology of economic liberalization and structural adjustment is shifting wealth and benefits into the hands of a minority class of elites who are accumulating great affluence at the expense of vast impoverishment of the population, social services, and public welfare. "Under the euphemistic label of 'structural adjustment' . . . states are required to impose domestic austerity with the effect of raising unemployment and domestic prices which fall most heavily on the economically weaker segments of the population."[46]

The function of electoral (or even liberalized monarchical) regimes is "to facilitate domestic public support for imperial policies [of economic liberalization] while retaining the armed forces as political insurance if the electoral regimes lose control or the disintegration of 'free market' economies provokes popular uprisings."[47] Algeria's and Egypt's militaries are key examples. In 1992 the military in Algeria seized power and canceled the scheduled elections to prevent an electoral victory by the Islamic Salvation Front (FIS):

> Blossoming under a democratic process that began with the advent of multiparty politics in 1989, the [Islamic] front had built a solid core of support among jobless and working-class voters. . . . Determined to prevent an election victory by the Muslim militants, military officers forced President Chadli Benjedid to resign in January 1992, cancelled the second round of voting and named a High State Council to rule by decree. A month later the Government banned the front and issued an emergency decree that gave it unrestricted powers to detain citizens and bar demonstrations.[48]

Algeria remains under military rule that has little political legitimacy in the eyes of many Algerians.

Since the middle of the 1980s, Arab resources have been appropriated by the West through Gulf War payments (for oil-exporting peninsular states), international debt payments, firm and resource equity and market takeovers, international capital deployments, and oil market control. The potential for long-term and large-scale inter- and intra-Arab productive public investment (except for oil) has evaporated. Inter-Arab or regional conflicts in turn do not bode well for the confidence of private investors (in states other than one's own), nor for state and Pan-Arab institutional support for investment in productive sectors of oil-poor states. "Arab

Solidarity" was shattered by the Gulf War of 1990–1991, and it may be a long time coming before a new sense of Pan-Arabism reemerges.

The Impact of Liberalization on the Social and Class Structure

The impact of economic and political liberalization on the social structure in general and the class structure in particular of the eastern Arab states is profound. The more recent impositions of structural adjustment regimens on varied Arab states escalated the rate of change and quickened trends that were set in motion in 1973, the year the oil revenues started to rise. Since that time, oil revenues and their derivative socioeconomic consequences underwent two phases and are now in the beginning of the third. These phases are popularly characterized to coincide with revenue levels as the "seven fat years" (1974–1981), the "seven lean years" (1982–1990), and the current "seven miserable years" (1991–1998).

As noted earlier, in the course of the last two decades, the regimes of the Arab socialist states slowly but persistently reordered their economic priorities away from state-controlled national development toward private capital. During that period several important social developments took place in the Arab world in general: the decline, or perhaps near elimination, of subsistence production; massive occupational shifts from agrarian to service and (to a much lesser extent) industrial activities; a massive exodus of surplus rural labor to urban conglomerations and to oil-exporting countries (and to Europe from North Africa); the transformation of rural social relations toward wage labor; the marginalization of Arab women from agricultural production; and the proletarianization and subproletarianization of the young, poor, and unskilled migrant. Of great significance to Arab social structure in oil-poor Arab states is the reproduction and expansion of the petty commodity producers and distributors (including, of course, in the service sector). These are the great mass of very small-scale self-employed shopkeepers, artisans, manufacturers, repairmen, transport and personal service providers, and family enterprises—the core of the growing "informal sector" of all the countries of the Arab world.

As significant as the expansion of petty commodity producers and distributors is the rise of new Arab bourgeoisie. In the oil-rich Arabian peninsula the new bourgeoisie is a class of contractors, middlemen, brokers, agents of foreign corporations, and wheeler-dealers. While in the oil-rich countries this class is composed of members of the ruling dynasties, their relatives, associates, advisors, and agents; in the oil-poor, labor-exporting countries, it is composed from among those repatriated from the oil states and those who capitalized on their access to the state to enrich themselves in the new order. They include many of the top officers in the military establishments. In both types of countries this new bourgeoisie is typically engaged in nonproductive economic activities.

Associated with these structural changes are several other noteworthy social features. The first is that this transformation of interlocked capitalist and precapitalist forms of production, labor processes, and distribution has not brought about an irrevocable rupture of the social relations, ideology, and culture associated with the previous order. To the contrary, they helped reproduce those traditional social relations of economic activity, social values, kinship, and religious and political behavior. Second, the structural changes resulted in differentiated and fragmented class structures and heterogeneous social forms of organizing, social views, and action. "Less energized by nationalist issues than the previous generation, this fragmented urban mass is also less likely to engage in class organization. It is more likely to engage in social and political action based on kinship or on neighborhood, street, ethnic, sectarian, or religious organizing."[49]

Third, these structural developments continue to take place at an important social conjuncture: Vast numbers of youth are coming of age for employment. Over 50 percent of the population is under 20 years of age. The plight in oil-poor countries of vast masses of barely skilled and unemployed youth lacking hope and future is a perfect social formula for frustration and political instability.

Finally, during the "seven fat years" of economic embourgeoisement, the Arab world experienced a period of rising standards of living, of consumerism, and of social mobility for some segments of the population even though large sectors did not benefit. As a consequence of these transformations the political culture of the region transformed dramatically: from an ideology of national liberation and economic and social development to one of possessive individualism, cynicism, and personal enrichment, and from secular Arab nationalism to Islamic fundamentalism.

The above-detailed processes of change had escalated during the "fat years" and lurched even further in the same direction when the "lean years" ensued in the early 1980s. A process of rapid social polarization developed not only between states of the region, oil-exporting versus labor-exporting, but also within each country as well.[50] Throughout the lean years and the imposed structural adjustments of the late 1980s and thus of free markets, the impact has been to polarize the labor force structure: a minority who benefited from the privatized market and from the economic institutions linked to the multinationals (including oil) and the great majority that did not.[51]

In addition to the *nouveaux riches,* export-oriented industrialists, commercial agriculturalists, merchants, agents, managers, professionals, lawyers, researchers, public relations specialists, technicians, and even skilled workers tied to multinational corporations and banks became increasingly affluent. Others employed by domestic public, mixed, and private institutions experienced downward social mobility, declining standards of living, declining or deteriorating social services, and rising economic insecurity. These include workers in all state agencies who often turned to second jobs or corruption to supplement their comparatively meager incomes in this period of rising costs of living.

While large sectors of the middle and lower strata have experienced declining fortunes since the mid-1980s, vast numbers of petty commodity producers and distributors (self-employed or wage workers) are swelling the ranks of those in the "informal sector." In Egypt, for example, the World Bank estimates the increase in the "informal sector" from nearly 2.5 million workers in 1976 to 3.4 million in 1986,[52] all of whom labor without social benefits including declining or nonexistent basic food subsidies and without steady incomes or employment. An Arab League report notes that the real rate of unemployment in 1990–1991 in Jordan, Yemen, and Lebanon was 30 percent, while in Egypt it was 20 percent.[53] Algeria's official rate of unemployment is over 20 percent.[54] While these high averages are partly a consequence of the dislocations of the Gulf War, the data for the future do not augur well.

The same Arab League report notes that the projected rate of increase in the labor force in the Arab world is 2.5 percent per year during the 1990s, requiring 2.5 million additional new jobs per year. Finally, the report also notes that the average rate of inflation for the Arab world was 20 percent during 1990–1991; however, certain countries had much higher rates (106.1 percent in the Sudan, 50 percent in Lebanon, 22.8 percent in Algeria). Among this mass of the less fortunate, it is women, the urban youth, and small peasant farmers who have been and will continue to be most hurt by the declining standards of living and employment opportunities triggered by economic restructuring and the free market system. In addition to this large army of workers in the "informal sector," increasing numbers of people are becoming involved in illegal and criminal activities.

Conclusion

This social polarization means, among other things, an increased wealth and income gap between those few affluent sectors of the population and the vast majority, hence increased inequalities among the social classes. Such structured and deepening social inequalities are not conducive to building a national consensus to sustain elite-instituted economic and political liberalization. To the contrary, these socially divisive and fragmenting processes seem likely to undermine the social basis of democracy in the Arab world.

There is, however, a new genre of writers who believe that leaders or regimes can—with appropriate political management—successfully institute economic adjustment and reform without being overwhelmed by opposition. This literature is largely prescriptive (in the manner of advice to modern princes) on how to phase in or sequence implementation of structural adjustment policies, use sequential rewards and punishments for coalition partners, manipulate the contradictions of political opponents, divide and undermine individual opposition groups and prevent their coalescing, neutralize or counterbalance opposition from below, and reduce the size of coalitions. Its key argument, as John Waterbury writes, is that "the task of political management is one of coalition management, as every regime has a set of allied interests and coalition partners that buttress its ability to govern."[55]

Regimes must therefore carefully calculate how the process of structural adjustment will affect various coalition members and adopt appropriate tactics of program sequencing or phasing, timing, policy packaging, rhetoric, and style all in order to block the coalescing of an oppositional coalition that could isolate and overwhelm them. Moreover, through these clever and manipulative tactics, regimes can restructure the old coalition into a new one—from one based on the military, the public sector, organized labor, and urban, white-collar interests, to one based on the military, commercial agriculture, private industrialists, and export sectors.[56] Thus they can survive, institute the economic reforms, and establish a new social, economic, and political order.

These latter-day Machiavellis recognize the difficulty of the task they propose. Unorganized labor, the urban unemployed, those in the informal sector, shantytown dwellers, students, and rural agricultural workers and peasants are absent from the governing coalition, will lose most from austerity and structural adjustment, will oppose the regime, and are the most violence-prone sectors of the population. Accordingly, "if economic grievances . . . become bound up with a religious or ideological movement . . . the violence [and, by implication, opposition to the regime] may become self sustaining and draw in ever larger segments of the populace."[57] Yet, such a caveat—currently taking place in Egypt and Algeria—practically obviates the thrust of the argument. Furthermore, manipulation of the political system and of coalitions can also be made from below by savvy grassroots leadership, as the FIS leadership did in Algeria before the army intervened. While the ideology of economic and political liberalization couples the two, the modern theorists of princely advice typically ignore the question of democratization and do not address (as Luciani argues) the critical nature of the link between political participation and fiscal efficacy. Instead, they are more anxious to find ways for a collaborative regime to institute structural adjustment programs.

Economic and political liberalization is imposed by ruling elites from above while the repressive state agencies that existed heretofore remain intact in the new electoral regimes and are used to suppress (and in some cases, as in Jordan and Morocco, co-opt) all opposition. Thus the externally conditioned democracy of the elites and the free marketeers is both suspect and illegitimate in the eyes of the disadvantaged and prone to challenge from below. Hence, elite democracy imposed from above is—in the context of structural adjustment, free market, and economic crisis—very vulnerable in the Arab world.

Yet in the longer term, the prospects for genuine political opening may be somewhat more optimistic. In the past, the provision of government social services and social welfare came to be regarded as *political rights* to economic security. Now, by instituting democracy from above as a "survival strategy," elites may have replanted the expectation of—and hence demands for—*democratic rights* within those same populations.

Notes

1. Samih K. Farsoun, "Class Structure and Social Change in the Arab World: 1995," in Hisham Sharabi, ed., *The Next Arab Decade: Alternative Futures* (Boulder: Westview Press, 1988), pp. 221–238; also "Oil, State and Social Structure in the Middle East," *Arab Studies Quarterly* 10, 2 (Spring 1988), pp. 155–175.

2. Foreign policy stands are also important for the opposition. Arab states' foreign policies are part of the mix of issues in the struggle between regimes and the opposition.

3. Chris Hedges, "Denied Elections, Algeria's Muslims Counterattack," *New York Times,* 12 May 1993, p. A3.

4. Currently, the electoral regimes in Jordan, Morocco, and Yemen seem to have integrated one part of the opposition into newly elected parliaments. Whether this system of co-optation will sustain, in the longer run, elite-instituted democracy remains to be seen.

5. Jordan may be an exception. Liberalization has gone relatively far (although hardly to liberal democracy), the structural adjustment program appears to be functioning quite well (the IMF now holds it up as an example), political reforms are broadly accepted, the regime is more popular than ever, and no strong opposition to economic reform has materialized. Jordan may be an anomaly at this conjuncture due to a number of factors including an influx of capital from ex-Kuwaiti Palestinians and expatriate Iraqis, the very popular position of the king's regime against the Gulf War, and the acceptance of and help to the hundreds of thousands of ex-Kuwaiti Palestinians by the regime. Finally, one cannot underestimate the consummate political management by the king of both economic adjustment and international political issues.

6. Farsoun, "Class Structure and Social Change in the Arab World: 1995," p. 231.

7. See John Waterbury, "The Political Management of Economic Adjustment and Reform," in Joan M. Nelson, ed., *Fragile Coalitions: Politics of Economic Adjustment* (New Brunswick: Transaction Books, 1989), pp. 39–56.

8. *Al-Sharq al-awsat* (6 April 1993), p. 12.

9. Paul R. Shaw, "The Political Economy of Inequality in the Arab World," *Arab Studies Quarterly* 6, 1–2 (Winter–Spring 1984), pp. 124–154.

10. World Bank, *Egypt: Alleviating Poverty During Structural Adjustment* (Washington, DC: World Bank, 1991), p. 224.

11. World Bank, *Egypt*, p. 180.

12. WEFA Group, *Middle East Economic Outlook* (April 1991).

13. World Bank, *Egypt*, p. 1.

14. World Bank, *Egypt*, p. xiii.

15. World Bank, *Egypt*, p. 113.

16. World Bank, *Egypt*, p. 93.

17. World Bank, *Egypt*, p. 228.

18. According to Tim Mitchell, "Between 1966 and 1988 . . . total Egyptian grain consumption increased by 148 percent. From 1974 onwards, Egypt began to import enormous and ever increasing quantities of grain, becoming the third largest importer after Japan and China. A small proportion of the increases in imports reflects an increase in per capita human consumption, which grew by 12 percent in this 22-year period. The bulk of the new imports was required to cover the increasing grain to feed animals. . . . Grain imports grew by 5.9 million metric tons between 1966 and 1988; non-food consumption of grains (mostly animal feed, but also seed use and wastage) grew by 5.3 million tons or 268 percent." Tim Mitchell, "America's Egypt, Discourse of the Development Industry," *Middle East Report* 169 (March–April 1991), p. 21.

19. Robert Springborg, *Mubarak's Egypt: Fragmentation of the Political Order* (Boulder: Westview Press, 1989).

20. Noteworthy is the dislocation of nearly five million people, Arab and Asian, as a consequence of the 1990–1991 Gulf War. See *Middle East Report*, issue on "Radical Movements: Migrants, Workers and Refugees" 181 (March–April 1993).

21. Immanuel Wallerstein, "The Collapse of Liberalism," in Ralph Miliband and Leo Panitch, eds., *Socialist Register 1992* (London: Merlin Press, 1992), pp. 44–75.

22. Said El-Naggar, ed., *Privatization and Structural Adjustment in the Arab Countries* (Washington, DC: IMF Publications Services, 1989).

23. Fawzy Mansour, *The Arab World* (London: Zed Books, 1992); see also Esmail Hosseinzadeh, "How Egyptian State Capitalism Reverted to Market Capitalism," *Arab Studies Quarterly* 10, 3 (Summer 1988), pp. 299–318.

24. Of course, the exception was Syria in the early 1980s, during which an Islamic rebellion was brutally crushed.

25. Certain political groups (Nasserists, Ba'thists, Socialists, Communists, and others) continue to uphold the nationalist ideology.

26. Farsoun, "Oil, State and Structure," p. 172.

27. Giacomo Luciani, "Economic Foundations of Democracy and Authoritarianism: The Arab World in Comparative Perspective," *Arab Studies Quarterly* 10 (Fall 1988), pp. 457–475.

28. Luciani, "Economic Foundations of Democracy and Authoritarianism," p. 463.

29. Ann M. Lesch, "Democracy in Doses: Mubarak Launches His Second Term as President," *Arab Studies Quarterly* 11, 4 (Fall 1989), pp. 87–107.

30. In spite of the State Department's Human Rights Report, the United States paid little attention to the human rights violations of its regional allies (Israel

especially, Egypt, Saudi Arabia, and even Iraq before the Gulf War) while it exposed and pressured its adversaries (especially Syria, Libya, and others).

31. Sami Zubaida, "Islam, the State and Democracy: Contrasting Conceptions of Society in Egypt," *Middle East Report* 179 (November–December 1992), p. 3.

32. Zubaida, "Islam, the State and Democracy," p. 4.

33. Zubaida, "Islam, the State and Democracy," p. 10.

34. See *Al-Mustaqbal al-Arabi* 158 (April 1992), special issue on civil society; *Al-Mujtama' al-madani fi al-watan al-arabi wa dawruhu fi tahqiq al-dimuqratiyya* [Civil Society in the Arab Nation and Its Role in the Achievement of Democracy] (Beirut: Center for Arab Unity Studies, 1993); *Al-mujtama' al-madani wa al-tahawwul al-dimuqrati fi al-watan al-arabi* [Civil Society and Democratic Change in the Arab Nation] (Cairo: Dar Suad al-Sabah, 1992).

35. Samih K. Farsoun and Lucia P. Fort, "The Problematic of Civil Society, Intellectual Discourse and Arab Intellectuals," paper presented at the Georgetown University Center for Contemporary Arab Studies (Washington, 1992). In general, however, the question of civil society and political liberalization has not been analyzed as an ideological and policy concept that appeared at a certain historical juncture.

36. See Yahya Sadowski, "The New Orientalism and the Democracy Debate," *Middle East Report* 179 (July–August 1993), pp. 14–21, 40.

37. Zubaida, "Islam, the State and Democracy," p. 5.

38. The advertisement in the *Washington Post* (6 April 1993), p. A18, placed by the ministry of information, State Information Service, Egypt, states:

A Man of Political and Economic Renewal

President Mubarak clearly defined and strengthened Egypt's democratic institutions. Popular participation was ensured through the formation of political parties, freedom of the press and the reaffirmation of the independence of the judiciary. The constitution ensures the respect of human rights and the role (*sic*) of law.

. . . Egypt, under President Mubarak has been conducting a profound economic reform, emerging private enterprise and integration into the world economy (*sic*). The first phase of this program has been successfully completed as recognized by the IMF and the World Bank, thus paving the way for further progress.

39. For Saudi Arabia in particular and the Gulf oil-exporting states in general, the policy of the United States is reflected in James Schlesinger's query: "An even deeper question is whether we seriously desire to prescribe democracy as the proper form of government for other societies. Perhaps this issue is most clearly posed in the Islamic world. Do we seriously want to change the institutions in Saudi Arabia? The brief answer is no: over the years we have sought to preserve those institutions, sometimes in preference to more democratic forces coursing throughout the region." James Schlesinger, "The Quest for a Post–Cold War Foreign Policy," *Foreign Affairs* 72 (1992/93), p. 20.

40. Robert W. Cox, "Global Perestroika," in Miliband and Panitch, eds., *Socialist Register 1992*, p. 33.

41. Cox, "Global Perestroika," pp. 30–31, 37–38.

42. James Petras, "The Transformation of Latin America: Free Market Democracy and Other Myths," unpublished manuscript, Department of Sociology, State University of New York, Binghamton, 1993.

43. Cox, "Global Perestroika," p. 31.

44. For Latin America see Petras, "The Transformation of Latin America."

45. David Gill, "Privatization: Opportunities for Financial Market Development," in El-Naggar, ed., *Privatization and Structural Adjustment in the Arab Countries*, p. 130. More recent Kuwaiti scandals involve the incredible "losses" (in billions of dollars) sustained by Kuwait's investments in Spain and in its London-based Kuwaiti Investment Office for Future Generations.

46. Cox, "Global Perestroika," p. 37.

47. Petras, "The Transformation of Latin America," p. 6.

48. Hedges, "Denied Election," p. A3.

49. Farsoun, "Oil, State and Structure," p. 226.

50. Saad Eddin Ibrahim, *The New Arab Social Order* (Boulder: Westview Press, 1982).

51. See the World Bank's comments on "potential losers," in *Egypt*, p. 93.

52. World Bank, *Egypt*, pp. 45–46.

53. *Al-Sharq al-awsat* (6 April 1993), p. 12.

54. Hedges, "Denied Election," p. A3.

55. Waterbury, "The Political Management of Economic Adjustment and Reform," p. 39.

56. Waterbury, "The Political Management of Economic Adjustment and Reform," p. 46.

57. Waterbury, "The Political Management of Economic Adjustment and Reform," p. 47.

4

The Regional
and International Context

14

Regional Influences on Experiments in Political Liberalization in the Arab World

F. Gregory Gause III

The pressures for greater political participation and representative institutions in Arab states are overwhelmingly domestic in origin, as are the most important barriers to such developments. In that context, regional influences play a secondary but potentially important role in the issue of democratization in the Arab world, a role that largely militates against movement toward greater political openness on the part of Arab regimes. Those negative influences can be grouped in three categories: (1) the prevalence of interstate conflict in the region; (2) the continuing importance of transnational ideological factors like Arab nationalism and Islam in the politics of the Arab world, and how those ideological platforms are used by some states to play a role in the domestic politics of other states; and (3) the prevalence in the Arab world of states that rely greatly on external rents for government revenue.

The analysis presented here is based on the premise that democratic experiments in the Arab world are the result of regime decisions—a calculus of costs and benefits made by leaders facing a myriad of domestic, regional, and international pressures in the political and economic realms. This premise does not deny that powerful social forces in Arab countries are pressing for more open and participatory political systems. However, it asserts that the immediate decision to open up the political process is made by leaders, who are calculating the costs and benefits to them personally of any such move, frequently as part of a negotiation with other elites both inside and outside the regime. Thus any opening of the political system must be seen, on balance, as increasing the leader's chances of overcoming whatever political or economic crises are challenging the stability of his rule. Arab leaders who allow political openings are gambling that the risks of maintaining the status quo are greater than the risks of what they hope will be cautious, gradual, and nonthreatening political evolution. The focus here is not on long-term historical or social factors either contributing to or militating against more open political systems in the Arab world, but rather on the immediate calculus of Arab leaders confronting difficult choices.[1]

The three regional factors mentioned above—the prominence of interstate conflict, the importance of transnational ideologies, and the centrality of the state in Arab economies and of external rents in states' fiscal strategies—all lessen the incentives for rational political leaders to accept political openings in their regimes. Each factor will be discussed below, followed by a discussion of the deviant cases in the Arab world, those states where liberalizing experiments have continued despite difficulties (Morocco, Jordan, Yemen, and Kuwait). While the recent appointment in Saudi Arabia, Oman, and Bahrain of *majlis al-shura* (consultative councils) represents an effort by those regimes to broaden the institutional avenues for popular participation in politics, in response to demands in those societies, they are not included in this analysis among liberalizing experiments because the members of those bodies are not elected by popular vote. Since both the Sudan and Lebanon have been engaged in long-running civil wars, they are not considered in this analysis either.

It must be emphasized that this chapter is not dealing with either purely domestic factors militating for or against political openings, nor with pressures emanating from the international system as a whole—be they economic, in terms of structural adjustment pressures, or directly political, in terms of pressure on human rights and political participation issues from the United States and Western Europe, or related to international demonstration effects from the changes in Eastern Europe since 1989. The intent here is to isolate the effects of *regional* factors on the prospects of democratizing experiments in the Arab world, so that those effects may be more easily considered in overall assessments of the prospects for democratization.

Regional Barriers to Democratization

The Prevalence of Interstate Conflict

Almost every Arab state over the past decades has been directly involved in some form of international conflict, though of varying intensities. From the Western Sahara dispute through Libya's episodic military confrontations with its neighbors, to the Arab-Israeli arena and the past decade of war in the Gulf, international conflict has been a major preoccupation of Arab leaders. That preoccupation is reflected in the size of their militaries in relation to their populations and in the proportion of the countries' economies committed to the military. Tables 14.1 and 14.2 show that the states of the Arab *mashriq* concentrate much more of their human and material resources on the military than do a set of democratic and democratizing non-Arab countries. The states of the Arab *maghreb* are closer to these non-Arab comparative cases in this regard.

Table 14.1 Armed Forces per 1,000 Population (1993)[a]

Selected Arab Countries		Non-Arab Comparative Cases	
Algeria	5.94	France	8.84
Egypt	14.55	Hungary	9.37
Iraq	22.11	Norway	7.14
Jordan	23.64	Poland	8.04
Kuwait	25.37[b]	South Korea	14.40
Libya	14.35	Turkey	9.3
Morocco	8.69		
Saudi Arabia	14.10[c]		
Syria	30.34		
Tunisia	6.83		
Yemen	6.71		

Source: International Institute for Strategic Studies, *The Military Balance 1993–94* (London: Brassey's for the IISS, 1993).
Notes: a. Includes both regular armed forces and standing paramilitary forces; excludes reserves, "civil militias," and "tribal levies."
b. Based on the Kuwaiti citizen population and stateless population, excluding foreign residents.
c. Based on the official Saudi citizen population figure of 12.304 million.

The literature on the effect of war on domestic political development is not encouraging regarding the prospects for democratization. That war and preparation for war have played a major role in the development of state structures is clear. War both drove and contributed to the centralization of state authority in Europe, but in ways that tended to strengthen the power of existing regimes, almost all of which were nondemocratic. While the shift to mass-based conscript armies in the nineteenth century is sometimes cited as one of the reasons behind the emergence of democratic pressures on the Continent, nondemocratic regimes during the nineteenth and twentieth centuries have been very successful at raising large armies through compulsory service.[2]

There are a number of reasons why a state that is engaged in war and/or that places a heavy emphasis on war preparation might be less

Table 14.2 Military Expenditure as a Percentage of GDP

Selected Arab Countries	1981	1982	1983	1984	1985	1986	1987	1988	1989
Algeria	1.8	1.9	1.9	1.8	1.7	1.7	1.7	1.7	1.7
Egypt	6.5	6.3	6.7	6.9	5.8	6.1	6.2	4.8	4.5
Iraq	12.3	18.4	24.3	29.1	26.0	24.2	24.3	23.0	—
Jordan	13.7	13.5	13.8	13.1	13.6	14.8	15.0	15.0	11.0
Kuwait	4.4	6.0	6.8	6.8	7.9	8.6	7.0	7.3	6.5
Libya	14.0	15.0	13.0	14.5	15.2	12.7	—	8.6	7.4
Morocco	6.6	6.5	4.9	4.7	5.4	5.1	5.0	4.2	4.3
Saudi Arabia	14.5	21.1	20.3	20.9	22.0	22.4	22.7	19.8	—
Syria	14.7	15.6	15.4	16.7	15.6	14.4	11.3	9.2	—
Tunisia	2.7	5.9	6.6	4.7	5.2	5.9	5.5	5.3	4.9
Yemen AR	12.6	14.7	14.2	10.4	8.4	7.3	7.2	—	—
Yemen PDR	19.7	18.7	19.1	17.1	16.7	22.2	18.4	18.5	—

Non-Arab Comparative Cases

	1981	1982	1983	1984	1985	1986	1987	1988	1989
France	4.1	4.1	4.1	4.0	4.0	3.9	4.0	3.8	3.7
Hungary	2.4	2.4	2.4	2.3	3.6	3.6	3.4	3.0	1.8
Norway	2.9	3.0	3.1	2.8	3.1	3.1	3.3	3.2	3.2
Poland	3.1	3.2	2.8	2.9	3.0	3.6	3.4	3.0	1.8
South Korea	6.0	5.8	5.3	4.9	4.9	4.7	4.5	4.6	4.4
Turkey	4.9	5.2	4.8	4.4	4.5	4.8	4.2	3.8	3.9

Source: Stockholm International Peace Research Institute, *SIPRI Yearbook* 1991 (New York: Oxford University Press, 1991).

likely to democratize. Wars tend to concentrate power in the hands of the executive, a power most leaders are loath to give up. Wars make it easier to stigmatize as treasonous, and then suppress, opposition forces. War preparation leads to greater state control over the economy, limiting the power and autonomy of private sector economic actors who might press for democratic reform. War and war preparation encourage the building of large coercive institutions—armies, national guards, secret police—and give such institutions, which are not necessarily antidemocratic but frequently tend toward that position, a large role in the political system. Leaders who can rely on the loyalty of such coercive institutions could be tempted to use them against domestic political opponents, rather than to allow free political competition that could lead to the end of their own rule.

In the Arab world, we see that the four states with the longest and most intense involvement in regional conflict—Egypt, Syria, Jordan, and Iraq—were hardly pressed to democratize by that experience. The tentative openings of the Egyptian political system in the late 1970s occurred *after*

Egypt had opted out of the Arab-Israeli conflict.[3] Jordan's liberalization experiment began in 1989, long after its last direct military involvement in the Arab-Israeli conflict. Similarily, Algeria's brief experiment with competitive politics in 1989–1990 was contemporaneous with the reduction of its role in the Western Sahara conflict. The apparent end of the Arab-Israeli conflict, a major change in the regional picture dating from the PLO-Israeli and Jordanian-Israeli agreements of 1993 and 1994, could remove the "war obstacle" to liberalization in many Arab countries. These recent changes will be discussed in this chapter's conclusion.

The centrality of regional conflict in the political agenda of Arab leaders over the last two decades posed two disincentives to their taking the risks of opening up their political systems. First, political transitions are messy—they encourage the airing of internal differences, call into question established priorities, and give the impression of domestic disarray. In the face of "enemy" pressure, real or imagined, it is easy for regimes to justify (or rationalize) the avoidance of such domestic "distractions" as open debate and political contestation in order to concentrate all the country's resources on the foreign "threat." This kind of argument was a staple of regime discourse in the Egypt of 'Abd al-Nasser and in Jordan from the late 1950s through the late 1980s, and remains so in Syria (though for how long is now an open question) and Iraq.

Second, the ability to suppress domestic opposition, or to believe that it can be suppressed, reduces the incentives for leaders to compromise with social forces pressing for political openings. Military institutions built ostensibly to meet external challenges can also be used by regimes to combat their domestic opponents. Armies in Jordan, Syria, Sudan, and Iraq have at times since 1970 been deployed in major, sustained confrontations with domestic opposition groups. The Algerian army is currently fighting a civil war against armed Islamic opposition groups and Egyptian paramilitary forces are engaged in an increasingly violent confrontation with their own Islamic opposition. In each of these cases the political leadership has assumed that it could defeat its domestic opponents militarily at a lower cost than it would have to pay to co-opt or compromise with them. That assumption is based, in part, on the regimes' calculations of the strength of their military and paramilitary apparatus.

The Importance of Transnational Ideologies

One of the historical characteristics of interstate politics in the Arab world, particularly in the *mashriq*, has been the rejection of the legitimacy of existing state entities by powerful political leaders and movements in the name of Arab nationalism. In the 1930s and 1940s the Hashemite states of Iraq and Transjordan spearheaded unity efforts directed toward Syria,

Lebanon, and Palestine. By the mid-1950s the unity agenda had been captured by the Ba'th Party and by the regime of Gamal 'Abd al-Nasser in Egypt, reaching its highwater mark in the Syrian-Egyptian unity of 1958–1961. Even during the period of the purported "death" of Pan-Arabism, Syria and Iraq experimented briefly and unhappily with unity in 1978–1979. None of these efforts was able to change the map of the Middle East, but they did define much of the agenda of regional politics during these periods.

Unity efforts were pursued to a large extent through efforts by the proposers to build support among constituencies *inside* the countries that were the targets of their efforts. Thus Transjordanian and Iraqi Hashemites developed client relations with Syrian, Lebanese, and Palestinian political notables as means to affect directly *domestic* decisionmaking in those states. In order to combat these efforts Egypt and Saudi Arabia developed their own client relations with other notables in those countries.[4] These links between leaders in one country and political actors in another were both driven and legitimated by the Arab nationalist contention that the rules of interaction among sovereign states prohibiting interference in the domestic affairs of others did not apply in the Arab world.

Inter-Arab politics of the 1950s and 1960s saw an escalation in this pattern of direct interference in the domestic affairs of other states legitimated by appeals to Pan-Arabism. While the Hashemites and their rivals played the unity game at the level of elites, the "politics of the notables," in Albert Hourani's phrase,[5] Nasser used Arab nationalist rhetoric and the new technology of the radio to appeal directly to citizens in other Arab countries, calling on them to oppose their governments on the basis of loyalty to larger Arab interests. The game of clientelist politics was still played, but a new and, for Arab leaders, more dangerous element had been introduced into inter-Arab rivalries. What had been in essence a game of elite musical chairs, with the losers subject to no more than some time out of power, was transformed into a struggle between the old elites and new players. Losing now meant the loss of elite status—regime change, the socioeconomic upheaval of land reform and nationalizations, even death—for those involved.[6]

The leaders of Arab states today for the most part came to power and received their rough-and-ready political socialization during this period of intense inter-Arab rivalry. For King Hussein of Jordan and King Fahd of Saudi Arabia (who was the minister of the interior for most of the 1960s), the pressures put on their regimes by Nasserist and Ba'thist opposition are not-so-distant memories. King Hassan of Morocco was subject to similar, though less intense, pressures from republican revolutionary Algeria in the 1960s and early 1970s. The Ba'thist regimes in Iraq and Syria under their current leaderships have spent 20 years attempting to delegitimize and destabilize each other. As recently as the Gulf War of 1990–1991, Saddam

Hussein attempted to revive the Nasserist tactic of direct appeals to Arab citizens to oppose their governments. Non-Arab states in the region have also adopted the tactic of developing client relations with domestic groups in efforts to affect the domestic politics of Arab states, as Israel's relations with various Lebanese parties and Iran's support, both under the Shah and the Islamic Republic, for Iraqi Kurdish and Shi'i opposition groups attests.

While the salience of the threat to regime security posed by transnational appeals based on Pan-Arabism is much reduced from the period of the 1950s and 1960s, many Arab leaders perceive a new transnational threat to regime security in the rise of Islamist opposition groups. The 1980s saw open efforts by the new revolutionary Islamic regime in Iran to encourage opposition groups, particularly Shi'i opposition groups, in Iraq, Kuwait, Bahrain, Saudi Arabia, and Lebanon.[7] Such pressures contributed to the closing of the Kuwaiti parliament in 1986 and added a new factor to the ongoing Lebanese civil war.

Since the Gulf War, accusations of Iranian interference in domestic politics have been heard more from North Africa than from the Gulf. The beleaguered regimes in Algeria, Tunisia, and Egypt regularly attribute their domestic troubles to Iranian and Sudanese support for Islamic groups in their countries. In March 1993 Algeria, which had excellent relations with the Islamic Republic of Iran in the 1980s, serving as mediator between it and both the United States (during the hostage crisis) and Iraq (during the Iran-Iraq War), severed diplomatic relations with Teheran. At the same time it recalled its ambassador from Khartoum, with the Algerian government issuing a public statement that accused both countries of supporting "terrorism" in Algeria.[8] By late 1992 Egypt, Tunisia, and Algeria, which had found themselves on opposite sides of the Arab divide over the Gulf War, had begun intensive cooperation on internal security matters. Tunisian prime minister Hamid al-Qarawi confirmed in a newspaper interview that the three countries were coordinating in the field of "combatting terrorism coming to these countries through the Sudanese-Iranian alliance."[9]

Egypt has been the most outspoken of the Arab regimes in charging foreign powers with interference in its internal affairs. On a number of occasions President Mubarak has spoken publicly about foreign powers directing the operations of violent opposition groups in Egypt.[10] In December 1992, General 'Abd al-Halim Musa, then Egypt's minister of the interior, told a committee of the Egyptian parliament that Iran and Sudan are directly involved in supporting "terrorist activity" in Egypt.[11] Sudan's president, General 'Umar al-Bashir, responded by publicly accusing Egypt of masterminding a coup plot against his government in April 1993.[12] In August 1993, 'Usama al-Baz, President Mubarak's political affairs director, again accused Iran of directly supporting Islamic opposition groups in Egypt.[13]

Iran has done its part to keep the war of words going. In June 1993, in a speech commemorating the death of Ayatollah Khumayni, Iran's supreme guide Ayatollah 'Ali Khamena'i said that Iran was providing "political and moral support" to Islamic movements in Egypt, Algeria, and Iraq, among other countries.[14]

The fear of ruling regimes that other countries might exploit political openings to affect their domestic politics is reflected in the legal barriers a number of Arab states have set up prohibiting contacts between opposition political parties and groups outside the country. In February 1993, Egyptian courts denied a license to the Awakening Party because the party's charter permitted the acceptance of foreign donations.[15] Jordan's national charter, adopted in June 1991 at the instigation of the king by all political tendencies in the country as a prelude to the legalization of political parties, specifically forbids any "structural or financial affiliation by the leadership or members of any party with any non-Jordanian." Jordan's political party law, adopted in 1992, reiterates this stricture.[16]

The truth or falsehood of these various charges is less important than the evidence they give of the continuing fears many Arab leaders have of foreign involvement in their domestic politics. Undoubtedly the origins of Islamic opposition movements in Arab states are overwhelmingly domestic. However, state leaders, who are making the decisions about political liberalization, can easily convince themselves, or see the possibility of convincing others, that Islamic opposition represents foreign meddling in their affairs. Whether such beliefs are legitimate or mere rationalizations for suppression of domestic discontent, they provide incentives for Arab political leaders to avoid liberalization of their political systems and to reverse liberalizing experiments where the opposition seems to be growing in strength.

It should also be noted that there are more direct ways in which common Arab identity is used by one Arab state to limit the possibilities of greater political openness in other Arab states. Syria justifies its military and political role in Lebanon by reference to the larger Arab interests (against Israel) being served, while using its influence to affect Lebanese elections. Saudi Arabia has quietly asserted its right in the past to have a role in the domestic politics of other states in the Arabian peninsula. There is circumstantial evidence of Saudi pressure on both Kuwait and Bahrain to curtail the power of their elected legislative assemblies in the 1970s.[17] Riyad was extensively involved in the domestic politics of the Yemen Arab Republic in the 1970s and appears to be trying to revive that involvement in the politics of the newly united Republic of Yemen, as will be discussed below.[18] Obviously the material opposition of an influential neighbor to political liberalization presents yet another disincentive for rational Arab leaders to open up their political processes.

External Rents

The previous two categories involved pressures against political liberalization that emerge from the interaction of Middle Eastern states. The central importance of exogenous rents in the fiscal profile of so many Arab governments emerges not from Arab states' relations with each other, but rather from their serendipitous position, quite literally, in the global political economy. Many Arab states are "positioned" over large amounts of oil and natural gas, giving the governments of those states a steady (though not at a constant level) source of revenue transferred directly to them from the world economy, not extracted from their domestic societies. Other Arab states, not so favored geologically, exploit their geostrategic "position" to extract revenue from the international system. Proximity to both Israel and the oil patch in the Gulf has allowed relatively resource-poor Arab states like Egypt, Syria, and Jordan, as well as the PLO, to bargain with the United States, other industrialized states, and—until the late 1980s—the Soviet Union for direct economic and military aid.

The importance of exogenous rents in the political economies of the major Arab oil and gas producers need not be belabored here. For non-oil states, aid from donor countries and loans from private and governmental sources represent a substantial percentage of state revenues, though less than the percentage provided by hydrocarbon revenues in the oil and gas producer states. Table 14.3 shows the extent of the reliance of selected Arab states on what the International Monetary Fund calls "non-tax revenue" and the same figures for a number of non-Arab democratizing or democratic countries. These Arab governments can be grouped into three categories of rent dependence: high-level rentiers, who rely on non-tax revenue for more than 50 percent of state budgets (Algeria, Kuwait, Libya, Saudi Arabia); mid-level rentiers, whose reliance is between 20 and 49 percent (Egypt, Jordan, Syria, Yemen); and non-rentiers, whose reliance is below 20 percent (Morocco, Tunisia). It should be noted that Iraq does not report revenue and budget figures, but it can safely be assumed that oil revenues and other non-tax revenue have accounted for more than 50 percent of Iraqi state finances over the last two decades.

The rentier state phenomenon is no guarantee of regime stability, as both the Iranian and Algerian cases show. Large-scale oil revenues do not necessarily "depoliticize" society, sapping individuals and social organizations of their desire to have a say in their country's politics, as some analysts have contended.[19] Even in the most rentier of the oil states, the Arab monarchies of the Gulf, demands for more responsible and representative government are heard.[20] What exogenous revenues do—be they in the form of aid, loans, or oil revenues—is reduce the need of the regimes that control them to respond to demands for political change from their societies.

Table 14.3 "Non-Tax Revenues" as a Percentage of Government Budgets

Selected Arab Countries	Percentage	Non-Arab Comparative Cases	Percentage
Algeria (1993)	57.6	France (1991)	6.95
Egypt (1989)	33.77	Hungary (1990)	15.53
Jordan (1990)	28.26	Norway (1990)	22.89
Kuwait (1986)	97.56	Poland (1988)	5.09
Libya (1990/91)	57.04	South Korea (1992)	9.73
Morocco (1987)	10.13	Turkey (1991)	12.54
Saudi Arabia (1993)	79.4		
Syria (1990)	25.77		
Tunisia (1991)	17.32		
Yemen (1991)	42.5		

Sources: Algeria, Libya, Saudi Arabia, Syria: Economist Intelligence Unit, *Country Profiles,* 1993–94; Egypt, Jordan, Kuwait, Morocco, Tunisia, Yemen, non-Arab countries: IMF, *Government Finance Statistics Yearbook—1992* (Washington, DC: IMF, 1992).

Since the regimes are not as reliant on domestic bargains to fund the state budget as they would be without exogenous revenues, they can more easily ignore calls for broadened political participation. Because regime decisions on how to spend exogenous revenues are an important, in some cases central, factor in their domestic economies, these revenues give the regimes an important political tool with which to vest the interests of important social groups in the continuation of the regime. Exogenous revenues also allow governments to devote a greater percentage of their budgets to the coercive and intelligence apparati. In a very real way, rents give regimes both more carrots and more sticks with which to deal with societal actors, lessening the need to open up their political systems.

These antiliberalization effects are not absolute. The relatively greater autonomy that exogenous rents provide for a regime vis-à-vis its society is bought at the price of greater dependence on international factors, be it the price of oil or the demands that foreign donors attach to their loans. The case of the liberalization of Jordanian politics since 1989 is an example of a regime risking a limited opening in the political process in order to share the responsibility for stringent economic policies imposed by international lenders. The Algerian example shows that a rentier state can so mismanage its domestic economy that it is forced to experiment with new participatory institutions as part of negotiating a different economic bargain with society. But the Algerian example also shows that the availability of exogenous rents makes it easier for a regime to reverse a liberalization process that threatens its hold on power, because the regime can still rely for fiscal support on the flow of rents from the international system.

Oil and gas revenues are more reliable rents, in political terms, for Arab regimes than international grants and loans. While the former are subject to price fluctuations, the latter frequently come with either explicit or implicit conditions related to the recipient's domestic politics attached. Foreign aid is sometimes linked to human rights issues; IMF structural adjustment packages frequently lead regimes to experiment with more inclusive political strategies to spread the blame for hard times. However, because of their strategic value to outside powers, a number of Arab states have been able to rely on international aid and loans even while reversing liberalizing experiments domestically.

The best example is Egypt. As a result of its support for the coalition in the Gulf War, Egypt had $7 billion in military debt to the United States and a further $10 billion in debt to other bilateral creditors written off. This windfall occurred despite the fact that most of the opposition parties boycotted the 1990 parliamentary elections, accusing the government of prejudicing the poll, and that the government had adopted a very confrontational policy with its Islamist opposition.[21] As recently as January 1994 Egypt received aid commitments of $2 billion to $3 billion from wealthy countries to support its economic reform program, and was looking forward to further debt relief from the Paris Club creditors.[22] Within two months of canceling parliamentary elections in January 1992, Algeria received a $1.5 billion loan from a consortium of European, Japanese, and U.S. banks to allow the government to reschedule debt payments.[23]

Regional Factors and Political Liberalization: A Preliminary Test

Three sets of regional factors have been identified as presenting rational disincentives to engaging in political liberalization experiments for Arab leaders concerned with remaining in power: the prevalence of interstate conflict, the importance of transnational ideologies, and the availability of exogenous rents for financing state budgets. Given the prevalence of all three in the Arab world, at least through the early 1990s, one can make a *prima facie* case that these factors at least contribute to the relative paucity of liberalizing experiments in comparison with other world regions during the last decade. Syria, Iraq, Libya, and Saudi Arabia all have devoted vast resources to their militaries, been involved in international conflict (Syria and Iraq more than the others), have been subject to transnational political pressures, and rank in the high or middle rentier categories. On every score regional influences work against liberalization in those states, and there has been none. This is not to argue that these regional influences are the primary reason why liberalization experiments have not occurred in these countries: Domestic factors are far more important. It is only to say that these countries do not present a challenge to the argument that regional influences work against liberalization in Arab states.

A more difficult question is what relationship these variables have to specific cases of political liberalization and the reversal of liberalization. The cases of reversed liberalization to be considered are Egypt, Tunisia, and Algeria. The cases of ongoing liberalization experiments are Jordan, Kuwait, Morocco, and Yemen (with the caveat that the results of the 1994 Yemeni civil war could spell an end to the liberalization experiment there). If we find that the three regional variables—war and war preparation, exposure to transnational ideological challenges, and high levels of rentier income—are less salient in these seven cases where no liberalization has occurred, then there might be a basis for concluding that these regional factors are important elements in determining where liberalization experiments will occur in the Arab world. If we find that these variables are more salient in the cases of reversed liberalization than in those of ongoing liberalization, we can draw tentative conclusions about the importance of these regional variables for the sustainability of liberalization experiments in the Arab world.

Of the seven cases, only Kuwait has been actively engaged in an international conflict over the past decade. Particularly since Algeria disengaged from active support for the Polisario at the beginning of the 1990s, Morocco has not faced a serious international military challenge to its control of the Western Sahara. The lack of active involvement in international conflicts thus helps to explain why liberalizing experiments have occurred in six of the seven cases, but this variable cannot help explain setbacks to liberalization in Egypt, Tunisia, and Algeria, which were not faced with international military challenges at the time of the reversals. Tunisia and Algeria devote less of their resources to military purposes than most other Arab states, yet they halted their liberalization experiments. Nor can this variable help explain the liberalization undertaken by Kuwait after the Iraqi occupation, where the feeling of vulnerability to outside attack still ran high.

One thing that the three cases of setbacks to liberalization have in common is their contention that outside powers (mainly Iran, but also Sudan) are intervening in their domestic politics and encouraging violent opposition groups. However, the accuracy of these charges is difficult to ascertain, so it is impossible to say that some particular level of foreign interference contributes to the reversal of liberalization. It is also interesting to note that in three of the ongoing liberalization experiments, outside power meddling on the basis of transnational ideological platforms has in the past been an important part of domestic politics: Jordan (Palestinians, Syria, Saudi Arabia, to some extent Israel), Kuwait (Palestinians, Saudi Arabia, Iraq, Iran), and Yemen (Saudi Arabia, and in relations between what were the two Yemeni states before 1990). We will discuss below why these states, in the past subject to ideological and political penetration, have moved ahead with their liberalizing experiments. Morocco, with its long history as a distinctive political entity, is less subject than many other Arab states to outside pressures based on transnational ideological platforms, but the same could be said about Egypt and Tunisia, where liberalization has suffered setbacks.

The cases demonstrate that a past history of external interference motivated and justified on transnational ideological bases is no bar to political liberalization. However, perceptions of foreign interference can serve as a justification and/or rationalization to reverse liberalization. Talk of such pressures—particularly "Islamic" pressures generated from Iran and Sudan —by regimes might be more of a signal than a cause of such reversals.

Exogenous rents play the major role in the fiscal structure of two of the seven liberalizing cases—one reversal (Algeria) and one continuing experiment (Kuwait). Rents play an important fiscal role in three other cases, not representing a majority of state income but, given their precarious economic situations, an irreplaceable marginal increment in state resources—one reversal (Egypt) and two continuing experiments (Jordan, Yemen). Rents play a much less significant role in the fiscal structure of the remaining two cases—one reversal (Tunisia) and one continuing experiment (Morocco). Clearly there is no necessary relationship between the fiscal basis of the state and political liberalization experiments. Exogenous rents can give leaders the option (perhaps illusory over the long term) of reversing liberalizing experiments while maintaining a steady revenue base for the state, but in the Tunisian case a regime that did not have a major source of exogenous rent also reversed a liberalizing experiment.

This preliminary survey of the effects of regional factors on liberalizing experiments in the Arab world indicates that there is neither a necessary nor a sufficient relationship between any one of them, or all of them together, and decisions by regimes to liberalize or to reverse liberalization. There does seem to be an elective affinity between the absence of international conflict and regime decisions to risk liberalization (the Kuwait exception is discussed below), but no guarantee that the absence of international threat will keep such experiments going. Both transnational ideological pressures and the role of exogenous rents in the state fiscal profile need to be seen as intervening variables. Only given certain domestic and international conditions will they play a role in decisions to liberalize and to reverse liberalization. One of the tasks of future research is to identify in what circumstances these regional variables play a role in such decisions.

Liberalizing Experiments and Regional Influences

If it is true that regional factors generally militate against liberalization, and help contribute in some limited, though by no means necessary, way to reversals of liberalization, how does one explain the continuing liberal experiments in the Arab world—Morocco, Jordan, Kuwait, and (perhaps, with the post-1994 civil war picture yet to clarify) Yemen? Remembering that regional factors are neither necessary nor sufficient conditions for liberalization, it is still important to consider how these exceptions have continued in the face of regional factors working against them.

The Moroccan case is the easiest to account for among the exceptional cases. Its commitment of resources to the military is not particularly large in comparison to other Arab states, and is well in line with a number of non-Arab examples of liberalizing experiments. Since the withdrawal of major Algerian support for the Polisario, the risk that it will be involved in international conflict is much reduced. Given its location on the western extreme of the Arab world, its strong Berber heritage, and its long history as an independent political entity, Morocco is less subject to transnational ideological pressures than other Arab states. Finally, the Moroccan state is less reliant on exogenous rents than most other Arab states. The regional factors that provide rational disincentives for leaders to experiment with political liberalization are less intense in Morocco than in most other Arab states.

The other three cases are more difficult to explain. Kuwait is a state that suffered a harsh military occupation, perceives a continuing military threat from Iraq, and devotes a large proportion of state resources to the military. It has been buffeted by Pan-Arab and Islamic transnational ideological pressures during its history and has as its most important regional ally a neighbor, Saudi Arabia, that is opposed to democratic institutions. Kuwait relies almost exclusively on exogenous rents for state finance. All the regional factors work against liberalization.

In the Kuwaiti case, the experience of the Iraqi invasion and subsequent liberation by coalition forces led by the United States has made both domestic and international factors for liberalization much more salient than regional factors. During the Iraqi occupation, the Kuwaiti regime needed the support of its people to make its case to the world for support. It thus committed itself, at a meeting of Kuwaiti notables in Jidda, Saudi Arabia, in October 1990, to restore the 1962 constitution and the elected (though by very limited suffrage) legislature mandated by it. In 1986 the regime suspended the constitution and attempted to replace the elected legislature with a partially elected, partially appointed body with much reduced legislative and oversight powers.

Once returned to power, the Al Sabah regime was constrained to make good on its promises. Kuwaiti political groups organized to press the government for restoration of the constitution. The regime itself was weakened by its poor performance during the Iraqi invasion and by the need to spend most of its reserves in the liberation. The physical and economic rebuilding of the country required more expenditures and some amount of belt-tightening. A return to constitutional procedures would make those steps more palatable to the population. Also, while the United States did not actively press the Al Sabah regime for democratizing moves, many in the Kuwaiti political elite believed that cementing the defense relationship with Washington would be helped by a return to constitutional life.

Importantly, the experience of occupation and liberation also served to strengthen the political identity of Kuwaitis as Kuwaitis, reducing the fears of the regime that a return to constitutional politics would be an avenue for fifth columnists to infiltrate the country. The almost unanimous rejection by Kuwaitis of the Iraqi claim and the shock many Kuwaitis felt when public opinion in other Arab states seemed to support Saddam Hussein both went a long way to discrediting Arab nationalist ideologies in the country. The Shiʻi minority, suspected by many Sunnis of harboring more loyalty to revolutionary Iran than to the state during the 1980s, proved themselves to be loyal citizens during the occupation. Iranian support for Kuwaiti independence during the crisis reduced fears that Teheran would attempt to mobilize Kuwaiti Shiʻa against the state, as it had tried to do at times in the 1980s. These affirmations of Kuwaiti political identity had their negative aspects, particularly in the strong feelings among Kuwaitis against the long-resident Palestinian population in the country, but they provided necessary reassurances to the Kuwaiti leadership that opening up the political process would not call into question the existence of the state or the existing political system. All these factors reduced the fears among the Al Sabah that a return to constitutional procedures would threaten their hold on ultimate power in Kuwait.[24]

In Jordan also one would expect, from a look at regional factors, that leaders would perceive numerous threats in a liberalizing course. Jordan has been directly involved in the Arab-Israeli conflict since its inception, and commits a substantial portion of its resources to the military. It has been subject to transnational ideological and political pressures of Arab nationalist, Palestinian, and Islamist varieties. It is in the middle level of Arab states in terms of reliance on external rents to finance the government.

Regional pressures are readily apparent in Jordanian politics. Two parties that applied for licenses under the party law of 1992—the Jordanian

Communist Party and the Jordanian branch of the Ba'th Party—were initially denied licenses because of their foreign links, though after an appeals process in which they reiterated their commitment to the regime and the political system their licenses were granted. Three of Jordan's new political parties are organizational offshoots of constituent groups of the Palestine Liberation Organization—the Popular Front for the Liberation of Palestine and the two competing branches of the Democratic Front for the Liberation of Palestine.[25] A prominent Islamist member of parliament elected in 1989, Layth a-Shubaylat, was arrested in September 1993, accused of conspiring with Iran to foment instability in the country. He was convicted and then pardoned by the king, and withdrew from political life.[26] King Hussein himself publicly accused Iran and Sudan of collaborating with local Islamists to subvert his regime.[27] It was widely supposed that King Hussein would postpone the parliamentary elections scheduled for November 1993 because of the uncertain effects of the Israeli-Palestinian Declaration of Principles signed in September of that year, though he chose to proceed with the elections as scheduled.

As in the case of Kuwait, domestic and international pressures for the liberalization experiment have outweighed the regional pressures against it in Jordan. The king adopted a clear strategy after the 1989 riots to link the austerity measures required of Jordan by the International Monetary Fund to an opening of the political system, to spread the responsibility for the economic difficulties that would follow.[28] With another difficult policy choice looming, the signing of an Israeli-Jordanian peace treaty, the king seemed to want an elected parliament to share in that responsibility also. The change in the Jordanian electoral law preceding the November 1993 elections, aimed at reducing the strength of the Islamist bloc, helped return a parliament less likely to oppose such a treaty.

Also, as in the case of Kuwait, the moves toward political liberalization in Jordan were preceded and accompanied by important decisions and events that tended to solidify political identity in the state, reducing the risks that outside forces would be able to exploit political openings. In the Jordanian case the great crisis of political identity came in the 1970–1971 civil war with the PLO. Since that time the regime has steadily pursued a "Jordanization" strategy in political life. That strategy culminated in the king's decision of July 1988 to renounce formally Jordan's claim to the West Bank. In his address to the country explaining his decision, the king cautioned that this step did not affect East Bank Jordanians of Palestinian origin: "All of them have citizenship rights and commitments, just like any other citizen regardless of origin." He asserted that safeguarding Jordanian national identity in the officially truncated East Bank state was "a sacred matter that will not be compromised," offering a thinly veiled warning to those who would challenge his definition of political loyalties that "order and discipline" would be the basis of that unity.[29] The Jordanian parliament, which since 1967 continued to have half of its seats allotted to West Bank representatives, was constitutionally altered so as to represent only the East Bank. The boundaries of the political system were now defined, after decades of tensions that stemmed first from the incorporation of the West Bank and then from the Israeli occupation and the concomitant growth of Palestinian political identity.

Two other factors were also at work in Jordan, reducing the dangers to the monarchy of political liberalization. First, the regime had a decades-long relationship with the Jordanian branch of the Muslim Brotherhood. As the Islamist trend, based organizationally on the Brotherhood, was the major "opposition" element in the electoral arena, the regime's confidence in its ability to manage the results of liberalization was greater than that of other Arab regimes facing Islamist opposition. Second, the king's personal popularity increased markedly with his stand in the Gulf War of 1990–1991, giving him greater freedom of maneuver regarding the liberalizing experiment. The disengagement from the West Bank, the history of monarchical relations with the Brotherhood, and the Gulf War experience all increased the confidence of the ruling regime that the risks of political liberalization could be managed.

Yemen is unique even among these exceptional cases. The liberalizing experiment there came as the result of the unification of the two previous Yemeni states in May 1990, neither of which was politically liberal. Since the unification was the outcome of negotiation, not a political or military victory of one side over the other, the ruling groups in the two former states had little choice but to agree to share power.[30] With the General People's Congress of North Yemeni president ʻAli ʻAbdullah Salih (who became head of the presidential council in the new state) and the Yemeni Socialist Party mutually checking each other, the field was open for other groups in Yemeni society to organize politically. With neither side able to impose its political control at the outset, it was agreed that elections would be held at the end of a two-year transition period for a legislature that would select a new presidential council. Those elections, once postponed, were held in April 1993. Local and international observers agreed that the polling was generally fair and that a variety of political currents other than the two ruling parties were able to participate.[31]

The results of that election added a new element to the Yemeni ruling coalition, the Yemeni Reform Alignment (*Tajammuʻ al-ʼislah al-yamani*), which won 62 seats (the General People's Congress took 123, the Yemeni Socialist Party 56, independents 47, and smaller parties the remainder of the 301 seats). The Reform Alignment is a coalition of tribal notables headed by the paramount shaikh of the Hashid confederation, Shaikh ʻAbdallah al-ʼAhmar, and urban Islamist groups. The new Yemeni government formed after the election included ministers from the three major political groups, and the Reform Alignment was allotted one seat on the five-member presidential council.

Despite the success of its first free elections, the liberalizing experiment in Yemen remains buffeted by continuing tensions between the two ruling parties of the former Yemeni states. The Yemeni Socialist Party won 90 percent of the seats in former South Yemen, and precious few elsewhere in the country, attesting to the difficulties in integrating the political life of the unified state.[32] President Salih acknowledged in an interview in July 1993 that the transition period "was accompanied by a number of negative points," including an increase in government corruption and violent political incidents, "as a result of combining two international entities and regimes into a single state and a single regime."[33] The armies of the two previous states were not merged, effectively reporting to command structures controlled by President Salih and the Yemeni Socialist Party, respectively.

The tensions between the two factions in the ruling elite erupted into a violent civil war in May 1994. As the fighting continued, the YSP leadership declared the secession of the former South Yemeni territory from the united state. The secessionist regime was defeated militarily in June 1994, with the capture of Aden and Mukalla by forces loyal to the government of the unified state. The YSP leadership that led the secessionist regime fled the country, and the new government formed after the civil war contained no YSP ministers, though many prominent party members had remained loyal to the San'a government during the fighting.[34] While the multiparty system remains in place in post–civil war Yemen, and a rump of the YSP continues to operate, the ultimate effects of the war in the liberalizing experiment in the country remain to be seen.

The difficulties that faced Yemeni liberalization before the civil war were domestic but had their origins in international tensions between the two former Yemeni states, which had a long history of direct interference in each other's domestic affairs and fought two brief border wars in 1972 and 1979. With the question of Yemeni political identity apparently settled by unity, neither of the former ruling elites could point to potential meddling by the other Yemeni state as a reason/rationalization to avoid a more open political system. It is interesting in this context, however, to note that the Yemeni political crisis of late 1993–early 1994 attracted a number of outside power mediators, including the Sultan of Oman and the King of Jordan, presumably at the request of the Yemenis themselves. The agreement between the Yemeni Socialist Party and the General People's Congress in February 1994 that was intended to end the crisis was signed in Amman, Jordan, not in Yemen. The civil war attracted the diplomatic attention of the entire Arab world, with accusations by both sides that the other was receiving military support from other regional states. (The San'a government accused the separatists of being supported by Kuwait and Saudi Arabia, and the separatists declared that Iraq, Iran, and Sudan were backing President Salih.)

Also complicating the liberalization process are the troubled relations the new state has with its powerful northern neighbor. Saudi Arabia, which had consistently opposed Yemeni unity efforts in the past, was caught by surprise by the May 1990 unity agreement. Even more troubling to Riyad was that the new state's first major foreign policy decision was to oppose the Saudi decision to invite foreign forces into the kingdom during the Gulf crisis. In response, the Saudis revoked the special status of Yemeni workers in the country, forcing approximately 750,000 to return to Yemen. The resulting loss of worker remittance income and increase in unemployment have severely damaged the Yemeni economy, an inauspicious background for political liberalization. During the Gulf War, the Saudi media gave prominent coverage to Yemeni exiles and tribal groups who opposed the regime's stand, signaling that Riyad was working against President Salih in Yemeni domestic politics.[35]

Saudi diplomacy during the civil war clearly tilted toward the secessionist regime in Aden. Riyad strongly urged a "ceasefire in place" during the fighting, which would have been to the advantage of the secessionists, who were losing on the battlefield. The San'a government (indirectly) and Saudi opposition groups (directly) accused the Saudi government of covertly providing weapons and money, along with its more public diplomatic support, for the breakaway regime in Aden.[36] Riyad did not overtly oppose the liberalizing experiment in Yemen before the civil war, and there is little evidence that its position during the war was motivated by fear of contagion effects of Yemeni "democracy," as many Yemenis contend. Historic Saudi opposition to Yemeni unity and Saudi antipathy toward 'Ali 'Abdullah Salih because of his position during the Gulf War are more than adequate reasons to explain Riyad's stance. However, the tensions between Yemen and Saudi Arabia could in the future serve to inhibit the development of the Yemeni liberalizing experiment in two ways: Saudi indirect intervention in Yemeni politics to weaken the Salih regime, and fears of such intervention leading Salih to reverse the liberalizing moves of 1990–1993. Two of the regional factors discussed above—involvement in conflict and fear of external meddling in domestic affairs—now militate against the continuation of the Yemeni liberalizing experiment.

The Saudis have not worked actively against political liberalization in Kuwait, where they have also in the past exercised influence in the domestic arena. The *salafi* movement in Kuwait, which takes its inspiration from the Wahhabi movement in Saudi Arabia, constituted itself as a political group called the Popular Islamic Alignment (*al-tajammu' al-Islami al-sha'bi*) and contested the Kuwaiti parliamentary elections of 1992, winning three seats and supporting a number of victorious independents.[37] There are no public indications of Saudi pressure on the Al Sabah to reverse the liberalizing course.

Two factors may account for this surprisingly passive Saudi stance toward liberalizing experiments on its borders. First, the Saudis have less money with which to affect the domestic politics of these states. The expenses of Desert Storm, on top of the expenditures during the 1980s to support Iraq in the war against Iran and to cushion the shock of falling oil prices on the domestic Saudi economy, have largely depleted the Saudi government's financial reserves. Money has been the primary instrument of Saudi influence in the domestic politics of other Arab states, and there is just less of it to go around now. Second, Riyad is cautiously and hesitantly opening up its own political process, with the appointment of the *majlis al-shura* in August 1993. While hardly a sign of incipient democratization in the kingdom, this move might signal a somewhat more lenient attitude in Riyad to political experiments in neighboring states.

In all three of the cases discussed above, regional factors have not been powerful enough to derail ongoing liberalizing experiments. In each case liberalization was preceded and accompanied by important political events that served to clarify and strengthen—at least in the eyes of the rulers who were making the liberalizing decisions—national identity. Unity in Yemen, the disengagement from the West Bank in Jordan, and the Iraqi invasion and subsequent liberation of Kuwait all removed at least some of the fears that the rulers had about the consequences to them and their regimes of partial openings in the political system. These examples, along with that of Morocco, demonstrate that the regional influences against political liberalization in the Arab world are not insuperable. The domestic political environment is the key to explaining the presence or absence of liberalizing experiments.

Conclusion

Three specific regional factors in the Arab world present disincentives to rational leaders considering liberalization of their political systems—the prevalence of international conflict in the Middle East, the power of transnational ideological platforms based on Arabism and Islam, and the centrality of exogenous rents in the fiscal profile of the state. Taken together they can contribute to an explanation of the relative lack of liberal regimes in the Arab world. However, their ability to account for specific cases of liberalization and the reversal of liberalization is minimal. States like Kuwait, Jordan, and Yemen, where regional factors militate against liberalization, have been able to sustain such experiments longer than countries like Tunisia, where regional factors seem more propitious for liberalization. These examples indicate that regional forces can only affect decisions on liberalization through their articulation in the *domestic* political arena of the states concerned. The research task is thus to identify the domestic political variables that affect how and to what extent regional factors play into the domestic arena, and from there into the leaders' calculus of costs and benefits, on the question of political liberalization.

Trends in the mid-1990s could further attenuate the power of these regional factors in blocking regional experiments in liberalization, in the areas of international conflict and the rentier phenomenon. Arab-Israeli peace treaties could lessen the fear of war in the region. However, neither Egypt's peace treaty with Israel in 1979 nor Jordan's more recent pact led to a flowering of democracy in either place. In fact, it has been argued that in both countries peace treaties with Israel were followed by limitations on, not expansions of, existing liberalization experiments.[38] Moreover, rivalries in the Gulf area and on the Arabian peninsula make it difficult to rule out the possibility of regional international conflict even if comprehensive Arab-Israeli peace is achieved. The jury remains out on the effect of the Arab-Israeli peace process on liberalization prospects.

While many Arab states remain highly reliant on external revenues to fund their budgets, the availability of rents has declined recently and could continue to decline. With the end of the Cold War, foreign aid is less available from outside powers (though Jordan clearly is counting on promised aid in the wake of its peace treaty with Israel). Oil prices have flattened out, with no immediate prospect of dramatic increase. Governments that in the past had used external rents to "buy off" domestic demands for political participation will find it much harder to pursue that strategy in the future, particularly given the high population growth rates throughout the Arab world. Less money spread around more people is not a promising equation for leaders looking to deflect participatory demands. Of course, financial troubles in rentier states do not necessarily lead to sustained liberalization, as the Algerian case demonstrates, but they can be an incentive, as they were in both Algeria and Jordan, for leaders to contemplate opening up the political process.

The regional factor that will continue to militate strongly against liberalization experiments in the Arab world is the continuing importance of Islamic opposition groups. Secular nationalist regimes tend to see such opposition as an extension of foreign powers, even though the overwhelming evidence is that Islamic opposition movements are homegrown phenomena. The fear of foreign intervention in domestic affairs will remain a reason, or at least a rationalization, for Arab leaders to avoid liberalization and turn back existing liberalization experiments.

Are there any regional factors encouraging democratic experiments in the Arab world? Yes, but more on the intellectual level than on the immediate political and material plane. There is an emerging regionwide intellectual consensus—among liberal and Islamic thinkers—about the failures of centralized planned economies and authoritarian polities. In many ways, the intellectual discourse in Algiers, Cairo, Amman, and Kuwait City on these issues is remarkably similar. Because the Arab world is a cultural unit, that intellectual ferment cannot be stopped at state borders. Agreement that the present models have failed does not imply agreement on the proper course to take from here. Liberals and Islamists disagree profoundly on many issues. Among Islamists there are those who are willing to experiment with democratic forms of rule and those who see such institutions as Western-inspired innovations against Islam. However, the growing intellectual consensus on the failure of current political models and the increasing belief in many intellectual circles of the connection among the concepts of limited government, economic development, strong civil society organizations, and political rights is a regionwide force pressing for democratic experiments. As of now, it is a relatively weak force.

Notes

1. This focus on the decision calculus of individual leaders follows from a strand in the democratization literature that emphasizes the contingent nature of transitions to democracy as, in effect, elite bargains aimed at meeting immediate political needs. See, for example, Guillermo O'Donnell and Philippe Schmitter, *Transitions from Authoritarian Rule: Volume 4—Tentative Conclusions about Uncertain Democracies* (Baltimore: Johns Hopkins University Press, 1986); and Samuel Huntington, "Will More Countries Become Democratic?" *Political Science Quarterly* 99, 2 (Summer 1984).

2. Charles Tilly, ed., *The Formation of National States in Western Europe* (Princeton: Princeton University Press, 1975), especially the introduction and conclusion; Otto Hintze, "Military Organization and the Organization of the State," in Felix Gilbert, ed., *The Historical Essays of Otto Hintze* (New York: Oxford University Press, 1975); Perry Anderson, *Lineages of the Absolutist State* (New York: New Left Books, 1974), especially chapters on Eastern Europe; Yousef Cohen et al., "The Paradoxical Nature of State Making: The Violent Creation of Order," *American Political Science Review* 75, 4 (December 1981).

3. This is not to argue that war preparation and war involvement did not affect political development in these states. Barnett argues convincingly that the Egyptian state sacrificed a fair amount of its autonomy to groups that developed to service its strategy of war preparation; Michael Barnett, *Confronting the Costs of War: Military Power, State and Society in Egypt and Israel* (Princeton: Princeton University Press, 1992). However, that does not necessarily lead to democratization.

4. Yehosua Porath, *In Search of Arab Unity, 1930–1945* (London: Frank Cass, 1986); Bruce Maddy-Weitzman, *The Crystallization of the Arab State System,*

1945–1954 (Syracuse: Syracuse University Press, 1993); Patrick Seale, *The Struggle for Syria*, 2nd ed. (New Haven: Yale University Press, 1987).

5. Albert Hourani, "Ottoman Reform and the Politics of the Notables," in William R. Polk and Richard L. Chambers, eds., *Beginnings of Modernization in the Middle East: The Nineteenth Century* (Chicago: University of Chicago Press, 1971).

6. Seale, *The Struggle for Syria*; Malcolm Kerr, *The Arab Cold War*, 3rd ed. (London: Oxford University Press, 1971).

7. Ramollah K. Ramazani, *Revolutionary Iran: Challenge and Response in the Middle East* (Baltimore: Johns Hopkins University Press, 1986); Martin Kramer, ed., *Shi'ism, Resistance and Revolution* (Boulder: Westview Press, 1987), chapters 7–12; John Esposito, ed., *The Iranian Revolution: Its Global Impact* (Miami: Florida International University Press, 1990), chapters 3–9.

8. *New York Times*, 28 March 1993, p. 14.

9. *Al-Hayat*, 17 December 1992, p. 6; 6 December 1992, pp. 1, 4.

10. See, for example, *al-Hayat*, 26 August 1993, pp. 1, 4; *New York Times*, 12 October 1993, p. A3.

11. *Al-Hayat*, 14 December 1992, pp. 1, 4. Musa subsequently was dismissed from his position in April 1993, after meeting with a group of prominent Islamist intellectuals who were trying to mediate between the government and the Islamic opposition in the wake of increased domestic violence in Egypt. In September 1993 Egyptian security sources reiterated their accusations against Iran about involvement in Egyptian domestic politics, but made a distinction between the Sudanese government, which they absolved of meddling in Egyptian domestic politics, and the National Islamic Front of Sudan, headed by Hasan al-Turabi, which they asserted was actively encouraging Egyptian domestic opposition. *Al-Hayat*, 12 September 1993, p. 6.

12. *Al-Hayat*, 25 April 1993, pp. 1, 4.

13. *Al-Diyar* (Beirut), 28 July 1993, in Foreign Broadcast Information Service–Near East and South Asia–93–150.

14. *Al-Hayat*, 5 June 1993, p. 4. Interestingly, he did not include Saudi Arabia or the smaller Gulf monarchies in his list.

15. *Al-Ahram* (Cairo), 3 February 1993 in FBIS–NES–93–021.

16. Excerpts from the charter can be found in Yehudah Mirsky and Matt Ahrens, *Democracy in the Middle East: Defining the Challenge* (Washington, DC: Washington Institute for Near East Policy, 1993), pp. 100–102.

17. Nadav Safran, *Saudi Arabia: Ceaseless Quest for Security* (Cambridge: Harvard University Press, 1985), pp. 268–269; Jill Crystal, *Kuwait: The Transformation of an Oil State* (Boulder: Westview Press, 1992), pp. 97, 99.

18. For a discussion of the Saudi role in the politics of both Yemeni states from the 1960s through the mid-1980s, see F. Gregory Gause III, *Saudi-Yemeni Relations: Domestic Structures and Foreign Influence* (New York: Columbia University Press, 1990).

19. See, for example, Giacomo Luciani, "Allocation vs. Production States: A Theoretical Framework," in Luciani, ed., *The Arab State* (Berkeley: University of California Press, 1990), particularly pp. 76–77.

20. F. Gregory Gause III, *Oil Monarchies: Domestic and Security Challenges in the Arab Gulf States* (New York: Council on Foreign Relations Press, 1994), chapter 4.

21. Stanley Reed, "The Battle for Egypt," *Foreign Affairs* 72, 4 (September–October 1993), p. 95.

22. *Reuters,* 26 January 1994.

23. *Radio Algiers Network,* 26 February 1992 in FBIS–NES–92–039.

24. For accounts of Kuwaiti politics after liberation, see Gause, *Oil Monarchies,* pp. 90–94, 101–105; Crystal, *Kuwait,* chapter 7; Shafeeq Ghabra, "Kuwait: Elections and the Issues of Democratization in a Middle Eastern State," *Digest of Middle East Studies* 2, 1 (Winter 1993).

25. See *Sawt al-sha'b* (Amman), 4 December 1992 in FBIS–NES–92–234; *al-Hayat,* 11 February 1993, p. 4; 24 March 1993, p. 10.

26. *Al-Hayat,* 3 September 1992, p. 1; 11 November 1992, pp. 1, 4.

27. *New York Times,* 24 November 1992, p. A9.

28. See Laurie A. Brand, "Economic and Political Liberalization in a Rentier Economy: The Case of the Hashemite Kingdom of Jordan," in Iliya Harik and Denis J. Sullivan, *Privatization and Liberalization in the Middle East* (Bloomington: Indiana University Press, 1992).

29. The full text of the king's speech can be found in FBIS–NES, 1 August 1988, pp. 39–41.

30. On the events leading up to Yemeni unity, see Charles Dunbar, "The Unification of Yemen: Process, Politics and Prospects," *Middle East Journal* 46, 3 (Summer 1992); and Robert D. Burrowes, "Prelude to Unification: The Yemen Arab Republic, 1962–1990," *International Journal of Middle East Studies* 23, 4 (November 1991).

31. See Sheila Carapico, "Elections and Mass Politics in Yemen," and Renaud Detalle, "The Yemeni Elections Up Close," both in *Middle East Report* 185 (November–December 1993).

32. Election results can be found in *al-Hayat,* 2 May 1993, pp. 1, 4; 3 May 1993, pp. 1, 4.

33. *Al-Hayat,* 16 July 1993, pp. 1, 4.

34. The Yemeni government formed in October 1994 included 28 ministers, nine of whom were from the Islah, with the remainder being either from the GPC or independents seen as close to President Salih and the GPC. *Al-Hayat,* 8 October 1994, pp. 1, 4.

35. See, for example, accounts of domestic Yemeni opposition to Salih in the major Saudi international newspaper *al-Sharq al-Awsat,* 18 September 1990, pp. 1, 4; 21 September 1990, p. 2; 6 March 1991, p. 5.

36. In a 7 September 1994 interview with the London-based Arabic newspaper *al-Quds al-'Arabi,* President Salih accused "two Arab Gulf states" of paying $3.9 billion in bribes and weapons to encourage secession. *United Press International,* on-line, 7 September 1994. The Saudi opposition group "Committee for the Defense of Legitimate Rights," headquartered in London, said that the Saudi government supplied the secessionist regime in Aden with "hundreds of Saudi armored vehicles and tanks and large quantities of ammunition," as well as money. CDLR, *Communique #9,* 28 May 1994. In a long article on the U.S.-Saudi relationship, the *New York Times* reported that Riyad had secretly transferred armored personnel carriers to the Aden regime and had financed the purchase from Bulgaria of MIG-29 aircraft for it. *New York Times,* 4 November 1994, pp. A1, A6.

37. Gause, *Oil Monarchies,* pp. 102–103.

38. See Wahid 'Abd al-Majid, "Aya 'alaqa bayn al-dimuqratiyya wa al-salam ma' Isra'il?" [What Is the Relationship between Democracy and Peace with Israel?], *al-Hayat,* 16 January 1995, p. 15.

15

Prospects of Democratization in the Arab World: Global Diffusion, Regional Demonstration, and Domestic Imperatives

Gabriel Ben-Dor

The idea of democratization is all the rage today.[1] Some of this popularity is due to the assumption that we are witnessing the birth of a new world order, which is characterized by the end of the Cold War, the decline of the ideological element in world politics, the rise of economic considerations, the reduction in the tensions of regional conflict and a form of global consensus about human rights, and concomitant political notions. Among these notions is some vague idea of democracy, more or less along the lines recognized in Western parliamentary and presidential regimes.[2] Hence it makes sense to ask the question to what extent such political trends can be expected to gain ascendancy in the Arab world, bearing in mind that political theory for the time being has failed to come up with a universally accepted definition of the democratic phenomenon.

It is possible to answer this question in many ways, based on many different paradigms of democracy, and just as many paradigms of the Arab world.[3] One can approach the subject from the point of view of the political structure and culture of the Arab world, regardless of the prevailing "world order," and explore the ideas of democracy as they are congruent (and to the extent that they are congruent) with the main components of the domestic political systems concerned. After all, democracy is a political regime, and a political regime by definition has to cater, above all, to the proper domestic constituency. One may argue with conviction that it is the basic fit between the parameters characterizing the traditions of that constituency on the one hand and the main characteristics of the foreign idea on the other that will determine whether or not that idea will ever become authentically part of the political system of the importer, so to speak.

However, political ideas, as we know, are not born in a vacuum, but rather are the products of concrete historical and sociological circumstances. The very existence of modern forms of political organization such as states, parliaments, parties, movements, and interest groups has been a product of complex processes of cultural and political diffusion. This tendency has been reinforced by the rapid growth in communications, which in turn has created political elites that are partly fed by the same intellectual sources as well as modes of popular culture. In addition, many of the key members of these elites were educated in the same schools, and were exposed to the same systems of ideas, as the elites of other countries and in this sense the proverbial "global village" has indeed come into existence. Hence the ancient distinctions between East and West are not as sharp as they used to be, because the impact of the West in both practical forms of political organization as well as cultural penetration has been so overwhelming as to make many of the classic ideas—and techniques—of the West an authentic component of culture around the world.

Global Diffusion and Regional Manifestations

In the light of this process, it is now possible to study the idea of "democratization" as a process of the global diffusion of ideas and cultural influences in dynamic interaction with the components of the concrete historical and sociological realities in various regions of the world. Certainly in the Arab world many boundaries were shaped by the vagaries of Western colonialism, initial political elites were educated by the West (and in the West), and the exposures to the workings of a modern state were primarily Western. In this sense, the existing state in the Middle East is basically the product of the West, in terms of its techniques as well as its basic ideas, albeit the concrete manifestation of these (namely the specific state in the Middle East) is, of course, the synthesis of these fundamentals with the unique circumstances surrounding the emergence of each state and in fact each regime in the region.[4] Yet the strong orientation to the birthplace of the fundamentals remains an important fact of life.

This strong connection is manifest in many ways. Elites in the Middle East are quick to learn the innovations in governmental technology, and they are closely attuned to what is happening in the world at large in terms of the technical progress manifest in the workings of others. The way that some of the key Arab regimes have maintained power over the years and even the decades (as in the cases of Syria and Iraq, to note just two salient examples) has been heavily influenced by outside sources of inspiration, assistance, and consultation. The impact of the colonial powers (France and Britain) was intertwined with the impact of the main outside supplier of arms (the late lamented Soviet Union and its erstwhile "allies"), as well as with the principal source of imitating "modernity," namely the United States and its material culture.[5] All the while, Arab leaders have maintained a high degree of sensitivity to the mainstream of political thinking in the West, because by and large they read in Western languages, think in terms of a worldwide constituency to which they appeal in their political and diplomatic maneuvers, and also because to many of them what the intellectuals and politicians of the mainstream think is important in the subjective sense. By this I mean that while they recognize that the primary constituency for maintaining power is to be found in their own countries as well as in the adjacent centers of Arab nationalism, the constituency for finding personal satisfaction in their achievements is partly to be found elsewhere, where the political fashions of the age reside.

Political fashions in this age are made largely in the English language, in the English-speaking countries, and primarily in the United States. It follows that when the fashions of the age change, the cultural and ideological orientations of the Arab world enter a difficult period. Change is never automatic, but it comes into being potentially. The old ways are now open to question, and the influence of the new ones begins to filter in. There is in most cases a time lag, because Arab leaders and intellectuals have to come to terms with the new realities in the world and think about their possible impact on their own countries, and this takes time. The agents of change (students, journalists, professors, diplomats, officers in training, civilian experts abroad) may lack the influence to bring the new ideas home quickly, and the sinking in of new messages via the electronic media (probably the most potent agent of change today) also takes time to gain a critical mass cumulatively over a given period. Eventually, though, the key people realize that in order to speak to the world constituency effectively a new language has to be adopted, and of course language is never value-neutral. A new language generally means a new politics, and when one loses the monopoly over language, one loses the ability to set the political agenda by exclusive control.

Moreover, every political elite needs a basis for legitimacy, and every political elite attempts to shape the patterns of legitimacy in the political community. Some pundits tend to treat this matter cynically, and they assume that political legitimacy is but a matter of manipulating the public in order to make life for the regime easier, particularly in political communities where the patterns of participation are poorly institutionalized. However, political leaders need to believe that they are doing the right thing, and that history will judge them favorably. By and large, while politicians may be cynical, at the same time they are attuned to the voices of the people in their own communities as well as the relevant constituencies across the border. Of course, this does not preclude cynical manipulation, but there is a need for something acceptable to be manipulated, and that something is the ideological basis of society. And that basis changes over time, largely in response to changes in the environment of the given political system.

The political elites in power in the Arab world have been at the helm for a long time. Some of them are royal dynasties and some of them are revolutionary regimes of military origins. Neither dominant type has come to power by democratic means, and neither has maintained power by democratic means as the term is commonly understood. The leaders themselves know this very well, notwithstanding the colorful ideological mumbo-jumbo that often accompanies political rhetoric in the various countries of the region.[6] At one point in time, it was possible to justify this fact of life by the transitional nature of the period, and hence the need to work out urgent problems of the political community before democratization could and would take place. Liberating all parts of the Arab homeland, dealing with the challenge of Israel, fighting corruption, and introducing rapid economic development in the face of scarcity of resources coupled with extensive population growth in key Arab countries would constitute a reasonable agenda that would precede the formalities of democracy as it is understood in the West.

Moreover, postponing democracy into the indefinite future made all the more sense in light of global trends. Many of the same arguments were heard all over the Third World, and the feeling of solidarity with those countries was not only an important ingredient of the political agenda, but also a source of inspiration as well as legitimation for key political forces in the Middle East, notably the Nasserists and Ba'thists whose own brand of nationalism and socialism was regarded as a peculiarly Arab version of a worldwide phenomenon that also could be discerned in such countries as Burma, Indonesia, Ghana, Yugoslavia, Tanzania, and many others. The idea that this was an authentic reply to the exclusive demands of the West for political legitimacy was widely believed—of course, it was very convenient to believe this in the first place in the light of the characteristics of the regimes themselves. The notion of an "Arab socialism" (just like an "African socialism") coupled with the slogans of Arab nationalism was a convenient shell (and a rallying cry) to assert being different from the imperialists as well as a fitting cover to the prevailing situation in the revolutionary regimes. And the need to react to this trend (what the late Malcolm Kerr used to call "the Arab cold war") in turn allowed all regimes to claim that the ideological struggle involved had to precede the niceties of a Western-type democracy.

Yet now these slogans sound hollow, and not just in the Middle East. The mystique of the Third World is over in much of the globe. The traditional examples and models have disintegrated, and the countries involved outside the Middle East—Ghana, Indonesia, Tanzania, Yugoslavia—no longer argue seriously that they are able to offer an alternative to Western-style democracy that is workable and legitimate. The disintegration of Yugoslavia into a medieval-type free-for-all in which Muslims are systematically persecuted and physically injured is particularly galling to those who believed that the Nasser-Tito relationship of the 1950s and 1960s was based on the emergence of an ideological basis for Arab regimes that could supply a degree of authenticity to those in honest search of an alternative to the old clichés of West and East alike. That this alternative and its spiritual-political cousins are as dead as a doornail is obvious. To the extent that the search for alternatives is serious, the only major direction left is that of fundamentalist Islam, which has indeed emerged as an enormously potent political force supplying a basis for political legitimacy that is wholly authentic to the region.

An even more important development has been the death of communism in Eastern Europe and the virtual disintegration of the Soviet Union.[7] The existence of the USSR as a political and strategic counterweight to the old imperialist world dominated by Americans and Europeans was obviously a favorable fact of life to such Arab regimes as Egypt, Syria, and Iraq, which, as a rule, played with great skill the game of flip-flop diplomacy that was inherent in the situation. Indeed, it is almost impossible to imagine the emergence of the regional and international stature of a Nasserist Egypt without the existence of the potent Soviet alternative to the West, without which the entire regional balance in the Middle East would have been so different as to render the eventual concrete historical development questionable. But that is only a part of the story. The Soviet influence also had a strong ideological dimension. Even though Soviet cultural penetration was minute compared to that of the West, and the Russian language never gained a foothold among Arabs comparable to English or even French, the ideological basis of the Soviet Union, emphasizing collectivism, the primacy of a vanguard party, the need to force an accelerated economic development by central state planning and the possibility of a "people's war" against the imperialists and their lackeys exercised a strong hold over the imagination of many politically involved Arabs.

In fact, it is a wonder that Soviet influence was not even stronger. In light of the fact that a significant segment of two generations of Arabs in key countries was trained in the Soviet Union and Eastern Europe, one can only wonder why the Soviet cultural penetration was not deeper and more enduring. The best pilots, the most senior officers, an elite group of doctors and engineers spent years in the Soviet Union, and then many more years in an intensive relationship with Soviet experts in the Arab countries as well as the Soviet Union itself. Yet the political elite at large (Nasser himself being a prime example) continued to smoke U.S. cigarettes, drive

U.S. cars, watch U.S. movies, and read U.S. newspapers and magazines—in English. This is very significant, because culture—even pop culture—means language, and language is never value-neutral. Hence the depth of Soviet penetration was always limited by the fact that Soviet culture was found basically unattractive and even inaccessible by most Arab leaders. Nevertheless, Soviet ideology was important and it did have a profound impact on the Arab world.

This is all the more remarkable in the light of the many difficulties that any communist-oriented ideology has always had to face in the Middle East. Communism is by nature a profoundly atheist doctrine, whereas Arab politics in almost every variation has been Islamic in some deep sense of the term, and in any case the masses of the constituency at large have remained Muslim in every sense of the term.[8] This fact alone sufficed to give communism a bad name and make it a pejorative term in Arabic. Also, the distance from the Soviet Union, the domination of the USSR by the successors of the Russian empire, which had always been known as the oppressor of Muslims in Central Asia, the complex legalism of the federal system coupled with the Soviet one, the scientific pretensions of Marxism-Leninism, and the oppressive nature of the Soviet presence in Eastern Europe all made Soviet ideology alien as well as suspect. In and of itself, it was no more attractive than the culture it represented, and was found manifestly inferior to its U.S. competitor.

Yet Soviet ideology represented the only significant and somewhat credible challenge to the heritage of the Western imperialists. It defied the claims of the West that the future necessarily belonged to the trends that it, the West, claimed to represent. It presented an alternative model of economic and social development that made a great deal more sense than the one presented by the West, which was based on concrete social circumstances that were so different from anything experienced by the Arabs. Hence its very existence led to a sort of ideological pluralism that was essentially seen as welcome. Also, Soviet ideology was basically prescriptive, future-oriented, and relevant precisely to the issues judged pertinent by radical Arab leaders: national liberation, anti-imperialism, forced and rapid economic development, the privileged role of the political vanguard vis-à-vis the "masses." By contrast, Western ideology appeared excessively and rigidly formal, dealing with form rather than substance, sanctifying the status quo rather than dealing with change, built on the successes of imperialism rather than its failure, and giving little consideration to the needs of the political elite in charge in what were widely regarded as revolutionary times. So a paradox came into being: An alien ideology that represented an unattractive culture spoken in a virtually incomprehensible language came to exercise a strange but enduring fascination over the imagination of a whole generation of energetic and ambitious leaders.

Perhaps the most important consequence of this fascination was simply to reassure the leaders in power in the Arab world that they were doing the right thing and that they were on the right track as far as history was concerned. The Soviet reading of history spoke of the collapse of the capitalist-imperialist West, which was music to Arab ears, and of the ultimate triumph of communism/socialism. One could always ignore the part of the doctrine that spoke of "scientific" socialism, Communism, and the other alien atheist doctrines and instead develop the specific variation of socialism that one could and wished to live with:[9] Arab socialism Nasserist style, Arab socialism Ba'thist style, Islamic socialism in its Saudi or Libyan variations, *Jamahiriyya,* and so on. It is not as if this were a serious attempt to bring to reality a measure of admiration for what was being done in the Soviet Union, but without the strength of the Soviets and the concomitant ideological posture it would not have been possible to present this sense of self-confidence among Arab elites either.

In the radical Arab countries all elites were basically revolutionary elites that had captured power and maintained power by force, although their links to the constituency in the country were, as a rule, far better than those of their predecessors in the so-called liberal period. It was necessary to find not only a justification for this disturbing fact of life, but also for the continuing obsession with power and force, at the expense of its possible relinquishing via some constitutional experiment akin to the Western ideas that most leaders had learned to subscribe to in the formative stages of their political socialization. The Soviet model gave a convenient justification, and its future ramifications via the various "socialist" versions allowed for the continued domination of the political life of the country in the name of legitimate ideals. Most important, it seems that the rulers themselves found it convenient to believe that what they were doing was indeed the "wave of the future," and that they were in good company, as the political order they had cultivated was basically akin to that of the Soviet empire, which also continued to inspire the key countries of the Third World. This affinity, of course, was reinforced by the extensive network of ties developed by the thousands of advisers who flocked from the Soviet bloc into the Arab world, as well as by the links with the relevant countries in Asia and Africa.

The collapse of the Soviet model was a blow of the greatest significance for Arab elites. However, change in the Arab world had begun long before the winds of change started to blow so strongly in the Eastern part of Europe. Military regimes grew older and had to mature somehow. They started to experiment with diverse models of civilianization. The Egyptian postmilitary regime opened up in the direction of some early Gaullist model, whereas the Ba'thists of Syria started building a one-party-dominated, "popular-front"-facaded party state truly reminiscent of Eastern

Europe.[10] To many observers, Saddam Hussein's Iraq eerily resembled Ceaucescu's Romania. Libya went its own way with the ideology of the *Jamahiriyya*, but the importance of that experiment has always been limited not only by the eccentricities of the leader but also by the fact that Libya is a small and remote country in terms of the mainstream of Arab politics. These changes were inspired by the authentic needs of domestic political development as well as by a reading of the trends in world politics relevant to each country. Unquestionably, the economic difficulties of Egypt and the wish to secure massive Western assistance and investment played an important role in the evolution of the regime there in the direction of a more open and competitive society, and of course the economic policies of *infitah* had a political counterpart in a more open presidential monarchy that accepted a fair dose of parliamentary participation and criticism—without relinquishing the ultimate reins of power.[11]

So at the time of the collapse of communism the Arab world was already a full political generation and more removed from the original military regimes, in the age of the postmilitary regimes. These were groping for formulas of legitimacy and participation, something the original military regimes had not satisfactorily resolved. While it would be an unjustified exaggeration to argue that the answers were found in the communist model, it did exercise a strong influence on the political patterns of the postmilitary regime in the Middle East. In the Egyptian case, the move away from anything having to do with the Soviets was clearly discernible in the 1970s. It became stronger with the peace treaty with Israel and the continuing experiments with a form of semi-open political community that tolerates a parliamentary regime with multiparty characteristics, and with a degree of freedom for the press that is completely out of step with the theory and practice of communism in Eastern Europe. The obvious weakness and the ultimate collapse of communism made a great deal of difference in that it reinforced the conviction of the Egyptians that they chose the right option in moving away from the characteristics of the communist model as well as from extensive practical ties with the Soviets.

On the other hand, the Syrian-Iraqi variety of the postmilitary regime did resemble the Soviet–Eastern European model in developing an essentially one-party pattern of dictatorship, with occasional openings in the direction of some popular front, allowing the existence and functioning of other parties under the leadership of the vanguard Ba'thists. One can argue to what extent the ruling party indeed has been institutionalized as a party proper, apart from the personality of the leader and the alliances and allegiances that he brought with him and forged in the course of maintaining power. Some argue that the party in Eastern Europe was infinitely better institutionalized, whereas in the Arab case the personal-ethnic element largely predominated. Be that as it may, clearly the Syrian and Iraqi elites derived much encouragement from the existence of regimes such as the one in Romania, and they must have experienced not just disappointment but also anxiety when that model was overthrown by a revolution uniting a popular uprising and the armed forces.

Of course one should not jump to hasty conclusions, because the differences between the circumstances of the cases are so great, but still, the changes in Eastern Europe, coupled with the practical consequences of the retreat of the Soviet Union from the Middle East and then its total collapse, led to gigantic changes. One major example of this would be the transformation in the political attitudes of one key Arab country, Syria, which went on to capitalize on the favorable opportunities presented by the 1991 Gulf War in order to introduce (some will say *accelerate*) a shift in its regional and international orientation, effectively reducing the traditional pro-Soviet orientation that had been an overwhelming fact of life for this regime practically since its inception.[12] It would be exceedingly naive to assume that changes of such magnitude can take place in virtual isolation from domestic consequences, particularly since the revolution of communications allows the population to follow the changes through the foreign media, at least to some extent.

This is an important factor in political change everywhere, and certainly the Middle East is no exception. The Arab countries have highly developed systems of communications and listening to the radio and watching television in them is a matter of habit for the masses as well as the elites. Moreover, a large number of observers have noted that the Arab political environment puts a premium on the spoken word; hence the importance of access to the words spoken across the world in general and in the Arab world in particular.[13] Such access, while by no means guaranteed in the tightly controlled communications systems in the region, still substantially exists because developments in the technology of transmissions have reached a stage where it is no longer practical, in most cases, to jam foreign broadcasts (among other things, for the fear of also jamming your own), and the miniaturization of radio receivers clearly calls the control of the state over broadcasting into serious question. In addition to this, atmospheric conditions in the Middle East are extremely favorable to long-range radio and television reception, so that the proverbial "global village" in the area exists at least in the form of a "regional village." It follows that political trends may generate their own momentum, and that the famous cluster effect, or epidemiological effect of change, is probably as important in the Middle East as anywhere in the world, particularly if we also keep in mind the common language and culture that substantially exist among Arab countries, helping to facilitate the maintenance of a common political agenda across state boundaries.

It would be a vast exaggeration to state that the "epidemic" of democratization is already under way. On the other hand, it is clear that various Arab countries have decided one way or another to experiment with diverse forms of opening up their systems to more participation and competition, something that seems to me well entrenched in the prevailing trends of world politics, and hence something that is likely to continue in one form or another. And it does appear that one major reason for this is the collapse of communism and the Soviet Union, something that leaves the arena clear for the ideological domination of the West at a time when the earlier grudges held by many Arab elites against the colonial heritage of the West are still very much a fact of life. Of course, the outcome of the new order in the countries that used to be communist is still most uncertain, and this is again something of the highest importance in terms of a "demonstration effect." If these countries manage to achieve success with some form of democracy, the tendency to experiment with more open systems in the Middle East is likely to continue and even gather momentum. On the other hand, if there is a major relapse in the key countries into some other form of authoritarianism, it is likely that this new form will be a potent competitor for democratic experiments still largely inspired by Western examples.

The key countries include the large successor states such as Russia and Ukraine, along with Belarus and Kazakhstan, the nuclear powers to have emerged from the grave of the Soviet Union. But that is not all. The five Islamic republics of the late Soviet Union enjoy a special relevance and privileged standing in this regard. In fact, some of the more active Islamic forces in the Middle East, among them Saudi Arabia and Iran, have pursued an energetic policy, trying to affect the patterns of future development in the area, as has been the case also with Turkey. It is obvious that the experience of these five republics will have special significance for the entire Middle East because of the continuing emergence of Islam as the most potent popular political force in the region, and also because of the accumulated experience of those Arab countries experimenting with a more open political system. These experiments (as in Egypt, Jordan, and Algeria) have invariably involved a confrontation of sorts between the regime on the one hand and some sort of Islamic fundamentalism on the other.[14] Although the degree of the fundamentalist penetration into Central Asia is not at all clear, it is obvious that the interplay of the collapse of communism, its vestiges, the influence of the Western models of capitalist democracy, and the diverse manifestations of political Islam is particularly salient in the making of the new political order in Central Asia. It is equally obvious that the factors at play there are more immediately relevant to the Islamic countries in the Middle East than the more complex, remote, if more visible, experiments with political transformation in the more alien political climate of Eastern Europe proper.

The outcome in all these cases is far from certain, nor is even a clear direction discernible at the moment. What is clear is that the only two major forces that have a massive impact on the thinking of the future leadership in the new countries are Islam and some form of Western democracy. As the Arab countries themselves (indeed, also Turkey and Iran) have had major difficulties in working out a practical synthesis or even coexistence between these two poles, any successful example of coming to terms with it would have to have a major impact as a demonstration of possibilities and directions inherent in the situation. The fact that the new synthesis, if indeed one is found, will be based also on extensive experience with the local forms of socialism will merely add more depth to the new form of political modus operandi. Yet it is, of course, possible that the new forms will not be found soon, and indeed, it is also possible to envisage a lengthy period of political disorder or even chaos in Central Asia, due to the difficulties of creating an authentic political community out of the collapse of the huge and diverse Soviet empire. In other words, it is conceivable that no clear outcome will emerge in either Eastern Europe or Central Asia, but that a protracted, unclear "transition period" will be the order of the day for quite some time, perhaps an entire political generation.

It is impossible to determine how such a state of affairs, which is not at all unlikely, will affect the politics of the Arab world. It appears safe to say that in this case there would be fewer relevant models to relate to, so that authentic indigenous sources of political development will become that much more important. One might also anticipate that, in the event of something resembling chaos in Eastern Europe and Central Asia, some of the Arab countries that have accumulated extensive political experience with Western models, such as Egypt, will prefer to look to the source, the West, more than to the derivations around the world, no matter how relevant from the technical point of view the latter may appear to be. In other words, the demonstration effect will be unmediated, perhaps less immediately relevant, but in a more pristine form.

It is not possible, of course, to find clear answers to any of these questions about the future. Yet one needs to make certain assumptions about the future trends that shape the political environment in which the Arab political system operates. If the assumption is that the present global trends will continue in more or less the same direction, then the conclusion is that the external influences pointing to the need to experiment with some form of democracy will get stronger,[15] that the cultural and ideological impact of the West will be unopposed by anything of significance that may have emanated in the past from Eastern Europe, and that the various components of the "good life" as understood in the West will continue to filter in to the consciousness of Arab elites and masses via the media of mass communications, without having an alternative ideological vision from its historical competitors. Moreover, it also makes sense to assume that the demise of communism in this rapid and at times brutal form will continue to pose psychological challenges to the ruling elites, in some cases shaking some of their self-confidence.

Of course, the collapse of communism, while obviously enhancing the appeal of Western-style political systems, does not do away with the highly negative legacy of Western imperialism in the Middle East. Nor does it erase the widespread feeling among many Arabs that the postcolonial West is inherently anti-Arab as manifest, above all, in pro-Israeli policies. Among Islamists, in particular, there may also be a view that Western society is materialistic and permissive, if not inherently corrupt and morally depraved.

Such negative associations between democracy and "things Western" are mitigated, however, by several factors. First, today's leaders are now three generations removed from the painful days of direct Western imperialism (and early Western-supported pseudo-democratic experiments). Second, even the salience of the Arab-Israeli conflict is changing amidst peace negotiations or agreements between Israel and its neighbors—*raison d'état* seems more broadly accepted than ever. Third, Arab leaders and intellectuals today realize the complexity of Western society with its good, as well as bad, aspects. Finally, there has been no really successful alternative to the (failed) communist and (more successful) democratic models. Islamic forces in the Arab world offer one, but at present they are all forces of opposition, lacking the responsibility of power. Moreover, there is increasing recognition among many Islamists that democracy may be utilized as a useful vehicle for transforming society into one that is more in tune with Islamic ideals.

Regional Diffusion and Domestic Imperatives

Needless to say, none of this should be taken to mean that we can expect rapid and massive democratization any time soon.[16] It does mean that the international environment will be more favorable for such a development, but of course domestic political order is primarily a matter of the authentic political development of the society in question, so that the more basic questions about the future of democracy have to be asked within the context of the political realities *inside* the Arab countries, even if the external circumstances clearly point to a certain direction of change. More specifically, the traditional literature points to two problem areas of major significance.

One is the set of characteristics that the Arab world shares with the rest of the so-called Third World, also referred to as the developing countries, non-Western countries, and other euphemisms.[17] If we ignore the difficult definitional questions for a moment, the gist of the argument is that democracy is not necessarily a universally marketable commodity but perhaps is merely the product of very unique circumstances prevailing at a given moment in history in a small part of the globe. Not more than two dozen or so countries are involved, and these happen to be located primarily in Western Europe and North America, as well as other countries stemming from the same tradition, as in the case of the English-speaking democracies in other continents. With a couple of notable exceptions, as in the cases of India and Japan, that is about all. Hence it is clear that countries that do not share the social and economic characteristics of the small group of democratic societies will have difficulty constructing a democratic system, and indeed we may well ask whether it is even reasonable for us to expect that this will be attempted in the first place.[18] In other words, the theory is not that there is something unique and different about the Arabs that makes it difficult for them to adopt democracy, but rather that there is something unique and different about those who are democratic, and that others should not be expected to subscribe to the same political values, and even if they do, they should not be expected to be successful until the socioeconomic foundations of their countries change substantially in the direction of those of the original democracies.

Of course, the Arab world is diverse; certainly in terms of income per capita, distribution of national income, and other socioeconomic indices it is split into many different categories. Likewise, in some cases its rates of literacy rival those of Europe, whereas in others they are typically low Third World rates. As a whole, though, the key Arab countries share the basic characteristics of those countries that in general have not adopted—or have not adopted successfully—Western models of democracy, and certainly the literature points out that until the socioeconomic conditions improve to the point where they resemble those of the original two dozen democracies, democratic experiments may not succeed for lack of favorable circumstances. This literature does not really explain how such huge exceptions as India function, though. It turns out that this "exception," which is the world's largest democracy, has just about all the typical characteristics of the socioeconomic realities of the Third World and, in addition, suffers from debilitating ethnic tensions as well as external threats and involvements in nationalist-religious disputes. Yet it has maintained a democracy that, although much criticized by purists, is impressive by any standard and certainly stands out as thought-provoking in the extreme. It is not sufficient for the literature to point out that India is an exception, because it is such a major "exception" that its patterns need to be explained in order to demonstrate the potential inherent in other countries.

The second major point is that of Islam. There can be no question as to the overwhelming importance of the Islamic heritage in the political culture and ideology of the Arab world. This was true even in the heyday of messianic socialist-nationalism, and is certainly that much more true with its decline, to be replaced by a resurgence of Islamic fundamentalism that appears to be easily the most vital and popular mass movement in the 1990s. If one can debate to what extent there is a clear relationship between Islam and democracy, certainly the relationship between fundamentalism and democracy is obvious not only to the outside analyst, but also to those in power who conduct the experiments in democracy. It is not easy to find a fully developed argument that is convincing on Islam and democracy. The arguments that Islam is collectivist and that it is not sufficiently concerned with the individual as the most important ontological unit in a democratic environment seem to be too sweeping and lack sufficient support from history and society.[19] Then there is the example of Turkey, a Muslim country in the Middle East that has experimented with democracy for decades.[20] The example is ambiguous. Some will point to the basic success of the country in creating strong foundations for democracy and a political-military elite devoted to its ideals. Others will point to the huge center-periphery discrepancies that make the basic ideals the property of a relatively small segment of the population, whereas the mass of the people (those with whom a democracy is properly concerned) remain committed to Islamic ideals, voting into power people who then have to be removed by force by the military as the most potent segment of an elite steeped in another culture.[21]

Many will argue that Turkish democracy is unstable and plagued with a lack of consensus not because of Islam, but precisely because it lacks the Islamic component. It is the invention and imposition of an elite dedicated to ideas totally alien to the masses of the population. Hence, the periodic revolts against the existing regime represent attempts at finding a political identity that does not derive from secular nationalism but rather from a more profound domestic force that is difficult to define, but one that certainly will have to include a very strong Islamic ingredient, as that is the language people apparently consider truly their own. It is clear that the Turkish model of democracy in a Middle Eastern Islamic society does not resolve the tensions and the issues, but rather raises the strong possibility that Turkey itself will have to undergo a massive political transformation before its democracy is stabilized in a form that is close to a societywide consensus. And that consensus, which is not yet clearly discernible, certainly does not include such ideas as the separation of Islam and state, something that the elite has wanted literally since the inception of the Republic, but the masses of the people seem to want little or no part of it.

Still, the example of Turkey can by no means be taken to imply that Islam as such is the main stumbling block in the transition to democracy. At best, one can make the argument that a blind attempt to copy outside models of democracy is bound to fail because, if it is based on the separation of church and state (which, by the way, is only one of several approaches to this complex subject), it ignores the strength of Islam, which, as a civilization rather than a mere "religion," cannot be separated from politics within the existing paradigms, no matter how diverse and liberal.[22] Hence an authentic Arab variety of democracy will have to find some honest and original solution to this problem. This is not impossible but at the present time the solution still seems elusive. Moreover, the pressure of Islamic fundamentalism sweeping large parts of the Arab world as a huge mass movement authentically and radically challenging the existing regimes does not allow the time needed to think slowly and carefully about future possibilities. Where Islamic fundamentalism does strike (which is in most places in the region), the future is now, and practical solutions are needed in the short run in order to allow regimes to survive, let alone experiment with legitimate and orderly transitions to democracy.

The literature[23] insists that outbreaks of Islamic radicalism have to do with societal crises such as the present crises of modernization (identity, legitimacy, social justice, and the like). The present crisis is not likely to go away soon because the problems are endemic to most countries. The lack of balance between population and resources, the question of participation in the political process of the territorial state, the relationship between Islam, state, nation, and tribe, the difficulties of dealing with Israel and everything it represents, the ambivalence of the attitudes to the West, the generally poor performance of the socialist-nationalist regimes are all facts of life (and in some cases, historical memories) that are likely to endure for a prolonged period.[24] It does not seem realistic to expect the wave of fundamentalist Islam to abate soon because the social conditions that breed it are going to be with us for quite some time. The arguments about the relationship between Islam and democracy are lengthy and complicated, and in some ways they are better left alone in the present context: Either they are dealt with in voluminous detail, or not at all. On the other hand, it is obvious that fundamentalist mass movements and democracy have indeed difficulties in getting along, and this is seen time and again in practice.

There have been notable experiments in various Arab countries to open up the political system. While the results could hardly have been called democratic by exacting theoretical standards, there is no question that the recent experiments in Egypt, Jordan, and Algeria indeed have indicated a shift toward genuine competition and their institutionalization in relatively free parliamentary elections.[25] Hence the results of these experiments are of some general significance, particularly since they represent quite different orientations to Arab politics in three countries with extremely divergent societies and histories. Yet they all ended in relative failure (in total failure, in the case of Algeria) because the results have been discouraging to the values of the ruling elites to such a radical extent as to call in question the wisdom of future experiments. This is significant because ultimately the motivations to experiment with different forms of political organization may originate from external sources, but the judgment whether to continue will as a rule be made on the basis of domestic circumstances, and when the two clash the domestic imperative of the rulers to survive is always bound to be stronger than the response to the external political fashions of the day.

The lesson of the three experiments is that open and democratic elections mean mass movements contesting elections, and that there are no authentic mass movements other than Islamic fundamentalism. Political movements are not created out of nothing, so when elections come the political forces able to contest them are those that are "authentic," regardless of the momentary orientation of the regime. It turns out that the only such movement is some variation of Islamic fundamentalism. It simply preempts the center of political activity when the masses are brought in (as they inevitably are in a general election), and as long as the alternative ideological forces continue to be weak, this is not likely to change. Indeed, some observers argue that this is *never* likely to change. Bernard Lewis,[26] for instance, argued a long time ago that the more popular a political force in the Arab world the more Islamic it is going to be. Hence, there may be a built-in, internal contradiction in democratization. On the one hand, it encourages the free organization of mass politics. On the other hand, it leads to a result that is not only unacceptable to the political values that supported the idea of democratization in the first place, but also the danger arises that the results will bring about the demise of democracy itself.

In the light of this paradoxical dilemma inherent in the nature of democratization in the Arab countries,[27] the experiments in Egypt, Jordan, and Algeria are not really surprising. They have demonstrated that opening up the system for electoral competition leads to the elections being successfully contested by those who are able to attract the support and loyalty of the masses. It turns out that neither the aura of revolution and national liberation (as with the FLN in Algeria) nor the tradition of respecting the rulers in power at the center (as in the case of Egypt) nor the respect for the dynasty that founded the state (as in the case of Jordan) are sufficient to overcome the attraction of fundamentalist Islam as a focus of identification and loyalty for the masses. This raises the question to what extent the ruling elites in these three countries were correct in arguing that allowing the fundamentalists to win would have led to the demise of democracy itself, because the fundamentalists would have imposed a Khumayni-like theocracy that would have put an end to the free and competitive nature of the system right there and then.

Of course, there are differences between the three countries mentioned. Certainly it appears that the case of the Islamic Salvation Front (FIS) in Algeria differs substantially from that of the Muslim Brothers in Egypt and Jordan. It is not certain that the accusations of disloyalty to democracy in the Algerian case are indeed convincing. Besides, one wonders how the basic decision on holding elections was made when it was known that the fundamentalists would participate and that it was not inconceivable for them to win in some sense of the term. Holding democratic elections, after all, means taking a risk that the results would not be in accordance with the values of those now in power, or else there would be little point in holding them in the first place. On the other hand, it is acceptable practice in even the most developed democracies in the West to exclude from participating in elections (and perhaps political life in general) those who do not subscribe to the principles of the constitutional order, and whose victory in an election might raise the specter of the end of democracy. Of course, this is *not* done in the middle of an election when the opposition seems well on its way to winning, or in the wake of an election in which the opposition wins "too many" seats. Excluding someone from contesting an election necessitates a careful cultivation of a national consensus that has to be supported by all the other main political forces in society, and this is a very complex and lengthy process that takes a long time, by the nature of things.

Understandably, the revolutionary upheavals and the lack of democracy in the Arab countries in the last two generations have generally prevented such a consensus from emerging, so that the reaction of the respective regimes in the three countries has not only left a bitter taste in the mouths of even the most sympathetic observers, but also has left a cynical residue of appearing to be less than sincere when talking about "democratization." Such cynicism also means dangers when it comes to the political socialization of the generation that has just experienced its first encounter with experiments in democracy and that will have to be the backbone of experiments in the future. Unfortunate experience with democracy in the formative stages has in the past had devastating negative consequences for a whole generation of young Arab leadership and it would be a supreme irony of history to have that experience repeated once again precisely at a time when the notions of democracy along Western lines are accepted more extensively worldwide than at any time since the classic age of colonialism.[28]

Yet one cannot expect rulers in power to legislate themselves out of power, particularly when this means handing over power to political forces that do not promise adherence to democratic principles. Of course, there is no way to tell whether they would stick to their promises, even if promises were made. Yet the example of Iran, which is the only example we do have of a fundamentalist regime actually in power in the Middle East (with the exception of the Sudan) is not encouraging. Certainly the patterns of the development of that regime are not in the direction of the worldwide trend to democratization. While the regime is undeniably more popular with the masses than its predecessor, it is not more democratic, and it does not really represent an improvement from the point of view of either the basic principles of constitutional government or the formal processes associated with a democratic political process. Of course, fundamentalists will argue that the example of Iran is not one that they would follow slavishly, and they may be right. However, the suspicions are heavy.

Much has been said about a liberal version of Islam. There have been many such versions in the past and undoubtedly there will be many more later. But this is not only a question of theory or theology. The real question is not whether a logical synthesis can be found between Islam and democracy (indeed, any religion and democracy bear a certain similarity to this dilemma), but whether the synthesis will be sufficiently attractive to the masses of those who have to vote people and parties into office if democratic elections are held. No one knows the answer to this question but there is little enough reason for optimism. A synthesis by definition invites complexities and compromises that are not easy to understand and these rarely inspire a mass following, particularly in the atmosphere of crisis that now prevails in key Arab countries. A liberal approach to religion is something that is not difficult to accomplish in the intellectual sense, but the resulting product may be all but impossible to market to the masses of the people as an ideological alternative to the prevailing messages. Hence it is a mistake to regard the question of Islam *as such* as central. Rather, it is the question of mass politics that is the secret to a possible transition to enduring democracy when democratic experiments are undertaken. If an effective alternative to radical versions of Islam is not found, democratic competition appears to be doomed. The nature of that alternative is far from clear but the quest will have to go on.

One other major factor has to be mentioned. One principal difficulty with the transition to democracy is the collectivist approach to politics that is the natural result of an order of priorities geared to protracted international conflict. The Arab-Israeli conflict is a classic case of a "protracted conflict" that has engaged the attention, energy, and other resources of the protagonists to an extent that can only be called "obsessive," without regard to the basic justice of the claims raised by the parties.[29] The investment of such huge resources in something that has endured for so long, and that is not likely to produce a sense of justice any time soon, has had debilitating consequences for all involved. It has also had very negative implications for democracy. It is well-known that when the guns thunder, the muses fall silent. This also means that when a society is engaged in international struggles for decades, no matter how just the cause may be or seem to be, the creative talents and energies of its best and brightest will be harnessed for the most part to promote the cause on the international scene rather than to resolve the domestic problems. Although the two were connected in the past, the connection appeared to be for the most part unidirectional. This means that in practice the various fiascoes in the Arab-Israeli conflict inspired domestic change, but not enough thought was given to the possibilities for democracy inherent in the potential reduction in the intensity of the Arab-Israeli conflict.

One possible exception to this general statement was the Sadat initiative, which clearly had a strong domestic motivation, even though not necessarily one oriented to democracy as such. One may argue to what extent the aftermath of the peace treaty between Egypt and Israel has really enhanced the chances for democracy in Egypt, and the record appears to be mixed. Of course, that peace is only partial and the tensions associated with the conflict continue to plague Egyptian society and its intellectual leadership. Moreover, substantial elements in the Egyptian body politic, among them the fundamentalists whose power is evidently on the upsurge, are vehemently opposed to the peace treaty. Yet it is not possible to imagine the serene environment needed for a democratic government within the trials and tribulations engendered by the bitterness of protracted conflict that involves nations, religions, ethnicity, and ideology. As there is very little likelihood that a solution to this conflict can be found in the foreseeable future along lines that will satisfy the major historical objectives of the Arab countries, it will be necessary to find some compromises and creative solutions that will allow the conflict to abate so as to free up energy and other resources for domestic transformation.[30] The changes in world politics in the wake of the demise of the Soviet empire and the growing emphasis on the need to find negotiated solutions to regional conflict have already created a certain momentum in this direction, but the question is far from settled.

Conclusion

No one can foresee the future with certainty. We can only make conjectures about the future (based on the past and the present)[31] and assume that we have missed no sharp discontinuities, such as unforeseen technological innovation or the appearance of new ideological forces. Assuming that the future will be strongly related to the present, we can hypothesize that the changing international environment and the disappearance of old ideological and political forces has created a positive momentum toward experiments with democracy in the Arab countries. While these experiments do not necessarily satisfy all the criteria of the formalities of constitutional democracy, they do involve opening up the political system for freer elections and greater participation and communications by more diverse political forces in society. The success of these experiments depends predominantly on the ability of the given societies to generate mass ideologies that can compete with Islamic fundamentalism within a democratic framework and on the possible reduction in the tensions of the Arab-Israeli conflict with its obsessive ideological radicalism. This is a tall order, and at the moment there seems to be no convincing reason for excessive optimism.[32] Yet precisely the antecedents of the present situation, such as the Sadat initiative in 1977 and the popular revolt in Eastern Europe culminating in the collapse of communist dictatorship there, demonstrate the creative potential inherent in the present global and regional conditions. The prospects for democracy in the Arab world may still not look very bright, but they are now brighter than at any time since the late 1940s. One can only hope that the opportunity will not be missed.

Epilog

This is a paper by an Israeli professor of political science on some of the most painful problems of Arab society. By the nature of things, many Arab intellectuals (and also many Western intellectuals who are sympathetic to Arab societies) do not like statements by Israelis about domestic Arab problems, let alone about the ideological foundations of those societies. I am not surprised by that—indeed, I would be surprised if things were otherwise in the light of the tortuous history of the Arab-Israeli conflict and the resulting ideological and intellectual perversions that plague any attempt at a normal academic intercourse. Still, I would like to assure the prospective reader that the writing of this paper was motivated neither by the secret joy of dealing with the soft underbelly of a rival set of countries, nor by any arrogant ambition to preach to others from the lofty fortress of one who is smugly satisfied with his own society, but rather by a genuine desire to assess a situation in a society that I honestly wish to be successful in its challenging efforts to find its own way to a more democratic form of government. I do admit to a bias in favor of democracy as a better form of government than any other, but this is a general statement, and it does not mean that I "condemn" other forms of conducting political intercourse, especially under historical circumstances that make democracy very difficult to implement.

Why bother to read (and think about) a paper by an Israeli scholar on peculiarly Arab problems? For one, he may have something to say that stems not from "Israeliness" but from being a reasonably well-trained political scientist. Second, an Israeli perspective (not *the* Israeli perspective, but *an* Israeli perspective) may be interesting simply because it is different, or assumed to be different, so that its comparison to other points of view may be revealing. Third, Israelis live in the Middle East (they differ much less from others in the Middle East than is normally assumed, and certainly their problems with democracy, strained by the Arab-Israeli conflict, are relevant to the rest of the region, at least to some extent) and their insights into the problems of the area, discounting all possible biases, are probably sharper than those of totally objective and "detached" outsiders. (It seems to me that the record of Israeli scholarship on the history, sociology, and politics of the Middle East easily bears this out.) Finally, any serious and sustained attempt at an Arab-Israeli scholarly intercourse is valuable in its own right. In that spirit, Arab scholars should be encouraged to have their say on the problems of democracy in Israel. I, for one, am looking forward to reading the fruits of their labor, and I promise to treat them in the spirit in which my efforts will, I hope, be received by them.

Notes

1. This chapter is a general survey of global and regional trends affecting the chances for a more democratic Middle East, and a more democratic Arab world, in particular. The author is aware that literally every word in this statement (democracy, Arab world, etc.) is subject to controversy and problems of definition and measurement. Yet it is not the intention here to enter into any of these ontological and epistemological controversies, as the shortage of space would not allow this treatment. Consequently there are but a very few references to the relevant literature. However, for a survey of the most widely prevailing trends see the special issue of the *Middle East Journal* 47, 2 (Spring 1993) devoted to this problem. A fuller analysis of the ethical and moral questions involved is to be found in Gabriel Ben-Dor, "The Modern State in the Middle East: The Need for a Human Face," York Centre for International and Strategic Studies, Occasional Paper, April 1993. For a convincing exposition of the key concept of civil society see Edward Shils, "The Virtue of Civil Society," *Government and Opposition* 26 (Winter 1991).

2. Of the innumerable works attempting to define or characterize democracy my favorite (meaning the one that I believe to be the most useful) is Robert Dahl, *Polyarchy* (New Haven: Yale University Press, 1971).

3. See Saad Eddin Ibrahim, "Crises, Elites and Democratization in the Arab World," *Middle East Journal* 47, 2 (Spring 1993).

4. See Gabriel Ben-Dor, *State and Conflict in the Middle East* (New York: Praeger, 1983).

5. Gabriel Ben-Dor, "Civilianization of Military Regimes in the Arab World," *Armed Forces and Society* 1, 3 (Spring 1975).

6. See Elie Kedourie, *Democracy and Arab Political Culture* (Washington Institute for Near East Policy, 1992).

7. See Samuel P. Huntington, "Democracy's Third Wave," *Journal of Democracy* 2, 2 (Spring 1991).

8. Timothy D. Sisk, *Islam and Democracy: Religion, Politics and Power in the Middle East* (Washington, DC: U.S. Institute of Peace, 1992).

9. The seemingly endless struggle between these is brilliantly documented and explored in one of the true classics of Middle East politics: Malcolm Kerr, *The Arab Cold War*, 3rd ed. (London: Oxford University Press, 1972).

10. See Ben-Dor, "Civilianization of Military Regimes in the Arab World."

11. Sami Zubaida, "Islam, the State and Democracy: Contrasting Conceptions of Society in Egypt," *Middle East Report* 179 (November–December 1992).

12. See Raymond Hinnebusch, "State and Civil Society in Syria," *Middle East Journal* 47, 2 (Spring 1993).

13. See the literature quoted in Gabriel Ben-Dor, "Political Culture Approach to Middle East Politics," *International Journal of Middle East Studies* 8, 1 (January 1977) and Tawfic Farrah and Yasamusa Kuroda, *Political Socialization in the Arab States* (Boulder: Lynne Rienner, 1987).

14. See, for instance, Daniel Pipes, *In the Path of God: Islam and Political Power* (New York: Basic Books, 1991); Judith Miller, "The Challenge of Radical Islam," *Foreign Affairs* 71, 2 (Spring 1993); and John Esposito and James Piscatori, "Democratization and Islam," *Middle East Journal* 45, 3 (Summer 1991). Of course, the literature on this continues to be voluminous and full of controversy.

15. Augustus R. Norton, "The Future of Civil Society in the Middle East," *Middle East Journal* 47, 2 (Spring 1993), p. 216.

16. See Gudrun Krämer, "Liberalization and Democracy in the Arab World," *Middle East Report* 174 (January–February 1992).

17. The literature on this complex and ancient subject is so huge that it is hopeless even to refer to it. However, some of the residue of this literature is quoted and analyzed perceptively in Krämer, "Liberalization and Democracy in the Arab World," as well as in Elie Kedourie, *Politics in the Middle East* (London: Oxford University Press, 1992). The single best-known work on the subject is Seymour Martin Lipset, *Political Man* (New York: Anchor Books, 1961).

18. See Samuel P. Huntington, "Will More Countries Become Democratic?" *Political Science Quarterly* 99, 2 (Summer 1984) and his classic *Political Order in Changing Societies* (New Haven: Yale University Press, 1968).

19. There is, of course, an extensive literature that is critical of these generalizations, and much controversy abounds around this. See, for example, the critique of the political culture approach in this volume by Lisa Anderson. This article can be considered a prototype of such literature.

20. See Engin Akarli and Gabriel Ben-Dor, eds., *Political Participation in Turkey* (Ankara: Bosphorus University Press, 1974).

21. This appears to be a classic case of what the literature in political sociology refers to as a "center-periphery cleavage."

22. Nor should this be taken in a simplistic vein. As Norton and others point out (Norton, "The Future of Civil Society in the Middle East," p. 211), democracy is not only a matter of formal political systems, but also one of a complex interplay of associations and institutions that are a buffer between state and citizen. Surely the Islamic flavor of these institutions (and hence of civil society as such) cannot and should not be expected to "go away" or "wither away," as the ancient formulation by Engels and Lenin would probably have it.

23. See, inter alia, Esposito and Piscatori, "Democratization and Islam."

24. This was pointed out emphatically in 1962 by Manfred Halpern in his *The Politics of Social Change in the Middle East* (Princeton: Princeton University Press) and has not been refuted since.

25. See Ibrahim, "Crises, Elites and Democratization in the Arab World."

26. "The Return of Islam," *Commentary*, January 1976.

27. And not only there, as the example of mass movements in Western Europe in the 1930s eloquently demonstrates.

28. As is well known, there was an earlier age of liberal experiments in the Arab world (in the immediate postcolonial period) that ended in a resounding failure. It seems to me that the literature on that period should now be critically evaluated as an important stepping stone toward a sophisticated theoretical structure on the future of Arab democracy.

29. See Gabriel Ben-Dor and David B. Dewitt, eds., *Conflict Management in the Middle East* (Lexington, MA: Lexington Books, 1987) for the elucidation of the concept of protracted conflict (invented by Edward Azar) and its consequences for the Middle East.

30. See Gabriel Ben-Dor and David B. Dewitt, eds., *Confidence Building in the Middle East* (Westport: Greenwood Press, 1994).

31. Reinhardt Bendix, *Nation Building and Citizenship* (New York: Wiley, 1962).

32. See Michael Hudson, "After the Gulf War: Prospects for Democratization in the Arab World," *Middle East Journal* 45, 3 (Summer 1991).

Conclusion

16

Trends, Trajectories, or Interesting Possibilities? Some Conclusions on Arab Democratization and Its Study

Rex Brynen, Bahgat Korany, and Paul Noble

This volume has explored key issues and debates regarding the role of culture, civil society, economic forces, and the broader international system in shaping current or potential processes of political liberalization and democratization in the Arab world. But is such attention really warranted, either theoretically or substantively?

Democracy and the Study of Arab Politics

At a theoretical level, several objections might be raised to the study of democracy and Arab politics. Perhaps an intellectual preoccupation with democracy (or its lack) blinds scholars to other, equally important, political processes. It can be suggested that recent attention to democracy is inappropriate or overoptimistic, given contemporary political realities—realities characterized by the violent collapse of the reform process in Algeria and Yemen, by regression or stagnation in Tunisia and Egypt, and by, at best, mixed signs in Jordan, Morocco, and Lebanon. An even more sweeping critique would suggest that recent scholarship on political reform has become a virtual "democratization industry" sustained by a combination of academic fad, grant-seeking scholars, would-be consultants, and government agencies seeking an intellectual underpinning to their current efforts to promote pro-Western political forces and market economies.[1] Or perhaps, as Islamist and other intellectuals have sometimes been heard to complain, it simply conceals an ethnocentric desire to impose Western values and Western political dominance on the Middle East.[2]

All of these concerns are valid. As noted at the outset of this volume, the study of democratization has certainly entered academic fashion in contemporary political science—although not without reason, given transitions in Latin America, Eastern Europe, and elsewhere. Attention to issues of democracy and "good governance" on the part of Western governments reflects a variety of motives, including both a liberal hope that the global triumph of capitalism and democracy will ultimately usher in a (Western-led) global system characterized by greater peace, freedom, and prosperity, and a more cynical use of human rights issues to punish unfriendly (but not friendly) regimes.[3] Specific government-supported programs in this area, such as the U.S. Agency for International Development's "Democratic Institutions Support Project" for the Middle East, usually emphasize economic liberalization as a vital concomitant of political reform.[4] Moreover, most scholars who study democratization—non-Arab and Arab alike—harbor a clear normative bias in favor of liberal democratic outcomes. This preference undoubtedly finds some implicit or explicit expression in their work, particularly in their selection of research topics. Consequently, there is a real danger that the democratic aspirations of scholars will lead them to read an unjustified democratic teleology into their subject matter, conceptualizing liberal democracy as a sort of natural "endpoint" of political development rather than focusing on the underlying social struggles that comprise the real raw material of all politics. Similarly, scholarship on democracy sometimes seems based on the uncritical presumption that democracy is a universally empowering process, benefiting one and all (excepting, perhaps, former dictators).

None of these criticisms, however, really invalidates the study of political liberalization and democratization in the Arab world. Rather, the value of such study ultimately depends on the insights that it generates. These insights are not confined to "democratization" alone but contribute to our understanding of a range of issues: the interrelationship between culture and politics, the factors shaping social organization, the political economy of state-society relations, or the complex and dynamic interface between the spheres of "domestic" and "international" politics, among others. If democratization is comparatively rare in the Arab world, this demands study; if it is not, it is important to understand how its processes are similar to or different from those elsewhere. In doing so, it is essential to emphasize the struggle between political interests that shapes both liberalization and repression, and to explore the implications of this not only for regimes and elites but also for subaltern and intermediate groups within society too. Normative predispositions along the way are to be expected, as with any scholarship; indeed, their effects are less pernicious when such preferences are explicit. The best response to these sort of concerns, we suggest, is to adopt interdisciplinary and critical perspectives— to question intellectual and ideological assumptions, highlight debates, and encourage methodological, theoretical, and political pluralism.

Looking Ahead

Where is Arab politics headed as it approaches the twenty-first century? In many ways, the question itself is inappropriate, given the numerous significant differences across the many countries that comprise the "Arab world." As noted in the introduction, any analysis of political trajectories must be done in a manner that is sensitive to historical legacies, structural settings, and contemporary contexts. Moreover, when they do occur, political transitions are themselves contingent on the players themselves, their strategies, tactics, bargains, and confrontations. For those reasons, the second volume of this project focuses on a number of different countries—Algeria, Egypt, Jordan, Kuwait, Lebanon, Morocco, Palestine, Sudan, Syria, and Yemen—so as to illuminate their individual and comparative experiences.

Still, having reiterated the extent to which particular contexts will shape particular political trajectories, there are a number of observations that can be made for the region as a whole. The first, evident in several of the contributions to this book, is the extent to which discourse on democracy exists across the Arab world. This discourse—sustained by a common language and sense of Arab identity, shaped and reshaped by external diffusion, regional demonstration, and local conditions—locates questions of pluralism and expanded political participation squarely on contemporary political agendas. At the same time, however, such discourse is in a profound shape of flux, with a variety of fundamental issues—Islam and pluralism, the protection of minorities, gender issues, cultural authenticity, and institutional structures, to name but a few—subject to intense discussion and debate. Moreover, there is considerable distance between democratic discourse and "politics on the ground," with the space between them profoundly shaped by regime policies, opposition strategies, socioeconomic forces, and a host of other factors. In short, many political futures remain possible.

A second broad set of effects, also noted by multiple contributors to this book, is the impact of economic malaise and consequent pressures for structural economic adjustment. While analytical differences exist as to both the social effects of structural adjustment and the nature of any connection between political and economic liberalization, it is clear that economic crisis and the policy responses that it generates can have the effect of reshuffling the status quo, opening up new (but uncertain) political avenues. Political liberalization, even democratization are possibilities. So too are political and economic stagnation, new authoritarianisms, or even descent into social chaos.

Finally, several authors have pointed to the regional dimensions of political change in the Arab world, including linkages between regional conflict and domestic politics. Thus, perhaps the ending of the Cold War will, by reducing external support for authoritarian client states, force political elites into domestic political compromise. Or perhaps long-term success in the Arab-Israeli peace process would, by reducing regional tensions, reduce the imperatives of "national security" that have been so often invoked to justify internal political controls. However, some caveats are in order here too. While the post–Cold War world has seen the end of some forms of external support (Soviet support for Iraq, Syria, [former] South Yemen, and Libya), it has seen the consolidation of others (U.S. support for the GCC states). Moreover—as the 1990–1991 Gulf War demonstrated —the Arab-Israeli conflict may be the primary source of regional insecurity in the Middle East, but it is far from the only one. Moreover, the process of Arab-Israeli conflict resolution will, as the parties move toward an uncertain end, certainly involve internal and external insecurities all its own. In the short and medium term, this too could be used to justify repression and containment.

It is possible to point to several cases—constrained pluralism in Egypt, liberalization and elections in Jordan and Morocco, the reestablishment of limited parliamentarianism in Kuwait, the transition from Israeli occupation to Palestinian self-government—where political liberalization has been unfolding. But in all of these countries another problem presents itself: After an initial period of "easy" political opening, regimes find themselves resisting a "deepening" (or "democratization") of the reform process. In most of these countries, political elites are reluctant to release too much power, or to allow too much energy or autonomy in civil society. The state remains strong enough to revert to more authoritarian measures if required. A degree of ambiguity between the "carrot" of limited pluralism and the "stick" of authoritarianism is purposefully cultivated: repression if necessary, but not necessarily repression. This, combined with careful political co-option and the attractions of patronage, creates conditions under which civil society and political oppositions are reluctant to press matters to a climax. This reluctance is further reinforced in many cases by the fear that the existing regime ultimately stands as the only guarantor of political stability. Secularists fear the rise of Islamist influence; Islamists fear an Algerian-style clampdown; communal minorities fear majoritarianism. This sort of constraint is particularly strong where an established monarchy has defined the very structural foundations of the political system, where societies are divided by deep social cleavages, or in other cases where no clear consensus exists over possible alternative political orders. Under such conditions, liberalized autocracy may seem preferable to political chaos, and civil war seemingly too high a price to pay for expanded political participation.

These sorts of problems are not, of course, unique to the Arab world. On the contrary, they have been characteristic of political development in many other countries. In the European context, such questions—for example, the changing balance between royal prerogative and parliamentary power in Britain, and the gradual extension of the franchise to the mass population—often took centuries to resolve. Even in Latin America, the most recent transitions to democratic governance have taken place after more than a century and a half of postcolonial constitutional development and political struggle.

This is not to suggest that the Arab world, decolonized comparatively recently, is bound to observe similarly lengthy timeframes. It is to suggest, however, that analysts must look not only for dramatic shifts and transformations, but also for extended struggles and incremental change. Indeed, processes of change are unlikely to be either unilinear or unidirectional.

Given this, and given both the ambiguous character of the regional factors identified above and the inherently contingent nature of transition processes, it would be premature to speak of an inexorable democratic "trend" in the Middle East. Instead, the preceding analyses suggest that "interesting possibilities" and potential "trajectories" of eventual democratization may more accurately portray the potential for political change now present within the region.

Notes

1. Robert Vitalis, "The Democratization Industry and the Limits of the New Interventionism," *Middle East Report* 187/188 (March–June 1994).
2. For a discussion, see Aziz al-Azmeh, "Populism contra Democracy: Recent Democratist Discourse in the Arab World," in Ghassan Salamé, ed., *Democracy Without Democrats? The Renewal of Politics in the Muslim World* (London: I. B. Tauris, 1994), pp. 124–126.
3. For a fuller discussion of this see Rex Brynen, "Democracy in the Arab World: The View from the West," in World Affairs Council, *al-Dimuqratiyya fi al-watan al-'arabi* (Amman, forthcoming) from which sections of this chapter are drawn.
4. For a critique of this sort of free market evangelism see Vitalis, "The Democratization Industry and the Limits of the New Interventionism," as well as Al Miskin, "AID's 'Free Market' Democracy," *Middle East Report* 179 (November–December 1982), "Softening Structural Adjustment," *Middle East Report* 180 (January–February 1993), and "Chemionics Revisited," *Middle East Report* 186 (January–February 1994).

The Contributors

Lisa Anderson is associate professor of political science at Columbia University and vice-chair of Middle East Watch. She is author of *The State and Social Transformation in Tunisia and Libya* and numerous articles on politics in the Middle East. She is currently completing a book on political liberalization in the Arab world.

Gabriel Ben-Dor is professor of political science and former rector, University of Haifa. He is the author of *The Druses in Israel* and *State and Conflict in the Middle East*, and a contributing editor of *Conflict Management in the Middle East*, *The Palestinians and the Middle East Conflict*, *Political Participation in Turkey*, and *Confidence-Building in the Middle East*. He is also the author of more than 70 articles on political development and international relations in the Middle East.

Daniel Brumberg is assistant professor in the department of government at Georgetown University. Previously he was a visiting professor at Emory University and a visiting fellow in the Carter Center. He has published articles on religion and politics and on political economy and reform in the Middle East, and is currently working on a book on Islam and democracy.

Rex Brynen is associate professor of political science at McGill University. He is author of *Sanctuary and Survival: The PLO in Lebanon*, editor of *Echoes of the Intifada: Regional Repercussions of the Palestinian-Israeli Conflict*, and coeditor of *The Many Faces of National Security in the Arab World*. In addition, he has contributed articles on Middle East politics to the *Arab Studies Quarterly*, the *Canadian Journal of Political Science*, *International Perspectives*, the *Journal of Refugee Studies*, the *Journal of Palestine Studies*, and elsewhere.

Janine Astrid Clark is a post-doctoral research fellow with the Inter-University Consortium for Arab Studies (Montreal) and assistant professor of political science at the University of New Hampshire.

Samih K. Farsoun is professor and chair of sociology at the American University, Washington, D.C. His most recent work includes an edited volume, with Mehrdad Mashayekhi, *Iran: Political Culture in the Islamic Republic*. A forthcoming publication is a coauthored book, with Christina Zacharia, *Palestine and the Palestinians: A Political Economy*.

Lise Garon is a professor of public communication at Laval University. As a specialist of the North African public arena, she studies the role of the press in political change, the public discourse on human rights, and the manufacturing of consensus in either pluralist or monolithic contexts, among other areas.

F. Gregory Gause III is assistant professor of political science at the University of Vermont. He is the author of *Saudi-Yemeni Relations: Domestic Structures and Foreign Influence* and *Oil Monarchies: Domestic and Security Challenges in the Arab Gulf States*. In 1993–1994, he was fellow for Arab and Islamic Studies at the Council on Foreign Relations.

Mervat F. Hatem is associate professor of political science at Howard University, Washington, D.C. She is one of the editorial consultants of *Feminist Studies*. She has published many journal articles on state feminism in Egypt, the nationalist discourses on gender in the Arab Middle East, and the gendered implications of economic and political liberalization in Egypt. Her most recent publication is "Towards Post-Islamist and Post-Modernist Discourses in the Middle East" in *Arab Women: Old Boundaries and New Frontiers*, Judith Tucker, ed. She is presently working on a study of gender as an element of modern governmentality in contemporary Egypt.

Michael C. Hudson is professor of international relations and government and Seif Ghobash Professor of Arab Studies in the School of Foreign Service at Georgetown University. He is a former director of Georgetown's Center for Contemporary Arab Studies and former president of the Middle East Studies Association. Among his many publications, he is author of *The Precarious Republic: Political Modernization in Lebanon* and *Arab Politics: The Search for Legitimacy;* coauthor of *The World Handbook of Political and Social Indicators*; and editor of *The Palestinians: New Directions*. He is currently writing a book on political participation in the Middle East.

Saad Eddin Ibrahim is president of the Ibn Khaldoun Center for Developmental Studies and professor of political sociology at the American University in Cairo. He is author of several books and articles on Egypt, the Arab world, and the Middle East and has served as secretary-general for the Arab Organization for Human Rights and the Arab Thought Forum.

Salwa Ismail is a research fellow of the Centre for Developing Area Studies, McGill University. She has written a number of articles on contemporary Arab and Islamist discourses and is currently preparing a monograph on the question of renaissance and heritage in contemporary Arab thought.

Bahgat Korany is professor of political science at the Université de Montréal, and director of the Inter-University Consortium for Arab Studies. He is coauthor and editor of *The Foreign Policies of Arab States*. He is also author, coauthor, or editor of *Régimes politiques arabes* and *Social Change, Charisma and International Behavior*. In addition, he has authored more than 30 articles in such journals as the *Revue française de science politique*, the *International Social Science Journal*, the *Journal of South Asian and Middle Eastern Studies*, and *World Politics*.

Gudrun Krämer is professor of Islamic studies at Bonn University. She is author of *Egypt under Mubarak: Identity and National Interest* and *The Jews in Modern Egypt*, among other works.

Giacomo Luciani is deputy director, International Strategies, at ENI Spa in Rome. He is editor of *The Arab State* and author of *International Oil Companies and Arab Countries*, among other works.

Paul Noble is associate professor and chair of the Middle East Studies Program at McGill University, and associate director of the Inter-University Consortium for Arab Studies. He is coeditor of *The Many Faces of National Security in the Arab World* and has contributed articles to *Arab Studies Quarterly*, *International Perspectives*, and a number of edited volumes.

Mustafa Kamel al-Sayyid is professor of political science at both Cairo University and the American University in Cairo. He is the author and editor of several books in Arabic as well as articles in Arabic, English, and French on aspects of Egyptian and Arab politics, interest groups, and the political economy of development.

Christina Zacharia is a Ph.D. candidate in sociology at the American University, Washington, D.C. She is currently working on a coauthored book with Samih K. Farsoun, *Palestine and the Palestinians: A Political Economy,* and is planning to write her dissertation on Palestinian communities in the diaspora.

Index

'Abd al-Nasser, Gamal, 99, 218, 239, 242, 254, 267, 287–288, 311
'Abd al-Rahman, Sheikh 'Umar, 102
'Abd al-Raziq, 'Ali, 115
'Abd al-Salam, Bel'aid, 160, 248
'Abduh, Muhammad, 94, 97
Abu al-Nasr, Muhammad Hamid, 121
Abu Bakr, Caliph, 117
Abu Dhabi, 212
AbuKhalil, As'ad, 22
Africa, 194, 313. See also maghreb
Ahmad, Sa'd Muhammad, 140
al-'Ahmar, Sheikh 'Abdallah, 299
Ajami, Fouad, 23, 66
'Alawis, 158, 248, 250
Algeria, 8, 16, 36–37, 39–40, 43, 46, 50, 54, 68, 102, 135, 138–142, 144–145, 187, 212, 224–225, 233, 249–250, 262–263, 270, 272, 275–276, 287, 289–292, 294–296, 304, 333, 335; economic policy in, 222–223, 238, 244–246; mass media in, 149–165; military in, 157–158; recent politics in, 48–49, 246–248; statistics, 213, 216, 284–285, 292. See also Front de Libération Nationale (FLN); Islamic Salvation Front (FIS)
Algerian Human Rights League, 153, 159
Algerian Journalists' Movement, 152
'Ali, Caliph, 97
'Ali, Kamal Hassan, 139
'Ali, Muhammad, 100, 134
Almond, Gabriel, 63, 65, 67
Al Sabah, 297, 302
Amin, Samir, 99
Amnesty International, 50, 52
Anderson, Lisa, 9
Arab Democratic Nasserite Party, 50
Arab identity, 290, 335

Arab-Israeli conflict/peace process, 20, 23, 34–36, 53–55, 95, 151, 215, 220, 265, 284, 287, 297, 303, 310, 318, 324–327, 336
Arab League, 264, 275
Arab nationalism, 36, 134, 268, 273–274, 283, 287–290, 296–297, 310
Arab Organization for Human Rights, 6, 52
Arab socialism, 121, 233, 239, 267, 271, 310, 320–321
Arab Socialist Union, 242
Arab Women's Solidarity Association, 202
'asabiyya (group identity), 83
al-Asad, Hafiz, 51, 219, 248–250
al-'Ashmawi, Muhammad Sa'id, 115
'Ashur, Habib bin, 140
Asia, 82, 155, 313; Central, 312, 316–317; East, 5; economic development in, 219, 232, 253–254; Southeast, 224
Awakening Party, 290

Babiker Badri Scientific Association for Women's Studies, 191–193, 204
Baha'is, 118
Bahrain, 143, 284, 289–290; statistics, 213, 216
al-Banna, Hasan, 119–120, 122, 173
Barakat, Halim, 69
Barry, Brian, 64
al-Bashir, 'Umar Hasan, 51, 194, 289
Ba'th (party), 51, 220, 233, 248–249, 298, 310, 313–314
bay'a (oath of allegiance), 7, 94, 97, 169–170
al-Baz, 'Usama, 289
Belhadj, 'Ali, 102
Benachenhou, Mourad, 248
Ben-Dor, Gabriel, 10, 20, 69

343

About the Book

Long-dominated by authoritarian regimes, the Arab world is now experiencing a variety of factors—both internal and external—that pose the challenge of change. Significant degrees of political liberalization have occurred already in Egypt, Lebanon, Jordan, and Kuwait, although the extent to which this presages eventual democratization is far from self-evident. Elsewhere—for example, in Syria—regimes have resisted demands for expanded public freedoms, and in still other countries—notably Sudan, Algeria, and Yemen—democratic experiments have been aborted or derailed by civil strife.

This book focuses on the major factors shaping liberalization and democratization in the Arab context, as well as the role played by particular social groups.

Rex Brynen is associate professor of political science at McGill University. He is author of *Sanctuary and Survival: The PLO in Lebanon.* **Bahgat Korany** is professor of political science at the University of Montreal, and director of the Inter-University Consortium for Arab Studies. His books include *How Foreign Policy Decisions Are Made* and (with M. Flory, et al.) *Regimes politiques arabes.* **Paul Noble** is associate professor of political science and chair of the Middle East Studies Program at McGill University, as well as author of numerous articles on Arab politics.